God's Loving Word

Discovery House Publishers

Books, music, and videos that feed the soul with the Word of God

Box 3566 Grand Rapids, MI 49501

God's Loving Word

Exploring the Gospel of John

by

Ray C. Stedman

with

James D. Denney

God's Loving Word
Exploring the Gospel of John
Copyright © 1993 by Elaine Stedman

Library of Congress Cataloging-in-Publication Data

Stedman, Ray C.
　God's loving word / by Ray C. Stedman ; with James D. Denney.
　　p.　cm.
　ISBN 0-929239-79-2
　1. Bible. N.T. John—Commentaries. I Denney, James D. II. Bible. N.T. John.
English. New International. 1993. III. Title.
BS2615.3.S784　1993
226.5'077—dc20　　　　　　　　　　　　　　　　　　　　93-20920
　　　　　　　　　　　　　　　　　　　　　　　　　　　　　CIP

Unless otherwise indicated, Scripture is taken from the
HOLY BIBLE, NEW INTERNATIONAL VERSION.
Copyright © 1973, 1978, 1984 International Bible Society.
Used by permission of Zondervan Bible Publishers.

Discovery House Publishers is affiliated with
RBC Ministries, Grand Rapids, Michigan 49512

Discovery House books are distributed to the trade
by Thomas Nelson Publishers, Nashville, Tennessee 37214.

Printed in the United States of America

97 98 99 00 01 02 / CHG / 10 9 8 7 6 5 4 3 2

Dedication

To Robert DeVries and James Denney, whose vision and editorial skills, respectively, have combined to make possible this uncommonly rich publication; and to every reader who has a hungry heart for God's loving Word.

Elaine Stedman

Contents

Chapter One

Who Is Jesus?

John 1:1–4

The Danish Christian philosopher Sören Kierkegaard tells the story about a king who fell in love with a peasant maiden. This king was the wealthiest, most respected, most powerful king in the entire region. No one dared oppose him or speak a word against him. But this king—as powerful and respected as he was—had a problem: How could he tell this maiden that he loved her? And how could he know for sure that she loved him?

The very fact that he was a king—rich, famous, and powerful—was a barrier.

He could lead an armed escort of knights to the door of her humble cottage, and he could demand, by his authority as king, that she marry him.

But that wouldn't do. The king didn't want a fearful slave for a wife. He wanted someone who would love him, someone to share his life, someone who would be happy and eager to spend her days at his side.

He could shower her with gifts and jewels and beautiful robes and—

No, no, that wouldn't do either. He didn't want to *buy* her love. He wanted her to love him for *himself,* not for his gifts and his wealth.

Somehow he had to find a way to win the maiden's love without overwhelming her, without destroying her free will. Somehow he had to make himself her equal.

So the king clothed himself in rags and went to her as a peasant. But the truly amazing thing is this: The king did not merely *disguise* himself as a poor man. He actually *became poor!* He loved this maiden so much that he renounced his throne, his wealth, and his kingly power to win her love!

This story is a beautiful parable of the story of Jesus as it is told by Jesus' friend John in his gospel. Jesus the King, the Creator, the source of Light and Life, has come to earth—not in disguise, but truly as one of us. God himself has come as a poor, humble, limited human being, subject to hunger, pain, temptation, and death. He has come because He loves us—and He has come to win our love. As we work our way through the gospel of John, we will see the love of God unfolding to us on every page.

The Intimate Gospel

Of the four gospels, John is in a class by itself. It is written in a different style and with a completely different emotional feel than the three "synoptic gospels," Matthew, Mark, and Luke. *Synoptic* means "to see together." Those three gospels are called "synoptic" because they "view together" the same story from three slightly different perspectives. Though each has its own distinctive voice and unique purpose, the three synoptic gospels are similar in the way they "report" the life of Christ.

The gospel of John, however, stands completely apart. Its style, its selection of events, and its viewpoint are all radically different from those of Matthew, Mark, and Luke. Most of all, it is written for a very different *purpose* than the other three gospels. John himself tells us his purpose in writing his gospel in chapter 20, verses 30–31:

> Jesus did many other miraculous signs in the presence of
> his disciples, which are not recorded in this book. But these
> [signs] are written that you may believe that Jesus is the
> Christ, the Son of God, and that by believing you may have
> life in his name.

In this passage, John tells us, first, that his method is *selection.* He did not set out to write a comprehensive history, but a selective profile of his Friend, Jesus. He tells us, second, that his purpose is *regeneration:* vital, fulfilling *life* in the name of Jesus, the kind of life Jesus meant when He said, "I have come that they may have life, and have it to the full."[1]

Another feature that sets this gospel apart from the synoptics is the firsthand familiarity of its viewpoint. John's gospel reads more like a personal diary than an encyclopedic history—and with good reason. It has such a personal flavor because it was written by the disciple of whom it was said, "Jesus loved him." John was the closest intimate of our Lord during the days of His ministry, and the tone of the writing reflects the bond of friendship between John and his Lord. That is why this book has often been referred to as "The Intimate Gospel."

For three months in 1950, I had the privilege of living and traveling with Dr. H. A. Ironside, the famous Bible teacher and former pastor of the Moody Memorial Church in Chicago. He suffered from cataracts in both eyes and was nearly blind, so I was his chauffeur, his secretary, and his companion— and he was my mentor. During that time, we spent almost all of our time together, and I watched him and listened to him intently. I studied his example as a Bible teacher and as a man of God. I saw his human warmth and compassion and—on occasion—his human weaknesses. His impact on my life was unforgettable.

As memorable as that experience was for me, I believe my three months with Dr. Ironside are just a faint and feeble echo of an infinitely more profound experience of companionship and mentoring that the apostle John enjoyed for three and a half years at the side of Jesus of Nazareth. The momentous impact of John's close, daily friendship with Jesus can be seen on virtually every page of John's gospel.

John was an old man when he wrote this gospel. Biblical scholars believe he wrote it from the city of Ephesus sometime between A.D. 85 and 90. Following the destruction of the temple of Jerusalem in A.D. 70, John settled in Ephesus to guide and oversee the Christian community there. Ephesus was a major city of the Roman Empire, located on the west coast of Asia Minor (modern-day Turkey).

At the time of the writing of John's gospel, the gospels of Matthew, Mark, and Luke were already written and widely circulated throughout the early church. In addition, all the letters of Paul and Peter had also been written and circulated. Because it was written so late, and because there are many important events in the synoptic gospels that John does not bother to retrace, some Bible scholars suggest that John forgot some of the events in the life of Christ.

It is true that forty or fifty years have probably passed since the events John records in his gospel. But is it actually possible that John *forgot* any of those events? John's gospel, remember, is the record of a story John lived almost every day for more than three tumultuous, exciting, astounding years. The vivid colors and emotions that saturated those events—miraculous healings, the dead brought back to life, the Lord's triumph among the crowds, the heartbreak of the cross—how could these events *not* have been burned deeply and unerasably into John's mind?

Powerful emotions—joy, fear, shock, grief—burn memories into our brain as if with a branding iron. Just think back to some of the most memorable days in your life—days tinged with emotion. Could you ever forget what you saw, heard, and felt on the day

• you were married?
• your first child was born?
• you heard that President Kennedy had been shot?
• you heard that the space shuttle *Challenger* exploded?

No, of course you couldn't forget such feelings, such events. Neither could John forget the powerful events he witnessed at the side of Jesus? John didn't forget a thing.

Moreover, John was helped in the writing of his gospel by the Spirit who was promised by Jesus when He said, "But the Counselor, the Holy Spirit, whom the Father will send in my name, will teach you all things and will remind you of everything I have said to you."[2] John and the other apostles who set down the text of the New Testament were aided not only by vivid, unforgettable memories, but by the Holy Spirit himself, who brought to their minds the life-changing words that Jesus spoke. They meditated many long hours over those events, often retelling and reliving the words and deeds of Jesus among themselves.

Out of the deep reservoir of his memories and through his deep connection with the Holy Spirit, John was able to set down his unique and intensely personal story of the life of his Friend and Lord, Jesus.

The Central Question: Who Is Jesus?

John begins his gospel with an eighteen-verse introduction. This prologue is so rich in meaning and significance that we will spend this entire chapter in just the first four verses.

The central question of John 1:1–18 is *Who is Jesus?*

John answers this question by portraying Jesus as the central figure of human history, and the central focus of God's eternal plan. Here in these verses we encounter the crucial fact of Christian faith: Christianity is not a philosophy or a body of teachings. Christianity is about a Person. If you take the Person of Jesus out of Christianity and leave only His moral teachings (as many people through the years have tried to do), Christianity cannot stand. Trying to understand and practice Christianity without accepting the significance of Jesus himself—His birth, His life and ministry, His death, and His resurrection—is like saying, "I want to understand mathematics—but let's leave out the numbers," or, "I want to understand why it is light during the day—but I don't want to hear any of that nonsense about the sun." Christianity at its core is not merely about what Jesus taught, but about *who Jesus is.*

It is impossible for any objective person to deny that Jesus was the most extraordinary, influential, and revolutionary individual to stride the stage of human history. More books have been written about Jesus than any other figure of the past. More music has been composed, more pictures have been painted, more great drama has been written about Jesus than any other person. We mark off our history in years either before or after the birth of Christ.

Have you ever wondered why? Why does this one man occupy such a unique and unforgettable place in history? Why does He not fade into the dim past as others have? No other leader in history is even considered in the same breath with Jesus—not Alexander the Great, not Julius Caesar, not George Washington, not Gandhi. There is something about Jesus Christ which sets Him apart from every other figure in human history. Unlike all other leaders of the past, Jesus remains as much a focus of interest and influence in our society as our contemporary leaders.

Why? What marks this one person as the most powerful personality ever to appear on this planet?

That is the question John answers for us in the prologue to his gospel.

Jesus Is God

In the first four verses of his gospel, John tells us in clear and uncompromising terms who Jesus is: Jesus is God.

1:1–4 *In the beginning was the Word, and the Word was with God, and the Word was God. he was with God in the beginning.*

Through him all things were made; without him nothing was made that has been made. In him was life, and that life was the light of men.

Those of us who have been raised in the Christian tradition may not realize how radical and astonishing these words sounded to the first century ear. Remember, these verses were not written about some epic hero out of the mists of time, but about Jesus, the carpenter from Nazareth. To John's audience, the story of Jesus was not an ancient legend, but yesterday's headlines.

And John knew this carpenter on an intimate basis, having lived with Him, talked with Him, traveled with Him, and watched His life. If anyone had the opportunity to observe any human faults or failings in this man, it was John. Yet here is the remarkable conclusion of Jesus' friend John:

Jesus is God!

How does John make his case? First, he tells us that Jesus is the Word of God: "In the beginning was the Word." In the original Greek, John calls Jesus the *logos,* which means "word"—God's expression of himself.

A word is a symbol—either written or spoken—which expresses thought. Thought cannot be communicated until it is put into words. There are several Scripture passages which ask the question, "Who has known the mind of the Lord?" The answer: no one. Nobody knows what God thinks until He tells us with His *logos,* His Word.

After all, who can know your mind or my mind unless we express our thoughts in words? The only way you can know my thoughts on the gospel of John, for example, is to read the words in this book.

In a similar way, when Jesus came among us as a man He expressed to us what was in the mind of God. As the book of Hebrews tells us, "In the past

God spoke to our forefathers through the prophets at many times and in various ways, but in these last days He has spoken to us by His Son."[3] He was God's utterance on earth, revealing to us what Paul calls "God's secret wisdom, a wisdom that has been hidden and that God destined for our glory before time began."[4]

If we want to understand reality, we must understand God's thoughts, for whatever God thinks *becomes* reality. God thought about a universe and the stars and the earth, and they sprang into being. God thought about the laws of physics, and those thoughts became real. He thought about animals and sea creatures and human beings, and they came into being. Everything that exists began as a thought in the mind of God. The results of His thoughts are all around us—and *we* are the realization of His thoughts as well.

Jesus, too, is an expression of God's mind to us. In the life of Jesus we can see and hear God's love, God's power, God's compassion, God's justice, and God's forgiveness. Jesus is the ultimate expression, the clearest Word God could ever speak to us. He came to unfold the mind of God to us in terms that cannot be mistaken.

Notice the parallels between the opening lines of John's gospel and the opening lines of Genesis, the first book of the Old Testament. Both begin with these sweeping words: "In the beginning . . . ." At the outset of both books, you gain a sense that the story which follows is a story of vast scope and significance. The human stories found in both Genesis and John are connected to a much larger story—the story of God's eternal plan as it is being worked out in history. This is not just a narrative of events that began 2,000 years ago or 6,000 years ago, but the grand disclosure of a plan that has been operating since the beginning of time and space itself.

In the opening lines of his gospel, John tells us that the Word has always, eternally existed: "In the beginning was the Word." The beginning of what? The beginning of everything! We see appearances of this eternal Word even in the Old Testament, before Jesus was born. Before He came as a man, the Word was not called Jesus. Rather, you find references to "The Angel [literally, 'messenger'] of the Lord" or "the Son."[5] Jesus was the eternal Son of God before He came to earth, even before time and the universe began.

You and I had no history before we appeared on the earth—but Jesus did.

I remember as a boy wishing I had been alive to witness some of the exciting events of World War I, but it was all over before I arrived on the scene. To the young people of today, the events I witnessed and the times I lived through—the Great Depression, World War II, the wars in Korea and Vietnam, and the Watergate era—are just stories of the past. These events were history before many people now old enough to vote were even born! But Jesus had a history and an existence even before He came to earth.

Three Persons—One God

In verse 1—at the very beginning of his gospel—John grapples with one of the deepest mysteries of God: the Trinity. He says, "the Word was with God, and the Word was God."

At this point, a problem arises. What John is saying is that the Word is distinct from the Father—two separate Persons. Yet there is a mystery here as well, for John also indicates that the Word was so intimately involved with the Father that their thoughts and their purposes were one. That is what Jesus himself said in John 10:30: "I and the Father are one."

Is Jesus saying that He and the Father are one and the same? Some people are understandably confused on this point. "How could both Jesus and the Father be God?" they ask. "How could the Son be His own Father?" The confusion lies in the meaning of the word *one*. Some people think that when Jesus says, "I and my Father are one," He means they are one and the same. But they are not. They are two separate persons.

What does the word *persons* suggest to you? Does it suggest physical bodies? The fact is, bodies are not essential to persons. Our essential nature is not that of a physical body, but that of a spirit. The essence of a person is not a head, trunk, limbs, and organs. The essence of a person is that person's "I-ness," that person's awareness, feelings, motives, loves, desires—all the intangible yet utterly real aspects that make up a unique self, a personality.

In verse 1, John declares that the eternal Son, Jesus, was a person, and the Father was a person, and they were one in purpose and action.

The final line in that verse is a blunt and astonishing statement: "and the Word was God." No doubt about it! Some religious sects, such as Jehovah's Witnesses and the Unitarians, deny this great truth that Jesus was God. They try to dilute the power of this statement by reinterpreting those words or by explaining them away. For example, Jehovah's Witnesses take the position that John is saying, "Jesus was a god," not, "Jesus was God." They suggest that John was introducing a concept bordering on polytheism, the belief in many gods, and that Jesus was just one among them.

Yet there is no other way to translate these words without violating the laws of Greek grammar and the theological statements of other Scriptures. John is taking great pains to make his point clear, and the point is this: There is only one God, and Jesus was one with that God, and *Jesus was God.*

I once attended a meeting between leaders of the Christian and Jewish faiths. Eleven prominent rabbis from Reformed Jewish congregations in places such as Washington, New York, and Chicago met with evangelical Christian leaders at a location in Los Angeles. Our objective was to discuss the differing points of view between Jews and Christians and to build understanding. It was a warm and congenial meeting, and it proved to be only the first of a series of such talks.

During the session, one of the rabbis read a statement of Christian doctrines to us and asked the evangelical Christians in the room to state whether or not they agreed with those statements. When the rabbi came to a statement that read, "We believe that God exists as three Persons in one," he said, "I'm sure you understand we would differ with you a great deal at this point." That was probably the understatement of the day!

The first reason Christians and Jews differ on this point is that one of the three Persons is Jesus Christ, who is not acknowledged by the Jewish faith as the Messiah. The second reason is that one of the essential affirmations of the Jewish faith is that there is only one God. In fact, that is the core affirmation of three of the five great religions of the world, Judaism, Islam, and Christianity. Of the other two religions, Hindus believe in many gods and Buddhists believe there is no god, that man is his own god. But Jews, Muslims, and Christians all believe there is only one God.

But there is a profound difference in the Christian view of God. When we examine the Christian definition of that one God, we find not one but *three* Persons.

The Jewish faith objects to the triune concept of God. It states that there is only one Person in the Godhead, and that Person is the Father alone. But because of the testimony of Scripture, the evidence of the life of Jesus, and even statements within the Old Testament, Christians have come to understand that God has revealed a complexity in His personage. We conclude that He exists as three Persons, sharing the same divine essence, so that there is one God expressed in three individual Persons.

We see the first hint of the plural nature of the Godhead in the very first chapter of the first book of the Old Testament. There God says, "Let us make man in our image, in our likeness."[6] A plurality of Persons within one God is clearly indicated right from the beginning.

This is a hard concept to grasp, and there is nothing in our everyday experience to help us. I recall the story of the mother who was ironing while her little son was sitting on the floor with a notepad and crayons, drawing pictures. "What are you drawing?" she asked.

"I'm drawing a picture of God," said the little boy.

"How can you do that?" asked the mother. "Nobody knows what God looks like."

The boy smiled up at his mother and said, "They will when I get through!"

Many have tried to draw a picture of God to help people understand the Trinity, our Christian God in three Persons. (The word *Trinity* is really just a brief way of saying "tri-unity" or "three-in-one.") For example, C. S. Lewis, in his book *Miracles,* said that God "contains 'persons' (three of them) while remaining one God, as a cube combines six squares while remaining one solid body."[7] This picture helps somewhat, but falls far short (as Lewis himself would admit) of ever completely encompassing the incredible mystery of the Trinity.

"This is the deep end of theology, no doubt," writes J. I. Packer, "but John throws us straight into it. . . . John sets the mystery [of the Trinity] at the head of his gospel because he knows that nobody can make head or tail of the words and works of Jesus of Nazareth till he has grasped the fact that this Jesus is in truth God the Son."[8]

Jesus Is the Creator and Sustainer

In verses 2 and 3, John declares that Jesus is the Creator of all things. This statement accounts for Jesus' forceful and remarkable personality. It accounts for his miraculous acts. It accounts for so many things that are simply incomprehensible apart from the creative power of God himself.

Jesus, says John, is the originator of all things: "He was with God in the beginning. Through him all things were made; without him nothing was made that has been made."

Again we see a parallel between the opening lines of John and the opening lines of Genesis. Eight times in the opening chapter of Genesis we read about God's creative activity:
- "And God said, 'Let there be light' " (1:3).
- "And God said, 'Let there be an expanse between the waters to separate water from water' " (1:6).
- "And God said, 'Let the water under the sky be gathered to one place, and let the dry ground appear' " (1:9).
- "Then God said, 'Let the land produce vegetation' " (1:11).
- "And God said, 'Let there be lights in the expanse of the sky' " (1:14).
- "And God said, 'Let the water teem with living creatures, and let birds fly above the earth' " (1:20).
- "And God said, 'Let the land produce living creatures' " (1:24).
- "Then God said, 'Let us make man in our image' " (1:26).

In these lines from Genesis, we see God the Son at work, just as John describes Him in verses 2 and 3: He is the *logos,* the eternal Word, speaking into being what the Father had conceived and designed in His amazing, infinite mind.

Any scientist who studies nature is continually astonished when he views the complexity of life, the marvelous symmetry of energy and matter, the order that is embedded within all visible matter: the molecule, the atom, the structure of a flower or a star. As the English essayist J. B. Priestley observed, "Believing that life and the universe are a mystery quite beyond our grasp keeps you humble. And really, the arrogance of thinking it's an accident! The conceit of thinking we know everything!"

All the deep wonders of the universe were once just a thought in the mind of God. That thought never would have been expressed as physical reality if the Son had not spoken it into being. He spoke, and the world appeared.

This amazing Man, Jesus of Nazareth, in the mystery of His being, was not only a human being here on earth. He was, John tells us, the One who created the universe at the beginning. He understands it. He knows how it functions. He directs, guards, and guides the creation to this day. He keeps it going and holds it in existence.

I have always been fascinated by the great linear accelerator that runs out toward the mountains behind Stanford University. I have often thought about the immense energies which power that great scientific instrument as I have driven up Highway 280 between Palo Alto and San Francisco. This linear accelerator is, loosely speaking, a great "atom-smasher." Using enormous voltages of electrical energy, the accelerator moves particles along a long tunnel, increasing the speed of the particles until they approach the speed of light. These high-speed particles smash into a target—the nucleus of an atom—at the far end of the tunnel.

The energies used to smash these atoms are measured in "mega-electron volts" and "giga-electron volts"—that is, in millions and billions of volts! Why does it take so much power to break apart an atom so that its component particles can be studied? Science has asked that question for decades, and the answer is still unknown. All that is known is that there is a force that scientists do not yet understand which holds all things together.

The apostle Paul tells us in Colossians what that force is: "In him [Jesus] all things hold together."[9] The book of Hebrews says, "The Son is . . . the exact representation of [God's] being, sustaining all things by His powerful word."[10] And John says, "Through him [Jesus] all things were made; without him nothing was made that has been made." The world around you, the book you hold in your hands, and your very body itself are all held together by His word and His power.

Life and Light

The third thing John says in these verses is that Jesus is the source of life and light—two essential ingredients to our existence. "In him was life," says John, "and that life was the light of men."

What is life? We all think we know the difference between life and death—until we are asked to define what life is or explain where life comes from. A scientist can analyze all the elements that make up a living being— but even if he puts it all together in the proper proportions, he cannot create life. The elements are there, the chemistry is there, but something is missing. It will not grow. It will not function. It is not alive.

Life is one of the great mysteries of science and philosophy. No one knows what life is. But the Word of God declares that God the Son is the source of life.

Plants have life; the Son gave it to them. Animals have a higher form of life; He gave it to them. People have a still higher form of life, and He is the source of it. Jesus stands at the beginning and the end of every human life. Our life goes back to Him when it has ceased on earth.

And with the life of the Son comes the light of the Son. Light, as John uses it, is a symbol of knowledge, understanding, and truth. You and I can go to school and learn because we have physical life, human life. But John tells us that Jesus is the source of eternal life, a higher level, a life that never ends. As John declares in his letter, "He who has the Son has life; he who does not have the Son of God does not have life."[11]

So eternal life comes only from Christ. When you have life from Him, then you also have access to the source of light—the light of God's truth. That's why there is no possibility of understanding the workings of the universe in which we live without eternal life from the Son of God.

Throughout the Scriptures, we are invited to pursue the truth and to discover the wonders of the universe and the life God has created. We can pursue understanding in such fields as science, medicine, art, literature, and politics—and there is nothing wrong with any of these pursuits. But there is more, there is a deeper understanding. If we stop at the level of human knowledge and human understanding, then life is narrow and limited, and we will never truly understand the workings of God in the world. It is only as we seek that deeper level of truth, the level of divine light that is found in Scripture, proceeding from the lips of Jesus, that we can truly put all the pieces together. Only then can we understand God's purposes in the world, as well as our own meaning, our own place in God's purposes.

In the opening lines of his gospel, John introduces us to a mystery: This amazing man from Nazareth is not only a man but God himself. The Creator has become a part of his own creation. The Originator of life and light has submitted himself to death and the darkness of a tomb. The source of deepest wisdom has limited himself to learning as a little child. Not until He explodes from the tomb is the fullness of His life and light manifested in resurrection power.

Now it is clear why more books have been written, more music composed, more paintings painted, more drama presented about *this* Man than any other person in history. Now it is clear why this one Man occupies such a unique and unforgettable place in history. Now it is clear why no other leader in history is even considered in the same breath with Jesus. He is not only the focus of interest and influence in our society, but in history, and in the universe. He is not only the center of our faith, but the source of life and light. As the poet John Donne once wrote,

> Twas much, that man was made like God before,
> But that God should be made like man, much more!

Jesus is the ultimate crisis—the decision that must be made, the question that must be answered, yes or no, accept or reject—in every human life. Every human being must sooner or later deal with Jesus of Nazareth.

Chapter Two

Hello, Darkness

John 1:5–13

Here are the words of one of the most famous and powerful people in history:

> I know men, and I tell you that Jesus Christ is not a mere man. Everything in Christ astonishes me. His spirit overawes me, and His will confounds me. Between Him and anyone else in the world there is no possible term of comparison. He is truly a being by himself. I search in vain in history to find a parallel to Jesus Christ, or anything which can approach the gospel. Neither history, nor humanity, nor the ages, nor nature offer me anything with which I am able to compare it or to explain it. Here everything is extraordinary.

Those words were spoken by Napoleon Bonaparte during a conversation with one of his generals at the end of his career. At the time he spoke these words, Napoleon was in exile on the tiny island of St. Helena in the South Atlantic. There are other remarkable statements about Christ that the exiled leader of France made in his final years. It is my opinion, and the opinion of many who have studied Napoleon's life, that he became a Christian during his exile.

Even the most amazing and forceful personalities in history—the Napoleons of past and present ages—are driven to their knees in awe and humility by the amazing reality of this one Man, Jesus Christ. Something within us instinctively responds to the words and the life of Jesus. Something within us is touched by His love, by the force of His personality, by the purity of His character. Something within us is magnetically drawn to the One who made us—and then was made like us.

In John 1:5–13, the Lord's friend John tells us not only who Jesus is eternally—the Word made flesh, God become a man—but what Jesus came to accomplish on earth.

1:5 *The light shines in the darkness, and the darkness has not understood [or overcome] it.*

In these words we find the first hint in John's gospel of the struggle between belief and unbelief in the world. John has said that Jesus is the light of men, the source of all understanding of true reality. He is the basis of the knowledge of truth. To a world full of darkness and confusion, John declares that it is only in the light of Jesus that we begin to see things the way they are.

Feeling Our Way in the Darkness

It is hard for many of us to accept that we live in a world of darkness. We are proud of our achievements, our social, technological, and scientific progress. We point to our impressive achievements in computers, in communication technology, in space travel, in medical science. We compare these achievements to the state of human knowledge and engineering of fifty years ago, or a century ago, or a thousand years ago, and we say, "See how far we've come!" We point to our great libraries and universities, and we say, "How can anyone say we live in darkness?"

Yet, if we are honest, we have to admit that regardless of our impressive social and scientific advances, we have made no progress whatsoever in conquering the basic ills of the human condition: Fear. Hate. Crime. Conflict. War. Racism. Injustice. Sin.

We do not know the answers. In fact, we often feel we don't even know the questions. We are like children lost in a dark wood, feeling our way around, hoping to recognize some landmark, yet despairing of ever finding our way back to the path. We don't know what we may find in the dark, behind the next shadowy tree or bush. We hope to find a rescuer—but we fear that there is nothing awaiting us but a beast or a deep abyss.

Listen to the politicians. Listen to the scientists. Listen to the economists. Listen to the news commentators. No one truly understands all the immense complexities and problems of our world today. No one is in control. Even our kings and presidents seem to be feeling their way in the darkness.

The opening line of the 1970s song by Simon and Garfunkel is still relevant today: "Hello darkness, my old friend / I've come to talk with you again." That is how millions feel today: The darkness is our constant companion, a shadow that never leaves us, and from which we have no hope of escaping.

The darkness is not only outside us, surrounding us, but it is within us as well. Some time ago in my counseling office, I actually heard a husband—a professing Christian—say to his wife, "Why are you getting so upset at me? What's the big deal? All I did was have an affair!" That is true darkness—a darkened heart, a darkened understanding. Any man who does not comprehend the pain and destruction he creates when he defiles the marriage bed is living in the darkness of self-deception.

This kind of darkness pervades our entire culture, our entire world. Easy divorce, permissive sex, a decline of moral standards in our entertainment media and our political leaders and cultural heroes—all of these factors are dissolving the glue that holds society together, destroying our families, and sabotaging a whole generation of children and young people. Anarchy and violence are on the rise and standards of behavior are on the decline. This is darkness. Clearly, the words of the gospel of John are as relevant today as when John first wrote them to the dark and evil world of the first century Roman empire.

A Witness to the Light

I believe the NIV text misses the truest sense of the word it translates "understood" (or, in the margin note, "overcome") in verse 5. Certainly, it is true that the darkness cannot understand the light, nor can the darkness ultimately overcome and defeat the light. But there is an even deeper significance to John's message in these words than either "understood" or "overcome" conveys.

The original Greek word that is translated "overcome" actually means "to lay hold of, to lay hands on, to seize." One can "lay hold" of something as a hostile act. Or one can "lay hold" of something in order to possess it. By comparing this passage with other New Testament passages, I have come to conclude that it is this second sense of the word—"laying hold" in order to possess something—that John intends in this verse. John is telling us that the darkness cannot get hold of the light, cannot appropriate it, cannot possess it, cannot apprehend it.

In 2 Corinthians 6:14, the apostle Paul asks, "What fellowship can light have with darkness?" The two are mutually exclusive. The moment you introduce light, darkness must flee. Darkness and light cannot exist together. We, who live in darkness, are incapable of possessing the light—unless it descends to us and places itself within our reach.

And that, as we shall see in the next few verses, is exactly what the light chose to do for us who live in darkness.

1:6–8 *There came a man who was sent from God; his name was John. He came*

as a witness to testify concerning that light, so that through him all men might
believe. He himself was not the light; he came only as a witness to the light.

Here, John the apostle refers to another John—John the Baptist, whom the prophet Isaiah predicted would come to "prepare the way of the Lord." John the Baptist's ministry was to take the deep, profound truths of God and make them clear and plain so they could be grasped by the people in their darkness.

The name John means, "God is gracious." The grace of God was exhibited when He sent a man—John the Baptist—to go before the Light—Jesus—to make the light plain and clear to our understanding. John the Baptist stooped to our weakness, put the truth at a level we could understand, and placed the light of God within our grasp.

When a child is just learning to read, you do not hand that child *The Collected Works of William Shakespeare* and say, "Here's something to read. Get started." No, you don't start a child at the most advanced level. You start a child at the simplest level, the ABCs. And that's just what John the Baptist did. He came and began with the ABCs. Here are the ABCs of John the Baptist.

A
Admit your need.

Admit you are confused, bewildered, blind, and needy. Admit you cannot solve your own problems. That is summed up in the word John preached again and again: "Repent!" Admit the fact that you are in trouble. Admit it that you can't find your own way out. Admit it that none of the solutions you have applied by your own strength have worked in your life. Admit your need.

B
Believe.

Believe in the One who gives life and light. Believe in the One who has come to meet you right where you are. Believe in God the Son, Jesus Christ.

C
Correct your behavior.

"Correct your behavior." That is what John preached to the people in their darkness. To the soldiers and leaders he said, "Stop oppressing the people."

To the rich he said, "Give freely and generously to the poor." To all he said, "Correct your behavior on the basis of the new life and new light you have received from God."

These are the ABCs of John the Baptist's message and ministry. It was not the most exhaustive and complete truth, nor was it the deepest and most profound truth—but it was a place to start, and it was the place where John began.

The writer of the gospel of John says that John the Baptist identified the true light. He told the people who the light was, because Jesus did not have the outward appearance of light and brilliance. Jesus did not come into this world like a sunburst, or like some visitor from outer space. He did not step out of cloud or a flying saucer so everyone could see how radically different He was from run-of-the-mill humankind. Jesus came looking like us. He *was* one of us. That is why people failed to recognize Him for what He was. He needed a witness.

Can you think of another time Jesus commissioned witnesses on His behalf? It was in the opening verses of the book of Acts. Even though He had already demonstrated His character and His Godhood through His unique life, even after He had conquered death by rising out of the grave, He still needed witnesses. So in Acts 1:5 and 8, He stood before twelve faithful men and said, "John baptized with water, but in a few days you will be baptized with the Holy Spirit. . . . You will receive power when the Holy Spirit comes on you; and you will be my witnesses in Jerusalem, and in all Judea and Samaria, and to the ends of the earth."

A witness makes the light plain, and encourages belief in the light. A witness does not draw attention to himself but directs attention to what is *truly* important. John the Baptist is that kind of witness. He denies His own importance. As the apostle John observes in verse 8, "He himself was not the light; he came only as a witness to the light." This is the same humble, obedient spirit we see in the apostle Paul who wrote, "For we do not preach ourselves, but Jesus Christ as Lord, and ourselves as your servants for Jesus' sake."[1]

One of the things that alarms me about so many television and radio programs that attempt to preach the gospel is that they often seem to focus on the *witness*—the preacher, his looks, his dynamic preaching style, his clever way with words—rather than on the One he is supposed to witness to. But not John the Baptist! He is a witness who preaches Christ while denying himself. As a result, people stream out of the cities, towns, and villages. They flock to the hot desert places where there is not an air conditioner or a snow-cone stand in sight.

What draws these people out of their homes and into the desert? Only this: a witness with a wonderful message about a light—a light that shows a way out of darkness!

Have They Not Heard?

The apostle John now resumes his revelation of Jesus' true nature and purpose in the world.

1:9–11 *The true light that gives light to every man was coming into the world. He was in the world, and though the world was made through him, the world did not recognize him. He came to that which was his own, but his own did not receive him.*

Here is the first reference in John's gospel to the incarnation of Jesus. He was "the true light that gives light to every man." What is this "light" that the "true light" gives to every human being? It is the light of creation. It is the witness that God's creation gives to the existence, the power, and the awesome intellect of God. Jesus is that light, because He is the Creator behind all creation. The creation speaks of God, and Jesus is the creative Word which spoke the creation into being.

This point in John's message raises a question that many people—both Christians and non-Christians—wonder about the Christian faith: "What about those who have never heard the gospel? How can you say that people who do not know Jesus Christ in a personal way are condemned in eternity if they have never *heard* of Jesus Christ in this life?"

What these people are really saying is, "Isn't God being unfair? We can understand how God could say that people are responsible if they have heard the gospel, if they have Bibles to read or a Christian witness to listen to. But what about those in remote places, people who have never been reached by missionaries, those who have had no opportunity to hear about Jesus? Is God going to condemn them too?"

The answer, as John expresses in this passage, is that there are no people who have not heard about God. You may find this a surprising statement, yet this is exactly the point that Paul argues so eloquently and definitively in Romans 10. After asking, "Did they not hear?", the apostle Paul answers his own question: "Of course they did." Then he quotes two lines from Psalm 19. To make it unmistakably clear what both John and Paul are talking about, let's look not only at the lines Paul quotes, but at the first four verses of Psalm 19:

> The heavens declare the glory of God;
> the skies proclaim the work of his hands.
> Day after day they pour forth speech;
> night after night they display knowledge.

> There is no speech or language
> where their voice is not heard.
> Their voice goes out into all the earth,
> their words to the ends of the world.

John, Paul, and the psalmist all agree: There is no one who has not heard of God. His witness is not only in the mouths of people like John the Baptist, but it is also woven throughout nature itself. Regardless of what language you speak, you can look up into the skies and read the message written among the stars: "God is!" This message goes out into all the earth, even into places where no Christian missionary has set foot.

I spent most of my ministry in the southern San Francisco Bay area—a corner of the world with probably more scientists per square mile than any other region in the world. The Stanford research facilities are practically in my own backyard. A short drive to the south is the world-famous Silicon Valley. A hop, skip, and a jump to the northeast is Lawrence Livermore Laboratories. For decades, I was surrounded by some of the finest scientific minds in the world.

I confess to you that I am amazed and a little perplexed that so many scientists—men and women who work on an intimate, daily basis with the marvels of nature, the miracles of modern medicine, and the wonders of high technology—have concluded that the universe came into existence by blind chance! Astronomers explore the heavens—the very heavens that declare God's glory and proclaim the work of His hands—yet many astronomers insist that the billions of galaxies which wheel through the heavens in orderly arrangement just happened! Biologists study the complex interactions of plant and animal life, while talking about the genetic "code" that is written in a strand of DNA—yet many biologists refuse to acknowledge the existence of a "Code-Maker."

All of this complex, fine-tuned order is the result of "blind chance," say unbelieving scientists. And they say Christians believe in miracles! To me, an atheist's faith in "blind chance" is much more miraculous than a Christian's belief in a Cosmic Designer! As someone has observed, it is comparable to having a tornado blow through a junkyard and assemble a space shuttle! What is it that blinds human beings to the testimony of nature?

John tells us that God has a witness in the form of the "light" (or revealed truth) of creation. But he also tells us that the "light" that is revealed by creation has also been personified in Jesus. The light has walked among us. The light has demonstrated God's power by commanding the wind and the waves to be still. The light has turned water into wine, has taken simple elements of bread and fish and fed thousands of people, has delivered men and women from crippling disease and blindness and death. The Creator, says John, has stood in our midst—the true light that came into the world.

He was in the world and the world was made through Him, yet the world did not know Him. This spiritual blindness—this strange darkness of unbelief—is still in the world today. Many still do not recognize their own Creator even as He speaks to their hearts today.

His Own Did Not Receive Him

What's more, the Creator came to His own people as the Messiah, the promised One, and was not received. "He came to that which was his own, but his own did not receive him," says John 1:11. This is clearly a reference to the people and to the land of Israel. Jesus came to the place where God had put His name, to the land that had been promised to Abraham. He came to the temple that was dedicated to God the Father. Yet His own people—the chosen people who had been instructed for centuries about the coming suffering Servant of Jehovah who would take their sin upon himself—would not receive Him.

In the previous chapter, I mentioned a discussion I had in a meeting with eleven Reformed Jewish rabbis in Los Angeles. We had a very rich and cordial exchange of viewpoints. During that discussion one of the rabbis joked, "You know, when the Messiah comes, we Jews will say to Him, 'Welcome,' and you Christians will say, 'Welcome back.' But the Messiah will say, 'No comment.' "

I laughed—but I did not agree! I believe that when the Messiah returns, He will say what is recorded in the prophecy of Zechariah. In that day, says Zechariah, the Jews will ask Him, "What are these wounds on your body?" And the Messiah will answer, "The wounds I was given at the house of my friends."[2] Truly, Jesus came to His own people, and they did not receive Him.

So we are confronted right away in John's gospel with the darkness of the world—a darkness resulting from blindness. The Gentiles are blind because they will not acknowledge their Creator, even though He has given a convincing demonstration of His power in nature and in the appearance in our midst of God the Son. The Jews are blind because they cannot see their own long-promised Messiah—even though He has fulfilled all the messianic prophecies of the Old Testament.

Does this mean that Jesus was a failure at what He set out to do? Absolutely not! God always accomplishes His purpose. Despite the world's rejection, despite the Jews' denial of His Messiahship, there were those who believed and received Jesus, the eternal Creator, as their Lord.

1:12–13 *Yet to all who received him, to those who believed in his name, he gave the right to become children of God—children born not of natural descent, nor of human decision or a husband's will, but born of God.*

Here is yet another of the many strange paradoxes of Scripture: Again and again it seems that God allows everything to appear to be totally lost. (This may happen in your own life as well, so you had better be ready for it!) Just when it appears that all is lost, that all your hopes are dashed, that all your dreams are doomed to failure—that's when God starts to work! And that's what God does here. Though the Messiah was rejected and the Creator was spurned, still God was at work in the midst of that rejection, producing an entirely new creation, a whole new society of people.

It starts, as John tells us, like the old creation: with a birth. Every human being comes into the world by birth. There is no other way. And every human being who would enter the new kingdom must come in by *re*-birth. (Later in the book of John, we will see Jesus astonish one of the leaders and teachers of Israel with the news that he must be "born again.")

John goes on to list the many ways people mistakenly *think* they can come to God. He says, first, that the new birth is "not of natural descent" (some translations say, "not of blood"). That means not by inheritance, not by human ancestry. You cannot get into the kingdom of God, or be born into the family of God, by being raised in a Christian family. You can't inherit the kingdom of God like you would inherit brown eyes or a dimpled chin. You can grow up in a Christian home, attend a Christian school, spend all your life involved in Christian activities, but you are not a member of the kingdom until you are truly "born again."

Second, the new birth is not by "human decision." You cannot make yourself a Christian by positive thinking or by making a resolution or by deciding to live a good life. The kingdom has been opened to you by God's decision, by God's own sovereign will. It is a gift to you by God's grace—not something you accomplished by your own volition.

Third, the new birth is not by "a husband's will," or as some versions translate it, "the will of man." When you were born into this world, it was not your idea; it was your parents' choice. But when you are reborn into the new kingdom, there is no other human will involved. Your parents may pray with you and instruct you and take you to church every Sunday, but they cannot cause you to be "born again." Nobody can make you a Christian. No pastor, elder, bishop, archbishop, priest, or pope can make you a Christian. You cannot be reborn by a ceremony, by reading a creed, by standing up or sitting down, by going forward or by kneeling at a bench. None of that makes you a Christian.

John says that God's children can only be "born of God." It is a new birth, accomplished by God within the human heart. Because it is all God's doing, no one else's, it is an accomplishment beyond any human effort, any human cleverness, any human manipulation.

The new birth is available "to all who received him," says John. Not merely all who "believe" in Him, but all who *receive* Him. Many people say, "I believe in Jesus. I believe He lived, died, and rose again. I believe He was who He said He was." But that doesn't make you a Christian.

Only when you receive Him, yield to Him, and surrender yourself to His lordship do you truly become a Christian. "He who has the Son has life," said the apostle John in his first letter. "He who does not have the Son of God does not have life."[3] It is just that simple. If you receive Him, invite Him to be Lord, and ask Him to take over control of your life, you will enter the kingdom of God. You will be re-born.

The rebirth experience takes place deep in the human spirit. God accomplishes this miracle. It is not something you can do, and you may not even feel it happening. Just as a mother does not feel the moment when a baby first begins to form within her, when the egg and sperm unite and the cells begin to multiply, you cannot always sense the precise moment when the process of re-birth begins. There may not be a rush of ecstatic emotions. There may not be any sensation of change at all.

But the new life has begun, and God knows the moment and God nurtures the new life and God controls its growth. New life has sprung up within you, and with it comes light—the light of God's truth and spiritual understanding—for as John says, "that life is the light of men."

The Bible will take on new meaning for you. Once you receive new life, the Book will provide new light. It will make sense where it never made sense before. What was once dull and uninviting will take on a new radiance and fascination. That is the mark of a new birth.

In time, and by God's grace, that new life will change you and mold you into the likeness of Christ himself. It is a growth process that takes time and patience. You do not suddenly, by magic, become a new creature. You grow after your re-birth just as a baby grows after the first birth. God has designed it so. But God's promise to you is sure: "To all who received him, to those who believed in his name, he gave the right to become children of God."

Think of the encouraging power of those words: "the right to become." That is what God gives. He does not wave a magic wand over us and change us, like Cinderella's fairy godmother changed a pumpkin into a coach! He begins a process. At times, it is a difficult process.

We resist that process, like babies sometimes resist growing up. Sometimes I think babies are a little over-romanticized. If we parents are honest, we must admit that there are times when babies are not very nice creatures to be around. Someone once said, "A baby is a digestive apparatus with a loud noise at one end and no sense of responsibility at the other!" But babies are human beings—and eventually they grow to become *mature* human beings.

So it is with the new creation.

If you have never received Jesus as Lord of your life, then why not do so now? Don't wait till the end of this book! Do it now, so the rest of the gospel of John will make more sense to you!

But most of all, receive Jesus now so that the rest of your *life*—including your *eternal* life—will make sense. Surrender to Jesus. Ask Him to take control. Experience the second birth. Apply the ABCs of faith. Begin the process of daily becoming more and more like Jesus.

Don't worry that you don't know how to be a Christian. Don't worry that you don't know how to act like a Christian or how a Christian is supposed to pray. Just talk to God, tell Him what's on your heart, tell Him you mean business and you want Him to be in control of your life. He'll hear and He'll act and He'll do all the work.

Welcome to the family of God.

Chapter Three

The *Real* Jesus

John 1:14–18

Will the real Jesus please stand up?"

If you're from the baby boom generation or older, then you probably recognize that line as a take-off from the old television show *To Tell the Truth.* In that show, three mystery guests would take their seats on a stage, and a celebrity panel—people like Kitty Carlisle and Orson Bean and Tom Poston—would fire questions at the three mystery guests and try to find out which was the person he claimed to be, and which two were imposters.

Imagine if Jesus appeared on *To Tell the Truth!* Would you and I be able to tell which was the real Jesus and which was an imposter? What if one of the men claiming to be Jesus looked exactly like all the Christ-images in religious paintings and stained glass windows—the "gentle Jesus, meek and mild" image? He's inoffensive, bland, perhaps a little wimpy. Could *this* be the *real* Jesus?

Well, then, what about the next Jesus? He's a fiery-eyed radical who preaches revolution and overthrowing the establishment. His favorite one-liner is, "Woe to you, hypocrites!" Could *this* be the *real* Jesus?

Then what about the third man? What is he like? Is he the *real* Jesus? When the announcer says, "Will the *real* Jesus please stand up," will he be the one who rises?

If he is the Jesus we encounter in the gospel of John, then yes, He is the *real* Jesus.

Over the past two millennia, many false and contradictory images and conceptions have been built around Jesus. But here, in the gospel of John, we are encountering Jesus as He appeared and was known by a man who saw Him face to face, who traveled with Him, who heard Him teach. Like the early disciples, we can stand alongside John and see Jesus in all His deity, in all His humanity.

By examining Jesus through the lens of John's gospel, we can clear away many of the misleading images of Jesus that have been planted in our minds over the years. But it's not easy.

It's a little like restoring an antique table. When you first bring it home from the antique shop or the garage sale, you see that the wood of that old table has been darkened and obscured by time, neglect, dirt, and layers of old varnish. But if you take a rag and some varnish remover and carefully strip away the layers of grime from that piece of furniture, you will find the true beauty of the natural wood that has been there all along.

The same is true of our image of Jesus. With a little honest effort, we can strip away the layers of bias and tradition that hide the pure, unvarnished *truth* about Jesus from our eyes. We can remove those misconceptions we have absorbed over the years from cultural influences, or our parents, or our peers. We can return to the source, the eyewitness account of a man who walked with Jesus and talked with Him on a daily basis, face-to-face.

As we approach this gospel, let's ask God for new eyes to see His truth. Let's invite Him to open this gospel to us as if it were written yesterday, as if we were meeting Jesus for the first time. And let's ask Him to *change our lives* with the truth He has for us there.

Not a Bore

In his book *Faith, Hope and Hilarity: The Child's Eye View of Religion,* entertainer Dick Van Dyke laments the way we have taken this fascinating, exciting individual—Jesus Christ—and turned Him into a boring subject for religious instruction. As an example, he cites the case of a young Sunday school student "who saw his teacher setting up the figures for a biblical story, and said, 'Don't tell me we're gonna have that Jesus stuff again!' "[1]

If we truly understood the *real* Jesus, then "that Jesus stuff" would be the most thrilling and riveting adventure ever told. Unfortunately, we Christians have somehow taken this exciting story and made it boring. As Dick Van Dyke recalls, "When I was a boy, Sunday School was the dullest dryest time of all. I never heard anybody say, 'I was inspired . . .' or 'I learned something.' We would pass around the lesson for the day and each child would read a verse. We were reading from the King James Version, without understanding the grammar or half the words, and they were never explained to us."[2]

I think that is a crime—to take the story of Jesus and make it boring, to turn it into "that Jesus stuff." If there was one thing the *real* Jesus was not, He was not dull! As Dorothy Sayers wrote in her book *Creed or Chaos,*

> The people who hanged Christ never, to do them justice,
> accused Him of being a bore—on the contrary; they thought
> Him too dynamic to be safe. . . . He was tender to the unfortu-

nate, patient with honest inquirers, and humble before Heaven; but He insulted respectable clergymen by calling them hypocrites; He referred to King Herod as "that fox"; He went to parties in disreputable company and was looked upon as a "gluttonous man and a winebibber, a friend of publicans and sinners." . . .

He cured diseases by any means that came handy, with a shocking casualness in the matter of other people's pigs and property; He showed no proper deference for wealth and social position; when confronted with neat dialectical traps, He displayed a paradoxical humour that affronted serious-minded people, and He retorted by asking disagreeably searching questions that could not be answered by rule of thumb.

He was emphatically not a dull man in His human lifetime, and if He was God, there can be nothing dull about God either.[3]

The Glory Within

As we have already seen, Jesus is presented to us in the prologue of John's gospel as the Word, the expression of the mind of God; the Giver of Life and Light; the Creator who said, "Let there be . . ." and spoke everything into being. Beginning with verse 14 of chapter 1, John draws us even closer, and gives us an even more intimate glimpse into this amazing man, Jesus.

1:14 *The Word became flesh and lived for a while among us. We have seen his glory, the glory of the one and only Son, who came from the Father, full of grace and truth.*

The key phrase in verse 14 is the phrase "and lived for a while among us." In the original Greek, the word *lived* literally means "tabernacled." A tabernacle was a tent. In other words, John tells us that Jesus "pitched His tent" among us for a while. Jesus, said John, was a "human tent," a temporary dwelling place that came among us for awhile—then moved on. There is really nothing unusual about this idea. We are all "human tents." We inhabit these tent-bodies of ours for a time, and then we, too, move on.

To use a different metaphor, you might say that our bodies are "earth suits." Just as astronauts wear space suits to enable them to function in space, we have been given "earth suits" that are marvelously designed to enable us to function in the conditions found on this planet. The part that is intrinsically us is not the earth suit itself, but what's inside the suit. If I waved my arms at you, you would think, "There's Ray, waving his arms." But that wouldn't be me. That would just be my earth suit, functioning under my control. My earth suit—my body—is just the outer covering in which my spirit dwells. It is the earth suit, the tabernacle, the tent of Jesus that John lived with, talked with, walked with, and touched.

Yet the tent of Jesus could not hide the glory inside. It was the inner glory of Jesus that caught John's attention and made Him the amazing and unique Person He was. If you have ever been in a campground at night, then you have an image in mind of what John means when he says, "We have seen his glory." Picture it: the night is dark and moonless, and there are no streetlights to chase the gloom. But all around you are tents—tabernacles!—lit from within by Coleman lanterns. They glow like jewels in the darkness, filled with an inner warmth and illumination—an inner glory—that shines through the fabric.

That's what John saw when he looked at Jesus. He saw the glory within Jesus, shining through the fabric of His "tent" and lighting the darkness of our world. Then, using four striking images, John explains to us the nature of the glory of Jesus.

God and Humanity Unite

John uses this image first: "The Word became flesh." The Creator of the universe, the outpouring of the mind of God, became a creature made of soft, vulnerable baby flesh. What a staggering thought! In the original Greek text, those two words—"Word" (*logos*) and "flesh" (*sarx)* appear side by side: "*logos sarx* became." The Word, the creative thought and energy of the universe, became one of the most fragile of all His creations: a human baby.

Amazingly, that is what God had in mind from the very beginning. He designed human beings to be the bearer of himself. People have a capacity for God—and that is one of the stamps of our uniqueness. No animal has that capacity. No animal has any concept of God as we human beings have. Let evolution explain *that* if it can!

Every human being has a capacity for God and a hunger after God. Whether we know it or not, we are longing, searching constantly all through our lives for something that will meet what philosopher and theologian Blaise Pascal called "the God-shaped void" in the human heart. That capacity was designed into us by God—just as a flashlight has an empty space designed into it where the batteries are supposed to go—because God intended you and me to be His dwelling place.

In Jesus Christ, the concept of God dwelling within the human race takes on profound new meaning: God and humanity have united in a single human being.

In his letters, John the apostle says that this truth is so fundamental to our faith that a denial of it constitutes an anti-Christian heresy: "Every spirit that acknowledges that Jesus Christ has come in the flesh is from God, but every spirit that does not acknowledge Jesus is not from God. This is the spirit of antichrist."[4] Here is the test of heresy: If any teacher, church, denomination, or religion teaches that Jesus is not God made flesh, then that teaching is false.

The glory that John saw shining from within the "tent" of Jesus' humanity was the eternal glory of the living Word of God.

The Glory of the Son

The second image John uses to describe the glory of Jesus is the phrase "the glory of the one and only Son." As everyone knows, sons often display the traits of their fathers. A son may look like the father, may have a similar-sounding voice and similar mannerisms. A son may even display some of the same character qualities and abilities as his father. You can often tell a lot about a father by meeting his son.

Dr. R. A. Torrey was the founder of the Church of the Open Door in Los Angeles, and the founder of the Bible Institute of Los Angeles, now known as Biola University in La Mirada, California. Dr. Torrey was an associate of D. L. Moody, and was one of the great Bible teachers of the past generation. I never met Dr. Torrey, but some years ago I had the privilege of meeting his son. Everyone who knew both Torrey Senior and Torrey Junior agreed that the son looked exactly like the father. Even his expressions, his personality, and the timbre of his voice reflected his father. Because I knew his son, I have always felt that somehow I knew Dr. R. A. Torrey.

That is what John is saying here: the glory that he saw in Jesus was an exact reproduction of the glory of the Father, because the Son reflects the Father.

Full of Grace and Truth

The third image John uses to describe the glory of Jesus is the phrase "full of grace and truth." The glory that shone in Jesus, that was recognized by most of the people with whom He came in contact, was the same glory that characterized God the Father: *grace and truth.*

There are many good definitions for the word *grace.* Someone has defined it as "that which God does within you—without you." Another helpful definition is that famous acrostic: G-R-A-C-E—God's Riches At Christ's Expense. Perhaps the simplest definition of all is that grace is "the generosity of love." The greatest evidence of grace in the Bible is contained in the words, "For God so loved the world that he gave his one and only Son, that whoever believes in him shall not perish but have eternal life."[5] That is grace: Love giving itself.

Truth is the manifestation of reality, the unveiling of what is actually there, the stripping off of all the facades, illusions, and phoniness. Jesus was full of both grace and truth. He was the ultimate revelation of what is real. And He is the fullest expression of love giving itself, pouring out, reaching out to others. That is the glory that John saw in Jesus.

These words connect with John's words in verse 4: "In him was life, and that life was the light of men." Grace and truth are really nothing more than life and light. Life is a revelation of the love of the Creator, His gracious gift to all His creatures.

And light is the comprehension of reality, the illumination of truth. Have you ever said, "I wish I had more light on this subject"? By that you mean, "I wish I understood it better. I wish I could see the truth of this matter more clearly." Truth is light. The glory that shone from within the tent of Jesus was grace and truth, life and light. And in Him it was *full;* He was "full of grace and truth."

"He Who Comes After Me"

The fourth image John uses to describe the glory of Jesus is taken from the words of Jesus' forerunner, John the Baptist.

1:15 *John [the Baptist] testifies concerning him. He cries out, saying, "This was he of whom I said, 'He who comes after me has surpassed me because he was before me.' "*

The scholars differ as to how to translate these words. Notice that John's words seem to be carefully chosen to suggest Jesus' place in time relative to John the Baptist: "He who comes after me . . . he was before me." In other words, John the Baptist said, "This one who comes after me in time was before me in time." To the people listening to John the Baptist, this must have sounded like a riddle or a puzzle, designed to make his listeners think.

Have you ever wondered why crowds of people were attracted to the message and the personality of John the Baptist? I have been to Israel six times and have traveled all through that desert region where John preached. Having felt the extreme heat of the desert, and having seen the barrenness of the landscape, I have always been amazed that people would walk great distances from the cities of Jerusalem and Jericho to listen to this shaggy, rugged preacher with the strange eating habits. What was his secret?

I believe the secret of John the Baptist was that he had a message that was targeted at the deepest needs of the human heart. He talked about a dramatic change that was coming to Israel—a change that would be brought about by an amazing Man, a change that would affect the lives of everyone who heard his words. People were hungry for what John had to say, and he said it in such a captivating, challenging, enigmatic way that they had to think deeply about it. They had to wrestle with it. They had to come to grips with it.

John's riddle in verse 15 is actually a profound statement of the truest, deepest nature of Jesus: "He who comes after me," John the Baptist says, in effect, "is actually the Eternal One, the One who came before me and before all that is." Here is John the Baptist's image of the glory of Jesus Christ—the glory of God himself, come to live as a suffering and limited member of the human race.

In his prologue, the apostle John is weaving together several strands of imagery into a tightly braided cord. There is the imagery of life and light, of grace and truth, of the Word who became flesh and who lived—tabernacled, pitched His tent—among us. This imagery spoke very clearly to the culture of John's time. It resonated with Old Testament imagery of a God who came and tabernacled among the people of Israel in the wilderness. If you turn to the book of Exodus, you will find the story how the entire camp of Israel wandered through the desert for forty years, and during their wandering, the Lord God pitched a tent—a tabernacle—in the midst of them.

That remarkable tabernacle was a moveable building made of animal skins and beautiful woven cloth. It was constructed with rods of silver and decorated with gold. The tabernacle was divided into two rooms, the Holy Place and the Holy of Holies. To show how remarkable and how different it was from anything the Israelites had ever seen, there hovered over it a cloud—misty and vaporous by day, fiery and brilliant by night. This pillar of cloud and fire marked the tabernacle as the dwelling place of God. It was a foreshadow, an indicator of a time to come when God would come as a man and tabernacle among His people as a "tent" of flesh and blood.

In verse 15, John the Baptist is introduced to us, proclaiming and preparing the way for the One who will come after him, but who was also eternally before him—God in His tabernacle, dwelling among His people, the God-man Jesus Christ. I believe the apostle John underscores these words of John the Baptist because this is how the apostle first discovered who Jesus was.

For some Christians, the conversion experience was a gradual process of emergence into the full light of a relationship with God. But many Christians can look back to a moment in their conversion experience when the truth about Jesus burst upon them like a flash of lightning. We know that John the apostle was first a disciple of John the Baptist, and later became a disciple of Jesus Christ. So it may well be that John the apostle includes these words of his first mentor, John the Baptist, because these were the words which first revealed the truth of Jesus to his heart.

Law and Grace

In verses 16 through 18, John goes on to tell us what it means to each of us that the eternal God has become a man and dwelt among us.

1:16–18 *From the fullness of his grace we have all received one blessing after another. For the law was given through Moses; grace and truth came through Jesus Christ. No one has ever seen God, but God the only Son, who is at the Father's side, has made him known.*

Notice the reappearance in verse 17 of the words "grace and truth," and the contrast which John draws between "grace and truth" on the one hand, and the law and Moses on the other. Whereas grace is the generosity of love, the law is hard, cold, unyielding, and without mercy. In short, the law makes demands; grace releases us from the demands of the law.

Perhaps the most apt symbol of the law in our own society would be the Internal Revenue Service. Every April 15, every American citizen must file a tax return and hand over what the law requires. If we fail to do so, we are subject to a penalty. "Do this and thou shalt live," saith the IRS.

In a similar way, the law of God, which was given by Moses, is cold and unyielding. Moses did not originate that law. It is God's law, and He entrusted it to Moses, then Moses handed it down to the people. Thousands of years after Moses was laid to rest, the law remains. It makes demands. It shows no mercy. Ours would be a grim fate if the law was the end of the story.

But, says John, "grace and truth came through Jesus Christ." He is the grace channel and the truth channel. Take Jesus out of the picture and there is no more grace, no more truth. What John is saying in these verses is that the Principle of Supply and Demand operates within God's economy. The law represents demand. But grace represents supply. It is the grace of Jesus Christ that supplies and fulfills the demand of the law. Grace releases us from the demands of the law—demands which are nothing less than absolute perfection.

Many people think that law and grace are contradictory, that they are opposing principles. The fact is, law and grace complement and supplement one another. Law makes its demands, rightfully and justly, and no one can meet them, but grace and truth are given to meet that demand.

Exodus 20 tells the story of the giving of the law on Mount Sinai. Read that account and you will see that the law came to mankind amid fire, smoke, thunder, earthquake, fear, and trembling.

Immediately after the law has been explained in Exodus 20 to 25, we come to Exodus 26, where the Lord gives His people detailed instructions for building the tabernacle—God's gracious provision to meet the demands of the law. Many people think that the Old Testament is about the law and the New Testament is about grace. But here we see that Jesus and His grace are clearly foreshadowed in the Old Testament. That tabernacle is a picture of Jesus, the meeting place where God's demands are fully met in terms of the sacrifice of blood, of a life poured out, of costly grace being expended on our behalf.

In Jesus, the apostle John saw the fulfillment of the tabernacle—so much so that he described Jesus as having "tabernacled" among us. He has come among us, bringing grace and truth, so that the demands of the law over our lives have been met. Now we can say with John, "From the fullness of His grace we have all received one blessing after another," or as some translations put it, we have received "grace upon grace."

And not only have received grace upon grace, blessing after blessing, but as verse 18 tells us, Jesus has given us a parallel gift: truth. "No one has ever seen God," John explains, "but God the only Son, who is at the Father's side, has made him known." No one has ever seen ultimate reality, but Jesus the Son has come to reveal the truth behind all things.

Deep Truth

In our society, we have collected an enormous amount of knowledge, yet the profoundly deep truths—the answers to the ultimate questions that human beings have pondered for thousands of years—continue to elude the philosophers of our time as completely as they eluded the philosophers of ancient times. You might think that as scientific knowledge has increased, as we have gained a deeper understanding of physics, astronomy, and cosmology, we would be closer to understanding who designed the universe, why, and what our place is in it. Yet it seems that the more scientists learn, the more they find out they *don't* know!

For example, scientists are constantly pursuing truth about the fundamental nature of the material universe. When I was in high school I was taught that the atom was the smallest particle in the universe. It was considered indivisible. Today, of course, "splitting the atom" is a part of our everyday jargon, and many of us run our household appliances on electricity that was generated by atomic power. Scientists have discovered that the atom is made up of electrons, protons, and neutrons, and that there are still more exotic particles such as in the nucleus of the atom. They have discovered other particles too, with exotic names like quarks, leptons, mesons, gluons—a whole "particle zoo," as physicists facetiously refer to it. The list of particles grows year by year as physicists conduct their high-energy experiments. Clearly, the more knowledge we accumulate, the more we realize how little truth we really know. Our ignorance of deep reality and deep truth is like an endless regression, stretching to infinity.

When I think of the endless regression of our ignorance about the fundamental nature of reality, I am reminded of a simple experiment you can conduct with a video camera and a television set. Use a cable to hook up the camera to the TV so that the TV displays a live picture of what the video camera sees. Point the camera at the TV, and you will see a picture of a TV screen displaying a picture of a TV screen displaying a picture of a TV screen—on and on to infinity! Our minds cannot even grasp what we are seeing—certainly there must be an end to these images somewhere! Theoretically, however, this regression of images can go on and on forever.

In a similar way, it seems as if the more we know about the universe, the less we know about deep truth. No wonder John says that no one has seen God at any time. He "lives in unapproachable light," as Scripture says.[6] It may well be that this "unapproachable light" refers to the deep truth about God which cannot be discovered by science or any other form of human inquiry. It is only revealed by Jesus Christ.

The one and only Son of God who dwells at the heart of reality, who lives in the bosom of the Father, has made God known. Jesus has exemplified and expressed and explained the Father. Through His words and His life, He has revealed God to us. When we come to Him through Jesus Christ, we discover a loving Father; around us are a Father's arms; a Father's wisdom guides our way; a Father's power protects us and guards us; and a Father's insight warns us of the dangers that surround us. Like an earthly father teaching his little child to walk, our Heavenly Father takes delight in us as we take our tentative steps of faith. That is the Person Jesus reveals to us when we come to Him.

The *real* Jesus Christ is the eternal Word, the Creator, the Life-Giver and the Light-Bringer—and the most thrilling and profound story ever told is the story of the Word made flesh. He has tabernacled among us, illuminating our darkness, and fulfilling the demand of the law with His grace.

No one has seen the Father, but John lived side by side with the Son. The more we understand of the real Jesus Christ, as He is portrayed for us by His close friend and disciple, John, the more we will understand of the ultimate loving reality that is God the Father.

Chapter Four

Call the First Witness!

John 1:19–34

A remarkable religious phenomenon emerged in the United States in the year 1948. That was the year a young evangelist began preaching under a tent near the Hollywood area of Los Angeles. Though sparse at first, the crowds quickly grew. Among those who attended were prominent Hollywood celebrities, many of whom made public professions of faith in Jesus Christ.

At first—as so often happens with events of this kind—the press totally ignored the revival that was proceeding from the big tent in southern California. But when some of the well-known names of Hollywood became involved, the media began to take an interest. Reporters were sent to investigate and interview this dynamic young preacher, who dressed in pistachio-colored suits, wore flaming red ties, and spoke with a pronounced Carolina accent. The reporters discovered that God was doing something astounding through this man, and thousands of lives were being changed.

That was the beginning of Billy Graham's career. Soon, he was invited to preach in cities all over the nation, and eventually all over the world.

The Billy Graham of the first century A.D. was a man named John the Baptist. Though he didn't wear green suits and red ties, John the Baptist was as colorful in his era as Billy Graham has been in our own era. John wore animal skins and lived on a peculiar diet of grasshoppers and wild honey. Like Graham, this young man had a very powerful message, which seemed to attract many people. At first they came out by the dozens to hear him, then by the scores. Soon, crowds numbering in the hundreds and thousands were streaming out of the cities of Judah and Galilee to hear this remarkable preacher in the desert.

Eventually, the response—and John's popularity—became so immense that even the religious establishment of Jerusalem had to take note. They sent a delegation to investigate. In John 1:19–23, John the apostle records the moment when the religious leaders of the Jews first confronted John the Baptist.

44

1:19–23 *Now this was John's testimony when the Jews of Jerusalem sent priests and Levites to ask him who he was. He did not fail to confess, but confessed freely, "I am not the Christ."*

They asked him, "Then who are you? Are you Elijah?"

He said, "I am not."

"Are you the Prophet?"

He answered, "No."

Finally they said, "Who are you? Give us an answer to take back to those who sent us. What do you say about yourself?"

John replied in the words of Isaiah the prophet, "I am the voice of one calling in the desert, 'Make straight the way for the Lord.' "

The people who confronted and questioned John the Baptist were an official delegation from the Sanhedrin, made up of priests and Levites, who had been sent by the high priest himself. The leaders of the Jews were not very happy with John. They regarded him as an outsider and a troublemaker. He had never gone to seminary, had never been authorized by any responsible body, and had never been ordained. He had simply arisen out of the desert, from among the common people—and suddenly crowds were flocking to hear him preach! He was a threat to the establishment, and the establishment could no longer ignore him.

The delegation asked John the Baptist, "Who are you?" It is not hard to imagine an implied sneer in the tone of these words. It may well be they were asking John, "Who do you think you are, anyway?" It is clear they had asked him about the popular rumor that John the Baptist was in fact the Messiah. John's reply, which John the apostle emphatically underscores: "He did not fail to confess, but confessed freely, 'I am not the Christ.' "

John Is Not Elijah

So the religious leaders tried again. "Then who are you?" they pressed. "Are you Elijah?" They asked this because the last two verses of the Old Testament—Malachi 4:5–6—contain a promise that Elijah would come again: "See, I will send you the prophet Elijah before that great and dreadful day of the Lord comes." Elijah would have a special ministry of turning the hearts of fathers to their children and the hearts of children to the fathers—that is, a ministry of rebuilding the homes of a decadent nation. That prophecy had been written four hundred years earlier, and throughout those four centuries there had been a sense of expectation in Israel that Elijah—that rugged, fearless prophet of old—would return. No wonder so many people, when they saw John with his rugged countenance and his bold message, asked, "Is this Elijah?"

John's reply is clear: "I am not."

This is an important statement, because those who believe in the New Age doctrine of reincarnation often refer to New Testament passages which seem to refer to John the Baptist as if he were Elijah. They hold that John was really the reincarnation of Elijah. But there is nothing ambiguous about John's reply in verse 21: "I am not Elijah."

Reincarnation, of course, is a nonbiblical doctrine—what the Bible calls a "doctrine of demons"[1]—a false religious notion concocted by deceitful spirits trying to mislead people. Though belief in reincarnation has become widespread in our culture, we must recognize it as Satan's substitute for the doctrine of resurrection. You cannot believe in *both* the resurrection of the body *and* in reincarnation. They are mutually exclusive concepts.

Why, then, do some passages in the gospels treat John as though he were Elijah, and refer to him as such?

The answer is given very clearly in the opening chapter of Luke's gospel, where Luke records the visit of the angel Gabriel to John's father Zechariah. The angel predicted that this old couple, who were long past the days of childbearing, would have a child by a miraculous birth. His name was to be called John, meaning "God is gracious." God, not Zechariah, selected that name. The angel said of John, "He will go on before the Lord, in the spirit and power of Elijah."[2]

Here is the fulfillment of the Old Testament predictions that before the Lord would appear, Elijah the prophet would come. John's ministry was like Elijah's, and he went before Jesus in the spirit and the power of Elijah—but he was *not* Elijah.

A Voice in the Wilderness

After John the Baptist had denied he was the Messiah and denied he was Elijah, the delegation of religious leaders asked him, "Are you the Prophet?" This question was a reference to the popular expectation that one of the prophets was going to return—an expectation based on the statement of Moses in Deuteronomy 18:15—"The Lord your God will raise up for you a prophet like me from among your own brothers."

Some thought the Prophet would be Jeremiah. Others, because they did not know which prophet would return, called him, "that prophet." To this question, John's response is simply, "No." Notice the increasing bluntness of his answers. "I am not the Christ." Are you Elijah? "I am not." Are you the Prophet? "No."

Finally they say, in effect, "Who are you, then? We've been sent to find out who you are. We can't go back to Jerusalem without an answer." We can discern a lessening of their belligerence here. They began by saying, "Who do you think you are?" but they end up saying, "Come on, give us a break. We need to tell them something about you."

To this John replies, in the words of Isaiah, "I am the voice of one calling in the desert, 'Make straight the way for the Lord.' " In other words, "If you want to know my job description, read the prophet Isaiah. It's written there for you." This indicates that John had learned about who he was and what he was to do by reading and studying the prophecy of Isaiah.

Undoubtedly his parents had told him the wonderful story of his birth, and the predictions of the angel. He knew from childhood that he was a chosen vessel of the Lord, that he was filled with the Holy Spirit from his mother's womb. But when he asked himself—as he must have as a young boy—"What does God want me to do?", he found the answer in the prophecy of Isaiah: "Make straight the way for the Lord." In other words, John discovered that he was to be a highway builder, preparing a straight highway in the desert for God.

It is important to note that this highway was not intended to enable human beings to travel to God, but for God to reach us. Isaiah tells us how highways are built: "Every valley shall be raised up, every mountain and hill made low; the rough ground shall become level, the rugged places a plain."[3] Ask a modern transportation engineer and he will tell you that is exactly how a highway is built: the low spots are filled in, the high spots are leveled, the crooked ones are straightened out, and the rough ones are made smooth.

This vivid and descriptive word-picture of John's ministry to people is still an apt description of the way repentance works in the human heart today. If you feel worthless, depressed, and insignificant, if you feel your life is meaningless, if you are in a valley—then look to God and He will lift you up! "Every valley shall be raised up." God will meet you there.

If you feel proud and self-satisfied, perfectly sufficient to handle your own affairs, then you need to come *down* in order to find God: "Every mountain and hill made low." God will meet you there, and nowhere else. If you are handling things in a crooked manner, if you are devious in your business dealings and untrustworthy in your relationships with others, then repent. That is what John preached: "Repent!" Straighten out your life. God will meet you right there.

That is the kind of highway God used John to build in the desert places of human lives. That was John's ministry throughout his life. And the symbol he used was water baptism—a symbol which depicted a life being washed clean of the old ways.

"Why Do You Baptize?"

In verses 19 through 23, John the Baptist clarifies his own role and identity. Beginning with verse 24, John goes on to accomplish the mission for which he was born: To present and announce Jesus Christ to the world. In the centuries since John the Baptist lived and died, many men and women have served as witnesses to the person and character of Jesus. But when God called John the Baptist, He said, in effect, "Call the *first* witness!" John the Baptist was the first among thousands to bear witness to Jesus Christ. In fact, he was the forerunner and herald of Jesus.

1:24–25 *Now some Pharisees who had been sent questioned him, "Why then do you baptize if you are not the Christ, nor Elijah, nor the Prophet?"*

Baptizing was a new thing in Israel. No prophet or religious leader had ever baptized before. Under the law there were certain washings provided for those who were unclean or who had defiled themselves in some ceremonial way, and new converts were required to wash themselves before entering the ranks of Judaism. But nobody went around baptizing as John the Baptist did. When they asked him, "Why do you do this?" they were emphasizing the rite of baptism that John the Baptist performed. John's response is recorded next.

1:26–27 *"I baptize with water," John replied, "but among you stands one you do not know. He is the one who comes after me, the thongs of whose sandals I am not worthy to untie."*

John takes the question, "Why are you baptizing?" and turns it around to point to Jesus, to elevate Jesus—and to humble himself. When John begins by saying, "I baptize with water," you naturally expect him to go on to speak of the one who will baptize with the Spirit—but he doesn't do so at this point. That will come the next day, as we will see.

In the construction of the original Greek text, the emphatic word in this verse is not *water* but *I*. "I baptize with water," he says. And implied in the emphasis John gives to these words is a sense that John is saying, "I am simply dealing with externals. That is my ministry. But there is one standing among you"—and here John uses the present continuous tense—"there is one standing among you right now whom you do not know, whose dignity, whose person is such that I am not worthy to untie His shoestrings."

He Stands Among You

John the apostle records that this event took place at a very significant location.

1:28 *This all happened at Bethany on the other side of the Jordan, where John was baptizing.*

The old name for Bethany is Bethabara, which means, "the place of passage." Tradition held that this was where the Israelites entered the promised land under Joshua. John the apostle identifies Bethany as a significant location, and it was there that John the Baptist first pointed out who Jesus was. Joshua was a symbolic type of Jesus—a forerunner of the true Leader who would lead His people into the Promised Land.

It is clear from this passage that Jesus was physically standing in the midst of the crowd—a fact which helps us to determine when this event took place. By comparing John's gospel with the other gospels, it is clear that the incident recorded here took place at least six weeks after Jesus had been baptized by John in the Jordan River. (John will say the next day that it had already taken place.) According to the other gospels, Jesus left immediately to go into the desert for that remarkable experience of forty days and forty nights, tempted by the Devil.

All of these events took place *before* the delegation came from the Sanhedrin to investigate John the Baptist. By the time of the event in John 1:19–28, Jesus had come back from the desert and was now standing in the crowd. John recognized Him and said to the delegation, "Among you stands one you do not know. He is the one who comes after me, the thongs of whose sandals I am not worthy to untie."

How did John know that? He undoubtedly learned it from his studies in the Messianic prophecies of Isaiah. John's words—"among you stands one you do not know"—must have sent chills up and down the spines of those present. Can't you see them craning their necks and looking around to see who he was talking about? John does not identify Jesus any further at this point.

Read through the prophecies of Isaiah and you will see what John learned. Isaiah predicted the coming of one who would be born as a babe to a virgin. He would grow up and "the government will be on his shoulders. And he will be called Wonderful Counselor, Mighty God, Everlasting Father, Prince of Peace."[4] He would be the one to emerge in Isaiah 53 as the bearer of all human sin: "We all, like sheep, have gone astray, each of us has turned to his own way; and the Lord has laid on him the iniquity of us all." He would be the one in Isaiah 63 who would come out of Bozrah with crimson-stained garments, the one who had been treading out the winepress of God's judgment.

John the Baptist learned all of this from Isaiah. He says, in effect, "Like Isaiah, I am merely a voice in the wilderness. Listen to what I say—not because of who I am, but because I am talking about one who is far greater than I. He is so far above me that, compared to Him, I am like a servant—such a lowly servant I am not even worthy to untie my master's shoes." In other words, John is pointing to the long-awaited Messiah!

Someone Is Coming!

From the very beginning of the Old Testament, there is a sense of hope and expectation, like the sound of approaching footsteps: *Someone is coming!* To Adam and Eve as they are driven out of Eden, there is the promise that Someone is coming who will one day bruise the serpent's head. That hope increases throughout the prophetic record as prophet after prophet declares yet another tantalizing hint: *Someone is coming!* By the time the book of Malachi is written and the Old Testament canon is closed, that mysterious *Someone* has not yet come, and the Old Testament remains a book of unfulfilled prophecies.

But then, out of the wilderness, comes John the Baptist. He comes preaching and baptizing—and he makes an astounding announcement: *Someone* stands among you, and He is the long-awaited fulfillment of the prophecies of Scripture! And he goes on to proclaim a second and even more astounding truth about Jesus.

1:29–31 *The next day John saw Jesus coming toward him and said, "Look, the Lamb of God, who takes away the sin of the world! This is the one I meant when I said, 'A man who comes after me has surpassed me because he was before me.' I myself did not know him, but the reason I came baptizing with water was that he might be revealed to Israel."*

If you read through the Old Testament, you will find it a record of unexplained sacrifices. Abel, the son of Adam, offered a lamb to God and God smiled upon that sacrifice. Abraham made offerings unto God. The children of Israel were taught at the foot of Mount Sinai to slay and offer certain animals to God. Morning and evening and on great feast days, animals were sacrificed in the temple in Jerusalem. A river of blood runs all through the Old Testament—but nowhere is the need for these sacrifices explained.

Many people are offended by the pervasive presence of animal sacrifice and the spilling of animal blood in the Old Testament. Some ask, "Why does God demand the shedding of blood?" The answer is that every sacrifice was a testimony that *Someone was coming* who would supply that explanation! With the coming of Christ, at last there is an answer to the cry of Isaac, as Abraham his father was taking him upon the mountain to offer him, "Father, where is the lamb?" Remember Abraham's reply to his son? "God will provide a lamb."

Centuries later, as John saw Jesus coming toward him, knowing who He was, having baptized Him six weeks earlier, he announced to the crowd, "Behold, the Lamb of God, who takes away the sin of the world!" John saw in Jesus the fulfillment of all the previously unexplained sacrifices of the Old Testament.

The Baptism of the Spirit

When John says, "I myself did not know him," he means, "I did not know him as the Messiah, as the Lamb of God." John was Jesus' cousin; they must have known each other as boys. In those tightly knit Hebrew families it would have been unthinkable that they did not know each other. But even Jesus' own brothers did not understand who He was, though they grew up with Him. John says, "I didn't know who He was. I had heard some strange things about Him, as I had learned some strange things about myself, but I didn't know who He was until I came baptizing with water. I was sent to baptize in order that I might come to know who He truly is—the Lamb of God, who takes away the sin of the world."

1:32–33 *Then John gave this testimony: "I saw the Spirit come down from heaven as a dove and remain on him. I would not have known him, except that the one who sent me to baptize with water told me, 'The man on whom you see the Spirit come down and remain is he who will baptize with the Holy Spirit.' "*

Baptized by the Holy Spirit of God himself! Here was a promise of the fulfillment of one of humankind's oldest longings—the longing to experience God's indwelling presence, the longing after inner righteousness and holiness, the longing to seize that evil, self-centered tendency within ourselves and eliminate it. Have you ever experienced that longing? I certainly have!

There have been times I wished I could have a "sin-ectomy"—a surgical operation to remove my tendency to be sharp, critical, and caustic. But there is no way to cut sin out of the human heart with a knife. It takes God himself to do that. It is the work the Spirit was sent to do.

Here John is saying, in effect, "I deal with the externals. That is as far as I can go. But when I baptized Jesus, I saw the One who can change us internally—the Spirit of God—come down like a dove and light on His shoulder. The One who sent me to baptize told me, 'When you see the Spirit come down, you will know that *Someone has come* to baptize men and women with the Holy Spirit and change them from the inside.' When that happened I knew who that *Someone* was—my own cousin, Jesus of Nazareth."

Paul, in his first letter to the Corinthians, picks up the same refrain when he writes, "For we were all"—ALL!—"baptized by one Spirit into one body . . . and we were all given the one Spirit to drink." You cannot be a Christian and not be baptized by the Holy Spirit. You may not *feel* differently, because this baptism doesn't take place in your emotions, but in your spirit. It is a change that takes place deep within your inner self—a change that God does when He uproots you from the family of Adam and implants you in the family of God.

Later in John's gospel we will hear Jesus say, "If a man is thirsty, let him come to me and drink. Whoever believes in me, as the Scripture has said, streams of living water will flow from within him." And then comes John's commentary on Jesus' words: "By this [Jesus] meant the Spirit, whom those who believed in him were later to receive."[5] That is the baptism of the Holy Spirit!

The Son of God

In this passage, John the Baptist has identified Jesus as the *Someone* whose coming has been foretold and awaited throughout Old Testament times; as the sacrificial Lamb of God; as the One who baptizes with the Holy Spirit. And in verse 34, John the Baptist identifies Jesus with one more title.

1:34 *"I have seen and I testify that this is the Son of God."*

Jesus, says John the Baptist, lays rightful claim to deity. Every Hebrew would understand that if you say, "He is the son of peace" or "the son of encouragement," you are saying He is *characterized* by peace or by encouragement. You are making a statement about that person's intrinsic nature. So if Jesus is the Son of God, then He is God himself! That is what John the Baptist claims.

"Among you stands one you do not know," John said to the crowd. Jesus stood among that crowd, and He stands among us, too. The God and Creator of the universe has come into our world as one of us—subject to our pain, our sorrows, our poverty, and even death itself. He has come from the Father to bring us His love, forgiveness, and healing. Twenty centuries after John presented Jesus to the people who thronged the banks of the Jordan, the truth of His words still resonate in our own hearts.

He is God in the flesh. And He stands among us.

Chapter Five

The Man Other Men Followed

John 1:35–51

The proverb that says, "To plant for a year, plant wheat. To plant for a decade, plant trees. To plant for a century, plant people."

As we come to the concluding portion of John chapter 1, it will be clear that Jesus Christ planted not just for a year, nor a decade, nor even so much as a century. Jesus planted for the millennia, and indeed for all time. In this passage, we will see Jesus call men unto himself, and He will plant them at the crossroads of time, and these few men will change the course of history for the next twenty centuries.

The First Two Disciples

John tells us that Jesus began with two men who had already been in training under John the Baptist.

1:35–40 *The next day John was there again with two of his disciples. When he saw Jesus passing by, he said, "Look, the Lamb of God!"*

When the two disciples heard him say this, they followed Jesus. Turning around, Jesus saw them following and asked, "What do you want?"

They said, "Rabbi" (which means Teacher), "where are you staying?"

"Come," he replied, "and you will see."

So they went and saw where he was staying, and spent that day with him. It was about the tenth hour.

Andrew, Simon Peter's brother, was one of the two who heard what John had said and who had followed Jesus.

It is clear from this account that John the Baptist intended these two disciples to leave him and join Jesus. In chapter 3, John the Baptist makes that well known statement, "He must become greater; I must become less,"[1] and he has already begun living out that statement here. John knew that his role was to announce the Messiah, then step aside. Once the Messiah appeared, his own ministry would fade.

John the Baptist had already gathered a band of men around him as his disciples. Now he indicates to his followers that the time has come for them to follow the Messiah—and he does so in a vivid, impressive way. We have already seen that he had introduced Jesus to the people in a four-fold manner: as Messiah, as the Lamb of God, as the One who baptizes with the Spirit, and as the Son of God. Of those four he now chooses one, and it is interesting to see which one. He does not say, "Behold, the Messiah." He does not say, "Behold, the One who baptizes with the Spirit." He does not even say, "Behold, the Son of God." He says, "Behold, the Lamb of God."

John understood that the first problem—and the most difficult problem— people have to settle with God is the problem of sin. The only access we have to the Living God is through the forgiveness of sin. Only when we recognize and confess our sin and accept the sacrifice of Jesus on our behalf do we have an open door into the Kingdom of God. We will never truly know Jesus until we encounter Him as the Lamb of God, the sacrifice that was slain because of our own sin.

Two of John's disciples heard him call Jesus the Lamb of God, so they left their old mentor, John the Baptist, and began to follow Jesus. One of these disciples was Andrew, the brother of Peter. But who was the other disciple? We are not told. His name is not given here. Ironically, the very anonymity of this disciple is the strongest clue to his identity.

As you read through the gospel of John, you will notice that nowhere does the apostle John ever mention his own name. He always refers to himself in an indirect, oblique way, such as, "the disciple whom Jesus loved," or similar words. Since he does not give the name of the other disciple who left John the Baptist and followed Jesus, Bible scholars overwhelmingly agree that this second disciple must be John himself.

The Crucial Question

When John and Andrew heard John the Baptist identify Jesus as "the Lamb of God," those words must have struck a responsive chord within them, for they immediately followed Jesus. Whereas John the Baptist inspired their interest in Jesus, it was Jesus himself who inspired their allegiance. He drew them to himself, first of all, by asking them a question: "What do you seek?"

Those are the first words of Jesus in the gospel of John and they are profound, remarkable words! They are quite probably the very first words Jesus uttered in His public ministry. Like so many of Jesus' most profound words, as recorded in Scripture, they come in the form of a question.

I have always been fascinated by the questions God asks of human beings. The four simple words of this question go right to the heart of a human life. "What do you want?" Or, put another way, "What are you looking for in life?"

Have you ever asked yourself, *What am I looking for? Why am I here? What do I really want out of life?* Those are the crucial questions of your life and mine, and the answer to those questions will govern the way we live our lives and face our deaths.

What do most of us want out of life? For many people, life is a matter of climbing out of bed, eating breakfast, going to work all day, coming home in the evening, having dinner, reading the paper, watching TV, going to bed—and reliving the same dreary cycle the following day. Why are so many people content to spend their lives this way? Is that all we want out of life?

What do *you* want out of life? That's the question Jesus asks you today, just as He asked those two disciples two thousand years ago. As you ponder your answer, let's see how this question affected Andrew and John.

The Disciples' Answer

The answer these men gave Jesus was a very cautious answer. They replied not with an answer but with another question. They said, "Rabbi, where are you staying?"

I suspect it was probably Andrew who asked that question, because he appears throughout the gospels as a warm, friendly, approachable human being. He is the one who received the little boy who had five loaves and two fishes when Jesus fed the five thousand. He is the one who brought Peter to the Lord. He is very approachable—but he is also cautious.

No wonder Andrew is revered as the patron saint of Scotland! In that Hebrew body there dwelt the soul of a canny Scotsman! He does not give his allegiance easily or too quickly—but when he does, he is loyal to the hilt!

In my years as a minister in a community located on the San Francisco Peninsula, I have experienced my share of earthquakes. Many of those earthquakes were centered around a great geological fault that runs along the coast of California. There are few people in this country who have not heard of the notorious San Andreas Fault! But did you know what San Andreas means? It is Spanish for "Saint Andrew"! It is well named.

The disciple Andrew, the brother of Peter, was much like that fault. He was deep and quiet. There was not much action on the surface—but when he *moved,* something happened!

Jesus' response to Andrew's question shows how well He understood Andrew. When Jesus was asked, "Rabbi, where are you staying?" he replied, "Come and you will see." That is an invitation to investigate. Jesus welcomed the seeker, the inquirer, the one who hungered to dig deeper and know more. What a fitting response to the kind of men John and Andrew were! They were men of curiosity and keen interest, men who were not easily convinced—but once convinced, they were passionate about their beliefs and convictions. Jesus was instantly—and sensitively!—responsive to their need.

I've met many people like John and Andrew. They have open minds and they are willing to learn about Jesus Christ—but they cannot be pushed or persuaded against their will. They need to examine the claims of Christ on their own merits. They need time to investigate and make up their minds. If they become convinced of the truth of Jesus' claims, then they will commit themselves, body and soul, to the Lord and His message. I respect people like that, and I believe they should be given the time and the freedom they need to make up their own minds. That is the way Jesus dealt with Andrew and John.

According to this account, the two disciples went and stayed with Jesus all day. What they found was so fascinating they could not tear themselves away. According to John, it was the tenth hour when they went. It is somewhat difficult to know just what time that was. If it was Jewish time, then it was four o'clock in the afternoon. If it was Roman time (as I think it was, because John wrote his gospel for a wider world than the Jews), then it was the same as we count, ten o'clock in the morning.

During the time that Andrew and James spent with Jesus, they became absolutely captivated by the person of Jesus. We are not told what they asked Him, nor what He said to them. But the words Jesus shared with them and the personality He disclosed to them were so riveting and appealing that they ended up spending the entire day with Him. At the end of this encounter, Jesus has won His first two disciples.

Enter Peter

Now another major player in the gospel story makes his entrance—Simon Peter.

1:41–42 *The first thing Andrew did was to find his brother Simon and tell him, "We have found the Messiah" (that is, the Christ). Then he brought Simon to Jesus, who looked at him and said, "You are Simon son of John. You will be called Cephas" (which, when translated, is Peter).*

Peter, without question, is the best-known disciple of all. We all feel close to Peter—the man who suffered from hoof-in-mouth disease! Someone has said that whenever Peter appears in the gospel story, he always comes in with a thud! There are three words which make it easy to remember the process by which Peter came to Jesus: *sought, brought,* and *caught.* Peter was *sought* by his brother; he was *brought* to the Messiah; he was *caught* by what he saw and heard.

There may be a third man involved here, too. Notice that it says, "The first thing Andrew did was to find his brother Simon. . . ." The original Greek, in fact, is a little more emphatic: "He *first* found his own brother Simon." There is strong manuscript evidence for interpreting it this way: "He was the first to find his own brother." This implies that John also hurried to find *his* own brother. It is almost as though John and Andrew *raced*—each attempting to be the first to find his own brother and bring him back to Jesus.

John had a brother named James. (James and John were both sons of Zebedee.) Andrew and Peter, James and John, as we learn from the other gospels, were all fishermen from Galilee. On this day they are down in Judea, east of Jerusalem, by the Jordan River, where John was baptizing. But their home was in Galilee, seventy miles to the north. Undoubtedly they had brought their fish to market in Jerusalem, where they sold most of their catch. There they must have heard of the ministry of John the Baptist. Perhaps the fishing was slow, so they went out and joined John and became his disciples for a while. This speaks of the spiritual hunger and searching after meaning these men felt in their own hearts.

Andrew's first words upon finding his brother Simon Peter were, "We have found the Messiah!" Can you imagine the excitement in Andrew's voice as he called out those words? And can you imagine Simon Peter's astonishment at that news?

Andrew has spent one afternoon with Jesus, and now he comes running full-tilt to find his brother with the news that the Messiah—the One whose coming the Scriptures have prophesied for centuries—was among them *right now!* Obviously, Jesus made quite an impression in a short time!

Andrew brought his brother to Jesus and introduced him. "Rabbi," Andrew might have said as he pulled his brother into the Lord's presence, "I want you to meet my brother Simon." So Jesus looked this burly young fisherman up and down. "So you are Simon, are you?" said Jesus, immediately seizing on the meaning of his name—for Simon means "listener," "hearer," one who is constantly attentive to what is going on around him. "Well, from now on, you shall be called Cephas (or Peter)." Simon's new name—Cephas in Aramaic or Peter in Greek—means *rock.*

Perhaps what Jesus is saying to him is, in effect, "So you are Simon, a listener. You are tuned in to what everyone around you is saying. You are easily affected by the opinions and attitudes of others." Remember the actions of Peter when Jesus was being tried before the crucifixion? He was warming himself by a fire when a young woman came up to him and said, "Haven't I seen you with him?" Immediately Peter was affected by what this woman said, and he denied his Lord. This is the natural temperament of Peter. He is easily influenced, impetuous and impulsive, running after every word he hears.

Jesus read his heart instantly and said, "Your name is Simon, but you shall become a rock." Peter is going to be an anchorman, an immovable foundation upon which others will build, a steadying influence to everyone around him. Imagine Peter's astonishment as he was introduced to this Man for the first time—and the Man looked directly into his heart and read his weakness and also recognized his potential and possibilities. Peter's heart was instantly captured.

I've met many people like Peter. They have a capacity for great strength of character, but that strength is often undermined by their impulsiveness and undependability. They have never learned to listen to the right voice, so they listen to everybody. They putter through life and restlessly change from this to that until they fritter their life away. What they are looking for is a cause to which they can commit themselves.

In the hands of Jesus a person like Simon Peter can become as solid and steady as a rock. When such a person hears the right Voice and follows that Voice above all other voices, he or she takes on the character of a Cephas, a Peter. That person becomes—like the famous insurance company symbol—as solid as the Rock of Gibraltar!

The Invisible Man

1:43–44 *The next day Jesus decided to leave for Galilee. Finding Philip, he said to him, "Follow me." Philip, like Andrew and Peter, was from the town of Bethsaida.*

Notice that John specifically says that Jesus found Philip. Philip didn't find Jesus—he was *found*. Philip came from the same city as Andrew and Peter (and, presumably, James and John, since they all came from the same area).

One of the exciting things about studying the Bible is asking yourself questions about it. The questions that naturally occur to us as we read this passage are: Why does John tell us where Philip was from? Why does he tell us that Philip came from the same town as Andrew and Peter? Why does he say it this way?

The answer to these questions may be found in asking the obvious return question: Why didn't Andrew and Peter bring Philip to Jesus? They all lived in the same small town and probably were acquainted with each other. Andrew and Peter had just found the most exciting person they had ever met, the Messiah, the Promised One for whom the nation had been waiting for centuries. Why didn't they bring Philip to Jesus?

The answer: Philip is the kind of man nobody ever remembers to bring. He is quiet and shy—the kind who is easily overlooked, ignored, or forgotten. The only record of Philip's actions is found here in the gospel of John. The other gospels simply list him as one of the disciples. To read the other gospels, you might think that Philip is something of a "nobody." But, of course, in God's sight, *nobody* is a "nobody." Everybody—even quiet, shy Philip—is *somebody.*

This passage reveals Philip to be intelligent and perceptive. Later in John's gospel, he asks some very keen questions of Jesus. Yet he is virtually invisible. He should be the patron saint of all the quiet, shy people! Perhaps you identify with Philip—the man no one thought to invite. Because no one ever thought of Philip, Jesus went out and found him. If you are feeling forgotten and ignored by the people around you, then you can be assured that Jesus is seeking you, and He will find you.

"Follow Me!"

Once, I was speaking on the campus of Biola University in southern California. After my talk, while the audience was dispersing, a young man came up to me with a very serious, earnest expression on his face. Looking into his eyes, I recognized a hunger there.

He asked me, "How can I become a spiritual man?" I could sense in that question a deep longing in his heart to have spiritual power, to be the kind of man God wanted him to be.

"That's not your responsibility," I replied. "You don't make yourself into a spiritual man; nobody does. The words you need to hear are the words that Jesus said to His disciples: 'Follow me.'"

Those are the words Jesus spoke to Philip. Nobody really gave much thought to Philip. He was an invisible man. Yet he was intelligent, sincere, and spiritually hungry. Jesus saw him and addressed to him the words that captured Philip's heart: "Do you want to be a spiritual man? Do you long for spiritual power? Then you do the following, and I'll do the making. Come. Follow me!"

In the other gospels it is recorded that Jesus said to certain fishermen when He called them to action in Galilee, "Come, follow me. I will make you fishers of men." He didn't say they would do it. He said, "I will do it." One of the encouraging things about being a Christian is that you don't have to plan what you are going to do or be in life. You do not have to run through a computer all the ingredients it takes to become a spiritual person and then program yourself for it. All you have to do is follow your Lord and obey Him. Read His Word. Do what He requires, put aside those things He tells you to put aside. He will make you a spiritual person, just as He made Philip a spiritual man when he followed his newfound Lord.

"Come and See!"

We have already seen that Andrew became the first evangelist among the apostles when he ran to bring the good news of Jesus Christ to his brother Peter. Now we will see Philip became the second evangelist.

1:45–46 *Philip found Nathanael and told him, "We have found the one Moses wrote about in the Law, and about whom the prophets also wrote—Jesus of Nazareth, the son of Joseph."*

"Nazareth! Can anything good come from there?" Nathanael asked.

"Come and see," said Philip.

If you have studied the lives of the twelve apostles, as recorded in the four gospels, you may have noticed that the name "Nathanael" does not appear in any of the lists of the Twelve. That is because in those lists he is called "Bartholomew"—Bartholomew being his "patronym," which is like a surname, the name that indicates who his father is. *Bar* is Aramaic for "son of." Nathanael Bartholomew is the son of Tolmai, and Bartholomew is the English standardization of the Aramaic term meaning "son of Tolmai."

When Philip brings the good news to Nathanael, he bases his appeal to Nathanael on the authority of the Scriptures. "We have found the one Moses wrote about in the Law," he says, "and about whom the prophets also wrote." Then Philip identifies Jesus in a local context: "Jesus of Nazareth, the son of Joseph."

Well, that was too much for Nathanael! He had come from Cana of Galilee, a little village just over the hill from Nazareth. Having grown up just two miles from Nazareth, Nathanael knew the place well.

On my own visits to the Holy Land, I have been through both Cana and Nazareth. Today, Cana is a tiny village, out of the way and off the beaten track, whereas Nazareth—due to its fame as the home town of Jesus—is now a large city which covers the hillsides that used to encircle it. In those days, however, the situation was reversed. Cana was a center of commerce while Nazareth was a dusty little village with a bad reputation.

Nathanael's voice drips with scorn as he says, "Can anything good come out of Nazareth?"

But Philip wisely avoids arguing with Nathanael. Instead, he simply replies, "Come and see." Philip knew that Jesus could stand on His own feet and make His own case. It didn't matter where He came from. If He was the Messiah, people would recognize it just by meeting Him.

The Man with X-ray Vision

1:47–51 *When Jesus saw Nathanael approaching, he said of him, "Here is a true Israelite, in whom there is nothing false."*

"How do you know me?" Nathanael asked.

Jesus answered, "I saw you while you were still under the fig tree before Philip called you."

Then Nathanael declared, "Rabbi, you are the Son of God; you are the King of Israel."

Jesus said, "You believe because I told you I saw you under the fig tree. You shall see greater things than that." He then added, "I tell you the truth, you shall see heaven open, and the angels of God ascending and descending on the Son of Man."

Do you see a pattern developing?

Every time someone is brought to Jesus, He seems to look right through that person—almost as if He had X-ray vision! And He makes a penetrating pronouncement upon that person's character. Jesus knows what is in people. He reads the mind and heart and character. As John says elsewhere in his gospel, Jesus "did not need man's testimony about man, for he knew what was in a man."[2]

Many people view this passage as an example of Jesus exercising the omniscience of deity—the capacity that God has to know all things. While I clearly believe in the deity of Jesus, I do not believe He exercised omniscience in His earthly ministry. There are specific times in the gospels where Jesus says that He did not know a certain fact. I believe that when He came as a human being, the Son of God set aside many of the prerogatives of deity, including the prerogative of omniscience.

I am convinced that when Jesus "X-rayed" the souls of these men, He was so aware of the makeup and nature of humanity that He could accurately read the signals we all use to telegraph information about ourselves. He could "read" body language and the subtle cues of inflection in a voice. He could read a man's demeanor and the emotions revealed in his eyes. We all telegraph information about ourselves, even if we do not mean to. An astute judge of human nature and human behavior—as Jesus certainly was!—can tell many things about a person from a single glance, a handshake, or a word.

Jesus could read people instantly and accurately in a way no one else could. And when He saw Nathanael coming to Him, He read the character of Nathanael like a book: "Here is a true Israelite, in whom there is nothing false." There was no deceitfulness in Nathanael, no tendency to hide or be devious.

Nathanael's immediate response was, "How do you know me?" Clearly, Nathanael felt that Jesus had hit the nail on the head. He was a man who worked diligently at building both a reputation and the consistent inner reality of integrity and honesty.

Jesus replied, "I saw you while you were still under the fig tree before Philip called you."

Again, many Bible scholars feel this is a sign of Jesus' divine ability to see beyond the natural. The assumption is that Nathanael was over the hill, hidden from natural sight—yet Jesus saw him in some divine way. I don't believe this to be the case. The reason I do not is because of the word *saw* John uses when Jesus says, "I saw you while you were still under the fig tree . . . ." The word in the original text is not the Greek word for "saw"—meaning to visually observe or see. The word really means to perceive, to understand.

If we amplify this text by using the best sense of the original Greek words, what Jesus truly says to Nathanael is: "I saw you with my eyes, visibly, over there, talking with Philip. I saw Philip telling you something, and I saw your response. I could not hear your words but I saw you. And in that I *understood* who you are, I *grasped* the kind of person you are." This is the evidence that convinces Nathanael. This honest man of integrity, Nathanael, had finally encountered someone who can see the truth that is inside people—and Nathanael was drawn to a man of such insight and perception.

Nathanael's response confirms his own forthrightness: "Rabbi," he replies, "you are the Son of God; you are the King of Israel"—that is, the Messiah. Jesus commends him for that simple, immediate response of faith: "You believe because I told you I saw you under the fig tree. You shall see greater things than that." He is saying, in effect, "Do you believe because I said I saw you under the fig tree? That's wonderful, Nathanael. But faith like that is going to be shown greater things yet."

And Jesus goes on to describe the "greater things" Nathanael will see: heaven opening, and the angels of God ascending and descending upon the Son of Man. This is a reference to the dream the Old Testament patriarch Jacob had centuries earlier. Genesis 27 and 28 tell us that Jacob left home, fleeing the wrath of his brother Esau. He was headed for his uncle's home in far-off Aram. On the way, at a place called Bethel, he had a dream in which he saw a ladder reaching up to heaven. On the ladder he saw the angels of God ascending and descending.

Jesus said to Nathanael, in effect, "You will understand that dream when you learn of me. You will understand that I am the way to God for man, and the way for God to reach man. I am the bridge spanning the gulf between God and humanity." Jesus used an image from the Hebrew Scriptures that would be understood by all His disciples.

Four Observations

In this brief account we encounter the first disciples Jesus called unto himself. In closing this chapter, there are four observations to make from this passage that apply to our lives at the end of the twentieth century.

First observation: The Twelve that Jesus called to Him and instructed and poured His life into were men, not women. I realize this observation runs counter to the spirit of the age in which we live. It may even make some readers upset. But as I have studied the Scriptures, I see that our Lord consistently called men into places of ultimate leadership in His church.

This is not because men are smarter, or better, or more gifted than women, because they are not. God has given gifts of ministry to both men and women, and our Lord employs them both in His church. Yet the ultimate positions of leadership and authority in the church are, according to Scripture, reserved for men.

Clearly, Jesus treated women with a kind of respect and value that was unheard of in His time and culture. Jesus elevated the status of women in a culture where women were often treated as property and as second-class people. You see it in His dealings with His women followers, with the woman at the well, with the woman caught in adultery. Often, He taught women about matters that some of His male hearers were too spiritually blind to hear and understand. Indeed, women were the first evangelists, the first to return from the empty tomb with news that Jesus had risen. So there is a tremendous recognition of the value and worth of women in our Lord's ministry and in the Christian tradition. But the roles of leadership and authority are reserved for men.

I don't pretend to understand all of God's reasons for this. But I do know that, through the centuries, whenever this principle has been forsaken there has been weakness in the church. When men are true to what they are called to be, strong churches result.

Second observation: These were ordinary men. There is nothing unique about them. They were not the makers and shakers in their society. They were not unusually gifted, intelligent, respected, or powerful. They were ordinary. Jesus could have called His disciples from any group He happened to be with and they would have been successful apostles, just as He made these men to be. That is because the secret does not lie in the men but in the Lord who understands men, who uses them and empowers them to be what He wants them to be.

Third observation: Jesus never treated any two people alike. Andrew was cautious. Peter was impetuous. Philip was shy. Nathanael was guileless. Jesus spoke differently to each of them. He understood them. He treated them as unique individuals. He did not try to force them into a mold or crank out twelve identically xeroxed clones as we so often do to people today. He treated them differently because He understood who they were.

Final observation: Just as He called those men so long ago with the words, "Follow me," Jesus calls you and me today. Men and women alike are called to be His disciples, His followers.

And as He calls us to follow Him, He X-rays our souls and sees the strengths and the weaknesses within us. Just as Jesus knew what was in people in the first century A.D., He knows what is inside you and me today. He knows what to send into our lives. He knows what experiences will best shape our character and strengthen our faith. The people He wants us to be with, difficult and obnoxious as they may be, He has allowed to cross our path.

Following Jesus means accepting where He takes us and what He gives us. We trust Him, we obey Him, we put ourselves in His hands. His promise is that He will act in love for our best interests, for our good, and for His eternal purpose. He will accomplish whatever He sets out to do, making each one of us complete in Him, so that we can fulfill the potential and possibilities He created in us.

That is what it means to be a disciple of Jesus Christ.

Chapter Six

Water Becomes Wine

John 2:1–11

The German composer Johannes Brahms was invited to the home of a great wine connoisseur for dinner. After dinner, the connoisseur had some of his choicest bottles brought up from the cellar. He dusted off one cherished and well-aged bottle and carefully dispensed a few ounces into the composer's glass. "I want you to know," the host said as he poured, "that this is the finest bottle I own."

Brahms lifted the glass to the light, examined its clarity, inhaled the bouquet, then took a sip.

The connoisseur waited for Brahms' comment—but Brahms set the glass down without a word.

"That wine is the Brahms of my cellar," the host added, intending to compliment both the wine and his distinguished guest. "How do you like it?"

"You'd better bring out your Beethoven," Brahms replied.

As we open chapter 2 of John's gospel, we find the well-known event when Jesus took ordinary well-water and miraculously transformed it into wine—and not just any old wine, but a wine worthy to be called the Brahms, Beethoven, and Bach of anyone's cellar! As famous as this story is, there are new depths of meaning in this story that we can apply to our lives today.

The Third Day

2:1–5 On the third day a wedding took place at Cana in Galilee. Jesus' mother was there, and Jesus and his disciples had also been invited to the wedding. When the wine was gone, Jesus' mother said to him, "They have no more wine."

"Dear woman, why do you involve me?" Jesus replied. "My time has not yet come."

His mother said to the servants, "Do whatever he tells you."

Thus begins the story of the first miracle of Jesus. The scene has shifted from Judea, where John the Baptist was baptizing in the river Jordan, to the town of Cana, seventy miles north, in the region of Galilee. Jesus and His disciples have walked this entire distance.

John begins his account of this miracle with the words, "On the third day . . . ." It is rather significant that John mentions the "third day." John is referring, of course, to the third day after Jesus left Judea. It was a two-day walk to Galilee, and they would have arrived on the morning of the third day. John made particular mention of the third day because it had symbolic meaning. Remember that John the apostle wrote his gospel much later than the other gospels were written—some thirty or forty years after these events took place. By then he had opportunity to review the events that he had been teaching and preaching about for all those years and to select from his memories those things that were the most significant. There is a great economy of language in John's writing, and we can be sure that if he includes a fact or detail in his gospel, he does so for a reason.

John's reference to the third day suggests an allusion to the three days between the crucifixion and the resurrection. Even in the prophetic Scriptures of the Old Testament there is a reference to the third day as the day Israel would be spiritually healed and returned to her Lord.[1] Here, then, is the first hint in this account of the significance of the first miracle—the miracle when Jesus changed water into wine. It was to be a miracle of transformation, a miracle which symbolized bringing life out of death.

Here Comes the Groom!

The occasion of this miracle was a wedding—a Middle Eastern wedding. Weddings in the Middle East are very different from our Western affairs. In Western weddings, the bride is the prominent figure. When she enters, clad in all her glory, the whole congregation stands and the organ thunders, "Here comes the bride" and every eye is focused on her.

But in Middle Eastern weddings, the theme is, Here Comes the Groom! The groom is the featured attraction, and the bride merely shows up for the wedding. Not only is the groom the featured person, but he also pays for the whole affair! (As the father of four daughters, I have been trying to introduce that custom into our culture, but it has not taken hold yet!) Some Middle Eastern weddings go on for two or three days, or even a week, and the relatives on both sides of the family join together for a big, long, loud—and expensive!—celebration. That is the kind of wedding John is talking about here.

As Mary figures rather prominently in this story, it may well be that this was the wedding of one of Jesus' younger brothers or sisters. It may have even caused a bit of a complication when Jesus showed up at the wedding with five disciples who weren't on the guest list! He had just called these men to himself, and they had then walked two days from Judea. Obviously, Jesus had no way to phone or fax word that He was bringing a few friends to the party. So they just showed up.

As is usually true in the culture of the Middle East, no one seems to mind a few extra guests. Hospitality is a cardinal virtue in that society, and people are always willing to put a little more water in the soup and see that any unexpected guests are well cared for. So the disciples arrived with Jesus as unexpected—but welcome—guests.

That explains, of course, why the wine ran out. A two- or three-day celebration calls for a fair amount of wine, and five or six extra people can put a strain on the supply. Mary seized the occasion to say—very significantly!—to her son Jesus, "They have no wine." She does not ask Him to do anything about it. She simply informs Him that the wine has run out.

Some Bible scholars suggest that what she meant is that Jesus and His disciples ought to leave. In other words, Mary may have been hinting that the disciples were unwanted additions to the marriage feast, that they had strained the hospitality of their hosts and ought to leave.

Others say that Mary did not expect any miracle at this time because Jesus had never done any miracles before. And that, of course, is quite true. There are apocryphal gospels (that is, fanciful accounts of Jesus' life which were not accepted into the canon of Scripture, and with good reason) and some of these apocryphal gospels speak of Jesus doing miracles as a boy. In one story, for example, the boy Jesus and His friends were making toy pigeons out of clay. But when Jesus finished His pigeons and waved His hands, they flew off into the sky. There is no question that this and other such apocryphal stories are pure fantasy, for John clearly says that this is the first miracle Jesus performed.

However, this account demonstrates that Mary expected Jesus to do *something* to help. Personally, I believe she did in fact expect Him to do something startling and supernatural. Certainly, by this time, Mary's expectations had been greatly awakened. She had probably been told of what happened in Judea—how Jesus was baptized by John the Baptist, how the heavens opened and a dove lighted on Jesus' head, and how a voice uttered those remarkable words, "This is my beloved Son." She remembered the promises that were given to her by an angel, when she was told that her son would be the Messiah.

A Mother's Expectations

So, as the stage is set for Jesus' first miracle, His mother Mary expects Him to *act*. Perhaps she doesn't know exactly *what* she expects Him to do, but she expects *something*. Along with all the other Jews of that day, she probably expects Him, as the Messiah, to claim the throne of David, to drive out the Roman oppressors, and to fulfill the Messianic prophecies of the Old Testament. (Those prophecies predicted miracles of healing, of peace, of the lion lying down with the lamb, of the desert blossoming like the rose.) Now that Jesus has taken the initiative and called His own disciples, she naturally expects Him to assume His Messianic role and fulfill His destiny.

The fact that Jesus clearly understands her can be seen from His answer: "Dear woman, why do you involve me?" That is not a rude or disrespectful answer. In that phrase which in English is translated, "Dear woman," Jesus uses a common title of respect. It is the same term He uses from the cross when He says to Mary, "Dear woman, here is your son."[2]

When He says, "Why do you involve me?" that is simply a Hebrew way of saying, "You don't understand." So what He is saying is not that He will not act, but that when He does act, it will not be in a way that she expects. He is telling her, in effect, "What I do will not accomplish what you are hoping for. It will not persuade the nation that I am the Messiah." Miracles were indeed part of God's plan. Miracles would be performed, but they would not convince the nation.

Mary seems to be satisfied with His response, and says to the servants, "Do whatever he tells you." I have a number of Catholic friends who pray to Mary, asking her to intercede with Jesus on their behalf. I often tell these friends that there is only one time in Scripture that Mary ever interceded with Jesus—and in the end, her message to the people around her was, "Do whatever He—Jesus—tells you to do." That is good advice!

A Quiet, Dignified Miracle

The miracle is about to take place. As always, Jesus begins with whatever is at hand.

2:6–8 *Nearby stood six stone water jars, the kind used by the Jews for ceremonial washing, each holding from twenty to thirty gallons.*

Jesus said to the servants, "Fill the jars with water"; so they filled them to the brim.

Then he told them, "Now draw some out and take it to the master of the banquet."

They did so.

Notice the simplicity of this account. Everything was done with a quiet, simple dignity. Jesus said, "Fill the jars with water." And the servants filled them to the brim with a total of 120 to 180 gallons of clear, pure water. Then Jesus said, "Now draw some out, and take it to the master of the banquet."

There was no prayer, no word of command, no hysterical shouting, no laying on of hands, no binding of Satan, no hocus-pocus or mumbo-jumbo. Just a simple command and a simple action. Jesus did not even touch the water. He did not even taste it afterward to see if a miracle had occurred. He simply said, "Take it to the master of the banquet." The water simply became wine.

How did this happen? I believe it happened within the limits of a natural process. Let me explain with an illustration.

During the Depression of the 1930s, when everybody in the country was trying to make their meager earnings go as far as possible, many people were easy prey for con-men. A common fraud that was perpetrated on the gullible was the Gasoline Pill. The con-man would demonstrate how the pill worked by letting the "mark" (the person to be defrauded) drink from a jug of water. Then the con-man would drop a Gasoline Pill into the jug and would launch into his patter about how this amazing little pill was going to put all the oil companies (which were charging the extortionate rate of 20 cents a gallon for gasoline!) out of business forever.

The con-man would then fill the "mark's" car with gasoline from the "water jug"—and the car would run! What the "mark" didn't know was that, during the con-man's patter, the water jug was switched for one containing real gasoline. Many people who bought the phony Gasoline Pills ruined their engines when they filled their gas tanks with water!

The point is this: What the Depression-era con-man claimed to do was far more miraculous than changing water into wine. Chemically, water and gasoline have absolutely nothing in common. Gasoline is a volatile, flammable, man-made liquid—a complex chemical distilled from crude petroleum, rich in carbon atoms. By contrast, water is a natural, abundant, simple compound made of two parts hydrogen to one part oxygen. Regardless of what magical pill you put into it, a gallon of water does not contain the raw materials to make gasoline. There is no magical pill that can turn hydrogen atoms or oxygen atoms into carbon atoms.

But the miracle that Jesus performed when He turned water into wine is a miracle that goes on every day in nature. Visit any vineyard in any part of the world, and you will see this miracle going on. The grapes grow month by month as they take water up from the soil. As the grapes ripen and swell with water, they add natural sugar to the water. When the grapes are gathered and crushed, the sweet flavored water—called "juice"—is released so that it can be fermented by the actions of natural yeasts. The result is a beverage—clear and fragrant—that is anywhere from 86 to 92 per cent water.

This is characteristic of the miracles of Jesus.

In his book *Miracles*, C. S. Lewis has pointed out that every miracle of Jesus is simply a short-circuiting of a natural process. At Cana, the natural miracle that normally involves water, vines, grapes, sun, and fermentation over a period of months was compressed into a special miracle involving nothing more than stone jugs full of well-water. Lewis says, "Each miracle writes for us in small letters something that God has already written, or will write, in letters almost too large to be noticed, across the whole canvas of Nature."[3]

That is what Jesus does at Cana: As the Lord and Creator of all nature, He overleaps the elements of time, growth, gathering, crushing, and fermentation. He takes water—a commonplace inorganic substance—and without a word or gesture, in utter simplicity, the water becomes wine, a sparkling organic liquid, a product of living processes, belonging to the realm of life. Thus He demonstrated His authority—as God!—over the processes of nature.

Now, there are some who claim that Jesus didn't change water into real wine, that all He did was change it into very good grape juice! I consider that claim so ridiculous as to be hardly worth answering. They do *not* serve Welch's grape juice at Jewish weddings! They never have and they never will!

Elsewhere in the New Testament, we find warnings against the overuse of wine and against drunkenness—a clear indication that the wine of that day was indeed an intoxicating alcoholic beverage. Wine was a commonplace drink, one that believers partook of along with everyone else in that culture. Our Lord certainly did change water into real, genuine wine.

The Best for Last

The real force or "punch" that this miracle packs is not so much in the fact that water becomes wine, but that the water becomes a very *good* wine. This miracle is not just a gosh-wow special-effects miracle from a Steven Spielberg movie. It is a graceful, artistic triumph, a demonstration of the creative genius and elegant flair that the Lord of Nature lavishes upon His miracles. We see the Lord's stylish and tastefully prepared miracle at work here.

2:9–10 *And the master of the banquet tasted the water that had been turned into wine. He did not realize where it had come from, though the servants who had drawn the water knew. Then he called the bridegroom aside and said, "Everyone brings out the choice wine first and then the cheaper wine after the guests have had too much to drink; but you have saved the best till now."*

Can't you just see the master of the banquet taking a wine glass and sipping it, then swirling it around, inhaling its fragrance, tasting again, and pronouncing, "Ah! Chateauneuf-du-Pape 1966! And here I thought we were getting down to the dollar-a-gallon Muscatel!"

The servants, according to John's account, were smiling to themselves. They knew what had happened—but it was not their place to say anything. Still, they confirmed the fact that out of stone jugs of plain water had come *wine*—and an excellent vintage at that!

The account even hints at the bewilderment of the bridegroom. After tasting the wine, the master of the feast called the bridegroom and said, in effect, "Usually, people serve the good stuff first, while the guests still have enough wits about them to taste it. But you've saved the best for last! Bravo!"

What did the bridegroom reply? Perhaps he said, "We will serve no wine before its time." But I think not. The fact is, John does not record any reply—and perhaps that *was* his reply: total speechlessness! The bridegroom knew that all his best wine had already been served and consumed. Now—out of nowhere!—an even *better* wine appears! He must have been bewildered by this turn of events, yet he was smart enough to keep his mouth shut and to take credit for the good wine.

Miracles with Meaning

The significance of this miracle is recorded in one verse.

2:11 *This, the first of his miraculous signs, Jesus performed at Cana of Galilee. He thus revealed his glory, and his disciples put their faith in him.*

Three factors in that verse demand our attention. First, John says that the miracle was a *sign*. That is, it was a parable acted out in real life. Signs are not merely miracles. They are miracles with profound *meaning*. They are intended to convey truth that would not otherwise be known.

While a student in seminary, I visited the battlefield outside the city of Houston, Texas. There, at San Jacinto, General Sam Houston defeated the Mexican army and won independence for Texas. The Texans have erected a huge memorial tower on the site and with typical Texas humility they placed a sign on the front of the tower which reads, "This tower is ten feet taller than the Washington Monument."

That is what signs are for: to tell you something that you wouldn't otherwise know; to manifest a significance that might otherwise be hidden. That is what John means when he says that this miracle was a sign. It illustrates the normal result of the combination of human and divine activity. Men can fill water jars but only God can turn water into wine! Men do the ordinary, the commonplace—but when God touches our deeds, He brings them to life and gives them flavor, fragrance, and effect.

The meaning of this miraculous sign is that it is an indication of what the ministry of Jesus is going to be like whenever He touches a human life—not only during His lifetime on earth, but also throughout the centuries to come. Thus it affects us today as well. Allow God to touch your situation and all the humdrum, commonplace activities of your life can be charged with a new power that makes them fragrant, flavorful, enjoyable and delightful, giving joy and gladness to the heart.

The second factor John notes regarding this sign is that it "revealed his glory." In chapter 1, John told us what the glory of Jesus is: It is grace and truth. Here in this event we will see both His grace and His truth. His grace is manifested in the fact that He brought with Him five unexpected guests to the wedding. They had no gifts to bring, so He seized on the fact that there are six stone jars waiting. That is why He had them filled to the brim with water and then changed that water into wine. In doing so, He gave the most generous gift of anybody at the wedding: the best wine in the whole countryside—one jar for each of His five unexpected guests, plus one for himself, six jars in all. What a gracious touch that is!

But with His grace comes His truth. In this, His first miracle, Jesus manifested the truth about himself: He is the Lord of Nature. To quote again from C. S. Lewis's *Miracles,*

> If we open such books as Grimm's *Fairy Tales* or Ovid's *Metamorphoses* or the Italian epics we find ourselves in a world of miracles so diverse that they can hardly be classified. Beasts turn into men and men into beasts or trees, trees talk, ships become goddesses, and a magic ring can cause tables richly spread with food to appear in solitary places. . . . If such things really happened, they would, I suppose, show that Nature was being invaded. But they would show that she was being invaded by an alien power. The fitness of the Christian miracles, and their difference from those mythological miracles, lies in the fact that they show invasion by a Power which is not alien. They are what might be expected to happen when she is invaded not simply by a god, but by the God of nature; by a power which is outside her jurisdiction; not as a foreigner but as a Sovereign. They proclaim that he who has come is not merely a king, but *the* King, her King and ours.[4]

We humans have a strange habit of ascribing the wonders of the natural world around us to some undefined power or force that we call Nature. People say, "What a wonderful thing is Nature, which can produce such beautiful scenery." Or, "Nature has produced an amazing array of wonders in the animal kingdom." We look at a redwood tree and say, "Isn't Nature amazing!" But that is a tautology—a nonsensical statement that chases its own tail. The redwood tree wasn't produced by Nature, it is part of Nature. To say that Nature made the tree is to say Nature made Nature—or that the tree made itself. Ridiculous!

Someone has well said, "Nature is the glove on the hand of God." Imagine you are in your garden, spading the earth or pulling weeds with work gloves on. Somebody strolls by and notices how beautiful your garden is, and the comment this person makes is, "Isn't it marvelous that your glove can create such beauty! Imagine a glove being able to spade up a garden, and pull up weeds!" You would reply, "Glove, nothing! It was my own hand, at the end of my own arm, that did this work! My hand just happened to be wearing this glove!" Commenting on the wisdom and creativity of Nature is like commenting on the gardening skill of a work glove.

The third element of this miracle John calls to our attention is this: "his disciples believed in him." They believed that here was the Son of God, with authority over all the works and forces of God's hands. That is the meaning of this miraculous sign. The disciples were already following Him—but when they saw this miracle, they believed even more deeply than before. They saw that here was One who could handle life. Here was One who could take a commonplace thing and make it a source of joy and glory.

The Best Is Yet To Be

You've heard the expression, "the days of wine and roses." This world is constantly telling us, in one way or another, that youth is the time when one can drink the wine of life. Youth is the time we can really experience excitement, adventure, and passion. But when I sit at our table for the evening meal with my family—my dear wife (who becomes more beautiful with each passing year), my daughters, and my grandchildren, we experience together the best that life has to offer. We enjoy a family time of laughter, of sharing memories, of enjoying one another's company, of sitting in a comfortable home experiencing God's goodness in our lives and our hearts. At such times, the richness of God's love comes over me and I find my heart lifted to Him. And I whisper, "Father, you have kept the best wine until last!"

I think so often of Robert Browning's words,

> Grow old along with me,
> The best is yet to be,

The last of life
For which the first was made!

This is the significance of this sign for us. Our Lord—the Lord of Nature, the Lord of Life—has taken the commonplace, ordinary moments of commonplace, ordinary people like you and me, and with His touch He gives them full flavor, fragrance, strength, and beauty. He transforms the mere water of our lives into wine—and an excellent vintage at that!

He will do this in the life of anyone who will faithfully walk with Him, follow Him, and believe in Him. If you think you have missed God's blessing for your life, just wait! Follow Him. Listen to Him. Obey Him. Live for Him. And remember: He saves the best for last!

Chapter Seven

The Temple Cleansing

John 2:12–25

Joanie was a teacher and a dedicated Christian, very involved in her church. She had been raised in a Christian home and had known Jesus Christ as her Lord, Savior, and Friend for as long as she could remember.

Soon after Joanie's Bible study group began digging into the gospel of John, it became clear to the rest of the group that something was troubling Joanie. "What's the matter, Joanie?" asked Helen, the group leader.

"Well, it's chapter two," said Joanie. "I just wish we didn't have to study that part."

"What?" replied Helen in puzzlement. "You mean the miracle at Cana?"

"No," said Joanie. "The other part. Where Jesus gets angry and chases people out of the temple with a whip."

"You'd rather not study that part of John?"

"No," said Joanie. "I love Jesus, and I love the stories of how He heals people and loves the children and forgives people's sins. But I just don't like to hear about how He becomes angry and violent. That story always makes me feel bad."

Joanie is not alone. Many people have a hard time reconciling the love and grace of Jesus with the anger of Jesus. Yet the story of His cleansing of the temple is a crucial element in understanding the *truth* of Jesus. It is a story with profound implications for our lives today.

A Refiner's Fire

John organizes his account of the clearing of the temple around three factors: (1) where Jesus was; (2) what Jesus did; and (3) what the disciples learned by watching what Jesus did. Here John condenses about a week of time into two short verses regarding the whereabouts of Jesus.

2:12–13 *After this he went down to Capernaum with his mother and brothers and his disciples. There they stayed for a few days.*

When it was almost time for the Jewish Passover, Jesus went up to Jerus-alem.

We can easily fit into verse 12 some of the other gospel accounts of our Lord's second calling of the disciples. Matthew, Mark, and Luke record that as Jesus was walking along the sea of Galilee, He saw the brothers, James and John (the sons of Zebedee), and Peter and Andrew (the sons of Simon), fishing. And He called them to follow Him.

This second calling must have occurred when—after the miracle at Cana—Jesus moved down to the north end of the Sea of Galilee and stayed for a while with His mother and His brothers in Capernaum. Then, having called these disciples to a more permanent relationship with himself, He left with them for Jerusalem to celebrate His first Passover in the role of the Messiah, the Promised One of God.

Jesus had been in Jerusalem many times during the years before His public ministry began. He had been to the temple and had often seen the corruption there—the money-changers and vendors who turned the House of God into a carnival side-show. But in all of His previous visits to the temple, He had never taken any action against this corruption. This trip to Jerusalem, however, was different. This time He was going as the Messiah—and He was going to fulfill an Old Testament prophecy about the Messiah:

> "See, I will send my messenger, who will prepare the way before me. Then suddenly the Lord you are seeking will come to his temple; the messenger of the covenant, whom you desire, will come," says the Lord Almighty. . . .
>
> He will be like a refiner's fire or a launderer's soap. He will sit as a refiner and purifier of silver; He will purify the Levites and refine them like gold and silver. Then the Lord will have men who will bring offerings in righteousness.[1]

When Jesus arrived in Jerusalem, He came as a refiner's fire, to purify the Levites, the temple priests, so that the people could bring their offerings to the Lord in righteousness. This is the background for what our Lord did when He cleansed the temple.

The First of Two Cleansings

John has told us where Jesus was. Now he goes on to tell us what Jesus did.

2:14–16 *In the temple courts he found men selling cattle, sheep and doves, and others sitting at tables exchanging money. So he made a whip out of cords, and drove all from the temple area, both sheep and cattle; he scattered the coins of the money changers and overturned their tables. To those who sold doves he said, "Get these out of here! How dare you turn my Father's house into a market!"*

Jesus was clearly angry at what He found in the temple. He immediately began cleansing it—not only of the trafficking in money-changing and selling animals, but also of the extortion and racketeering that went along with it. The other three gospels record that our Lord cleansed the temple at the end of His ministry, in that momentous last week before His betrayal and crucifixion. Some of the scholars feel that John's account is of the same event, but John records it as having occurred at the beginning of our Lord's ministry.

These apparent discrepancies are difficult to reconcile with our belief that the Scriptures are without historic error. It is hard to understand why John would use language that sounds as though this event occurred at the beginning of our Lord's ministry. The answer, of course, is that there were two cleansings of the temple: Jesus cleansed the temple both at the beginning and at the end of His ministry.

A close look at the other gospel accounts reveals that there is a considerable difference in these events. In the synoptic gospels, a different Old Testament scripture is referred to. There is no mention of a braided whip. And Jesus makes a different claim for himself in that cleansing of the temple at the end of His ministry. On that final occasion our Lord made a great and final pronouncement in regard to the nation of Israel. Standing in the temple, having for the second time driven out the merchants and the money-changers, He spoke these dramatic words: "Behold, your house is left unto you desolate. You shall not see me again until you say, 'Blessed is he who comes in the name of the Lord.' " Then He went out to the Mount of Olives, and from there to the upper room, to the betrayal, and to the crucifixion the next day.

Here in John's gospel, however, is an account of anger and violent action on the part of Jesus at the beginning of His public ministry.

Extortion and Racketeering

John records the fact that this cleansing occurred at the time of a Passover feast. He undoubtedly wants to remind us that at the Passover, every Jewish household spent the day before the feast meticulously going through the house, seeking out any kind of yeast or substance that could cause fermentation, then cleansing every such manifestation from the home. This was absolutely necessary to properly celebrate the Passover.

So when Jesus enters Jerusalem, He enters a city in which every household is involved in a process of cleansing. By contrast, when He arrives at the temple, the very House of God, He finds it filled with clutter and noise, dirty-smelling animals, money-changers and merchandise. No one in the temple seems to be concerned that the House of God is itself in need of cleansing!

So Jesus became angry.

He was not only angry about the confusion, the clutter, the noise, and the smells. He was most particularly angry at the extortion and racketeering that was going on. Here is how the extortion racket worked:

Once a year at Passover time, every Jewish male was required to go to the temple and pay a half-shekel temple tax. The tax could not be paid in Roman or Greek coin but had to be paid in a special temple coin. So it was necessary to change the secular coins for temple coins. Money-changers were allowed to use the temple grounds as a convenience for those who had only secular coins to pay with. The problem was that the exchange rate they charged was outrageously high—often nearly 50 per cent above the face value of the coins being exchanged! The temple collected enormous revenues from this practice.

Another exploitative practice was the selling of animals for Passover sacrifice. If people had an animal of their own to bring, they didn't have to buy an animal at the temple—but the animal they brought had to pass inspection by the priests. The animal could not be sacrificed if it had a blemish or imperfection. Since the priests profited from the sale of animals by merchants in the courtyard, the priests had a built-in motive for rejecting as many animals as possible that were not sold by the temple merchants. You can be sure that if a priest looked hard enough, he could find *some* tiny imperfection on almost *every* animal!

As a result of these practices, even people who brought their own animals usually had to buy one of the approved animals from the temple herd, which were sold at inflated prices. It was barefaced extortion—legalized robbery, using religion as a gun. The victims were frequently the poorest of the poor. No wonder our Lord's anger was inflamed! So great was His anger that He made a whip out of the cords that held the animals together and He drove the swindlers and extortionists out of the temple.

Anger Under Control

Here we see a different Jesus than most people like to think about. We are comfortable picturing Him as the "gentle Jesus, meek and mild," the loving, understanding, forgiving Jesus. We'd prefer to serve a Jesus who lets us get by with anything, who winks at our sins and says, "Hey, you're not so bad. Don't be too hard on yourself."

But the *real* Jesus is not an indulgent, permissive Santa Claus-type character. The *real* Jesus of the gospel of John is a Jesus who demonstrates anger and who drives out oppressors and thieves.

Yet, even while we squarely confront the fact of Jesus' anger, we should recognize that His anger is not like our own anger. His *anger was under control.* He didn't rage and strike out blindly. His lash may have stung, but He didn't wound anyone.

He didn't even deprive anyone of their property. The animals He drove out could easily be collected again. The money He poured out on the temple floor could be gathered up and recounted. He didn't open the cages of the birds and let them loose, but ordered them taken away. He didn't destroy. He made a point: Don't turn God's House into a flea market. Don't use religion to make a fast buck.

Consuming Zeal

John has told us where Jesus was and what He did. Now John tells us what the disciples learned by watching Jesus as He cleansed the temple. In verse 17, we see the first of three lessons that were burned into the disciples' minds as they watched the Lord cleanse the temple—Jesus has a consuming zeal for purity.

2:17 *His disciples remembered that it is written: "Zeal for your house will consume me."*

Can you imagine what the disciples felt while their newfound Master was lashing the money-changers and animal vendors out of the temple? Were they shocked? Awestruck? Embarrassed? They had not been with Him very long, and they did not know Him well. Though they were attracted by the magnetism of His personality and the miracle they had seen at Cana, and though they were convinced He was the Messiah, they had not worked out all the theological puzzles surrounding this amazing Man. He was full of surprises.

What did they think when their Master strode into the temple as if He owned the place and began driving out the people whom the temple priests themselves allowed to do business there? No doubt, the first question on their minds was, "What will the authorities do about this? "Certainly Jesus doesn't expect to get away with this!

But as they watched Him lashing out at the swindlers and racketeers in the temple courtyard, a fragment of Scripture floated up into their minds—a verse from Psalm 69: "Zeal for your house will consume me."

For centuries, this psalm had been regarded as a Messianic psalm, a prophecy of the coming Messiah, and of His suffering. This verse—"Zeal for your house will consume me"—speaks of the fact that the Messiah would be seized, driven, and compelled by a zealous love for worship of the one true God, and respect for His house of worship. When that line from God's Word came to their minds, they suddenly understood that the One they had chosen to follow would never compromise with evil.

Herein lies one of the great paradoxes of our Christian faith. Throughout John's gospel, we see that anyone—*anyone!*—can come to Christ: murderers, prostitutes, swindlers, liars, alcoholics, drug addicts, sex addicts, cynics, snobs, religious hypocrites, and anyone else *as long as he or she realizes there is something wrong with his or her life and wants God to come in and change it!* Anyone who wants to be free can come to Jesus.

But as the disciples saw Jesus cleansing the temple, a realization must have dawned on them: Suddenly they understood—perhaps for the first time—that if you come to Jesus, be assured He is not going to leave you unchanged. He is not going to settle for clutter, compromise, dishonesty, and racketeering in your soul and your lifestyle. Whatever defiles and corrupts the "temple" of your body and soul will be purged. This purging may not take place immediately. In His love, He deals with us patiently. But equally according to His love, He never lets us remain complacent with sin and inner corruption. If we mistake His patience for indulgence and acceptance of our sinful habits, then we are in for a surprise.

When we commit ourselves to the lordship of Jesus, He receives us in love. But we dare not forget that He also comes into our lives with a zeal for purity. Many of us, like the Pharisees of Jesus' day, maintain an outer appearance of righteousness. But within our lives, hidden from public view, is the clutter of sinful habits: a lust for pornography or adultery; a lack of integrity in business dealings; an addiction to rage or indulgence or abuse. These habits have been a part of our lives so long that we think God will just wink at them and accept them. But God loves us too much to allow these sins to continue forever. If we do not wish to experience the chastening, loving lash of His righteous zeal, then we must clean house ourselves.

Delayed Reaction

The second lesson the disciples learned when Jesus cleansed the temple was that Jesus operated in a much longer time-frame than the rest of us do.

Many of His statements and actions involved a delayed reaction rather than immediate implementation. We see this principle in the dialogue between Jesus and His Jewish opponents.

2:18–22 *Then the Jews demanded of him, "What miraculous sign can you show us to prove your authority to do all this?"*

Jesus answered them, "Destroy this temple, and I will raise it again in three days."

The Jews replied, "It has taken forty-six years to build this temple, and you are going to raise it in three days?" But the temple he had spoken of was his body. After he was raised from the dead, his disciples recalled what he had said. Then they believed the Scripture and the words Jesus had spoken.

It's astounding how blind everyone was to the meaning of this event! For centuries, the Jews had expected their Messiah to come and fulfill certain prophecies, including the prophecy that the Messiah would come and purify the temple. The Messiah came and did just that—and the religious experts didn't even recognize Him! Instead, they asked Him, "What sign can you show us? How can you prove you are the Messiah?" Our Lord's answer was to give them a *future* sign, a *cryptic* sign—the sign of His death and resurrection.

Jesus gave the Jews a sign—but it was a sign with a delayed reaction. The meaning of Jesus' sign would not be clear to the Jews, not even to Jesus' own disciples, until after He was crucified and raised again.

The True Temple

"Destroy this temple," said Jesus, "and I will raise it again in three days." The temple Jesus spoke of was His own body. In this statement He gives us a profound truth that we dare not forget. God does not live in buildings. The true temples of God are *human beings.* Jesus was the prototype among human temples, but your body and mine are temples of God too.

All around the world are churches, cathedrals, edifices of stone and steel and glass—some costing millions of dollars. Pick any one of those buildings and odds are you can find a brass plaque somewhere on a wall that says, "Erected to the glory of God." I find such plaques irritating. Scripture teaches that God is not glorified by buildings. Even when Solomon dedicated the great temple in Jerusalem, he acknowledged this fact: "The heavens, even the highest heaven," he said, "cannot contain you. How much less this temple I have built."[2]

A building merely symbolizes the dwelling place of God. The real temples of God are human beings, composed of body, soul, and spirit. That is why Paul said, "Do you not know that your body is a temple of the Holy Spirit, who is in you, whom you have received from God?"[3] You do not have the right to defile that temple, says Paul, because it does not belong to you. "You are not your own," he continues. "You were bought at a price. Therefore honor God with your body."[4] It couldn't be more clear: Your body is a temple, and that is where God is glorified.

When I was a little boy I was told, "Behave yourself in church! Don't whisper or squirm in church!" Years later I made an amazing discovery: A believer in Christ is *never out of church!* A Christian in the body is always in the temple of God.

Looking Beyond the Facade

The third lesson the disciples learned is recorded next by John.

2:23–25 *Now while he was in Jerusalem at the Passover Feast, many people saw the miraculous signs he was doing and believed in his name. But Jesus would not entrust himself to them, for he knew all men. He did not need man's testimony about man, for he knew what was in a man.*

Following the first miracle in Cana and His assuming of the role of Messiah by cleansing the temple, Jesus launched into a public ministry involving miraculous signs: healing the sick and lame, and restoring sight to the blind. Many people were attracted to Jesus because of His miracles—but Jesus did not entrust himself to the masses. He knew that the masses were fickle. Many would come and believe and ask Jesus to be their Lord—but their lives would not change, and eventually they would drift away. Jesus knew that, because He knew what was in the hearts of men and women. Jesus was not fooled by outward professions and appearances. He had a penetrating understanding of the workings of the human heart.

Nothing has changed from that day until this day. We are still dealing with a God who cannot be fooled. If we honestly confess our sin, He will deal with us with loving forgiveness. If we defend and minimize our sin, we can only expect to receive His chastening, cleansing lash. God knows what is within you and me.

As the disciples watched the cleansing of the temple, they learned some astonishing, wonderful truths about God. They learned that even though God is loving and forgiving, He is a God to be revered and feared. Though He is a God of mercy, He is also a God of majesty. The disciples first experienced the warmth and acceptance of God's grace, but after the cleansing of the temple, they had a deeper and more solemn understanding of God's justice and purity.

May you and I take away the same solemn truth from our encounter with the real Jesus—the Jesus who not only loves and forgives, but refines and purifies and stakes His claim upon the totality of our lives. The Jesus who calls the little children to himself is the same Jesus who braids a whip out of cords and is consumed with a zeal for the purity of God's rightful worship. Let us, as believers and disciples, give all of who we are to all of who He is.

Chapter Eight

Born of the Spirit

John 3:1–16

A fter his public repentance and spiritual awakening following the Watergate scandal, Charles Colson wrote a book—the first of many books he would someday write about living the Christian faith in the rough-and-tumble arena of the real world. That first book became a best-seller and launched a new ministry for the former Nixon White House "hatchet man," ministry of prison reform and prison evangelism. The title of Colson's book: *Born Again.*

Largely because of the success of *Born Again,* the election of the "born again" President, Jimmy Carter, and the rise of televangelism during the 1980s, the term "born again" moved beyond the confines of evangelical and fundamentalist Christian circles and into the vernacular of secular society. In recent years, the print and broadcast media have seized upon the label "born again" as a term of scorn and derision. It's no longer fashionable to call yourself "born again," because the anti-Christian media has redefined the term to mean a narrow-minded religious bigot.

Despite the abuse and distortion the phrase "born again" has suffered over the past few years, it remains a term filled with powerful spiritual significance and meaning. I love the words "born again" because of what those words have meant in my own life and experience. It is a beautiful word picture that was coined by Jesus himself to describe a radical spiritual transformation that has taken place in my own life and in the lives of every person who has truly committed his or her total self to the lordship of Jesus Christ.

And we find that term used for the first time in John chapter 3, in the famous story of the night visitor who came to Jesus in search of the truth.

A Ruler of the Jews

In the first three verses of John 3, we meet a man named Nicodemus. Although he is a Pharisee, a ruler of the Jews—and as a class, the Pharisees were the mortal enemies of Jesus—Nicodemus came as one who was spiritually seeking and intellectually honest.

3:1–3 *Now there was a man of the Pharisees named Nicodemus, a member of the Jewish ruling council. He came to Jesus at night and said, "Rabbi, we know you are a teacher who has come from God. For no one could perform the miraculous signs you are doing if God were not with him."*

In reply Jesus declared, "I tell you the truth, unless a man is born again, he cannot see the kingdom of God."

John notes two important facts about Nicodemus: who he is and what he says.

First, Nicodemus was a powerful man in Jerusalem society—a Pharisee and a ruler of the Jews. He was a member of the Sanhedrin, the council of seventy men who ran the religious affairs of the nation and who had religious authority over every Jew anywhere in the world. That council was almost entirely made up of Pharisees.

If ever there was a group which deserved the label "religious fanatics," it was the Pharisees. They were a select group, never numbering more than 6,000. Each had taken a solemn vow before three witnesses that he would devote every moment of his entire life to obeying the Ten Commandments as a way of pleasing God.

The Pharisees took the Law of God very seriously. They sought to apply the Ten Commandments in every area of life. Those commandments, of course, speak about worshiping the true God and avoiding idols, honoring parents, and refraining from lying, adultery, and various other sins. They are written in a rather general way. The Pharisees, however, liked to have things defined in very specific terms. So a group of people arose within the Pharisee order called the Scribes, and it was the Scribes' job to study the Law and spell out how the Ten Commandments applied to every specific situation in life.

The Scribes took their work very seriously and compiled a very thick book, which the Jews still have today, called the *Mishnah*. To give you a sense of just how detailed and specific the *Mishnah* is, it devotes 24 chapters just to the subject of not working on the Sabbath! But there's more! In addition to the *Mishnah*, the Scribes also wrote a commentary on the *Mishnah*, called the *Talmud*. The *Talmud* devotes 156 pages to the subject of the Sabbath alone!

Clearly, the Pharisees were very zealous and serious about keeping the Law of God. In their interpretation of the commandment which forbids work on the Sabbath, the Scribes decreed that any form of labor which a man engaged in to make his living was forbidden. For example, a farmer or a fisherman could not tie a knot on the Sabbath, because knots are used in tethering farm animals and handling fishing nets. There were, however, certain exceptions to the knot-tying rule. If it was absolutely necessary to life, you could tie a knot on the Sabbath. Knots that could be tied with one hand were permitted, but not two-handed knots. A woman could tie a knot in her girdle or in a scarf that she tied around her neck.

In time, people began to look for loopholes in the laws of the Scribes— and many of these loopholes were incredibly silly! A man might need to draw a bucket of water out of a well, but he was not permitted to tie a rope onto the bucket because that would be violating the Sabbath. But if he tied the rope to a woman's girdle and then tied the girdle to the bucket, he could draw up water!

These meticulous, rigid—and often ridiculous!—interpretations consti- tuted the whole life of the Pharisees. And this is the religious climate that pro- duced a Pharisee named Nicodemus.

"Unless a Man Is Born Again . . ."

Once you understand the rigid, legalistic system of the Pharisees, it is amazing that Nicodemus would come to Jesus at all! The Pharisees regarded themselves as spiritually and morally superior to other men because of their inflexible adherence to the Law of God. Yet this particular Pharisee and ruler of the Jews came to Jesus with a heart full of astonishing humility and sincer- ity.

John tells us that Nicodemus begins with a courteous, respectful introduc- tion. "Rabbi," he says, "we know you are a teacher who has come from God. For no one could perform the miraculous signs you are doing if God were not with him." This is an amazing statement. Notice the word "we"—"we know that you are a teacher." Nicodemus is probably speaking for himself and other members of the Sanhedrin. He is admitting that the Pharisees—who vehe- mently oppose the spiritual freedom Jesus represents—know in their hearts that Jesus really is a teacher from God.

Nicodemus regarded Jesus as a teacher with authority, because God put His seal of approval on Him by doing miracles through Him. None of the other members of the Sanhedrin could work miracles. This was something new in Nicodemus's experience.

But even more alien to Nicodemus's training and experience was the reply of Jesus: "I tell you the truth, unless a man is born again, he cannot see the kingdom of God." According to everything Nicodemus had been taught, being accepted by God depended entirely upon adhering to an exhaustive body of rules and regulations. Now this miracle-working teacher appears, dis- pensing with that entire body of legality, and claiming instead that to be accepted by God, one must be "born again."

Born again?!

With a single sharp and penetrating phrase, Jesus has sliced through all the layers of rules and legalistic attitudes that have accumulated around the mind of Nicodemus. Like a sword, those words have pierced this Pharisee's heart.

Notice the words Jesus opens with: "I tell you the truth," or as it is translated in other versions, "Truly, truly," or, "Verily, verily." In the original language, Jesus says, "Amen, amen," an emphatic idiom used to underscore the importance of what is to follow. Jesus is saying, in effect, "I am about to reveal to you a fundamental reality of life. Listen carefully."

After highlighting His statement with this verbal neon light, Jesus goes on to say that the new birth is absolutely essential in order to enter the kingdom of God. The Greek word John uses that is translated *again* conveys several profound shades of meaning. It means to do something a second time; to begin something in a radical and totally new way; and to do something from above. So when Jesus says, "born again," He is saying many things at once: to be born a second time, to be born in a radical and totally new way, to be born from above, from God. Jesus is telling Nicodemus that the new birth is radical and transforming, and it is something that God does, not we ourselves.

To be in the kingdom of God, of course, is to belong to God. It means to be under His rule and lordship. Paul speaks of being rescued "from the dominion of darkness and brought . . . into the kingdom of the Son."[1] Thus, Jesus was referring to a transfer of citizenship, a radical departure from what we once were.

Jesus sensed in Nicodemus a deep hunger, a spiritual emptiness. Here was a man who was doing his level best to obey what he thought God wanted. Yet he had an empty and unsatisfied heart that led him to seek out Jesus by night, at the risk of the displeasure of his peers. Jesus—who we learned in previous chapters possessed a keen and penetrating insight into the hearts of people— sensed what was going on inside this seeker of truth. So Jesus did not waste any time in telling Nicodemus that he was operating on a false premise, and needed to make a radical change in his life. "You are wasting your time," He said, in effect, "if you think you can enter the kingdom of God the way you are. You cannot do it by keeping rules and regulations. You must be born again."

The third chapter of John was the favorite text of John Wesley, the great Anglican evangelist who cofounded, with his brother Charles, the Methodist movement. He used to travel throughout England, Wales, and Scotland, preaching, "You must be born again." Someone once asked him, "Why do you always preach on the words, 'You must be born again'?" Wesley's answer: "Because . . . you must be born again!"

That is what Jesus is saying here.

But Nicodemus misunderstood. With an obviously puzzled look on his face, he asked Jesus to explain what He meant by the words "born again."

3:4 *"How can a man be born when he is old?" Nicodemus asked. "Surely he cannot enter a second time into his mother's womb to be born!"*

Clearly, Jesus' strange phrase "born again" has had its effect: He succeeded in upsetting the normal course of Nicodemus's thinking. Taking Jesus literally, Nicodemus now wants to know, "How can I go back into my mother's womb and start life already? I'm already old and gray!" Of course, Nicodemus's befuddlement and misunderstanding give Jesus the perfect opening to explain the reality behind His symbol of being "born again."

Jesus was laying the groundwork for a radical and profoundly disagreeable truth: It's not enough to change what we do. Keeping the Law and the rules of the *Mishnah* and the *Talmud* are not enough. The reason we fail to do what is right is that there is something wrong with who we are. So it is *what we are,* not just what we do, that must be changed. This is a fundamental truth, the basis of the doctrine of sin, the doctrine that says that we all, as human beings, are a lost race.

Admit Your Need

Jesus once again prefaces and underscores His words with the phrase, "I tell you the truth . . . ."

3:5–8 *Jesus answered, "I tell you the truth, unless a man is born of water and the Spirit, he cannot enter the kingdom of God. Flesh gives birth to flesh, but the Spirit gives birth to spirit. You should not be surprised at my saying, 'You must be born again.' The wind blows wherever it pleases. You hear its sound, but you cannot tell where it comes from or where it is going. So it is with everyone born of the Spirit."*

How can a man be born when he is old? Jesus' reply: By water and by the Spirit.

What does Jesus mean by "water"? Some have thought it to be a reference to the bag of waters that breaks just before a baby is born, and thus a reference to physical birth. According to this view, Jesus is saying we must be born both physically and spiritually, of the water and the Spirit. I cannot agree with this view. Why would Jesus say something so absurdly obvious as, "To enter the kingdom of heaven, you first have to be physically born"?

It is clear from the context that when Jesus talks about water, He is referring to baptism. John's baptism was the sensation of the nation in those days. Everyone was talking about it. In John chapter 1, you recall, the Pharisees had sent a delegation to ask John why he was baptizing. Now Jesus indicates to Nicodemus, a Pharisee, what water baptism signifies: Water baptism is a symbol of repentance and an honest admission of need.

I have roughly half a century in the ministry, and I have observed that the one barrier that prevents most people from being born again is their own unwillingness to admit their need. They don't want to admit that they are sinful and helpless, and that God must come into them and completely transform them. They cling to the idea that there is some good within them that God ought to accept. They see their lives as balanced on a set of scales. If they do more good things than bad things, the scales will tip in their favor and off to heaven they go!

But God says no, you need a total renovation. You need to repent. And baptism is a symbolic acknowledgment of that repentance. When we repent and receive the Savior, then we are born of the Spirit. And when we symbolize our repentance by baptism, we are born of water.

Jesus goes on to draw a clear and unmistakable distinction between the old and new birth. He says, "Flesh gives birth to flesh, but the Spirit gives birth to spirit." Everyone knows what physical birth is all about. Jesus came to reveal to us what spiritual birth is all about. It is the Spirit of God who produces spiritual birth, not our own works, not our own observance of the Law. If we are trying, in our unchanged, fallen nature, to please God, then we will fail. But if we allow God to recreate us through the new birth, we will become citizens of the kingdom of God. That is Jesus' message to Nicodemus.

The Wind Blows

Jesus uses yet another symbol to demonstrate that the new birth will result in a totally new lifestyle. Once born again, that person will never be the same. Perhaps as they were talking, Jesus and Nicodemus could hear the wind blowing through the narrow streets of Jerusalem. In any case, He said to Nicodemus, "The wind blows wherever it pleases." The wind is sovereign. No one can direct it.

Despite all the scientific and technological advances of our age, Jesus' statement is still true today. Weather forecasters can track a hurricane and warn people in its path to take cover. But even the United States government, with all its military and scientific might, cannot deflect a hurricane one degree from its course. It will blow wherever it wants to, we are helpless to control it. The will of the wind is sovereign over the will of man.

In the same way, we cannot control the purposes of God in an individual life. The Spirit of God will direct that life. So it is with everyone who is born of the Spirit.

The Astonishment of Jesus

Nicodemus is puzzled by Jesus' reply. John records his response next.

3:9 *"How can this be?" Nicodemus asked.*

Now it is Jesus' turn to be astonished! He responds to Nicodemus for the third time with the emphatic phrase, "I tell you the truth . . . ."

3:10–12 *"You are Israel's teacher," said Jesus, "and do you not understand these things? I tell you the truth, we speak of what we know and we testify to what we have seen, but still you people do not accept our testimony. I have spoken to you of earthly things and you do not believe; how then will you believe if I speak of heavenly things?"*

Jesus is astonished because He is speaking to a man who is a teacher and leader of Israel, a man who has given his life to studying the Old Testament—yet Nicodemus still doesn't get it! Surely, Nicodemus should know that Isaiah spoke about new life from God; that Jeremiah had predicted a new creation that would be given; that Ezekiel had said that God would take out the old heart of stone and give a new heart of flesh. Throughout the Old Testament there are statements about a new birth, a new beginning, a new creation, a new life that would come as a gift of God to those who would humbly receive it, acknowledging their need.

So Jesus says to Nicodemus, "How can you, a teacher of Israel, not know about these things?" This was a gentle rebuke to Nicodemus that he ought to have known better. Jesus continues: "I have spoken to you of earthly things"—that is, in symbols of birth and water and wind—"and you do not believe; how then will you believe if I speak of heavenly things?"

The Incarnation

Jesus then plainly reveals who He is and where He comes from.

3:13 *"No one has ever gone into heaven except the one who came from heaven—the Son of man."*

Here, Jesus speaks of the incarnation. God has visibly appeared on earth as a man. It is an accomplished fact. The one who came down from heaven, Jesus, has witnessed to the truth of God.

Then Jesus cites another manifestation—this one from the Old Testament.

3:14–15 *"Just as Moses lifted up the snake in the desert, so the Son of Man must be lifted up, that everyone who believes in him may have eternal life."*

Here is an unmistakable reference to the cross. In Numbers 21, when the people of Israel were being bitten by hundreds of poisonous snakes in the wilderness, Moses was told by God to take a pole and set on it a brass serpent. The serpent would, by itself, do nothing whatsoever for the people. It was merely a symbol. But the people were told if they would look at it—and thus make a personal application of its symbolic meaning to their own lives—they would find themselves healed from the bite of the poisonous snakes.

From Genesis to Revelation, a serpent is always a symbolic representation of sin. Jesus says, in effect, "When Moses lifted that serpent in the wilderness, he was displaying a symbol of me. I will be made sin for the sake of the healing of the people. When that happens, if you will look at me hanging on the cross and believe that I am dying for your sake, God will forgive your sins and heal you."

How To Be Born Again

This brings us to the greatest and most treasured verse in Scripture, John 3:16.

3:16 *"For God so loved the world that he gave his one and only Son, that whoever believes in him shall not perish but have eternal life."*

That is how to be born again.

A totally new life is available to you, and to everyone. If we acknowledge our need and receive Jesus as Lord, God himself will perform that transforming miracle in our lives. Nicodemus needed to understand that. So do you and I. There is no other way into the kingdom of God but through faith in Jesus Christ.

Our own efforts to earn our way to God are futile. Nicodemus had tried to earn his way to God all his life, and the result was emptiness. It was that sense of emptiness and futility that brought him into the presence of Jesus under the cover of darkness. There he learned how to fill the emptiness of his life with truth and freedom and friendship with the living God:

Believe in Jesus.
Receive Jesus.
Be born again!

Chapter Nine

The Best Possible News

John 3:16–36

Y ou and I are on Death Row.

We have lived lives of crime and sin. We have been apprehended, brought before the Judge, tried, and convicted. The Judge has pronounced sentence: Death.

Now we await execution. Just a few yards from our cell, at the end of the corridor, is the gas chamber. Time is dragging us inexorably, moment by moment, to the fate we have earned.

But wait—! Do you hear those footsteps? Someone is coming down the corridor! And listen—! The footsteps have stopped outside the solid steel door of our cell! The key is turning in the lock. The door creaks open. There in the doorway stands—

The Judge himself!

What is He saying? Can we believe our ears? Yes! He actually says to us, "You are free. You can go now. You are no longer under a sentence of death."

We walk out of the cell, hardly able to believe what is happening! But as we step into the corridor, another man walks into the cell. His eyes meet ours, and His gaze burns deep into our souls.

"Who is that man?" we ask, turning to the Judge. "And why is He going into that Death Row cell? What did He do that He deserves to be executed?"

"Why, that is the man who volunteered to take your place in the gas chamber," says the Judge. "He hasn't done anything wrong at all. He's a good man, the best man I've ever known." Tears well up in the Judge's eyes and He turns away. "I should know. That man is my son."

"For God so loved the world," says John 3:16, "that he gave his one and only Son, that whoever believes in him shall not perish but have eternal life."

A Mountaintop Perspective

John 3:16 is undoubtedly the most famous verse in all of Scripture. It was the verse which capped and concluded our discussion of what it means to be "born again" in the previous chapter. And it is also the verse which introduces the subject of the Good News of Jesus Christ in this chapter. That's why we are spending parts of two chapters in one verse of Scripture. When a verse is as rich and powerful as this one, it deserves additional attention!

There is a debate among Bible scholars as to whether the words of John 3:16 were actually spoken to Nicodemus by Jesus, or whether this verse marks the end of the dialogue between Jesus and Nicodemus and the beginning of John's own commentary. The original Greek text contains no punctuation marks, such as quotation marks, so it's easy to see why there might be confusion.

It seems to me, however, that the first word of John 3:16—the word "for"—ties this verse into the verses before it. That would mean that John 3:16 is part of the transcript of the words that Jesus himself spoke to Nicodemus. If so, then Jesus' discourse to Nicodemus continues on to verse 21, after which John changes the scene and begins a new narrative. The English text used in this book, the New International Version, agrees with this view, and puts the entire section from verses 16 through 21 within quotation marks.

This entire section presents to us two contrasting ways of life, two choices we have to make. On the one hand, we can choose belief, resulting in eternal life—not just an eternally long life in heaven after we die, but a glorious *quality* of life on earth, as we live for Him. On the other hand, we can choose disobedience, which results in living under the wrath of God, both now and forever.

The problem most of us face is that disobedience often seems like more fun than belief. Certainly, disobedience seems to be the approved and accepted choice in our fallen society. Some of us wonder, "If God made life, why did He make it so hard to be good and so much fun to be bad?" If that is our view, it is easy to take the next step and say, "Obviously, God is not fair. What a mean old crab He must be to make life that way!"

I've heard people say that, and you probably have too. But when people accuse God of being unfair, of being a cosmic killjoy, notice how far they have moved from the truth of John 3:16. John's gospel does not describe a hard, cruel God who is indifferent to our feelings and our sufferings. Rather it speaks of a God who loved us so much He would send His only son to take our place on Death Row. If *that* isn't love, what is? The negative perspective so many people have about God shows how confused and distorted our perceptions are as human beings.

Dr. Billy Graham tells the story of a friend of his who stood on a mountaintop in North Carolina, looking down on the road below. It was a winding road that twisted along the side of the mountain, and there were many blind curves along its course. The man could see three cars on the road, all approaching a blind hairpin curve, two from one direction, one from the opposite direction. One of the two cars pulled out to pass the other, unaware that a third car was approaching just around the bend.

The man on the mountain could see what was going to happen. Because of the narrowness of the road, there was no room for any of the cars to escape. He cupped his hands and shouted a warning, but it was hopeless. The drivers would never hear him. In seconds, there was a clash of grinding metal as all three cars met in the middle of the curve. It was a horrible, fatal crash.

That is the difference between God's perspective and ours. We are like drivers on a mountain road, approaching a blind curve. We know that God has warned us not to pass on the curve, not to take the curve too fast, not to drive recklessly. But we say, "God just wants to limit my freedom. He just wants to ruin my fun." And we proceed to our doom.

God has the mountaintop perspective, and He can see what lies around the bend. He has called out a warning to us—but it is a warning that we, in our own free-will, are free to ignore. And if we choose to ignore it, the results can be fatal.

When God looks at our world, He sees many things we try to ignore: He sees the hurt in people's lives, the shame that fills their hearts, the misery they are going through. He sees those who are living lives of meaninglessness and quiet desperation. He sees the murder, violence, hatred, bitterness, and anger. He sees the greed, oppression, child abuse, famine, death, and fear of every kind.

He sees the destruction and anguish we call down upon ourselves by ignorantly trying to find fulfillment in everything but himself. He sees the painful consequences we reap from the choices we make—choices to avoid and deny the truth about ourselves; choices to pursue selfish goals rather than pursuing God and righteousness; choices to exploit others to advance our own ambitions; choices to seek revenge rather than forgiveness. God sees that so much of the suffering and agony we feel is a result of *what we are* as fallen people, slaves to sin.

He could say, "They made their bed. Let them lie in it. Let them reap every last grain of suffering they have sown by their disobedience." But no, God's response to us is not anger or ruthless justice. According to this wonderful verse, God responds to us with compassion. He is moved with love for the whole world. He loves every race. He loves rich and poor. He loves the powerful and the powerless. He loves those whose hearts are broken and whose backs are bent by toil and suffering. He loves the Mother Teresas of this world, and He loves the Saddam Husseins. He loves the whole world, every human being, without exception.

True, not everyone whom God loves will take hold of the gift God has given and receive Jesus as Lord and Savior. But that does not change the fact of God's love. John 3:16 is a statement of God's love, a statement which flings its arms wide to embrace the people of every continent and island, every color and race, every background and status. "God so loved the world."

The Best News of All

"God so loved the world that he *gave his* one and only Son." That word *gave* is rich in meaning. God gave His Son to us in the incarnation, when Jesus came among us as a human baby. And He gave His Son *for* us when He sacrificed Jesus on the cross for our sakes. God, seeing our agony, wanted to rescue us—but the rescue would be costly. It cost pain, thirst, blood, and death. It cost darkness, separation, and unspeakable shame, when Jesus was made sin for us in our place.

But God accomplished what He set out to do for us through His Son. The grip of sin was broken. And that is the best news ever heard on earth.

This is the truth that underlies our greatest hymns. One of my favorites is the hymn of Charles Wesley which rejoices,

> And can it be that I should gain
> An interest in the Savior's blood?
> Died He for me, who caused His pain?
> For me, who Him to death pursued?
> Amazing love! how can it be
> That Thou, my God, shouldst die for me?

That is a beautiful, poetic restatement of the meaning of John 3:16. God is not angry with us. He loves us. He proved it in the most powerful way possible: by sending His Son to take our place in the execution chamber.

No Condemnation

The next verse gives us a crucial insight into how we should approach others with the good news of Jesus Christ.

3:17 *"For God did not send his Son into the world to condemn the world, but to save the world through him."*

I have seen many people try to "evangelize" others through condemnation. But this verse makes it clear that we should approach those who do not know God the same way God has approached them—with love, compassion, and understanding, not with a wagging finger of condemnation and accusation, not by telling people how terrible they are.

In every gospel vignette which shows Jesus' dealings with people—including people who were open, blatant sinners—He came sensing their hurt and need, their shame and loneliness. That is the way God feels and that is the way we should feel too.

Take, for example, the woman at the well in Samaria. She had been married to five different men, and was even then living with a man outside of marriage. Jesus recognized her sin, of course, but He also was able to look beyond it, to the throbbing, hurting human soul within this woman. Jesus was courteous to her, even while He spoke to her about her need and her lifestyle. There was no tone of shock or accusation in His voice—only compassion. And she responded to Him gratefully and joyfully.

Paul puts this very beautifully in his second letter to the Corinthians: "God was reconciling the world to himself in Christ, not counting men's sins against them."[1] Obviously, this does not mean that God is indifferent to sin. He knows we cannot be free until the sin issue has been solved in our lives. Throughout Scripture, we are reminded that Jesus came not to leave us in our sins, but to free us from bondage to sin. The point is that sin does not prevent us from coming to Him. God is always ready to receive us.

I once read a story about a young man who had quarrelled with his father and left home. He moved to another city, but he continued to keep in touch with his mother, and wanted very badly to come home for Christmas. His mother repeatedly asked the boy's father to forgive him. His father, however, would not forget the things his son had said to him and would not allow him to come home.

As it grew closer and closer to Christmas, the son called his mother several times. "Has Dad changed his mind?" the young man asked. "Will he forgive me? Can I come home?"

Each time, she sadly reported, "No, son, your father is still angry. Don't come home—just yet."

Finally, it was just two days before Christmas and the boy called his mother. "Can I come home yet?"

"Let me talk to your father one more time," said his mother. "Meanwhile, you take the train home. If he has forgiven you, I'll tie a white rag on the big elm tree beside the railroad tracks by the house. You can get off at the station and we'll be waiting for you."

"But what if there is no rag on the tree?"

"Then you'd better stay on the train, son."

So the young man set out on his journey. As the train drew near his home, his stomach was knotted with anxiety. Would the rag be tied to the tree? He watched all the familiar landmarks come and go. Soon, he knew, the old elm tree would come into view.

It was getting toward dusk, and he began to worry. What if it was too dark to see the rag?

But just then, the tree came into view. He blinked and rubbed his eyes. Could it be true? Yes! The old elm tree looked like a cherry tree in spring! It was "blooming" all over with white rags of forgiveness. The young man was home, truly home, at last.

That story resonates with the truth of John 3:16 and 17. God has removed all condemnation. All is forgiven. We are free to come home to Him.

The Choice

Yet, even though God has given His Son for us, there is still a response, a choice that we have to make. Jesus tells us about that choice next.

3:18–21 *"Whoever believes in him is not condemned, but whoever does not believe stands condemned already because he has not believed in the name of God's one and only Son. This is the verdict: Light has come into the world, but men loved darkness instead of light because their deeds were evil. Everyone who does evil hates the light, and will not come into the light for fear that his deeds will be exposed. But whoever lives by the truth comes into the light, so that it may be seen plainly that what he has done has been done through God."*

Verse 18 says that whoever does not believe is condemned already. The condemnation is not deferred until the end of life; it is already going on. The Bible takes the position that humankind is living under the wrath of God all the time. Psalm 90:9 states it plainly: "All our years pass away under your wrath." The wrath of God is the anger, anguish, and emptiness we feel when we go our own way rather than God's way. We do not have to wait for wrath. If we do not choose to follow Jesus, then we are already under that wrath.

If you are traveling on a wrong road and every so often you see a signpost that points the way to the right road, what should you do? Reason dictates that you follow the signposts to the right path. But you can still choose to stay on the wrong road—and many people do just that. They choose to ignore God's signposts, and they follow the path of destruction. Why? Why would anyone want to follow the wrong road, knowing that the signposts point the way to God?

Verses 19 and 20 give us the answer: "Men loved darkness instead of light because their deeds were evil. Everyone who does evil hates the light, and will not come into the light for fear that his deeds will be exposed." When the passage says, "Men loved darkness," it doesn't mean men as opposed to women (though my wife has sometimes read it that way!). Nor does it mean, "Some people love darkness rather than light." When the Bible uses the term "men," it generally means "humankind," the human race—that is, everyone, without exception.

We all dislike being shown to be wrong. I feel that way myself. I do not even want to be corrected in the way I pronounce a word. If you tell me that I have mispronounced a word, and prove me wrong from the dictionary, I will challenge the dictionary! We don't like to be proved wrong. That's just part of our fallen nature—and that's why we find it so hard to change. We defend what we are to the death, and we resist change with our last ounce of strength. We fear the light of God's truth, and the exposure of the evil within us, because that truth forces us to change.

Verse 21 is the hinge on which this passage turns: "But whoever lives by the truth comes into the light, so that it may be seen plainly that what he has done has been done through God." In other words, if we are willing to begin obeying the truth—even when that means that sin will be exposed in our lives—then change will take place, our lives will be brought into alignment with God's own character, and the deeds we do will increasingly be the kind of deeds that are done through God.

This process begins with a recognition, a conviction deep within us, that our lives are not right, and we do not like the way we are. We want to change, and we recognize that the only one who can change us is God himself, through Jesus Christ. If we pursue the truth, courageously and relentlessly, we will find ourselves drawn like a magnet to Jesus. In John 6:44, Jesus puts it very plainly: "No one can come to me unless the Father who sent me draws him." The sense that God is drawing you to Jesus is the desire within you to be free of your old self—a desire for change.

This must have come as a great encouragement to Nicodemus' heart. Here was a Pharisee who prided himself on his sincere and serious efforts to please God, yet he came to Jesus an empty, confused, and unfulfilled man. To do right, Nicodemus chose to risk the displeasure of his colleagues by coming to Jesus by night and talking with Him. Jesus encouraged him by telling him that those who do what is true will come to the light, that it may be clearly seen that their deeds are being worked by God. God was drawing Nicodemus to Himself.

"He Must Increase, I Must Decrease"

In verses 22 through 26, John the Baptist appears for the last time in this gospel (his imprisonment—which ultimately led to his death—is alluded to in

John's gospel but not related in detail as in the other gospels, especially Matthew and Mark). John reappears as a confirming witness to what John the apostle has recorded about Jesus.

3:22–26 *After this, Jesus and his disciples went out into the Judean country-side, where he spent some time with them, and baptized. Now John also was baptizing at Aenon near Salim, because there was plenty of water, and people were constantly coming to be baptized. (This was before John was put in prison.) An argument developed between some of John's disciples and a certain Jew over the matter of ceremonial washing. They came to John and said to him, "Rabbi, that man who was with you on the other side of the Jordan—the one you testified about—well, he is baptizing, and everyone is going to him."*

Some of John's disciples saw Jesus as a rival, and clearly experienced a sense of rivalry and jealousy. They were upset that Jesus—whom John had introduced—had set up a camp just a mile or two down the river and was winning more people than John the Baptist.

Competition is one of the most toxic forces to enter the family of God. Rivalry between ministries is one of the wedges Satan uses to break up the church and impede the progress of the gospel. The rivalry in this passage arises because the crowds that once flocked to hear John the Baptist are now following Jesus. John's followers had fallen victim to the numbers game: Who has the bigger following? Who is more popular?

There was also an argument over baptism. Evidently, a Jewish man questioned the meaning of Jesus' baptism, feeling that John's baptism was but an extension of the Jewish rite of purification, which was mentioned in the law. But now Jesus was baptizing—or, more accurately, His disciples were. John's disciples could not understand that, so they came to ask John about it.

3:27–30 *To this John replied, "A man can receive only what is given him from heaven. You yourselves can testify that I said, 'I am not the Christ but am sent ahead of him.' The bride belongs to the bridegroom. The friend who attends the bridegroom waits and listens for him, and is full of joy when he hears the bridegroom's voice. That joy is mine, and it is now complete. He must become greater; I must become less."*

What a beautiful example of Christian humility!

Here, John the Baptist gives us a three-fold reply to his disciples' concern over John's "rival," Jesus. First, John the Baptist declares that all position comes only from God: "A man can receive only what is given him from heaven." This is true whether you are a Christian or a non-Christian, and it has always been true. "The Lord sends poverty and wealth; he humbles and he exalts," says 1 Samuel 2:7. "No one from the east or the west or from the desert can exalt a man. But it is God who judges; he brings one down, he exalts another," says Psalm 75:6–7.

We like to think we can take credit for our accomplishments, yet who was it that gave us our intelligence, our health, our ability to work, and the good fortune that enabled our hard work to pay off? All credit goes to God, who humbles and exalts according to His own will. John the Baptist understood this principle. He knew he had been given a role in which he could find satisfaction and fulfillment by glorifying the Messiah. But John also knew that he himself was not the Messiah.

The second dimension of John's reply to his disciples: He reminds them that he knew his own role from the start. He says to them: "You yourselves can testify that I said, 'I am not the Christ [the Messiah] but am sent ahead of him.' " In other words, "If you think I'm greater than Jesus, if you think I'm the Messiah, then you are departing from what I have always taught you. I am like the best man at a wedding—not the groom himself! Jesus is the groom, and He has come to claim His bride. My job has been to stand next to Him and give Him glory—not take the glory for myself!"

The third dimension of John's reply is this: John is actually *joyful* and *glad* that he is being eclipsed by Jesus! He tells His disciples, in effect, "When I see crowds of people leaving me and going to Jesus, I think, 'That's great! That's what I came to do! My whole purpose has been to point people to Him—and look at them go! What more could I ask for?' "

Then John makes a statement that should be echoed by every Christian: "He must become greater; I must become less." Or, as the King James Version puts it so elegantly, "He must increase; I must decrease." That kind of humility doesn't come naturally to the fallen human spirit. Our tendency is to look for every opportunity to increase ourselves in any way we can! We all know people who are so hungry for attention and the glare of the spotlight that they want to be the baby at every christening, the bridegroom (or bride) at every wedding, and the corpse at every funeral!

But not John the Baptist. He says, "Point the spotlight at Jesus. Let me just fade into the shadows. I'm on the way out, and that's the way it should be." As a young preacher, I read a line of advice given by the Scottish theologian James Denney, and that advice has always stuck with me: "You can never at the same time convince people that you are a great preacher and that Jesus is a great Savior." It is one or the other. I hope that my own heart echoes this humble sentiment of John the Baptist: Jesus must increase; I and every other preacher and author and servant of Jesus must decrease.

"Whoever Believes . . . Has Eternal Life"

Finally, John the Baptist declares Jesus to be the ultimate Person in the universe, who speaks the ultimate truth.

3:31 *"The one who comes from above is above all; the one who is from the earth belongs to the earth, and speaks as one from the earth. The one who comes from heaven is above all."*

John is saying, in effect, "The word of Jesus is far greater than mine because He has come from the invisible realm, from heaven itself, where He sees all of life from an ultimate, eternal point of view. The truth He speaks comes from the storehouse of all truth—the heavenly mind of God. I, however, am from the earth. I see only a limited range of truth, but Jesus is truly *un*limited!"

John goes on to speak from his own personal experience.

3:32–35 *"He testifies to what he has seen and heard, but no one accepts his testimony. The man who has accepted it has certified that God is truthful. For the one whom God has sent speaks the words of God; to him God gives the Spirit without limit. The Father loves the Son and has placed everything in his hands."*

Jesus has seen and heard all that is within the mind of God. He personifies the wisdom and love of God. He is the eternal Word, calling into existence everything that is. Everything and all authority has been placed in His hands by the loving Father. And when Jesus speaks, the Spirit of God, whom God gives without limit to people, acts within people to confirm the word of Jesus.

I believe that if we could have been in the crowd when Jesus spoke, we would see that the mass response of the crowd would be, "Yes! Amen! That's right! That's the truth!" Something within the hearer confirms the word. Jesus did not need experts, authorities, or endorsements from the leading minds of the day to affirm His message. His words spoke to the heart and were confirmed by the inner witness of the Spirit.

3:36 *"Whoever believes in the Son has eternal life, but whoever rejects the Son will not see life, for God's wrath remains on him."*

The wrath that John speaks of is the natural condition of human life on earth, apart from God. Every individual who rejects Jesus Christ makes a choice to continue living in—and choking on—a gray smog of emptiness, depression, anger, pain, and death. That is the wrath of God—and it is not something God inflicts on us, but something we choose for ourselves when we reject His Son. God has made it possible for us to escape the wrath and step into the light of His grace and truth. It is up to us to choose life—or the wrath.

God so loved the world that He gave His only Son. If we believe in Him and follow Him, we will not perish, but receive eternal life. God has demonstrated a love for us that is beyond compassion. What is our response?

Wrath or eternal life: The choice is ours.

Chapter Ten

A Woman with Modern Problems

John 4:1–42

An American actress was once asked if she was not embarrassed to have been married seven times. She replied, "Why should I be embarrassed about all my marriages? All my friends are running around, having dozens of affairs, and never getting married. At least I marry my affairs!"

In John chapter 4, we encounter a woman very much like that American actress: a woman who has gone through marriage after marriage in a fruitless search for love. Though her story comes to us from an alien culture and the long-ago past, the woman John introduces us to in this chapter is someone we can relate to. She could easily be the woman who lives next door to you, or the woman who works at the reception desk in your office. She could be sitting next to you in your Bible study group, support group, or church pew. She could be a relative of yours, or that old college roommate you've been meaning to call. She could even be you.

In terms of her lifestyle, her spiritual needs, and her emotional pain, the woman in John 4 is as contemporary and relevant as any American woman of the 1990s. She is a lost, empty woman searching for love, and her story is rich in implications for our own lives—and for the lives of people we touch and talk to every day. In his encounter with this woman, Jesus will display for our instruction the Christlike method of evangelism. And as we watch Jesus reach out to this woman, we will be struck time after time with the issues of our own modern age—issues which include racial inequality, prejudice, the status of women in society, the decline of moral standards, human loneliness, and the hunger for love and acceptance.

An Encounter at Jacob's Well

4:1–6 *The Pharisees heard that Jesus was gaining and baptizing more disciples than John, although in fact it was not Jesus who baptized, but his disci-*

ples. When the Lord learned of this, he left Judea and went back once more to Galilee.

Now he had to go through Samaria. So he came to a town in Samaria called Sychar, near the plot of ground Jacob had given to his son Joseph. Jacob's well was there, and Jesus, tired as he was from the journey, sat down by the well. It was about the sixth hour.

In these verses, John calls to our attention three factors which set the stage for Jesus' encounter with a woman with modern problems.

First: The reason Jesus left Judea was to avoid a growing controversy. The Pharisees were upset over the apparent rivalry between the baptism of Jesus and the baptism of John. They could not understand it. They were choosing sides, and a conflict threatened.

This kind of controversy remains a major issue in the church today. Many denominations and individual Christians separate from each other over the mode and meaning of baptism. But Jesus walked away from this controversy—a silent, eloquent statement of His feelings on the matter! In fact, when John says Jesus "left" Judea, the original Greek word is even stronger, conveying that Jesus *forsook* or *abandoned* Judea. He would have nothing to do with petty, legalistic controversies over baptism.

Second: John calls attention to the route Jesus took on His journey to Galilee. He chose the most direct route, traveling through Samaria, which lies between Judea and Galilee.

What was once called Samaria is today a very famous and much-contested tract of land known as the West Bank, which Israel captured from Jordan and has occupied since the Six Day War in 1967. It is interesting that, while prime minister of Israel, the late Menachem Begin, reintroduced the practice of referring to this section of the Holy Land by its ancient name—Samaria—rather than "the West Bank."

Most Jews of Jesus' time, if they wanted to travel from Judea to Galilee, would take the long way around: eastward along the hot desert road from Jerusalem to Jericho, then north up the Jordan River valley, then turning east again toward Galilee, north of Samaria. This would take about five days, even though there was a direct route from Judea to Galilee that was only about 70 miles long—about two and a half day's walk. The reason most Jews chose the longer route rather than the more direct route was *prejudice,* pure and simple. The Jews did not want to associate with the Samaritan people, and would rather endure the hot, long uncomfortable road than let go of their bigotry.

Jesus, however, chose to take the short-cut through Samaria. In so doing, He also cut through the ignorant, narrow-minded prejudice of His day and actively demonstrated the inclusiveness and unconditional acceptance of God—the same acceptance He expressed to Nicodemus when He said, "God so loved the world," the whole world, including that corner of the world called Samaria.

Third: John calls attention to the place where Jesus stopped. It was a historic site called Jacob's Well, at the foot of Mount Gerizim. There, about a half mile west of the village of Sychar, at the well which Jacob had dug for his flocks and herds more than 1,700 years earlier, Jesus sat down to rest.

I had an interesting experience at Jacob's Well a number of years ago. I was traveling alone in a rented car through the West Bank, and I gave a ride to three Israeli soldiers carrying submachine guns. Though their camp was located right outside of town, they had never been to Jacob's Well. They didn't even know it was there.

When I told them I was going to visit the well, they were very interested and wanted to go along. I pulled up the car near by the Syrian Christian monastery that is maintained at the site of the well, and my three heavily-armed friends and I got out. When the Syrian priest saw an American approaching with a contingent of armed "bodyguards," he mistook me for an important dignitary! I have never been so royally treated in my life!

It was an awesome experience to stand on that ground and realize that I stood on the very place where Jesus met the woman at the well, nearly two thousand years earlier.

John records that it was about the "sixth hour" when Jesus stopped at the well. By Jewish reckoning, that would be noon, but John probably uses Roman time throughout his gospel. That would mean that Jesus stopped at about six o'clock in the evening. No wonder He was weary after a full day of foot-travel under the hot sun of Palestine. He was thirsty, so He sat beside the well to rest while the disciples went into the city to find something to eat. This gives us a beautiful picture of our Lord's humanity.

Living Water

In verses 7 through 26, John gives us an account of perhaps the most remarkable conversation our Lord ever had. As a Samaritan woman approaches the well to draw water, Jesus seizes the opportunity and initiates a conversation.

4:7–10 *When a Samaritan woman came to draw water, Jesus said to her, "Will you give me a drink?" (His disciples had gone into the town to buy food.)*

The Samaritan woman said to him, "You are a Jew and I am a Samaritan woman. How can you ask me for a drink?" (For Jews did not associate with Samaritans.)

Jesus answered her, "If you knew the gift of God and who it is that asks you for a drink, you would have asked him and he would have given you living water."

Already we can see how this story touches the exposed nerves of our own age. We see the prejudice of this society, which treats certain people as second class citizens because of their ethnicity and their sex. Here we see Jesus—the One who spent so much of His brief public ministry in a fight to break down barriers of injustice—as He shatters yet another barrier, a barrier between men and women, a barrier between divided cultures.

Jesus came as a teacher, which is why He is frequently called "Rabbi" (teacher) by those who approach Him. According to Jewish law, rabbis were never to talk to a woman in public—not even to their own wives or sisters. In fact, rabbinical law said, "It is better to burn the Law than give it to a woman." In that culture, women were regarded as totally unable and unworthy to receive and understand such lofty concepts as theology and religion. The status and regard in which women of that culture were held was abysmally low.

Ever since the days of Nehemiah, 450 years earlier, the Jews had regarded the Samaritans as a despised pseudo-Jewish cult. The Samaritans had been brought into the region by the Assyrians to populate the area after they had removed the Jewish population to captivity. The religious practices of the Samaritans were abhorrent to the Jews. The Samaritan scriptures consisted of only the five books of Moses, and the Samaritans had mingled idolatry with the Law of Moses. They had even erected a temple on Mt. Gerizim as a rival to the temple in Jerusalem. So the Jews regarded the Samaritans as heretics and defilers of the Jewish faith, and hated them even more than they hated the Gentiles.

No wonder the Samaritan woman is surprised when Jesus speaks to her!

But notice how Jesus treats her, how He is able to read her heart by reading her circumstances. Although there is another well in the village, this woman must come all the way out to Jacob's Well, a half mile away. Why? Because she is a moral and social outcast! Seeing her approach, Jesus instantly sized up the situation and understood that she was a sinner whom the Father had chosen to call to repentance. As Jesus himself said on one occasion, "I did not come to call the righteous, but sinners."[1]

Jesus probably knew more about this woman's history than the language of John's narrative suggests. Later, He tells her some facts about herself that

He evidently knew in advance. He had been through this small village several times, and had probably heard about her. Now, as she approaches from the village, He probably recognizes her and sees this as an opportunity, arranged by God the Father, for Him to reach out to her and minister to her needs.

So, as He always does when dealing with people, Jesus seizes whatever is at hand to make a connection—and make a point. Seeing a thirsty woman coming to draw water, He says these remarkable words: "If you knew the gift of God and who it is that asks you for a drink, you would have asked Him and he would have given you living water."

The "gift of God" Jesus refers to is the Holy Spirit. Later, in Acts 2:38, Peter addresses three thousand or more Jews on the Day of Pentecost and says, "Repent and be baptized . . . and you will receive the gift of the Holy Spirit." So Jesus is saying to this woman, in effect, "If you knew about the Holy Spirit and who it is that is talking to you, you would have asked Him to give you living water."

Whoever Drinks Will Never Thirst

But this woman misunderstands, just as Nicodemus misunderstood when Jesus said, "Be born again." He is speaking figuratively. She takes Him literally.

4:11–12 *"Sir," the woman said, "you have nothing to draw with and the well is deep. Where can you get this living water? Are you greater than our father Jacob, who gave us the well and drank from it himself, as did also his sons and his flocks and herds?"*

In her puzzled response, she reminds Jesus that the well is deep—and it is indeed, sixty feet in depth or more. If you do not have a bucket and a lo-o-ong rope, you cannot get the water out. When Jesus says "living water," she thinks of running water—that is, water from a fountain or stream as compared with still water from a well or cistern. She is saying, "You don't have anything to draw the water with, and there's no fountain or stream around, so where do you expect to get this 'living, running water'?"

Perhaps Jesus' words, "If you knew . . . who it is who asks you for a drink," sound arrogant to her ears. Perhaps she resents the way the Jews have looked down on her and her people for hundreds of years. If so, then her next question may have been asked with a note of skepticism—or even outright scorn: "Are you greater than our father Jacob?" Jacob was the great founder of the Jewish faith. The Samaritans, who had the five books of Moses, looked to Jacob as their father as much as the Jews did.

If there was sarcasm in the woman's question, then Jesus clearly looks past it and responds to her with aggressive compassion.

4:13–14 *Jesus answered, "Everyone who drinks this water will be thirsty again, but whoever drinks the water I give him will never thirst. Indeed, the water I give him will become in him a spring of water welling up to eternal life."*

Jesus' image of "living water" has gotten the woman's attention. Now He goes on to make His message more clear. He says, in effect, "I am not talking about the water in the well. Drink of that water and you will be thirsty again. I'm talking about a different kind of 'water' altogether."

The woman knows what it means to drink and be thirsty again. She has been coming to that well for years. Day after day, a half mile to the well and a half mile back home again, all for a single jug of water.

But Jesus says He has the gift of water—what He calls "living water"—and once you receive this gift, you will never thirst again. Jesus does not mean, of course, that a single drink cures your thirst for life. He is not saying that those who drink of this gift will never again experience a thirst in their souls. Rather, He is describing a situation that we Americans are so familiar with we take it for granted: piped-in running water!

We Americans have no idea what it means to be truly thirsty, to be surrounded by dry, cracked land without a drop of water in sight. Why? Because we have indoor plumbing and city water departments and viaducts and reservoirs—an efficient, twenty-four-hour-a-day water delivery system. At the slightest whim, you can turn a tap and—*voila!*—the water comes out!

That is the kind of situation—in a spiritual sense—that Jesus is describing. If you want to keep from thirsting, just have the water piped in—a constant, continuous flow of spiritual refreshment. Take a drink anytime you want, and you will never know true, parching thirst. Many Christians never seem to learn this truth. They never realize that there is a place where their inner thirst—their sense of restlessness, their desire for fulfillment—can be met instantly!

Jesus makes it clear that the source of this water is within—because when the gift of the Holy Spirit is given, the Spirit dwells within: "The water I give him will become in him a spring of water welling up to eternal life." As you drink of the Spirit, you experience a quality of life which the Bible calls *eternal life*. The term *eternal life* means much more than *everlasting life*. Eternal life is more than just life that goes on and on chronologically. It is life that has the *quality* of eternity: a rich, refreshing, profoundly meaningful, infinitely exciting life! Life that is saturated with God's own love, joy, and peace. Here is a beautiful picture: a well springing up to eternal life.

(By the way, notice that when Jesus addresses this woman, He does not change the pronoun to "she"; He uses masculine pronouns because that is a generic pronoun referring to both sexes. Whenever the Bible refers to the human race as "men" or individuals as "he" or "him," the feminine gender is always included.)

Piercing Her Darkness

The woman is still confused. She wants to know where she can find this "living water" Jesus has described to her.

4:15 *The woman said to him, "Sir, give me this water so that I won't get thirsty and have to keep coming here to draw water."*

She doesn't understand—and that's no criticism. Would you or I have understood any better than this woman, given the cultural context and that radically new message Jesus was sharing with her—a message of "living water"? Her understanding is hindered. She is living in darkness. And Jesus must find a way to penetrate her darkness. He must find a way to apply this message of "living water" directly to this woman's life and her needs. He will have to shake her up and open her eyes so that the light of His truth can enter her being.

So Jesus aims His next arrow straight at this woman's heart—and He scores a perfect bull's-eye.

4:16–18 *He told her, "Go, call your husband and come back."*
"I have no husband," she replied.
Jesus said to her, "You are right when you say you have no husband. The fact is, you have had five husbands, and the man you now have is not your husband. What you have just said is quite true."

How did Jesus know this? I don't believe it is due to divine omniscience, because I am convinced He didn't exercise divine omniscience during His earthly life. The likelihood is that Jesus had learned about this woman during previous visits to the area. Perhaps her lifestyle was so scandalous that she was a notorious and much talked-about item of gossip. Jesus had never met this woman before, but He knew she had been married five times, and that she was now living with a man without being married—and she was no doubt regarded as a moral pariah in the village.

Why did Jesus confront her with His knowledge of her lifestyle? It was not because He wanted to embarrass her, shame her, or condemn her. He had one purpose only: To help her face the central problem in her life.

The gospel tells us that the steps to redemption are twofold: (1) Repentance and (2) Belief. Repentance is a human act. Belief and regeneration are an act of God. Until we admit our need there is no way of releasing God to act and to regenerate.

Jesus knows that the woman must come to the place of repentance, so He proceeds to deal with the hindrance at the core of her life. "Go call your husband," He tells her. She claims she has no husband—which is technically accurate, though clearly disingenuous. She is trying to create an impression that she lives alone. Jesus responds with a twist of irony: He says, in effect, "Yes, you are speaking quite accurately when you say you have no husband—at the moment. Of course, there are five ex-husbands you neglected to mention, and there's also the matter of the man you are living with who is not your husband. But what you said is quite true—technically speaking."

With these words, Jesus penetrated the woman's denial, evasion, and defenses. In an instant, this woman knew she could not hide from this man and His keen, prophetic insight. He knew all about her—and yet when He told her about herself, He didn't seem to condemn her or ridicule her. He actually *accepted* her! Even her own people in the village didn't do that!

Jesus had reached this woman's innermost being. He had exposed the emptiness and the thirst in this woman's heart. Her defenses dropped. Her heart fell open like a book. This man had something that she wanted, something she needed. She was now prepared to hear the gospel truth.

A Woman Finds True Love

What is it that causes a woman to marry five different men in succession, and then to live with a man in an unmarried state? What was she looking for? What drove her so relentlessly from relationship to relationship?

It's clear now, isn't it, why the story of this woman rings true today. This woman could be someone you know. She could even be you. This woman is thirsty for love.

Perhaps she was raised by parents who rejected her or who broke down her sense of self-worth. Or perhaps her emotional wounds were inflicted during a difficult adolescence or a troubled marriage. Perhaps one or more of the men she married was an abuser. Perhaps she was emotionally and spiritually empty simply because she had no relationship with God. For whatever reason, this woman had a thirst for love and acceptance which had never been quenched. She had tried—and failed—to find love and acceptance through a succession of relationships with men.

Like so many in our own culture, this Samaritan woman knew what it felt like to "fall in love." She had experienced that sensation again and again—that sense of light-headed euphoria, the flutter in the heart, the throbbing of the pulse. Most of the popular music written throughout this century is written in praise of this powerful sensation called "falling in love."

But though she had "fallen in love" again and again and again, the Samaritan woman had not found *true love*. She had learned that heady intoxication of "falling in love" only lasts so long—and then something deeper and more real must take its place. If not, the relationship will die. This woman craved a secure and binding kind of love—a love to last a lifetime. But with each new relationship, with each new marriage, that hope became bleaker and more remote.

Finally, she had reached a point where she had given up on the commitment of marriage. She was just hoping to salvage some love from an unsanctioned relationship—a relationship with a typical "man of the '90s," the type of man who wants a relationship but is afraid of commitment!

All of this, Jesus saw in the woman at the well. He understood her loneliness. He sensed her fear—the fear that she was growing older and still had not found the security and sanctuary of an abiding, true love. He knew that her search for acceptance and self-worth and love had led her to seek the wrong kinds of love. In her desperation to find romantic fulfillment, she had made herself a moral outcast. Jesus made a decision to gently confront this woman with the very thing that was destroying her and ruining her life and her reputation. He took this opportunity to point her to true refreshment, true fulfillment, and true love. That was what she was thirsting for, and He had the gift of "living water" which alone could quench her thirst. Gently, simply, compassionately, and without the least hint of condemnation, Jesus pointed her to the truth.

"You Are a Prophet!"

4:19–20 *"Sir," the woman said, "I can see that you are a prophet. Our fathers worshiped on this mountain, but you Jews claim that the place where we must worship is in Jerusalem."*

The woman's response is revealing.

Most of the commentators take her response to be an evasion on her part, an attempt to change the subject in order to deflect further probing by Jesus. I once thought so myself, but I have come to see her response in a different light. I believe she is admitting that Jesus is right about her. She says, in other words, "You must be a prophet. You've seen me, you know my life, and you know my heart." Later, she will go into the village and call out, "Come, see a man who told me everything I ever did!" By her response, she is confessing that Jesus has spoken the truth about her.

I believe her next question, far from being an evasion, is an honest plea for help. She now understands that this talk about "living water" was a revelation of *spiritual truth*. Now she wants to know how she can have this spiritual water herself. She wants to know what she should do, where she should go, how she should sacrifice and worship in order to receive "living water" from God. And Jesus' reply is absolutely fitting to her searching, sincere question.

4:21–24 *Jesus declared, "Believe me, woman, a time is coming when you will worship the Father neither on this mountain nor in Jerusalem. You Samaritans worship what you do not know; we worship what we do know, for salvation is from the Jews. Yet a time is coming and has now come when the true worshipers will worship the Father in spirit and truth, for they are the kind of worshipers the Father seeks. God is spirit, and his worshipers must worship in spirit and in truth."*

Here, Jesus makes three remarkable statements. First: He says, in effect, "Your question about where to worship is soon going to be entirely irrelevant. The hour is coming when geography will no longer be an issue. Temples or buildings will not be necessary to worship God. You yourself—your body and spirit—will be the temple of God, and that is where you will worship Him." Jesus knew that, by His death and resurrection, He would abolish all mere *symbols* of earthly worship so that the *reality* of true worship could break through. Temples, buildings, and mountaintops would be irrelevant once God came to dwell within men and women.

Second: He said to her, in other words, "You worship what you do not know. Your knowledge is incomplete. You have some truth, but it is mingled with error." This often happens. Most cults teach a garbled version of Christian truth, mingled with error. But Jesus says, "The Jews at least know where to carry out proper symbolic worship, because they are the race by which God is carrying out His plan. They are the race which has produced the Savior."

Third: Jesus says, "Here is what true worship is: true worship is done in your human spirit." True worship comes from the heart, and it is honest, not put-on. It is not something you do with your body while your mind is somewhere else. It is not just showing up for church and mouthing hymns and closing your eyes during prayer while you think about the Forty-Niners game or the preparations you have to make for Sunday dinner. In every congregation, God is looking for those who mean what they are singing and what they are praying. He is seeking true fellowship with those who have put their trust in Him—not a lot of empty rituals performed in buildings with stained glass windows.

God is spirit, and so are we, at the innermost core of our being. Therefore, worship is the joining together of Spirit with spirit.

The woman still cannot quite believe that such a radical change is coming in the way people meet and worship their God. Certainly, this man must be referring to some distant time, such as the long-predicted time of the coming of the Messiah. John records the climactic moment of their dialogue next.

4:25–26 *The woman said, "I know that Messiah" (called Christ) "is coming. When he comes, he will explain everything to us."*
Then Jesus declared, "I who speak to you am He."

I cannot read this passage without feeling a shiver down my backbone. Some critics say that Jesus never claimed to be the Messiah, but the claim could not be made any plainer than it is in this verse: "I who speak to you am He." He has revealed himself unmistakably to her: He is the One foretold by the prophets. He is the One awaited and hoped for by generations. And He has come to Jacob's Well to talk to *her.* He is the Messiah!

"Come and See!"

In response, this woman immediately forgets her water jar and becomes an evangelist!

4:27–30 *Just then his disciples returned and were surprised to find him talking with a woman. But no one asked, "What do you want?" or "Why are you talking with her?"*
Then, leaving her water jar, the woman went back to the town and said to the people, "Come, see a man who told me everything I ever did. Could this be the Christ?" They came out of the town and made their way toward him.

Here we see the Spirit of God at work through this reborn woman. "Come and see!" she calls. "There is a man at the Well of Jacob who told me everything I ever did!" Called out of their homes by a woman they have considered an outcast, the people stream out the town and toward the well where Jesus waits. Why would they listen to this woman they have always ignored, even despised? Because there is a power in her—the power of "living water," the power of the Spirit of God—and that power energizes her words, drawing people out of their normal routines, overcoming their prejudices, drawing them toward Jesus.

A Lesson for the Disciples

The encounter between Jesus and the woman at the well became an invaluable object lesson for Jesus' own disciples.

4:31–38 *Meanwhile his disciples urged him, "Rabbi, eat something."*

But he said to them, "I have food to eat that you know nothing about."

Then his disciples said to each other, "Could someone have brought him food?"

"My food," said Jesus, "is to do the will of him who sent me and to finish his work. Do you not say, 'Four months more and then the harvest'? I tell you, open your eyes and look at the fields! They are ripe for harvest. Even now the reaper draws his wages, even now he harvests the crop for eternal life, so that the sower and the reaper may be glad together. Thus the saying 'One sows and another reaps' is true. I sent you to reap what you have not worked for. Others have done the hard work, and you have reaped the benefits of their labor."

The first thing Jesus taught them was that there is a deep satisfaction in obedience to what God wants—a satisfaction so rich it is like food! It fills you, it satisfies, it builds you up.

Then Jesus goes on to describe the spiritual harvest that awaits them. He uses a parallel out of everyday experience in that culture: planting seeds and harvesting crops. In a growing season, He says, four months elapse between sowing and harvesting—but in the spiritual realm the harvest can arise instantly, without warning! Time is irrelevant in the realm of the spirit. Though the order is the same—first planting, then harvest—the spiritual crop can sprout up in a wink, in a heartbeat. And when that happens, the sower and the reaper can rejoice together.

Another lesson Jesus gave the disciples was the joy of sharing labor, of ministering together. Jesus labored by teaching the woman and calling her to himself. Then she labored, going into the village and spreading the good news. The disciples—who were out grocery shopping while all this exciting ministry was going on!—arrived in time to baptize the new converts and reap a harvest where Jesus and the woman had sown.

All of these people—Jesus, the re-born woman, and the disciples—were in ministry together. They were an evangelistic team, and through the division of their labor, with each fulfilling his or her unique role, a village was evangelized. That is the way the gospel is spread: Some sow, others reap, but all labor together under God and can rejoice together.

A Changed Town

The story closes with a picture of an entire town that has undergone spiritual transformation.

4:39–42 *Many of the Samaritans from that town believed in him because of the woman's testimony, "He told me everything I ever did." So when the Samaritans came to him, they urged him to stay with them, and he stayed two days. And because of his words many more became believers.*

They said to the woman, "We no longer believe just because of what you said; now we have heard for ourselves, and we know that this man really is the Savior of the world."

Here we see a thrilling process of spiritual growth taking root in this Samaritan village. Many came to Christ by believing the testimony of others. They saw what God did in the woman's life, or in the life of someone who believed her testimony. They were affected by what they saw, and they too believed.

But their Christian walk did not end there. They began to experience the power of God's active presence in their own lives. They experienced a deep new level of personal growth and faith.

After two days with Jesus, the whole city was beginning to believe. Jesus had never experienced such an outpouring of repentance and belief among the Jews. Seeing these Samaritans—people whom the Jews despised, ignored, and walked two days out of their way to avoid—believing and responding, Jesus was uplifted and strengthened. Like the Jews, the Samaritans had seen the Messiah as a political liberator who would someday overthrow Roman rule. But now these new Samaritan believers saw the Messiah as the Savior of the world, the redeemer of all men and women who place their trust in Him.

What happened in the Samaritan village of Sychar can happen in our lives as well. The fountain of living water flows freely within every believer in Jesus Christ. Eternal life and abiding love are there for each of us. The lesson of the story of the woman at the well is as profound and relevant today as it ever was: Taste the living water! Worship in spirit and in truth! Drink deeply of One who has come and has proved himself the Savior of the world!

Chapter Eleven

The Encourager of Faith

John 4:43–54

om Landry, former head coach of the Dallas Cowboys, is an encourager. He once said, "My job as a coach is to make men do what they don't want to do, in order to achieve what they really want to achieve." Every football player wants to win the championship and earn his Super Bowl ring—but to get to the Super Bowl, a player has to do a lot of things he doesn't want to do: grueling, exhausting, boring, repetitive training. He has to absorb a lot of pain before he achieves the gain. And the job of a coach is to encourage his players—often at the top of his lungs!—to keep on doing what they don't want to do, so that they can win games and achieve their goals.

In the second half of John 4, we will see that Jesus was that kind of encourager as well. He was sometimes blunt, sometimes confrontational—but only because he loved people enough to give them what they truly needed in order to have saving faith. Jesus, as we are about to see, was not only the Object of faith, but the Encourager of faith as well.

Back to Galilee

Jesus and His disciples have just come off an enormous spiritual high, having seen an amazing spiritual awakening take place in a Samaritan village, beginning with the conversion of the woman at the well. It has been a time of rejoicing over an unexpected spiritual harvest.

I believe that even Jesus did not know for sure that something like that was going to happen. He is our model for Christian living and ministry, and I believe He lived in dependence upon God's leading, taking one day at a time, because He wanted to teach us how to do the same. Though He was fully God, I believe Jesus set aside the prerogatives of God—such as omniscience—when He became a man so that He could fully identify with us, and we with Him.[1] Jesus was showing us that the Christian life is a life of adventure and anticipation of what a creative God will do in our lives. We cannot guess what will happen next, but if we rely upon God, we can be sure that whatever happens will certainly be exciting!

A Prophet Without Honor

After two days of ministry among the people in the Samaritan village, Jesus is ready to move on to Galilee, the northern province of Israel. The towns of Nazareth, where Jesus had spent most of His life, and Cana, where He performed His first miracle, were located in the central part of Galilee.

4:43–45 *After the two days he left for Galilee. (Now Jesus himself had pointed out that a prophet has no honor in his own country.) When he arrived in Galilee, the Galileans welcomed him. They had seen all that he had done in Jerusalem at the Passover Feast, for they also had been there.*

Here John explains why Jesus went to Jerusalem in the first place. He had performed His first miracle in Galilee—yet His reception in Galilee was lukewarm. Why? As John notes in verse 44, "a prophet has no honor in his own country."

Jesus is stating a truth that many people have discovered: It is hard to gain acceptance and recognition in one's own home town, but if you make a hit somewhere else and return home, the folks you grew up with will see you in an entirely different light. That's just human nature, and that's why Jesus went to Jerusalem—not to gain fame, status, or popularity, but to gain a wider audience for the message of truth. He knew the people of Galilee would be more receptive to His message if He returned triumphantly from Jerusalem.

So Jesus left Galilee and went to minister in Jerusalem, beginning by cleansing the temple, and continuing by doing miraculous signs throughout the time of the Passover Feast. Then He returned to Galilee by the direct route leading through Samaria. He returned to His home region with a greatly enhanced reputation. As John notes in verse 45, "When he arrived in Galilee, the Galileans welcomed him." They had never welcomed Him before. In fact, as Luke 4 records, when He identified Himself as the Messiah in the synagogue of His home town of Nazareth, the people rioted and attempted to kill Him by throwing Him off a cliff.

But now, the people of Galilee—like people from all over Israel—had gone to Jerusalem for Passover and there they witnessed Jesus in action: cleansing the temple, healing the sick and blind, making the lame to walk. Now, as He returned home to Galilee, the Galileans saw Him in a different light—and they welcomed Him.

4:46–47 *Once more he visited Cana in Galilee, where he had turned the water into wine. And there was a certain royal official whose son lay sick at Capernaum. When this man heard that Jesus had arrived in Galilee from Judea, he went to him and begged him to come and heal his son, who was close to death.*

I believe Jesus selected Cana as His next stop for an important symbolic reason. Cana was the place where He had performed His first miracle, turning water into wine. That miracle was a revelation of Jesus as the Lord of Nature. It demonstrated His authority to command the forces of nature.

It is in Cana that Jesus again takes up His ministry.

A Father's Fear

At the same time, just twenty miles away in the city of Capernaum, an anguished father stands at the bedside of his young son, watching the boy slowly succumb to fever and disease. If you are a parent, you may have experienced the helplessness this father felt—the cold clutch of fear that grips your heart as you watch the suffering of your child, who means more to you than your own life.

The return of Jesus to Galilee apparently made quite a commotion, and the news reached the ears of this father, who was a royal official. He immediately rushed to Cana—possibly riding on horseback to save time—and located Jesus. He pleaded with Jesus to come to Capernaum and heal his son, who was lying at death's door.

After seeing the compassion with which Jesus responded to the woman at the well, you would expect Jesus to immediately drop everything and help this distraught father. But that's not what happens. What Jesus says next is almost unbelievable!

4:48 *"Unless you people see miraculous signs and wonders," Jesus told him, "you will never believe."*

What a harsh word to give a man who is on the verge of losing a child! Where is Jesus' compassion? This doesn't sound like Jesus at all! In fact, it seems He is turning a cold shoulder to the man's plea.

But all is not as it seems at first glance. Notice that Jesus addresses the man in the plural form. He says, "Unless *you people* see miraculous signs and wonders, you will never believe." Many English translations fail to convey the plural nature of the word *you,* and make it seem as if Jesus is only scolding this one poor, distraught man. But the NIV is very true to the original text at this point, making it clear that Jesus is not chiding the man, but is rather making an observation on a group of people—that group being the class to which this father belongs, the privileged class. It was the privileged class which, for the most part, treated Jesus with skepticism and opposed His work.

The NIV calls this man a "royal official," and the King James Version calls this man a "nobleman." In the original text, he is literally a "king's man," a member of Herod's retinue and a part of the governing class of Galilee. It is to this class that Jesus addresses this word of rebuke.

Why does Jesus rebuke those who demand signs and wonders in order to believe? Isn't that what miracles are for—to inspire faith? We would all like to see miracles—supernatural events that demonstrate God's direct intervention in nature and in human affairs. And yet this hunger for the wondrous and miraculous can often hinder rather than help our faith.

People are drawn by the thousands to the meetings and television broadcasts of so-called "faith healers," because these people have an insatiable craving for signs and wonders. Their faith depends on a regular dose of emotional and sensational healings: the eyes of the blind being opened, people jumping out of wheelchairs, people tossing their canes and crutches aside. Those who continually seek these kinds of signs and wonders are the prime candidates for being fleeced by the religious racketeers who offer "healing from God" while taking in millions of dollars in donations. These "healers" are generally accountable to no one for the money they receive, and they live the lifestyles of the rich and famous.

An Unexpected Answer

This father came to Jesus, pleading for healing for his son. Jesus' immediate response was to lecture the man on faith. Why?

I believe that, like Tom Landry at the beginning of this chapter, Jesus was acting as a "coach." He was encouraging this man to have faith—not the kind of faith that demands signs and wonders, but the deeper, truer faith that trusts God even without the demonstration of miracles.

What was the man doing when he came to Jesus, pleading with Jesus to heal his son? He was *praying,* of course! And one of the truths this man had to learn about prayer—and one of the truths you and I have to learn as well!—is that while God answers prayer, He doesn't always answer it in the way we expect. Our faith must be deep enough and wide enough and strong enough to embrace and encompass the answer God gives us in whatever way He chooses to give it.

Jesus was willing—as we will soon see—to heal the man's son. But He didn't say so right away—*because He wanted to do something greater in this man's life than merely heal his son.* He wanted to *transform* this father's life and faith. He wanted to coach this man toward a stronger, more durable faith. As the Savior and Shepherd of the human race, Jesus loved this man too much to allow him to leave his presence unchanged.

As part of the process of tempering and hardening the man's faith, Jesus said to him, "Unless you people see miraculous signs and wonders, you will never believe." The anxious father, however, was in no frame of mind to discuss miracles and faith with Jesus. All he could think about was the welfare of his little boy.

4:49 *The royal official said, "Sir, come down before my child dies."*

In the original language, the man uses a very plaintive and affectionate word for child. In other words, he is saying, "Come before my dear little boy dies." There is agony in his words. His heart is being stretched to the breaking point.

He has a kernel of faith—faith that this unknown miracle worker has powers that no one else has. He is desperate enough to leave his son's bedside and seek out the miracle worker. But it is not a strong faith. It is not a trust in the power of God. Rather, it is a last-ditch hope in an unknown stranger with reputed powers. He pleads with the miracle-worker to return to Capernaum with him, and if the miracle-worker refuses to come in person and touch the boy, this man thinks that all will be lost.

But Jesus doesn't want him to merely believe in a traveling miracle-worker. He wants this man to *trust,* completely and confidently, in the power of God.

4:50a *Jesus replied, "You may go. Your son will live."*

A more accurate translation would be, "You may go. Your son is living, he lives right now." Notice that in these words, Jesus both answers the father's prayer—and *denies* it at the same time! The man has not only prayed for his son to be healed, but he has unwittingly attempted to dictate the terms of that healing. I'm sure he didn't mean to dictate to Jesus; he simply couldn't conceive of Jesus healing his son without physically going to him and touching him. But Jesus refused to go with the man. He answered the man's prayer for healing, but He answered it on His own terms. He dismissed the man, saying, "You may go. Your son will live."

Does this seem harsh to you? The mercy of God often seems to us like a severe mercy. Once we understand what God is about, then His seeming harshness comes into focus as an even greater goodness and loving gift than we imagined!

Jesus was not being unkind to the man by refusing to go with him. He was giving him a rare and wonderful gift. He was giving him the privilege and opportunity to believe at a deeper level of faith. He was "coaching" this man into experiencing a stronger, more durable faith. The message of Jesus to this father was, "Don't just believe in what I can do for your little boy. *Believe in who I am.*"

Not What You Feel But What You Do

To summarize this conversation in modern English, it would be fair to say the exchange between Jesus and the official from Capernaum went something like this:

JESUS: "Are you one of those 'seeing is believing' kind of people? Or do you have a genuine faith?"

THE FATHER: "Sir, I'm just a desperate father. I don't want to argue with you or talk about what class I belong to. My poor little boy is dying and I need your help."

JESUS: "Then go back to your son. I don't have to go with you. He's already healed now. You don't have to see to believe. First believe—and then you will see."

Is Jesus a man who keeps His word? Is He a man with power to heal by His command, even from twenty miles away? These are the questions this father has to face and answer. And He does answer them.

4:50b *The man took Jesus at his word and departed.*

He let go of his demand that Jesus heal according to his own dictates. He trusted Jesus to keep His word. Personally, I suspect this man did not feel at ease. I imagine he went home with many doubts and questions on his mind. Perhaps, as he journeyed home, he said to himself, "Why did I leave Him? If I had just pressed Him a little more, perhaps He would have come with me. What if I get home and my boy doesn't get well? What if I get home and he's already gone?"

True faith does not mean an absence of questioning, any more than true courage means an absence of fear. Courage is the will to act in a positive, proactive way despite your fears. Faith is the will to act in a positive, proactive way despite your uncertain feelings. The man acted. He did what Jesus told him to do. Though he was uncertain, he obeyed the word of Jesus. Faith is not what you feel, it's what you do! Faith is obedience.

You probably know what it means to come to Jesus with a request—perhaps a desperate request. "Lord," you pray, "please answer this prayer, and answer it in this way. Lord, come here, do this, supply that, and do it all within this time frame." We all do this, I'm afraid. Out of the anguish of our hearts we can think of no other way for Jesus to respond than the way we have in mind. We say, "Come, Lord." But He does not come. And so, we doubt.

Jesus, our coach in the game of life, has something larger in mind for us than merely answering our prayers within the limited scope in which we pray them. He wants to do something greater in our lives than merely say "Yes" to our prayers. He wants to transform our lives and our faith. He wants to coach us toward a stronger, more durable faith. He loves us too much to allow us to remain unchanged.

The Rest of the Story

In verses 51 through 53, John gives us what radio commentator Paul Harvey calls "the rest of the story."

4:51–53 *While he was still on the way, his servants met him with the news that his boy was living. When he inquired as to the time when his son got better, they said to him, "The fever left him yesterday at the seventh hour."*

Then the father realized that this was the exact time at which Jesus had said to him, "Your son will live." So he and all his household believed.

One detail in this story tends to verify my suspicion that this man was plagued with uncertainty, even while he acted in faith and obedience to Jesus: He checked the hour when his little boy began to improve. If he hadn't felt at least some nagging doubts, he wouldn't have bothered to ask! He was looking for verification that Jesus really did what He said He would do—and everything checked! The fever left the boy at the precise moment Jesus said, "You may go. Your son will live."

Now the man understood—not merely what Jesus could do, but who Jesus was. This amazing man had authority over all illness, and He was not limited by distance or time. When the man came to this realization, says the apostle John in verse 53, "he and all his household believed."

But didn't he already believe? Didn't Jesus heal his son in response to the man's faith?

Yes—but the little kernel of faith this man began with was being nurtured by Jesus. Once the man arrived home and the miracle of his restored son became real, the man broke through to an even deeper level of faith. Suddenly, this man understood that he could trust God, and he could rely upon God to work out all the issues and crises in his life in ways far beyond what he himself could engineer or anticipate.

There is an interesting footnote to this incident. Some scholars believe that this royal official later became a leader in the early church, and that he is mentioned by name in Acts 13:1—"Manaen (who had been brought up with Herod the tetrarch)." In other words, he was the foster-brother of Herod the king, which would make him a "king's man," as he is literally called in John 4. We can't be certain that the royal official of John 4 is indeed Manaen, but if so, then we have just witnessed the moment Manaen came to Christ.

The Meaning of the Sign

In the closing verse of this chapter John affirms that this was more than just a miracle; it was a *sign,* which pointed out something significant about Jesus.

4:54 *This was the second miraculous sign that Jesus performed, having come from Judea to Galilee.*

The first sign was the changing of water into wine. As we have seen, there was an important meaning embedded in that sign. It pointed to a truth about Jesus that we would otherwise not have known—the truth that Jesus is the Lord of Nature.

The second sign, the healing of the official's son, also points to a new truth about Jesus: He is the Great Physician, with authority over illness that is far beyond the ability of human beings.

Another profound truth about Jesus in this story is that He is the Encourager of our faith. He is our coach. Just as Tom Landry said, the job of a coach is to make us do what we don't want to do in order to achieve a larger goal. We don't want to have to wait for answers to our prayers. We don't want to have our prayers answered in any other way but the way we ask them. But

Jesus, our coach in the game of life, is looking to that larger goal, and He is encouraging us to grow our faith.

That is why Hebrews 12:2 calls Jesus the Author and Finisher of our faith. He is the Source of our faith, and the Object of our worship—but He is also helping us to grow and perfect our faith in Him. Jesus, the Encourager of our faith, puts us through circumstances we don't want to go through, and makes us face things we do not like to face—but He does so because of his great love for us, so that we can achieve what we have always wanted with all our hearts: the strengthening of our faith.

Chapter Twelve

Do You Want To Get Well?

John 5:1–17

For hundreds of years, the pools of the village of Bath, England, have been considered to have healing properties because they are fed by natural mineral springs. To this day, thousands of people flock every year to bathe in the waters of Bath.

Nearly two hundred years ago, a famous English doctor, Sir Walter Farquhar, prescribed a three-week visit to the pools of Bath as a curative for one of his elderly female patients. The woman had complained for years of an ailment that had never been clearly diagnosed, so—unable to do anything else for her—Dr. Farquhar suggested that a stay in Bath might do her some good.

"But Doctor," the woman protested, "I wouldn't want to be out of your care for three weeks! You know how ill I am! What if I took a turn for the worse? Who could I trust to take care of me?"

"Ah, but there is an absolutely wonderful doctor in Bath," said Dr. Farquhar. "A very competent man. I guarantee that Dr. Lewis will give you the best of care. I'll give you a letter of introduction to take to Dr. Lewis. The letter will give him your complete medical history. It will be just as if I were treating you myself."

So the woman set out with a companion on the carriage ride to Bath. As they rode, the old woman's companion asked just what sort of ailment she was being treated for. "Well," the woman said, "Dr. Farquhar has never actually told me. But he gives my entire medical history in this letter to Dr. Lewis. Perhaps I should read it and find out—"

"Oh, no!" said her companion. "You mustn't do that!"

But the woman's curiosity was too strong. She took out the letter, ripped open the envelope, and read:

"Dear Dr. Lewis: The illness is all in her head. Keep the old lady in Bath for three weeks, then send her back to me. Truly yours, W. Farquhar."

In John chapter 5, we are going to visit—along with Jesus—another natural pool, where many who sought healing were convinced of its healing powers. It is the pool of Bethesda in Jerusalem.

5:1–3 *Some time later, Jesus went up to Jerusalem for a feast of the Jews. Now there is in Jerusalem near the Sheep Gate a pool, which in Aramaic is called Bethesda and which is surrounded by five covered colonnades. Here a great number of disabled people used to lie—the blind, the lame, the paralyzed.*

[Note: The best and most reliable of the ancient manuscripts do not contain verse 4, which reads:

From time to time an angel of the Lord would come down and stir up the waters. The first one into the pool after each such disturbance would be cured of whatever disease he had.]

Verse 4, which was probably not written by the apostle John, may have been inserted later to explain why the people had come to the pool of Bethesda. The people maintained a superstitious belief that whenever the water of the pools was "stirred"—that is, when it rapidly rose, then sank again—it was the result of an angel visiting the pool. According to the superstition, the first one to enter the pool after the "stirring" would be healed.

This is similar to the legends that have grown up around similar sites in our modern world. In the village of Lourdes in southern France, for example, there is a spa which many people believe has divine healing properties. And at the shrine of Guadalupe in Mexico City, thousands of crutches are stacked along the walls to mark that site as a place where people receive a healing from God.

Do people actually receive divine healing at places like the spa at Lourdes, the shrine of Guadalupe, or the pool of Bethesda? Let's examine the pool at Bethesda more closely and see what evidence we find. The pool of Bethesda, like many similar pools in the Jerusalem area, is fed by an intermittent underground spring. At various times, water is released in surges from hidden underground reservoirs under the city, causing these springs to rise and fall suddenly. This activity of the water—which was completely mysterious to the people of that time—gave rise to the superstition about an angel troubling the pool.

Undoubtedly, healings did occur there. Even today, healings take place in Lourdes and Mexico City when people go to such places in the belief that they can be healed. But most of these healings can be explained psychologically. In some cases, the "illness" may have been nothing more than a case of hypochondria—which, of course, was the diagnosis Dr. Farquhar made of the lady he sent to Bath.

But even more fascinating is the fact that researchers have shown that many genuine illnesses and ailments of the body can actually be healed when people believe strongly enough that healing is taking place. This is called the "placebo effect," and that is why whenever a new drug is tested, half the test group is always given a "placebo"—a fake "drug" such as a sugar pill—while the other half is given the real drug. If the real drug is no more effective than the "placebo" drug, then researchers know the drug doesn't work. The "placebo effect"—the power of mind over illness—is often so strong that the sugar pills frequently out-cure the real drugs!

So the fact that healings may have taken place at a site such as the pool of Bethesda doesn't mean that the healings were actually the work of God or angels. The pool might have been nothing more than a huge, water-filled placebo! In any case, the pool had established a reputation as a place where people could be healed at the time that Jesus paid a visit there in John chapter 5.

For many years the site of this pool was lost, buried under the debris of the centuries, but it was discovered and excavated in the 1960s. The pool is located to the north of the Temple Mount, near what is now called St. Stephen's Gate (which is built on the site of the Sheep Gate mentioned in verse 2). In these porches which were built around the pool, many of the people of our Lord's times used to gather during feast days, hoping for a healing miracle.

"Do You Want To Get Well?"

Now John introduces a man who needs the touch of the Great Physician.

5:5–6 *One who was there had been an invalid for thirty-eight years. When Jesus saw him lying there and learned that he had been in this condition for a long time, he asked him, "Do you want to get well?"*

Many people read this and assume that the disabled man has been at this pool for 38 years. But that's not what the passage says. It says he has been *ill* for 38 years. We don't know why. He is not referred to in this passage as "lame." Rather, he is weak, feeble, and unable to stand. He may have been stricken by some wasting disease such as polio, tuberculosis, or multiple sclerosis. Whatever his diagnosis, this man has been infirm for a very long time.

He is one among scores of lame, blind, paralyzed, and sick people, all waiting for the waters of the pool to heal them. Out of this entire crowd, Jesus selected this one man. He did not heal everyone. He didn't speak to everyone. He didn't preach to the multitude. He went only to one man.

This is an important point, for this story is intended to show us how God deals with human need and weakness. Undoubtedly, it was the helplessness of this man that drew Jesus to him. Perhaps you can identify with this weak and helpless man who lay beside the pool of Bethesda. Perhaps you know what it means to have a hurt that lingers and aches and won't go away. Perhaps you feel paralyzed in some area of your life. You are stricken by a sense of failure. Or sorrow. Or physical affliction. Or the cruel mistreatment of someone close to you. Or an addiction. Or a sinful habit such as lust, pornography, or adultery. In some sense, in some area of your life, you know how this invalid man feels.

It is to people such as this man—and people like yourself—that Jesus is drawn.

A Strange Question

Now notice the question Jesus asks the man: "Do you want to get well?" What a strange question to ask a man who had been sick for 38 years! Yet we know that Jesus never asked a foolish or pointless question in His life. Obviously it was important for this man to answer—at least to himself—this question.

As strange as it may seem, there are many people today who do not want to be healed. They do not want to receive divine help in their problems. They do not want to be helped out of their weakness. Outwardly, they may complain about their condition, but inwardly they love their weakness. They cling to the "victim" role, the "poor me" role, because they crave the attention that other people give them because of their problems and suffering.

Another reason some people do not want to be healed is that they fear change. They have become comfortable with their pain and their problems. To be healed would mean making changes in their lives and assuming responsibility for their lives. They could be delivered if they really wanted to—but it's much easier to stay mired in a trough of familiar unhappiness than to be healed and delivered and have to make major changes in their lives.

The question Jesus asked this man is the same question He asks you and me: "Do you want to be healed?" Do we want to be healed of that addiction? Do we want to be healed in our marriage relationships? Do we want to experience emotional and psychological healing? Do we want to be spiritually healed? Before we glibly answer "Yes," let's acknowledge that healing in each of these areas calls forth a commitment and some hard work and a willingness to change.

"Do you want to be healed?" I believe that if this man had said, "No, Jesus, to be honest with you, after 38 years I've become rather comfortable with my affliction," then I suspect Jesus would have gone his way and left the man in his weakness. You cannot help somebody who doesn't want to be helped. You can't help people who will not admit their need, who insist that they are doing all right and don't need anyone's help.

Jesus came to help the helpless, not the self-sufficient. He is the Solution for those who have given up trying to solve their problems in their own strength and wisdom. But Jesus can do nothing for those who are determined to make it on their own. If the Lord says to you, "Do you want to be healed?" and you answer, "Not yet," or, "I'm doing okay," or, "I'll let you know if I can't handle it," then He can do nothing more for you.

"Yes, But . . ."

The man at the pool of Bethesda answers Jesus' question.

5:7 *"Sir," the invalid replied, "I have no one to help me into the pool when the water is stirred. While I am trying to get in, someone else goes down ahead of me."*

The man's answer to Jesus' question is, "Yes, but . . . ." In other words, "Yes, I want to be healed, but I cannot. I've tried, I've done everything I know how. I want to get into that water, but I lack the ability. No one will help me. I've given up. I have no hope."

Many people are like that. They've given up all hope of being healed. They have resigned themselves to their pain or their weakness or their addiction.

It is amazing to me how many people casually feel they are in control of something that really controls them. They are like the person who says, "It's easy to stop smoking. I've done it hundreds of times!" What they are really saying is, "I give up. I've tried to change my situation, but it's hopeless."

A young pastor once told me that his problem was that he loved to read pornographic magazines. That's right, a pastor! Outwardly, he gave the impression that he was one of God's most dedicated servants. But inwardly, he was living a lifestyle of sin. He told me he could not pass a magazine store without going in and looking at filthy magazines, buying them and taking them home with him, and hiding them from his wife and children. He told me he had tried to stop but he could not. "What will I do?" he asked me.

I asked him if he really wanted to change, if he really wanted to be healed of his lust for pornography. His answer was like that of the man at the pool of Bethesda: "Yes, but . . . ." On one level, he hated what he did and was afraid his wife or someone else would discover his hidden sin. But on another level he was unwilling to give it up. Many people are right where this pastor was—wanting to be set free, yet on some level feeling either helpless or unwilling to fully make a break with the sin or the circumstance that is holding them down.

Asking the Impossible

So what is Jesus' response to a person who has lost all hope, who has given up on himself or herself? We see it in His answer to the man at the pool. Jesus didn't say, "I'll help you into the pool the next time the water moves." He could have, but He didn't.

He could have said, "Hang in there. Keep coming to the pool and you'll make it some day." But no, He didn't say that either.

He could have said, "Let's at least make you comfortable. Let's get you a new mattress to lie on and get you something to snack on while you wait." But no, He didn't do that either.

What does Jesus say, then? Notice His method: First, He asks the impossible. Second, He removes all possibility of a relapse. Third, He expects continued success.

5:8–9a *Then Jesus said to him, "Get up! Pick up your mat and walk." At once the man was cured; he picked up his mat and walked.*

First, Jesus tells the man to do what he has not been able to do for 38 years: Get up and walk!

What went through this man's mind when Jesus told him to do the impossible? Perhaps he thought, "If this man tells me to walk when I obviously can't walk, it must mean that He intends to do something to enable me to walk." Thus his faith is transferred from his own efforts to Jesus. Obviously, it was Jesus' will that this man should obey Him, and the moment the man's will agreed with the Lord's will, the power was there.

We don't know whether the man felt anything as the healing took place. There is no mention of any sensations of warmth or power flowing into him or anything so melodramatic. All we know is that strength came into his bones and nerves and muscles. Before he couldn't stand. Now he could.

Second, Jesus commanded the man, "Pick up your mat and walk." Bible teacher G. Campbell Morgan has said that the reason Jesus ordered him to take up his mat was "in order to make no provision for a relapse." The man might have said to himself, "I'm healed now—but I'd better leave my bed here in case of a relapse. I may need it tomorrow." Jesus didn't want to leave this man a back door through which he could escape back into his illness and his old ways.

Jesus is saying something important to all of us who need His healing: Don't make any provision to go back on your healing. Burn your bridges behind you. If you are giving up alcohol or cigarettes, don't keep a bottle or a pack in the basement. Say no to friends who have been luring you into evil. Don't go within ten blocks of the store that sells the magazines that tempt you. Cancel that cable channel with the sex-oriented movies you have trouble resisting. Cut off any possibility of going back. Let somebody know the new stand you have taken, and ask that person to check on you and hold you accountable. Find a counselor, support group, or recovery group that can keep you moving forward, not backward, in your healing process.

Third, Jesus says, "Walk." Don't expect to be carried. Get on your feet and walk. Many people want to be carried after they are healed. They expect everybody to gather around them and keep them going—and this is a common source of failure. If Jesus gives you the power to rise, He can certainly give you the power to walk daily and keep going—not looking to your friends or to anyone else to carry you, but looking only unto Jesus, the Author and Finisher of your faith.

Mounting Rejection

This chapter marks a major division in the gospel of John. In the first four chapters, Jesus has been presented to us as the Son of God, and He has presented Himself to the Jews as the promised Messiah. But now in chapter 5, John begins to trace a mounting climate of rejection toward the claims of Jesus. There is a growing mood of hostility in official circles against the ministry of the Lord. This rejection will gather around three remarkable acts of healing by Jesus: First, the healing here in John 5 of the man at the pool of Bethesda. Second, the healing of the man born blind in John 9. Third, the greatest of all His miracles, the raising of Lazarus from the dead in John 11. This mood of hostility toward Jesus will grow until it culminates in His death by torture upon the cross.

5:9b–11 *The day on which this took place was a Sabbath, and so the Jews said to the man who had been healed, "It is the Sabbath; the law forbids you to carry your mat."*

But he replied, "The man who made me well said to me, 'Pick up your mat and walk.' "

Jesus has healed this man—but He has also gotten him into trouble with the authorities! He has told him to do something which violates the Sabbath restrictions. At first glance it might seem that the Jewish leaders were right to criticize a man carrying his bed on the Sabbath, for the Law of Moses did say that the Jews were to keep the Sabbath and not do any work on that day. After studying that law, the teachers of Israel had—perhaps with good intentions— spelled out 39 different ways by which the Sabbath could be violated by certain types of work. One of the ways was carrying any kind of a load on the Sabbath day. Jeremiah 17:22 specifically warned, "Do not bring a load out of your houses or do any work on the Sabbath, but keep the Sabbath day holy, as I commanded your forefathers." So on the surface there appears to be some justification for their intervention in this case.

But the *true* motive of their hearts is about to be revealed. The healed man answers them, "The man who made me well said to me, 'Pick up your mat and walk.'" The Jewish leaders' intentions are revealed next.

5:12 *So they asked him, "Who is this fellow who told you to pick it up and walk?"*

Notice that their reaction is not, "How marvelous! Who is this man who can heal people? Tell us where we can find this miracle worker!" No, their reaction is, "Who's the wise guy who's telling you it's okay to disobey one of our regulations?" Their hearts are plainly revealed. They are religious bigots, intent on the letter of the law, but totally unconcerned about the mercy of God.

This kind of zeal for the letter of the Sabbath law can still be seen today. During a trip to Jerusalem in 1983, I decided to attend a cinema one evening, just as the Jewish Sabbath was drawing to a close. When I arrived, the theater was surrounded by a hostile crowd. The marquee lights had been shut down and the theater appeared to have been hastily closed down. There was some commotion and shouting, so I asked a fellow on the sidewalk what was going on. He told me that a contingent of Orthodox Jews had discovered that the theater was selling tickets just a few moments before the Sabbath ended. They were protesting and threatening to stone the theater because of their feeling that the Sabbath was being violated.

This was the legalistic attitude that confronted the man whom Jesus had healed. The law said that anyone caught bearing a burden on the Sabbath was to be stoned. Though this punishment was not often carried out, the man still had reason to be worried. Notice, however, that just as soon as this new believer got in trouble, Jesus was there to help him.

5:13–14 *The man who was healed had no idea who it was, for Jesus had slipped away into the crowd that was there.*

Later Jesus found him at the temple and said to him, "See, you are well again. Stop sinning or something worse may happen to you."

Jesus found him! The man had gone to the temple because the law required that one who had been healed had to make a thanksgiving offering. Jesus knew where to find him.

"Stop Sinning!"

The order of what Jesus says to the man is very important. He did not shake His finger at the man and say, "Sin no more. If you sin, you'll lose your healing." No, He said, "See, you are well again!" Jesus never says, "Sin no more," unless He first says, "You are made whole." He calls the man's attention to the fact that not only had he been physically healed, he had been spiritually healed. His sins had been forgiven. He had been cleansed, and he was a new man in his body, soul, and spirit. Only after a person has received the gracious and free gift of God's wholeness does Jesus then say, "Sin no more."

Here is an indicator of what was wrong with the man. Why did he lie helpless for 38 years? Because some sin was sapping the vitality of his life. This is not to say that the only reason people get sick is because of sin. Scripture makes it clear (see, for example, the book of Job) that sickness is not always the result of any sin committed by the sick individual. But sometimes—and I think the individual always knows, deep down, when this is the case—sickness is caused by sin he is involved in.

We do not know what kind of sin this man had been committing. Perhaps it was a bitter spirit toward somebody. Bitterness and resentment can sap all the energy and vitality of life and turn a person into an invalid. I have seen that happen. Perhaps it was a shameful habit he continually indulged in or an injury he had done to someone and had refused to make amends for. Our Lord reminds him that God is concerned about such areas in our lives.

Jesus makes it clear that the man's miraculous healing does not mean the end of all his problems and responsibilities to live a righteous life. He says, "Stop sinning or something worse may happen to you."

5:15–16 The man went away and told the Jews that it was Jesus who had made him well.

So, because Jesus was doing these things on the Sabbath, the Jews persecuted him.

This became the justification the Jewish leaders used for their persecution of Jesus: They hid behind a claim that Jesus violated the law. This, of course, was not their true motive for attacking Jesus. Their real grudge against Jesus was that He was taking their power. When the people flocked to Jesus, and began worshiping God in spirit and in truth, they no longer needed the restrictive legalism of the Jewish rulers. The leaders, rather than responding to Jesus' gospel, felt threatened by Jesus and chose to oppose Him.

The pretext the Jewish leaders used in attacking Jesus was that He broke the Sabbath law. Jesus ignored these regulations because they were not God's law but "the tradition of men"—and that gave the Jewish leaders all the excuse they needed to persecute Him.

Why is Jesus at war with "the tradition of men"? He explains here.

5:17 *Jesus said to them, "My Father is always at his work to this very day, and I, too, am working."*

Jesus is saying, "You Jewish leaders point back to Moses and to all that the rabbis have added to his law. But have a higher authority than Moses: God is doing this! Your traditions are a burden on people, but God is reaching down to liberate people. Our merciful and compassionate God has found this man and healed him. He is working and I am His instrument." That is one of the most profound statements in the gospel of John.

What Jesus said in that day is true for us today: God is working in our own times, at the climactic end of the twentieth century. God is working in international events. He is working in the pressures and problems that come to each one of us. He is working in the very circumstances in which you find yourself today. If you want to find real meaning in life, you need to find out what God is doing and start working with him. When you do this, you become an instrument in the hand of God as it moves through history.

The only experience that lasts, that gives true significance to life, is the experience of being a part of what God is doing. Only God's work will last. All that we do, all the monuments we build and works of art we create and music we compose, all will ultimately fall to nothing. Even our religious work—if it is not done through, for, and by God—will be just so much trash to be incinerated in the fires of judgment. Only what God does will last.

The question Jesus leaves each of us at the end of this story is, "In some area of your life, in some area of brokenness or temptation or anxiety in your life, do you want to be healed?" If your answer is yes, then Jesus' command to you is, "Stand up! Take up your bed, and walk!"

Chapter Thirteen

The Secret of Jesus

John 5:18–20

Now we come to three little verses in chapter 5. You may wonder, Why is Ray spending a whole chapter on three little verses?

Let me tell you: These three little verses are like a vast ocean of truth! I feel like a little boy who has been given a plastic bucket, then told to go to the beach and empty the Pacific Ocean before lunch! I have sat and stared at these verses and seen deep, amazing implications in them. And I have wondered how I can possibly bring out the beauty and the multi-layered depths of meaning of these verses in just one chapter!

But we must give it a try.

Without question, the most famous mathematical formula in the world is Einstein's simple equation, $E = MC^2$, which means "energy equals mass times the speed of light squared." This is the formula for transforming a given amount of matter (say, plutonium) into pure energy (such as a nuclear explosion). Such a simple little equation, just five little symbols in a row, yet it has totally changed our world—our political realities and our history.

Two tangible expressions of $E = MC^2$ over Hiroshima and Nagasaki in 1945 spelled the end of World War II. The threat of $E = MC^2$ ever since that time may well have prevented the outbreak (so far) of World War III. And this little formula has even changed our day-to-day lives. There is a very good possibility that when you switched on your lamp to read these words, you were using electricity generated by nuclear power, by $E = MC^2$.

Yet the profound meaning locked within these five little symbols is as nothing compared with the profound meaning embedded in the three little verses we now examine.

5:18–20 *For this reason the Jews tried all the harder to kill him; not only was he breaking the Sabbath, but he was even calling God his own Father, making himself equal with God.*

Jesus gave them this answer: "I tell you the truth, the Son can do nothing

138

by himself; he can do only what he sees his Father doing, because whatever the Father does the Son also does. For the Father loves the Son and shows him all he does. Yes, to your amazement he will show him even greater things than these."

These verses follow immediately the account of the healing of the man at the pool of Bethesda, an amazing manifestation of the power of God. Among those who witnessed this miracle were a handful of men whom John simply calls, "the Jews"—meaning the leaders of the Jews, Orthodox priests and members of the ruling class of the Jews. They looked on this miracle with narrowed eyes, whispering their displeasure among themselves, angered by what Jesus had done.

A Claim of Godhood

Verse 18 tells us that the Jewish leaders saw Jesus not only as a renegade who disobeyed the Sabbath regulations, but as a blasphemer: "He was even calling God his own Father, making himself equal with God." Their response: They wanted to kill Jesus.

Their misunderstanding of Jesus is absolutely amazing! They had watched Jesus call a powerless invalid to his feet and make him whole—and their reaction was not wonder or worship, but disgust and anger! Because Jesus had dared violate the regulations they had added to the Sabbath laws of Moses, they were furious to the point of murder. In the face of His proof of God-like authority over disease, they were angry because He claimed to be who He clearly was: the Son, coequal with God the Father.

(By the way, if you ever hear anyone challenge the fact that Jesus claimed to be God, point that person to this verse. It is one among a number of verses in John where Jesus clearly conveyed to those around Him His claim of Godhood.)

In reply to the misunderstanding and the anger of the Jewish leaders, Jesus explains Himself. It is one of the most magnificent, dramatic scenes in the Word of God. Here, Jesus confronts His hostile opponents and explains to them in simple terms how He operates. He didn't explain Himself in a defensive way. He wasn't trying to change the minds of His opponents. He knew that instead of being convinced, the Jewish leaders would twist and distort His words until they succeeded in bringing about His death.

What we see in this scene is an act of raw courage. In verses 19 and 20, Jesus answers His opponents, saying in effect, "I am only doing what the Father does. The Father is acting through me. And you will be even more amazed and confounded when the Father does even greater things through me!"

It took power—perhaps as much godly power as did the healing of the invalid—to stand before these murderous opponents and state His case. This is a further confirmation of what Jesus reveals to us in these verses: *the secret of His power.* It is the secret of how He lived His life. It is the secret of a life that was continually lived as a conduit, a channel for the power of God. That infinite power flowed from God the Father through Jesus the Son, who served as an outlet, a point of release, so that this infinite power could flow into the lives of men and women through the things He did—and the things He said.

Three Steps To Power: Step One

Notice that Jesus begins verse 19 with the words that I call "the formula of focused attention," which different translations render as "Verily, verily," "Truly, truly," or (as in the NIV, which is the text used in this book), "I tell you the truth." In the original language of the New Testament, Jesus literally says, "Amen, amen." He couldn't be more emphatic! He wants us to know that the words which follow are words of utmost importance. Jesus is about to unfold His secret. It is the secret of unlimited power, and He unfolds His secret in three steps.

Step One of His secret is *the folly of self-sufficiency.* He says, "The Son can do nothing by himself." This is probably the most radical statement in the Word of God. The first step in being a channel of God's power is a recognition that the human self is ultimately powerless and insufficient. In contrast to what the New Age and human potential movements teach, we have no godlike power within us. And we cannot appropriate God's power for our own selfish goals and uses.

You may mount to the top of whatever heap you aspire to, and gain the admiration and attention of all the world. But if you have not discovered this secret of God's power, your life will be unsatisfying and insipid. You will not find any satisfaction in life—and worst of all, your life will be of no use whatsoever to God. The gift of life you have been given will have been wasted.

When Jesus says, "the Son can do nothing by himself," He does not mean it is *physically* impossible for Him to act apart from the Father, any more than it is physically impossible for us to act apart from God. We can and we do. And Jesus could have, too. Later in this account, Jesus says the Father has given Him power to act "out of himself." Jesus could have created a whole universe over which He was God. He had the power to do so. But He chose never to exercise that power for His own benefit. Never!

Here we find His explanation of His refusal to change stones into bread, to leap from the temple to gain the applause of people, or to gain the whole world for Himself when Satan tempted Him during His forty-day fast in the wilderness: God gives His power to those who will not use it for their own benefit.

When Jesus says, "the Son can do nothing," He is not speaking of physical impossibility but of moral self-restraint. You probably know people of complete moral integrity. If you said to them, "I will give you a million dollars if you will cheat on your spouse, or if you will cheat your business customers, or if you will steal from your employer," they will look at you with horror and say, "I can't do that! I just *can't!*" Sure, they can—in a purely physical sense. But to do so would violate their integrity, their moral self-concept. It would be a cheapening and a contradiction of everything they stand for. In a moral sense, they can't do it.

That is what Jesus means when He says "the Son can do nothing by himself." He could, but He would not, and He never did. Instead, He made a choice to obey an inner vision. He said, "The Son can do nothing by himself; he can do only what he sees his Father doing." Jesus saw what God the Father did with an inner vision, and seeing into the heart of the Father in every situation, He immediately obeyed that vision.

What was this inner vision like? How can any of us truly know? But somehow, an impulse, a certainty arose within the spirit of Jesus which He knew was of the Father. It was an impulse that was consistent with the character of the Father as revealed in God's Word.

Many people today claim that God has told them to do something—even to commit murder or engage in sexual immorality. Many people experience emotional or psychological compulsions and believe that these compulsions are the voice of God, telling them what to do.

A man was once interviewed on a radio talk show, telling about the strange things he thought God had told him to do. The amazed interviewer said, "You actually heard God speaking to you in an audible voice, telling you to do these things?"

"Yes," said the troubled man, "but God doesn't talk to me anymore."

The interviewer asked, "Well, when did God stop talking to you."

The man replied, "When my psychiatrist put me on a certain medication, God stopped talking to me."

Here was a man who "heard" God telling him to do certain things—not because God actually spoke to him, but because he had a chemical imbalance in his brain that needed medical treatment.

It's dangerous for us to follow any impulse from our minds and emotions, thinking "God told us" to do it. The key truth about the inner vision of Jesus, of course, is that no impulse ever arose in His mind that was not in line with the external revelation of the Word of God. That is the ultimate guideline. Every impulse, every thought, every action must be tested according to Scripture. If that impulse, thought, or action agrees with Scripture, then it is of God. The Spirit of God *never* compels us to violate the Word of God before us; the Spirit of God and the Word of God always agree.

The secret to seeing God's power released in our lives is this: *Nothing comes from me, everything comes from God.* This may seem like a terrific leap to make—from the life of Jesus to your life and mine. Jesus was disclosing the secret of God's power in His own life—but He is Jesus, the Son of God! What does that have to do with mere mortals like us?

It has *everything* to do with us! Jesus is our model, our exemplar! His life was lived as a pattern for us to follow. We have the same relationship to Jesus, the Son, as He had to the Father. What the Father would do through Him the Son now wants to do through us.

I submit to you that here is a far more profound and shattering truth than the Einsteinian equation $E = MC^2$. Simple, yet astounding. At any point in our human need and limitation, the power of God is available, ready to meet our need. Jesus lived His entire life this way, and so can you and I. It was not merely in raising people from their sickbeds that He employed the power of God. He was a channel, an outlet, for God's power whenever He spoke to some lonely, heartsick, broken person and brought him or her to life and faith. It was the same power that put so much supernatural wattage into His words—words that electrified people like the disciples whom He called to Himself; people like the ruler of the Jews named Nicodemus; people like the Samaritan woman at the well.

Here is the secret of power! When you begin with an attitude of self-denial, with a confession of your own powerlessness and God's own infinite power—"I cannot, but God can"—God is able to release His power through us in a visible way. And Jesus goes on to say that even greater power is scheduled to be released!

"For the Father loves the Son and shows him all he does," says Jesus in verse 20. "Yes, to your amazement, he will show him even greater things than these." Later in the chapter, Jesus will reveal two of these "greater things" that will amaze His hearers: Jesus will be given power to give life and execute judgment. But in this verse, Jesus reveals the *source* and the *reason* for this divine release of power.

First, this power flows from God the Father's love for the Son. The Father Jesus talks about here is the Creator, the One whose brilliant mind conceived the glory of nature, the intricate structure of life, the complex blending and dovetailing together of the processes of the natural world. It is this creative Person who loves the Son and delights to communicate to Him and through

Him the creative power that counters the forces of evil, destruction, pain, suffering, death, and sorrow.

So it is with our relationship with the Son. Jesus is the Lord of life, the Lord of nature, the Lord of the universe, the Lord of history and of nations. He delights in communicating to us His power, His creative energy, His constructive solutions to the problems that oppress us and hem us in. We are normal, limited, powerless human beings—yet we have access to an infinite power, an infinite wisdom, an infinitely creative mind that fashions solutions to our problems which are far, far beyond our ability to imagine.

Three Steps To Power: Step Two

In these verses, we also find the second step to power: "The Father loves the Son and shows him all he does." God reveals to His Son *everything*—not all at once, certainly, but ultimately, everything is revealed to Him. As the writer of Hebrews says, "Yet at present we do not see everything subject to him [to humankind]. But we see Jesus, who was made a little lower than the angels, now crowned with glory and honor. . . ."[1] In the long view of God's plan, we see Jesus crowned. Eventually, that is the end of all God wants to reveal to the Son.

"Yes," Jesus continues, "to your amazement, he will show him even greater things than these." Jesus indicates that a *gradual revelation* is at work. It is a graduated process. Jesus the Man is growing in His understanding and strength. And as He does, He will participate more and more in the works of the Father until that moment when He hangs on the cross and says, "It is finished."

This is the process God outlines for us: His power is not handed to us as a package deal, so that we can use it for our own benefit and make a name for ourselves. God's power is released only when we use it as the Son did: for the glory of God, for the completion of the Father's will. When we do so, God gives us *more* power in a progressive way. We grow progressively in our ability to manifest the power of God.

That is why the person who walks with God becomes more beautiful, more Christlike, more rich in God's power and the fullness of life, even amid hostile opposition and the problems and pain of this world. That is God's pattern for us. He wants us to understand that the second step to unlimited power is a willingness to wait for God to gradually, progressively take more control of our lives so that He can gradually, progressively unleash more of His power through us.

Three Steps To Power: Step Three

Finally, the third step: "Yes, to your amazement, he will show him even greater things than these." Every manifestation of the Father's power (or the

Son's power released in us), will awaken a sense of wonder in those who witness it. A simple word, an act of compassion, a cup of cold water given to somebody in the name of the Lord, will leave an impact that will make people marvel. The third step to God's unlimited power is a recognition that when God unleashes His power through us, it flows out as a witness to others—and those who see it are amazed!

Most Christians are well acquainted with Romans 8:28—"And we know that in all things God works for the good of those who love him, who have been called according to his purpose." But many Christians have never studied the powerful truth of the very next verse: "For those God foreknew he also predestined to be conformed to the likeness of his Son, that he might be the firstborn among many brothers."

Just think what that means! God is not content to have only one Son. He wants *many* children, both men and women. And He wants these children to be like His firstborn, Jesus. He has "predestined" us, He has made a decision about us ahead of time, and He is intent upon it. He will not fail. The processes of change are now going on in your life and mine in order to mold us and shape us into the likeness of Jesus!

When you think about the fact that one day you are going to be—by sovereign God's grace, love, and power—conformed to the image of His Son, you are left with one question: How much *change* will that require? What sort of *change* will God have to bring into your life in order for you to become the Christlike person He intends you to be?

Because God *is* going to change us. And change *is* painful. We don't like to change. We prefer to be left alone in our comfortable mediocrity. We don't like to be prodded and jabbed and made to think about things we do not want to think about. But God is going to change us, and the purpose of that change will be to enable us to learn to live by the power of the Living God, to derive our power from God Himself. God is going to mold us into people who are open channels through which His power can flow unobstructed to a hurting world. In the process, He will show us how our lives can have true, eternal significance.

Once, when my wife Elaine and I were at Glen Eyrie, the beautiful mountain headquarters-retreat of the Navigators in Colorado Springs, we walked up the mountain trail leading to the grave of Dawson Trotman, the founder of the Navigators. We stood and we talked about our memories of Daws Trotman. I had been associated with him in those early Navigator days during World War II when I was stationed in Hawaii. And Elaine had been his secretary for a time in Los Angeles.

Just then, we heard footsteps behind us, and a young man emerged into the clearing, coming up the trail. We chatted, and I learned he was a pastor, attending a conference at Glen Eyrie. "Did you know Dawson Trotman?" he asked. Elaine and I both said we had.

"I never met him," the young pastor continued, "but I feel as if I have. I've read his books, and that man has changed my life."

We talked about Daws, about his life, and about his death at age fifty, when he was drowned in a boating accident in New York state while trying to save the life of a girl who could not swim. There, on the grave marker in front of us, were the words that summed up his life and his death: "Greater love has no man than this that a man lay down his life for his friends."

Finally, the pastor said to us, "Would you pray for me? Would you please pray that God would give me something of the spirit of Dawson Trotman? I really want to have an enlarged vision of the lostness and need of the world as he had. I want that hunger to reach people with the liberating Word of God that he had." So Elaine and I prayed with him. We prayed that God would indeed do what this young man asked.

And after we had prayed, and this man went on his way down the trail, I thought of the great work of the Navigators that has now reached around the world. In almost every country Navigators are discipling men and women, teaching them how to live as God intended men and women to live. What an impact that one life has had! We marvel at what God has done through the life of Dawson Trotman.

And as we open our lives to God's power, seeking to derive all we are and all we do directly from Him, relying not upon our own pitiful strength but upon His limitless power, the world will marvel at us as well, at what God has done through your life and mine! This is the kind of life Jesus modeled for us. He modeled it perfectly. And God in His grace has made it possible for you and me—however imperfectly, due to our human sin and fallibility—to learn to grow in this same limitless power that was revealed in Jesus.

Here, indeed, is a far greater truth than the truth of Einstein, the truth that E equals MC squared. The secret of Jesus is the secret of truly *infinite power*—and that power is available to finite human beings—to you and to me.

Chapter Fourteen

He's Got the Whole World in His Hands

John 5:21–30

In 1832, the great German poet and novelist Johann Goethe lay dying in his bed. There were several of his friends and family attending him in his darkened bedroom. After a long silence, Goethe reached out one hand to point to the shuttered windows. "More light," he said simply.

The nurse went to the window, opened the shutter, then turned back to the man in the sickbed. The light now fell upon his features. He was already dead.

We would all like "more light" on this subject called Death. And in this passage Jesus opens the shutters and sheds His light upon the fate of all of us.

5:21–23 *For just as the Father raises the dead and gives them life, even so the Son gives life to whom he is pleased to give it. Moreover, the Father judges no one, but has entrusted all judgment to the Son, that all may honor the Son just as they honor the Father. He who does not honor the Son does not honor the Father, who sent him."*

In the verses just prior to these, Jesus has challenged the whole thought-pattern of the Jewish leaders and of the crowd by saying, "Yes, to your amazement he will show him even greater things than these." Now we see what "greater things" Jesus is talking about—a miracle greater than the healing of a man who has been unable to walk for thirty-eight years! What could that miracle be?

The Son Gives Life

When Jesus says, "the Father raises the dead and gives them life," He is declaring the first of these "greater things." God has the power to give life to the dead. And when Jesus says, "the Father judges no one, but has entrusted all judgment to the Son," He is saying that Jesus is the final arbiter of eternal human destiny. Jesus is the Judge, with all judgment in His hands.

When Jesus speaks of "the dead" (verse 21), we have to ask: "Does He mean the *spiritually* dead or the *physically* dead?" In verses 24 through 27 He deals specifically with spiritual death. People who never think about the fact that they are ultimately and eternally accountable to God are spiritually dead. People who do not believe in the invisible realities of life but deal only with the material and the visible are spiritually dead. People who believe that their existence is bounded only by the womb and the tomb are spiritually dead. They are unresponsive to anything beyond what appeals to the body and the senses. That is spiritual death. Jesus has the power to give life to such people.

But in verses 28 through 30, Jesus is talking about the physically dead, "all who are in their graves." He claims He has power to give them life also. Thus both forms of death are included in the statement Jesus makes in verse 21: "the Son gives life to whom he is pleased to give it."

We have great difficulty today understanding how these words of Jesus sounded to those who heard Him that day. These are amazing claims! When you read them you are forced to conclude that Jesus was one of three things: a lunatic, a liar, or the Lord of Life. There are no other alternatives.

Jesus claims that life belongs to Him. He only lends it to us for a while. Imagine: This statement saws across the grain of the philosophies and dominant ideas of our own day, just as it did in Jesus' day. How many times have you heard on TV or radio or in books and magazines that your life belongs to you, and you can do with it whatever you want? That propaganda is fed to us all the time—but it's a lie! You did not invent your own life. It was handed to you as a loan. And one of these days, you'll have to give it back.

Spiritual life is what the Bible calls "eternal" life. It is a different level or quality of life. It is not merely, as it is frequently translated (especially in the King James Version), "everlasting" life. That conveys the idea that this present, earthly life will be extended infinitely. But that is not what "eternal" life means.

It is true that eternal life goes on forever, but the true difference between eternal life and earthly life is not its duration but the richness, fullness, and the beauty of the eternal life Jesus gives us. This special quality of life cannot be diminished by tragic circumstances or ended by death. Eternal life is not "pie in the sky, when you die, by and by." It is a quality of life that is given to us in the here and now. The claim of Jesus is that He alone has the power to give that kind of life.

The Son Has Authority To Judge

Because Jesus gives life "to whom he will," He has also become the arbiter of the destiny of human beings, the supreme Judge of all men and women. It is His knowledge of who is to receive eternal life and who is to remain without it that makes Him *the* infallible Judge of human destiny. These two roles of Jesus—Life-Giver and Judge—blend together. Each grows out of the other. If Jesus gives you life, you are on your way to heaven. If He has judged you to be forgiven—and therefore sinless—then He gives you life.

If you have received eternal life through faith in Jesus Christ, then you will never taste the emptiness and awful loneliness of death—and you will experience all the richness that knowing Jesus has to offer in *this* life. But only if Jesus gives it to you! He alone confers spiritual life on men and women.

If Jesus does not give you life then you remain exactly as you were: dead in your sin, condemned to a Christless hell, both in this life and in eternity. When Scripture speaks of hell, it means all of these things: life without God, without blessing, without richness, without fullness.

If Jesus' claim to be the Lord of Life is true, then He is clearly the most important Person in anyone's life. If your very physical existence has come from Him and your spiritual destiny is in His hands, then He is the most important Person you will ever have to deal with. More than that, He is the most important Person in the whole world, the central figure in all the universe.

In chapter 5 of the book of Revelation (which was also written by the apostle John), there is a tremendous scene where John takes us beyond the limits of earth and shows us the throne of God. The creatures of heaven are gathered around the throne, worshiping God. In the center of the scene, John sees a Lamb that has been slain. Here is his description:

> Then I looked and heard the voice of many angels, numbering thousands upon thousands, and ten thousand times ten thousand. They encircled the throne and the living creatures and the elders. In a loud voice they sang:
> "Worthy is the Lamb, who was slain,
> to receive power and wealth and wisdom
> and strength
> and honor and glory and praise!"
> Then I heard every creature in heaven and on earth and under the earth and on the sea, and all that is in them, singing:
> "To him who sits on the throne and to the Lamb
> be praise and honor and glory and power,
> for ever and ever!"

The four living creatures said, "Amen," and the elders fell down and worshiped.[1]

In this passage, we see Jesus standing astride the heart of the universe. Jesus has no peer, no equal. There is no leader or figure of religion who can compare—neither Mohammed, nor Buddha, nor the virgin Mary, nor Moses, nor the prophets, nor any other person of any period in history. This is why we cannot define a Christian as someone who *only* accepts the teachings of Jesus, or who *only* adopts His moral standards, or who *only* admires Him as a social reformer or religious leader. Jesus Himself does not allow us to do so.

Your Most Important Relationship

Jesus alone has the right to give the gift of eternal life. He alone is the eternal Judge. In 1 John, the apostle John writes, "This is the testimony: God has given us eternal life, and this life is in his Son. He who has the Son has life; he who does not have the Son of God does not have life."[2] Your relationship to Jesus Christ is the most important relationship of your life: It determines your ultimate destiny.

If that is true, the next great question facing us is, "To whom and on what terms does Jesus give eternal life?" The answer to that is given in one of the greatest verses in Scripture, John 5:24. It is one of my favorite texts, and one which I encourage you to commit to memory.

5:24 *"I tell you the truth, whoever hears my word and believes him who sent me has eternal life and will not be condemned; he has crossed over from death to life."*

Now we see what Jesus means when He says He "gives life to whom he is pleased to give it." This is no arbitrary selection on His part. He does not point at people and capriciously say, "You may live," and, "You must die." Clearly, you and I have a responsibility to fulfill.

To whom does Jesus give eternal life? To the man or woman, boy or girl, who hears His words and believes in the One who sent Jesus into the world. To the individual who accepts Jesus' credentials and acts on that basis to follow Him and be His obedient disciple.

Notice what happens when a person hears Jesus' words and obeys what He says: immediately, says Jesus, that person "has eternal life and will not be condemned." Jesus doesn't say that person will have eternal life some day when he or she dies. That person *has it,* right then, present tense. All judgment is past. That person has instantly "crossed over from death to life." Jesus has made the terms of eternal life unmistakably clear to His Jewish hearers, and to you and me.

All of us are born in the shadow of Death. It could come for us at any moment. We don't like to think about it, but that's the fact. Beyond our physical death lies the "second death"—eternal judgment—unless we have received eternal life. So the most important question you and I must settle is whether we have believed in Jesus and received from His hand the gift of eternal life.

The Hour Is Coming . . .

Jesus now extends His message of life and judgment well into the future.

5:25–26 *"I tell you the truth, a time is coming and has now come when the dead will hear the voice of the Son of God and those who hear will live. For as the Father has life in himself, so he has granted the Son to have life in himself."*

What does Jesus mean when He says, "A time is coming"? This is a clear reference to the Day of Pentecost, to the new thing that would happen when the Spirit of God would come in a new, fresh way and the gift of eternal life would be given to Jews and Gentiles alike. And not just the *Day* of Pentecost as an event in one moment and one place in history, but the "time" of Pentecost, as it would occur throughout the world and down through all the succeeding generations. Already the "time" of which Jesus spoke is nearly 2,000 years long. Throughout this "time," whoever hears Jesus' word and believes on the One who sent Him receives eternal life.

And Jesus goes on to say that this time, which is coming, "has now come." That is, it was already happening during Jesus' earthly ministry. He had already begun to give the gift of life. He had called disciples to Himself, and they came and were following. He had given the message of the new birth to a troubled religious leader named Nicodemus. He had given the message of living water to the woman by the well. They had believed and received the gift of eternal life. It was already happening. The spiritually dead were hearing the voice of the Son of God—and they were coming alive!

Then Jesus adds that, as the Son of God, as the One who is eternally with the Father, He has always had this ability to give life to the spiritually dead. This life is in Himself. He is the One who has always given eternal life, in the Old Testament as well as the New.

The Son of Man

Next Jesus adds a statement that is perplexing at first glance.

5:27 *"And he [the Father] has given him authority to judge because he is the Son of Man."*

What does Jesus mean when He says that God has given Him authority *because He is the Son of Man?* What does the manhood, the humanity, of Jesus have to do with God-given authority?

Just this: Because God has become a man, He understands how we must live, how we feel, and what we face. No one can say that Jesus is an unjust Judge because He can't understand our condition! He understands completely! He has been tempted—yet without sin. He has suffered pain and hunger and poverty. He has suffered grief and death. He knows how we feel. And because He is fully human as well as fully God, *He has the right* to pass judgment on us—on whether we should have the gift of life or remain in death. He knows when we have reached the place where we are ready to give up depending on ourselves and are willing to reach out and receive the gift of life.

We Can't Go Back

Many years ago in the San Francisco Bay area, a man murdered a young football player and raped the two young women who were with him. This criminal was arrested, tried, convicted, and sentenced to San Quentin Prison. He served over fifteen years for the crime—and then he came up for parole. An enormous hue and cry went up from the community, which was outraged at the thought that this murderer/rapist might again be loosed upon society. His parole was denied.

Several more times the parole board heard his case, and each time parole was denied, due to public pressure. Eventually, his case was taken all the way to the Supreme Court, and the denial of his parole was overturned. He was released from prison.

During this whole process, a reporter for the San Francisco Chronicle took an interest in the convict's case. He interviewed the man in prison shortly after his release, and one of the amazing facts that came out in the interview was that this convict now professed to be a follower of Jesus Christ. Near the end of the account, the reporter said, "The man who was released the other day is not the same man who went into that prison."

And he surely is not. Throughout the many times that his parole was denied, he waited patiently, without complaint. He understood the anger and the fear of those who wanted him to stay locked up. He was repentant over the terrible things he had done. And he was willing to wait upon God to work out the circumstances of his life. If God, by His grace, chose to give him a new life outside the prison walls, he would accept it gratefully, but he knew he had no right to demand it.

This man had received the gift of life, and despite his record of guilt, his life was changed and he was removed from under the judgment of God. Somewhere during his prison experience, he was reborn, and he crossed from death into life.

That is what eternal life is all about: A gift none of us can earn or demand, but can only receive from the hand of Jesus. That gift transforms us right to the very core of our being and makes us new again. Once we receive it, we can never go back to what we once were.

Empty Cemeteries

Jesus makes it plain that all physical life is in His hands, as well as spiritual life.

5:28–29 *"Do not be amazed at this, for a time is coming when all who are in their graves will hear his voice and come out—those who have done good will rise to live, and those who have done evil will rise to be condemned."*

When Jesus says, "Do not be amazed at this," it is easy to imagine the faces of His hearers as He has been speaking, as He has been laying claim to Godhood and to the prerogatives of Judge and eternal Life-Giver. The eyes of the people must have been wide with astonishment. Their mouths must have dropped open at His daring claims.

And now, as He tells them not to be amazed, He issues the most amazing claim of all: An hour in history will arrive when all the graves in the world will open and all the dead—the bad, the good, the evil, the kind, the generous, the thieves, the loving, the rapists, and murders—all, all, all shall come forth. Jesus is going to empty the cemeteries of the world. Not only will the spirits of men and women either live or be judged, but their bodies will be delivered to an ultimate destiny.

Those who have "done good," says Jesus, shall experience the resurrection of life. But what does it mean to have "done good"? Many people extract this verse from the context and make up their own ideas about what it means to "do good." They say if you have been fairly nice to your neighbor, do not beat your wife too often, speak kindly to people now and then, and try your best to obey the Ten Commandments, then perhaps the good you have done will outweigh the evil you have done, and God will let you into heaven.

But that is not what Jesus is saying. Remember, this is just a few verses away from where Jesus talks about the *gift* of eternal life. To "do good," of course, means to have received eternal life. Only those in whom the life of God is dwelling can "do good" in God's eyes. Those who have obeyed His word, walked in fellowship with Him, and shared His life are the ones who have "done good."

At the same time, those who have "done evil" are those who have refused His life, who have turned their backs on the truth. They have denied even the witness of nature and the witness of their own inner hearts. Even if they think of themselves as "good people" who do "good works," they will come forth to the "resurrection of judgment" if they have not received the free gift of eternal life in Christ.

No wonder Jesus amazed, frightened, and challenged His hearers on that day! This is a frightening image! The graves opened. The dead come forth. Every human being who ever lived is delivered to his or her eternal destiny, either heaven or judgment. This image should frighten and challenge you and me today! What is our response to this image that Jesus presents to us?

In His Hands

Shortly before he died in 1981, the great American playwright William Saroyan gave a final statement to the press. "Everybody has got to die," he said, "but I have always believed an exception would be made in my case."

There are no exceptions. Everybody dies. Period.

But in verse 30, Jesus gives us a final reassuring testimony to the fact that even though we must all die and meet our final destiny, Jesus will do what is right and just.

5:30 *"By myself I can do nothing; I judge only as I hear, and my judgment is just, for I seek not to please myself but him who sent me."*

There can be no argument against His judgment. No one can complain that it is unfair, because it is the work of both the Father and the Son. It is the judgment of the Father who created us, gave us life, and knows our hearts. It is the judgment of the Son who came among us and knows how we feel.

Jesus is the Life-Giver—and He is the Judge. We are in His hands. We sing about this truth in the familiar spiritual, "He's Got the Whole World In His Hands":

> He's got you and me, brother, in His hands,
> He's got you and me, sister, in His hands.
> He's got the little tiny baby in His hands,
> He's got the whole world in His hands.

Jesus holds our destiny in His hands. Will He be our Savior—or our Judge? It is up to you and to me to decide. It is a decision we make when we accept—or reject—the truth.

Whether in life or in death, we are all in His hands.

Chapter Fifteen

The Credentials of Jesus

John 5:31–47

A wealthy financier was once a defendant in a multi-million-dollar civil suit. At the trial, he was called to the witness stand and the first question was put to him by the counsel for the plaintiff. His reply:

"I decline to answer that question on the advice of my counsel."

The attorney asked, "Do you refuse on the grounds that the answer might incriminate you?"

"I decline to answer that question on the advice of my counsel."

"Is it on the grounds that the answer might cause you some public disgrace?"

"I decline to answer that question on the advice of my counsel."

Exasperated, the attorney asked, "Did your counsel tell you not to answer *any* of my questions?"

"I decline to answer that question on the advice of my counsel."

Clearly, here is a man who is reluctant to testify about himself! What a contrast between this defensive financier and Jesus, who has freely, daringly testified about Himself and His mission in the world! We have already witnessed some of His most amazing claims:

Jesus has testified that He is the Son of God; the One sent by the Father; the Source of all life, both physical and spiritual; the Judge of all the world; the focus of history; the One who raises the dead and will one day empty all the cemeteries of the earth.

As Jesus makes these claims, His hearers listen with open-mouthed amazement. Understandably, many are skeptical and ask, "How do we know you are telling the truth? What evidence do you give?" People who honestly ask such questions are to be commended. Many people—both in the first century and today!—make claims about themselves, including claims to be the Messiah, or even to be God Himself! They attract gullible, unquestioning followers and have even led many of these followers to destruction. A degree of reverent skepticism is healthy and desirable.

The First Witness

So how do we know whether to believe a person's claims? Seeing the skepticism on the faces of His hearers, Jesus proceeds to give them His credentials. He acts in accord with the law of Moses, who said, "A matter must be established by the testimony of two or three witnesses."[1] In this passage, Jesus introduces three witnesses to substantiate His testimony.

The first witness Jesus calls to the witness stand is . . . *Himself!*

5:31–32 *"If I testify about myself, my testimony is not valid. There is another who testifies in my favor, and I know that his testimony about me is valid."*

Our Lord first points to His own testimony about Himself—but then He immediately acknowledges that the testimony of a single witness is not sufficient to substantiate a matter. Testimony must be corroborated. Jesus proceeds to cite the corroboration which supports His claims, both for the sake of His first-century hearers and also for us in this day.

I have noticed a strange phenomenon over the years: People can hear the truth right out of the Scriptures for years and years, yet they never seem to believe it until they hear it from another voice. Sometimes I have invited guest speakers to preach in my place, and I have heard them preach the very same truths I have preached for years. And I have seen people's faces light up at the sudden "revelation" they had just heard. Afterwards they have said, "I never saw that before!" I always want to ask them. "Where have you been! I have been preaching that for years!"

But that's human nature, and I have learned to accept it and rejoice when someone discovers a new piece of the truth wherever they find it. We should not be dismayed just because people do not take our word alone on any matter, because God has ordained that "a matter must be established by the testimony of two or three witnesses."

So the first witness—Jesus—has testified. There are two more witnesses to call.

The Second Witness—and a Mystery

Jesus goes on to say that there is "another who testifies in my favor." Who is the mystery witness? Jesus does not refer here to John the Baptist, although John is mentioned in verse 33. Verse 36 makes it clear that Jesus is referring to a more substantial and credible witness than even John the Baptist: "I have testimony weightier than that of John."

Jesus further implies in verse 32 that when He hears the corroborating testimony of this other witness, He is inwardly strengthened. "I know that his testimony about me is valid," He says. The word for "know" means "to know inwardly, instinctively." It is this deep inner awareness that accounts for Jesus' boldness.

If you have an inner consciousness that what you say is true, you tend to speak boldly and confidently. This is what Jesus feels as He speaks about Himself. He is supported, strengthened, and emboldened by this mystery witness. In a few verses, Jesus will reveal the identity of this second witness, but for now He leaves us with a mystery as He proceeds to the third witness.

The Third Witness—John the Baptist

Here Jesus points to the testimony of the third witness, John the Baptist.

5:33–34 *"You have sent to John and he has testified to the truth. Not that I accept human testimony; but I mention it that you may be saved."*

In the early part of this gospel we saw that John the Baptist made four specific claims regarding Jesus: (1) he announced Jesus as the predicted Messiah, of whom the prophets had written; (2) he announced Jesus as "the Lamb of God," the sacrifice for mankind's sin; (3) John announced Jesus as the One who would baptize with the Holy Spirit; and (4) he announced Jesus as "the Son of God." Here, in verse 33, Jesus declares that all John said about Him is true!

Jesus goes on to say something that sounds a little strange to us, verse 34: "Not that I accept human testimony; but I mention it that you may be saved." Jesus is saying that He doesn't need John's testimony, but He mentions it because it may be a saving help to those who heard John.

I've seen it many times before: People who pay no attention to the voice of God speaking directly through the Scriptures or through their own consciences will often be moved by the testimony of a human witness. Though God doesn't need the testimony of human witnesses, He will often use human testimony to bring more people to Himself. This statement gives us a penetrating insight into the compassionate heart of Jesus. He is willing to use any approach as long as people will come to know Him.

Jesus goes on to give a beautiful affirmation of John.

5:35 *"John was a lamp that burned and gave light, and you chose for a time to enjoy his light."*

Notice Jesus' precise choice of words. John the Baptist was a lamp. He was not a light but a lamp. A lamp bears the light, but it is not the light itself. In fact, there are many lights which do not give light. You may have a lamp with a frayed cord or a bent shade in your attic or garage. It's a lamp, but it gives no light. It's not fit to stand in your living room. It's just taking up space somewhere.

There are many people like that. They are lamps, they were designed to give light, they have the capacity to shine—but they are not shining. They have taken themselves out of service. John was the kind of lamp who chose to shine brightly. He was a witness who told people how they could find and know the true light.

Would you like to be a shining lamp for God? There's only one way for you to shine: You have to *burn!* Let the truth of God fuel your heart until it begins to burn. We often sing, "This little light of mine, I'm gonna let it shine." When you understand what God is truly doing in this world, your heart will begin to burn—and then you will start to *shine.*

Jesus goes on to say that while many people were attracted to this light for a while, some grew tired of John. They listened for a while and then they went on to other things. To them, John was just a passing fad. Many people treat the truth of Jesus Christ in much the same way: They stop, look, and listen for a moment—until their attention is captured by the next craze or fashion.

Jesus cannot be relegated to the status of last week's news. He is the Lord of all things and all time. He is the light.

The Second Witness—a Closer Look

Jesus returns for another, closer look at the second witness, the truly crucial witness, for His case. This is the witness He spoke of when He said, "There is another who testifies in my favor."

5:36 *"I have testimony weightier than that of John. For the very work that the Father has given me to finish, and which I am doing, testifies that the Father has sent me."*

Now we see clearly who the "star witness" truly is. The best corroborating evidence Jesus presents on His own behalf is from the Father Himself. It is a witness who is invisible and universal. That witness is given in three different ways:

(1) Through the works Jesus does.
(2) Through the inner conviction of the Spirit.

(3) Through the witness of Scripture.

Let's look at each of these ways in turn:

(1) The Works of Jesus

Jesus has restored an invalid man to health. He has brought joy out of sorrow, and strength out of weakness. He has done this by the power of the Father. He has done the work the Father has given Him. And this work bears witness that the Father has sent Him, and that Jesus is who He claims to be.

You may say, "But that was two thousand years ago! If God would only witness like that again today, then I could believe in Him." Well, God does witness like that today.

I have a friend who is a prisoner in a state penitentiary in California. He had found some Discovery Papers, which are published by Peninsula Bible Church, in a trash bin. He rescued those papers and began reading them, and as a result, his heart was moved and he committed his life to Christ. He went on to lead many of his fellow-prisoners to Christ. Over the years, he and I corresponded a number of times.

In one of these letters, he told how several prisoners, including himself, took a Bible correspondence course. When they finished the course, the prison chaplain arranged a graduation exercise to encourage them. The prison authorities allowed them to have a special room, and they provided punch and cookies, and even a graduation cap and gown. Some of the friends and relatives of the prisoners attended the celebration.

This man was standing in line waiting to get some cookies when he felt a tug on his gown. Looking down, he saw a little eight-year-old girl wearing heavy leg braces and supported by crutches. She said to him, "Mister, could you get some cookies and punch for me?" He immediately did and sat down and began to talk to her about the love of Jesus and how Jesus went about feeding and loving and healing people. While he was speaking, she looked up at him and said, "Mister, if Jesus healed all those sick people, and if He still lives today, why can't He see that I'm crippled and heal me?"

Oh, Lord, what do I tell her, he thought. Then he felt the urging of the Holy Spirit. "Would you like me to pray for your legs?" he asked her.

"Oh yes," she said—and to his surprise, she began to remove the braces from her legs. The simple faith of this child inspired this man, and he placed his hand on her head and began to pray.

"I felt the power of God there with us," he later recalled. "The girl started praising God. She bolted out from under my hand and started running—without her braces! She held her crutches over her head and ran all around the visiting room!"

The child's mother, who was in the next room, heard her daughter shouting and thought something was wrong. She rushed into the room, saw her child running without crutches or braces—and she fainted!

"Brother Ray," he concluded in his letter, "I just wish you could have seen the people's faces. Everyone saw this girl as a poor crippled child. They didn't know what to make of a miracle happening right in front of their eyes!"

I've kept in touch with this man since then, and the little girl has returned to visit with her mother. She now walks normally. This prisoner has made no effort to publicize this incident or exploit it in any way. He simply rejoices to know that the power of God is still manifest today as it was in Jesus' time.

There are many miracles happening today. Sure, there are many phony miracles, too, performed by charlatans who want to cash in on the gullibility of the public. But that should not take away from the fact that God truly is at work in our time. He is still delivering people from pain and bondage wherever He chooses.

(2) The Conviction of the Spirit

Jesus declares the second way the Father bears witness next.

5:37 *"And the Father who sent me has himself testified concerning me. You have never heard his voice nor seen his form."*

What is this witness which uses no voice and is never seen? Jesus refers here to an inner, invisible conviction of the Spirit.

Some years ago I was sharing Jesus Christ with a very intelligent, highly educated electronics engineer. He prided himself on his high I.Q. and his ability to argue a point of view logically and intellectually. As we talked, he argued vigorously that he had no need of a Savior. But there came a point while we were talking, as he was still trying to maintain an intellectual argument, that he suddenly dropped to his knees and invited the Lord into his heart. For reasons that can never be rationally explained, all of his intellectual defenses suddenly crumbled. Why? Because the Holy Spirit had suddenly invaded his heart, convicting him of a need that his rational mind had refused to accept.

Such is the power of God to bear inner witness. When you are reading the Scriptures, listening to the voice of Jesus, you are not just playing games with religious theories. This is total reality; it is where the whole of life is explained and the answers are found.

(3) The Witness of Scripture

Finally, our Lord turns to the third way the Father witnesses to the credentials of Jesus.

5:38–40 *"Nor does his word dwell in you, for you do not believe the one he sent. You diligently study the Scriptures because you think that by them you possess eternal life. These are the Scriptures that testify about me, yet you refuse to come to me to have life."*

What a strange paradox! The Jewish leaders were painstaking students of the Scripture, spending their whole lives counting the very words and memorizing great sections of it, committing themselves wholly to it because they thought the knowledge of Scripture would give them life. Even today, there are many like them—students and scholars who search the Bible but never find Jesus. Someone has described the phenomenon this way:

> Trained men's minds are spread so thin
> They let all sorts of darkness in.
> Whatever light they find they doubt it,
> They love not light—just talk about it.

Jesus declares, "The Scriptures . . . testify about me," and it is easy to see that Jesus is the focus of the New Testament. But what many people fail to see—including those Jewish scholars of Jesus' time—is that Jesus is the focus of the Old Testament as well! If you want to have an exciting experience with the Old Testament, read it with the objective of looking for Jesus. I guarantee you will discover Him on every page. The entire Old Testament—that dramatic record of a nation separated from the rest of the stream of humanity and set aside to be a peculiar people unto God—is filled with references to Jesus. He appears in metaphor and type and shadow, in sacrifice and priesthood, and in clear and burning prophecy. What an amazing claim this is, "The Scriptures . . . testify about me."

The Enemy of Truth

How can so many people hear and read the Scriptures, yet turn away from the very One of whom the Scriptures speak? What is the problem?

The problem is the human will. In verse 40, Jesus says, "yet you *refuse* to come to me." It is a *choice* people make—a terrible, tragic choice. If they would just come to Jesus, they could have abundant life.

But they choose not to. Jesus explains why.

5:41–44 *"I do not accept praise from men, but I know you. I know that you do not have the love of God in your hearts. I have come in my Father's name, and you do not accept me; but if someone else comes in his own name, you will accept him. How can you believe if you accept praise from one another, yet make no effort to obtain the praise that comes from the only God?"*

Here Jesus puts His finger on the true reason for stubborn unbelief. Why would a man read the truth, know it to be true, know that it speaks of Jesus, know Him to be who He claims to be, and still refuse to come to Him? Jesus says the answer is that people want the praise of other people more than they want the praise of God. *Ambition* is the deadly enemy of truth! People want glory now, not heaven at some future time. They want fame, recognition, prestige, and respect. That, says Jesus, is the problem.

And there is a terrible danger in that, says Jesus: "I have come in my Father's name, and you do not accept me; but if someone else comes in his own name, you will accept him." In other words, "I have come with all the corroborating evidence of the Father and you have refused Me; but when someone else comes without any evidence at all, you will be fooled into embracing him!" Most Bible scholars view this as a reference to the Anti-christ—and I agree.

Jesus came with the visible evidence of the Word, of the Spirit, and of the Father. He came with the proper introduction: John the Baptist opened the door. Yet Jesus was rejected. "Very well," Jesus says in effect, "there is another 'messiah' coming, and he will make all kinds of claims of who he is and what he can do for you, saying everything you want to hear—and you will be seduced by him and wooed by him and ultimately betrayed by him."

That is the danger of rejecting truth when you know it to be truth: You hand over your will to the next religious con-man with an easy line of patter—and you open yourself up to destruction.

Now Jesus comes to the conclusion of His message.

5:45–47 *"But do you not think I will accuse you before the Father. Your accuser is Moses, on whom your hopes are set. If you believed Moses, you would believe me, for he wrote about me. But since you do not believe what he wrote, how are you going to believe what I say?"*

Here is an amazing paradox. Jesus says it is not He who will accuse the Jewish unbelievers in the time of judgment. No, it will be *Moses*—the very one they use as their excuse to persecute Jesus—who will become their accuser.

Many who are alive today will be in the same boat. I have heard people say, "When I stand before God I'll have a lot to say to Him. God has given me a raw deal in life, and I intend to tell Him so." The fact is, on that day they will stand absolutely mute before God, their own memories testifying that He is right and they have been wrong—tragically wrong!—all through their lives.

"If you believed Moses," says Jesus, "you would believe me, for he wrote about me. But since you do not believe what he wrote, how are you going to believe what I say?" I submit that this is a radical principle. Most people think that if a person does not believe something, what he needs is more proof, more information, more light on the subject. But Jesus declares that this will not work. If you do not believe the truth you now know, you will not believe greater truth when you hear it. If you do not respond to what you know to be true now, you will not respond when you hear further truth. And with that radical statement, Jesus brings His public discourse to a close.

Where does that leave us? We have the witness of the Father, the witness of John the Baptist, the witness of twenty centuries of testimony about the power of Jesus to deliver men and women from their chains, to heal them and make them whole. Hundreds of thousands of voices blend in unified witness to the fact that Jesus is who He claims to be. So where does that leave us, if we continue to pursue the empty, lost, confused voices of the world? Where does that leave us if we seek after positions of power and influence apart from the will of God?

These are searching words. I cannot make them easy words because Jesus did not make them easy. But they are words that force us to face ourselves in the light of reality. Where are you going in life? What are you doing with the only life you will ever have?

Let us face the choice which Jesus demands and submit ourselves to His Lordship—and to His love.

Chapter Sixteen

The Testing of Faith

John 6:1–15

Yogi Berra, the star catcher and hitter for the New York Yankees, once ordered an anchovy pizza at a Brooklyn restaurant. When the pizza was brought to his table, the waiter asked, "Mr. Berra, would you like your pizza cut into four or eight pieces?"

"Better make it four," Berra replied. "I don't think I can eat eight."

In John chapter 6, we encounter the story of one little Jewish boy who offers Jesus his "anchovy pizza"—five loaves of bread and two small fish. As this story unfolds, we will see Jesus break the bread and the fish—not into four pieces or even eight pieces, but into *thousands* of pieces, enough to feed a multitude. In the process, we discover how Jesus can multiply our own meager offering into blessings for the hungry people around us.

The Pressure of the Multitude

As we approach this account, it is important to note a major difference between the gospel of John and the other three gospels. The synoptic gospels focus largely upon our Lord's ministry in Galilee, following Him throughout His two-year ministry of healing and teaching in that region. They report a large number of different miracles that Jesus performed there.

But John selects only two miracles out of that entire two-year period: the miracle of the feeding of the 5,000, and the accompanying miracle when Jesus walked on the water to His disciples during a storm. This suggests that these are significant events, filled with great meaning.

6:1–4 *Some time after this, Jesus crossed to the far shore of the Sea of Galilee (that is, the Sea of Tiberias), and a great crowd of people followed him because they saw the miraculous signs he had performed on the sick. Then Jesus went up on the hillside and sat down with his disciples. The Jewish Passover Feast was near.*

That last sentence fixes this incident as occurring in the spring of the year, when the hills would be green with grass. The multitudes were following Jesus everywhere despite the fact that it was the Passover season, when they ought to have been on their way to Jerusalem. The law required that every male Jew celebrate the Passover there if he could possibly get away. So ordinarily these great multitudes would not be in Galilee but in Jerusalem.

John has included this detail to show why Jesus did what He did on this occasion. These great multitudes followed our Lord everywhere He went because they did not dare miss the tremendous excitement of the "signs" or miracles He performed. By this time, Jesus was feeling the pressure of the crowds and wanted to get away for a time. He wanted to be alone with His disciples. So they got into a boat to cross the northern end of the Sea of Galilee, heading for the eastern shore.

But the multitudes would not give up. As the boat left to cross the lake, the people ran along the northern shore—traveling, in fact, through rather rough country—trying to keep the boat in view so they could intercept it when it landed. Jesus and His disciples arrived on shore before the crowds got there, and they went up on the hillside together.

Soon, Jesus saw the crowd swelling along the shore and gathering at the foot of the hills—and His heart went out to them. He knew that ordinarily they would be in Jerusalem for the Passover, so it entered His heart to have a gigantic Passover feast right there in the wilderness! In verse 6 we read, "he already had in mind what he was going to do." And one of the things He planned to do was to use this occasion to give His disciples a "mid-term exam"!

Jesus Tests Philip

The disciples had been with Jesus for two years and had heard all His amazing words. They had seen the power of God demonstrated again and again and had themselves been sent out in ministry. So Jesus decided it was time to test their faith. He chose to examine Philip first.

6:5–6 *When Jesus looked up and saw a great crowd coming toward him, he said to Philip, "Where shall we buy bread for these people to eat?" He asked this only to test him, for he already had in mind what he was going to do.*

We are not sure why Jesus chose Philip as the first to be tested. It may be that Jesus found Philip to be the most advanced in lessons of faith.

Each disciple had his own unique personality. Peter, of course, was loud and brassy. He had his foot in his mouth most of the time. James and John were ambitious and fiery. They lost their tempers easily, which is why Jesus called them the "Sons of Thunder." Philip was a quiet, deep, and rather introverted fellow who hung around the edges of the group. Yet I believe Jesus saw in Philip a man of deep perception. The quiet kind are often the deep thinkers. Perhaps He chose Philip because Philip was the one who would most likely understand the underlying meaning of the dramatic events that were about to take place.

Whatever His reason, Jesus said to Philip, "Where shall we buy bread for these people to eat?" Jesus didn't really expect to buy bread. In fact, Jesus knew that Philip couldn't possibly answer the question. There were no villages and no bakeries nearby, and they had very little money besides. His question was clearly designed to confront Philip with a predicament that had no human solution.

Has that ever happened to you? Perhaps you are faced right now with a predicament which has no apparent solution. Perhaps you can identify with Philip at this point.

Philip Gets an "F"

Our Lord, of course, was thinking of how to minister to a real human need. But Philip, according to this account, immediately began to think of money.

6:7 *Philip answered him, "Eight months' wages would not buy enough bread for each one to have a bite!"*

Philip estimated the resources available—then he gave up in despair. He could think of no way this problem could be met. God forgive us for the Philip in us all! How many times has this happened in your experience? It has certainly happened in mine. In fact, it is happening around us right now.

As we contemplate God's message to us, we see that He commands us to feed the multitudes—not only physically, in war-torn or drought-parched regions of the world, but also spiritually, in corners of the world where people are hungry, starving, and thirsting for the gospel of Jesus Christ. Yet as we look at the enormity of the need, we feel so inadequate to meet it that we throw up our hands in despair! And we, like Philip, fail the test.

As I have traveled around the country, I have been distressed by the fact that very few churches seem to understand that the church exists to penetrate and saturate the world with God's truth. We Christians are the church, and we possess the truth, the bread that can satisfy all the hungers of life. We have a message of truth that millions of people desperately want to hear, and they will never hear it unless someone—someone like *you*—shares that message with them.

Many of these people are in far-off lands and speak a strange tongue. Perhaps the only way you will ever be able to help those people is by praying for and enabling trained missionaries to go out to them and share the Good News with them. But there are also people all around you—in your neighborhood, at your place of business, on your campus—who have never heard the Good News of Jesus Christ. If *you* don't actually reach out and touch that life and open your mouth and speak the Good News out of your own heart, those people may never have another opportunity to hear. *You* may be their only chance!

What do we do when we hear this command, "Feed the multitudes"? We respond like Philip. We translate the need into dollars. We think about "bottom lines" and committees and fund raising and organizations. We use impressive-sounding words: We must "set our agenda," we must "understand the parameters of the problem." And in the course of all our goal-setting and speech-making and demographic analysis, very little gets done.

Our Lord, however, says in effect, "Begin where you are, and begin with what you have." I am convinced that if the church would just do that across this country and around the world, a lot of those expensive programs and conferences and seminars would not be needed. We would soon transform our nation and our world by the simple sharing of the Word. After all, this is the way the news about Jesus was spread around the countryside. This is the way multitudes were attracted to Him. They had no electronic media, no television, telephone or telegraph, but they did have the most effective means of communication ever invented: tell-a-person! It's a powerful communication medium—one that you and I can still use effectively!

In this mid-term exam, Philip gets a big "F." I'm sure you and I would have fared little better. And consider this: If Jesus had given this command to feed the multitude to an atheist, would that atheist's reply have been any different from Philip's or yours or mine? For clearly, there is not one word in Philip's reply that reckons with the power of God. He offers only a dollars-and-cents assessment. What a revelation—and an indictment—of Christian unbelief!

Andrew Gets a "D"

Another of Jesus' disciples, Andrew, takes the "mid-term faith exam" and he fares a little better—he gets a "D"!

6:8–9 *Another of his disciples, Andrew, Simon Peter's brother, spoke up. "Here is a boy with five small barley loaves and two small fish, but how far will they go among so many?"*

There is not a lot of faith in his response—but there is a little! Andrew had been checking out the crowd. No wonder he has become the patron saint of Scotland: He demonstrates a thrifty Scot's aversion to spending money to feed this crowd! In fact, in the original Greek, Andrew uses expressions that are more easily translated into Scottish idiom than English: "Lord, there is a wee laddie here and he has five loaves of bread and two wee fishes." After checking the crowd, that was all the food he was able to scare up!

To Andrew, "five loaves of bread and two wee fishes" is hardly even a start. But, of course, that bread and those fishes were all that Jesus needed. God never asks us to stockpile resources before we begin to minister. He wants us to minister now with what little we have. If all He has to work with is one little boy's sack lunch—the first century equivalent of a few tuna sandwiches—then in the hands of the Lord, it will be enough.

A Quiet Miracle

Now John describes the miracle that took place next.

6:10–13 *Jesus said, "Have the people sit down." There was plenty of grass in that place, and the men sat down, about five thousand of them. Jesus then took the loaves, gave thanks, and distributed to those who were seated as much as they wanted. He did the same with the fish.*

When they had all had enough to eat, he said to his disciples, "Gather the pieces that are left over. Let nothing be wasted." So they gathered them and filled twelve baskets with the pieces of the five barley loaves left over by those who had eaten.

Notice the simplicity of our Lord's actions. We have seen this kind of gentle, quiet simplicity before in another miracle of Jesus: the changing of water into wine. In both this miracle and the miracle at Cana, there is no ballyhoo, no Hollywood-style special effects, no shouting or raising of hands. Jesus simply took the bread and fish, gave thanks to the Father—and began distributing the food.

By the time it was over, everyone had been fed, no one was hungry—and there was plenty of food left over! How did such a miracle take place? Where did the power come from to multiply five barley loaves and two fishes into a feast for 5,000 people?

Remember that in John 5, Jesus already declared the process by which He performed His works: He said He could only do what He saw the Father doing. In that inner vision of His heart He could see the Father feeding the multitude, meeting the need of the moment. He simply responded with thankful expectation that God would do what He said He would do.

Do you ever think of this story when you give thanks for a meal? Do you ever think of the grace and miraculous power of God that is required to put just one meal on your dinner table? We would all do well to remember, as someone has written:

> Back of the bread is the snowy flour,
> And back of the flour, the mill.
> And back of the mill is the field of wheat,
> The rain, and the Father's will.

How Did This Miracle Happen?

A young boy was once asked about his favorite Bible story. He replied, "I like the story where everybody loafs and fishes." Well, this little boy didn't get his facts quite straight, but I agree with him. This is one of my favorite Bible stories, too.

I have often wondered just when the miracle of multiplication took place. Did Jesus place the small amount of bread and fish in a basket and send the disciples out with little amounts of it to distribute it? And did it then keep increasing as people reached in and took food from the basket? Or did the food actually multiply and heap up as He blessed it? I wondered about this for a long time until I looked carefully at Mark's account of this story and discovered that Mark tells how Jesus did it.

In Mark 6 we read that Jesus "gave thanks and broke the loaves," and this statement is in what language scholars call the *aorist tense,* which is to say it was a single action, never repeated. Then Mark uses the *imperfect tense* as he says, "he gave them [the loaves and fishes] to his disciples to set before the people." Literally, "he kept on giving the loaves and fishes to his disciples." In other words, the miracle took place in our Lord's hands. As He held the simple meal in His hands, He broke off pieces and gave to the disciples—and He kept on doing that. There never was an increase in the amount in His hand, but there was always a continual supply until the whole multitude was fed.

Incidentally, the number of people given is 5,000 men, which means that there were almost certainly 3,000 to 5,000 women and children present as well. There could easily have been 10,000 people fed that day from those few loaves and fishes! And they did not receive one of those little meals you get on an airplane. They were fed until they were filled!

Another truth we find in this story is that we serve a God who cares about orderliness. In this account, we see that Jesus commanded the disciples to clean up the place, to save all the fragments, and to police the grounds so that nothing was left to mar the landscape God had made. He specifically commands that nothing should be wasted. This is a wonderful lesson not only in the power of God, but in the importance of the ecology, of good stewardship of God's gift of the earth.

There have been many attempts to explain this miracle on rational, non-miraculous grounds. Some have said that this was a "spiritual miracle" of sharing. They suggest that as Jesus was teaching the people, He so moved them that they abandoned their selfish habits and shared their own lunches with each other so that, in the end, there proved to be plenty for everybody. But Andrew's report that he had scouted out the crowd and found no food would lay that argument to rest. Moreover, it is clear that this crowd never had time to go home and pack a lunch—they were all too busy trying to keep up with Jesus!

Another suggestion is that this was really a "miracle of sublimation." In other words, Jesus' teaching was so powerful and compelling that people forgot about their hunger and went home saying, "His teaching is so rich and filling and satisfying that I'm not even hungry anymore!" Just a few seconds of thought is all it takes to sink this theory. As one little girl responded when her Sunday school teacher "explained" the miracle in this way, "Well, then what did they put in the baskets?"

Indeed! What did they put in the baskets, if an actual, physical miracle did not take place? Those who would explain away the facts of this event as they are reported in the four gospels are at a loss to account for the food that was left over.

C. S. Lewis offers a much more consistent explanation. He says this was a "miracle of the Old Creation," that just as He did when He changed water to wine, Jesus simply short-circuited a natural process and changed a little bread into a lot of bread. He writes:

> The two instances of miraculous feeding . . . involve the multiplication of a little bread and a little fish into much bread and much fish. Once in the desert Satan had tempted Him to make bread of stones: He refused the suggestion. "The Son does nothing except what He sees the Father do"; perhaps one may without boldness surmise that the direct change from

stone to bread appeared to the Son to be not quite in the hereditary style. Little bread into much bread is quite a different matter. Every year God makes a little corn into much corn: the seed is sown and there is an increase. . . .

That same day He also multiplied fish. Look down into every bay and almost every river. This swarming, undulating fecundity shows He is still at work "thronging the seas with spawn innumerable.". . . At the feeding of the thousands, incarnate God [Jesus] . . . does close and small, under His human hands, a workman's hands, what He has always been doing in the seas, the lakes, and the little brooks.[1]

Though this miracle included human effort and human preparation, Lewis suggests that this miracle was accomplished by the creative power of the Father—the same power that created all seed and grain and fish. It was a message written in small letters that has already been written in large letters across the face of the whole universe. Whatever the explanation, one thing is clear: the feeding of the 5,000 was an example of the creative will of the Father at work in the life of the Son.

The Reaction of the People

Now notice the effect Jesus' action has upon the crowd.

6:14–15 *After the people saw the miraculous sign that Jesus did, they began to say, "Surely this is the Prophet who is to come into the world." Jesus, knowing that they intended to come and make him king by force, withdrew again into the hills by himself.*

Here we see that the people have come to a proper conclusion—but then they follow it up with a completely *improper* response. Seeing this miracle, the people thought back to Deuteronomy 18, where Moses, having fed the people in the wilderness with manna from heaven, said to the people, "The Lord your God will raise up for you a prophet like me from among your own brothers."[2] A murmur spread through the crowd: "This must be the one of whom Moses prophesied!" And they were right! The feeding of the 5,000 was one of the signs of the Messiah.

But then they responded in completely the wrong way: "they intended to come and make him king by force"! When Jesus saw this, He separated Himself and went back up on the mountainside alone.

An Israeli friend of mine once told me that when Menachim Begin, the late Prime Minister of Israel, was at the height of his popularity, crowds would gather about him in the streets of Jerusalem, calling, "Hamelek Yisrael! The King of Israel!" Israel has been looking for a king ever since the days of David. When these people beside the Sea of Galilee were fed by Jesus, they thought, "Here is the one who can take care of all our needs. We don't have to worry again about eating. Let's take Him by force and make Him our king!" But our Lord would not consent to being used like that.

Upon recognizing the Messiah, they should have chosen to follow Him. But instead, they attempted to *use* Him for their own purposes! They wanted God to work for them according to *their* program and *their* schedule.

Our Response

Now, before we judge these people too harshly, we should ask ourselves: Don't we do the same thing? Have you ever become angry, impatient, or disappointed with God because He didn't give you what you asked for? Weren't you really expecting God to act for you on your program and your schedule? I don't know if you have done that, but I certainly have. This story is given to teach us the kind of relationship we are to have with God: We are not to make anything of God—we are not even to make Him king!—by force or by our will. Jesus is not simply a politician whom we have elected to do our bidding. He is our God, our Lord, and our Master.

Our greatest privilege is to see ourselves as His instruments, doing what He wants us to do, not using Him to do what we want to do. Certainly, that is the lesson this incident engraved upon the minds of these disciples. If they would be the Lord's disciples, if they would submit themselves to His Lordship and make themselves available as obedient channels of His power, then God himself—the Creator of the universe—was ready to do great things through them.

And God stands ready to do great things through us. He has chosen you and me to be His channels of blessing. That is the greatest joy we can know in life. Our privilege is to follow Him, to be used by Him, to allow Him to pour His power through us, so that we can share the bread of eternal life with a hungry world.

Chapter Seventeen

Treading Water

John 6:16–21

I n A. A. Milne's children's classic *Winnie-the-Pooh*, there is a scene in which a storm strands timid little Piglet alone in the midst of a flood. "It's a little Anxious," says Piglet to himself, "to be a Very Small Animal Entirely Surrounded by Water."

Perhaps you can identify with Piglet—and with one of the principal players in the scene we now come to in John chapter 6, Simon Peter. In this story, we will see Peter, too, surrounded by water and feeling "Anxious" with a capital A. Perhaps, like Piglet and like Peter, you know what it feels like to be surrounded by waters of adversity, with nothing to keep you from sinking but a rather flimsy, faltering faith. If so, then you will gain hope and insight as we take a closer look at one of the most famous and significant of Jesus' miracles—the miracle of walking on the water.

Gathering Darkness

John gives us the setting of this miracle here.

6:16–18 *When evening came, his disciples went down to the lake, where they got into a boat and set off across the lake for Capernaum. By now it was dark, and Jesus had not yet joined them. A strong wind was blowing and the waters grew rough.*

John wrote his gospel some 30 or 40 years after the other gospels had been written, so he didn't feel it necessary to repeat many of the details contained in the synoptic accounts. That is one reason why John's gospel is different from the other three. John expects us to derive many of the intimate details of these stories from the other gospels.

For instance, Mark indicates that when Jesus told the disciples to go to Capernaum, they were reluctant to leave. So "Jesus *made* his disciples get into

173

the boat and go on ahead of him."[1] Jesus had to persuade His disciples—and perhaps even order them into the boat with a sharply raised voice!

So the disciples obeyed, got into their boat, and started across to the other shore. As they rowed across the northern tip of the lake, staying in sight of land, they expected to encounter Jesus on the shore. Darkness was gathering and they still had not sighted Jesus.

The disciples had a problem. It was now so dark they could not see the shore. To make matters worse, a strong wind had arisen. In that region, the wind almost invariably blows from the north, out of the mountains of Lebanon and Mt. Hermon, down the valley and across the lake toward the south. As darkness settled in, the disciples were rowing hard, trying to get across to Capernaum, but the wind was driving them farther and farther south. Soon they lost sight of the shore and all possibility of picking up Jesus. Yet they continued to toil against the wind, trying to remain faithful to their Lord's command, even as the water grew rough and dangerous.

"Don't Be Afraid"

6:19–20 *When they had rowed three or three and a half miles, they saw Jesus approaching the boat, walking on the water; and they were terrified. But he said to them, "It is I; don't be afraid."*

Some commentators try to explain this phenomenon by saying that Jesus was not actually walking on the water, but was merely standing on the seashore. They cite the fact that the disciples were attempting to hug the shore, and they infer that it would have been easy to mistake Jesus, as He stood on a rock or promontory, as walking or standing on the water. As in most attempts to explain away the miracles of Jesus, there is something left unexplained. The problem with this theory is that it does not explain why the disciples were afraid when they saw Jesus.

The only possible explanation for the disciples' fear was that they were indeed in the middle of the lake, the storm was indeed raging, and Jesus was indeed approaching them on the surface of the water, just a few yards from their boat. These men were frightened—and you would have been, too! The account in Matthew's gospel tells us they thought Jesus was a spirit or a ghost.

Jesus immediately answered the disciples' fear with these words, "It is I; don't be afraid." These are words of profound reassurance. Jesus is saying, in effect, "This strange apparition which scares the living daylights out of you is I, Jesus! I have the elements—the boisterous sea and the buffeting winds—under my feet. I am in control of these events, so you have nothing to fear."

Peter Treads Water

The account in the gospel of Matthew tells us that when the apostle Peter looked out from the boat and saw Jesus approaching, he called out, "Lord, if it's you, tell me to come to you on the water." And Jesus immediately replied, "Come." Peter leaped out of the boat and began to walk on the water toward the Lord.

Notice that Peter started out boldly and confidently, as was his natural personality. Imagine how much faith it must have taken to place that first footstep upon the surface of the lake, trusting it to hold him up! Would you or I have had as much faith as bold, impetuous Peter?

But as Peter continued out into the water, with waves rising on every side, with the wind and the spray in his face, his confidence failed, his faith shrank . . . and he began to sink! If you've ever stepped out in faith, then had your faith buffeted and tossed by circumstances to the point where you felt yourself starting to sink, then you can identify with Peter. I've experienced that feeling myself, and I've heard testimony after testimony of people who have been there, too. And I can tell you this: Very often, the Lord in His wisdom and His tough love will allow a person to sink until he is all the way under the surface, and there is nothing showing but the bubbles.

This does not mean that God is cruel. This is actually God's grace and love toward us! God wants us to learn something whenever we experience that "sinking feeling," that withering of our faith. It is like when a swimming teacher "drown-proofs" a young child. Part of the learning experience is that the child is allowed to go under the surface briefly and come up sputtering. If you didn't understand the objective—helping the child learn to be safe and confident in a swimming pool—it would seem cruel. Yet the swimming teacher is close at hand to prevent disaster—and in the process, the child quickly learns to hold his or her breath the next time.

The text does not tell us how far Peter sank when his faith failed him. But when I imagine this scene, I picture Peter calling out, "Lord, save me!" as his head slips under the water. I see the bubbles breaking the surface . . . and then I see the hand of Jesus reaching down, grasping Peter's flailing hand, pulling him up out of the water. And as Peter rises, sputtering and coughing, I see Jesus shaking His head—but perhaps smiling as well—and saying, "Oh, Peter, you of little faith! Why did you doubt?"

Those are wonderful words for us, spoken not only for Peter's benefit, but for ours as well. This whole incident was designed to teach Jesus' disciples—and us!—the amazing resources that God wants to make available to those who trust Him.

A "Minor" Miracle

Here John tells us what happened next.

6:21 *Then they were willing to take him into the boat, and immediately the boat reached the shore where they were heading.*

The fear of the disciples was immediately relieved when they realized it was indeed Jesus who was walking on the water, and that He was in control of all events. So they eagerly received Him into the boat. Then, in the next instant, there was a further demonstration of the power of Jesus: "immediately the boat reached the shore where they were heading."

Note that word: *immediately.* After Jesus entered the boat, they were all suddenly, unexpectedly, *miraculously* at the other side of the lake, at their destination. The three or four remaining miles of the journey were suddenly accomplished, and they found themselves at the dock in Capernaum. It is a miracle within a miracle.

This aspect of the miracle on the lake is often missed by casual readers of the Bible because the other aspect of this miracle—walking on water—is so dramatic and amazing. Yet there is a lesson for us in the fact that when the disciples brought Jesus into their boat, they were suddenly at their destination.

That lesson will become clear at the end of this chapter. But first, let's examine this entire incident as a whole and ask ourselves: "What is the meaning of this strange and wonderful event?"

A Miracle of the New Creation

C. S. Lewis calls this a "miracle of the New Creation." Remember, he called the miracle at Cana and the feeding of the 5,000 "miracles of the Old Creation"—that is, miracles which employed the natural processes of the original Creation, only speeded up. When Lewis calls the miracle of Jesus walking on the water a "miracle of the New Creation," he means it is a miracle which signifies a *future* order. In the world of the Old Creation, the world before the Incarnation of Christ, water cannot support the human body. This miracle, he writes, is

> the foretaste of a Nature that is still in the future. The New
> Creation is just breaking in. . . . For a moment two men [Jesus
> and Peter] are living in that new world. St. Peter also walks on

the water—a pace or two: then his trust fails him and he sinks.
He is back in the Old Nature. That momentary glimpse was a
snowdrop of a miracle. The snowdrops show that we have
turned the corner of the year. Summer is coming. But it is a
long way off and the snowdrops do not last long.[2]

This, therefore, is a miracle intended only for those who believe—giving
us a glimpse of the New Creation that is coming. Unlike the feeding of the
5,000, which was a sign to believers and nonbelievers alike, this miracle is
designed to demonstrate to believers the resources that are available to them
through faith in Christ. It is a miracle designed to calm the uncertainty and
anxiety that so easily grips the heart in times of trouble.

As John reflected on this event, he realized that Jesus had deliberately set
this up for the disciples. He had sent them off against their will into the gathering darkness and the rising storm. He deliberately delayed His coming so
that they might learn to trust Him in time of trouble. And He wants us to learn
the same lesson.

We live in an uncertain world. Even with the collapse of Communism and
the easing of tensions between East and West, the world continues to be a
frightening place, filled with crime, disease, racial unrest, wars, moral decay,
corruption in high places, troubled families—pain and sorrow and suffering
on every side. Like the disciples, we often find ourselves in a sea of trouble in
the gathering darkness, looking for Jesus.

But Jesus is coming to us across the sea of our troubles. And Jesus says to
us the same words He said to His disciples: "It is I; don't be afraid. I am in
charge of all your circumstances. I won't leave you alone. I won't let you
sink." If our faith responds, as these disciples' faith responded, and we take
Him into our boat and welcome Him into our circumstances, we will suddenly
find ourselves on the other side of the waters of difficulty, steadied and
strengthened and at peace. We will find we have arrived at the goal—not by
our toiling and rowing and struggling, but by God's grace and love and power.

This story confronts us with a question: Where is our trust? Why are we
so much like Peter, who—even while experiencing for himself the miracle of
walking on water—lost his faith and began to sink beneath the waves? I identify with Peter. I feel so close to him. Perhaps you do as well. He is the disciple who seems to be our representative in the apostolic band, the one who
only opens his mouth to change feet!

Yet God is not content to let us sink. He is teaching us how to tread
water—to literally mount up out of our sea of fears and anxiety, to step out in
faith, to dare the impossible, to place the soles of our feet onto the shifting
surface of life and keep moving ahead! I have known people who have

learned the meaning of Jesus' comforting words, "It is I; don't be afraid."
They practice the presence of Christ. They dare great things for God, knowing
that Jesus is with them, that He is in charge.

Those who have learned this lesson of faith have a quiet peace in their
eyes, even when the darkness gathers and the seas of life turn rough and
threatening. They have a confidence in the face of trials, of sorrows, and even
death itself that everything is ultimately going to work out as God intends.
There is not a word of complaint or grumbling. They regard their circumstances as necessary to what God wants to do in their lives—which is always
for their own good and for God's glory. Such people are a joy to be around.
When you go to encourage and comfort them in their trials, you come away
with more encouragement than you gave.

Do you know why? Because they have already taken Jesus into their boat!
They have arrived at the goal which the rest of us are still struggling to find.
They have found love and joy and peace.

That is why John chose this sign out of Jesus' many miraculous signs to
include in his gospel. He wants to teach us the hidden resource of life, the One
to turn to when things become overwhelming and we find ourselves pressured
and stressed. When we accept that resource and invite the Lord of the New
Creation into our boat, we will find a resource the world knows nothing of.
We will find strength and peace and joy.

We will have arrived at our destination.

Chapter Eighteen

What Are You Working For?

John 6:22–40

During the French Revolution, mobs rioted and demonstrated outside the palace of Queen Marie Antionette, protesting the poverty in which they lived. The queen, who was widely hated because of her frivolous and extravagant lifestyle amid the suffering of her subjects, asked one of her courtiers why the people were rioting.

"Because they have no bread," was the reply.

History remembers Marie Antoinette for her hard-hearted and indifferent reply: *"Qu'ils mangent de la brioche!* Let them eat cake!"

In the opening verses of John chapter 6, we saw a crowd of people saying to Jesus, in effect, "We have no bread." But the reply of Jesus was very different from that of Marie Antoinette. He had compassion and concern for the people. And through the power and will of God the Father, He provided bread for the people.

Bread is the symbol of that which sustains life. As we approach the closing section of John 6, we come to one of the great discourses of our Lord, His sermon on the "Bread of Life."

"Because You Had Your Fill"

Jesus' discourse takes place in the synagogue at Capernaum on the north shore of the Sea of Galilee. If you go to Israel, you can locate and stand on the very site where this message was delivered. A synagogue has been excavated there, and though the present ruins probably date from a century after the events described here, that site has been reliably fixed as the exact place where the previous synagogue stood, and where Jesus gave this great message.

John gives us the background of this discourse next.

6:22–25 *The next day the crowd that had stayed on the opposite shore of the lake realized that only one boat had been there, and that Jesus had not entered* *it with his disciples, but that they had gone away alone. Then some boats from Tiberias landed near the place where the people had eaten the bread after the Lord had given thanks. Once the crowd realized that neither Jesus nor his disciples were there, they got into the boats and went to Capernaum in search of Jesus.*

When they found him on the other side of the lake, they asked him, "Rabbi, when did you get here?"

The crowd that had been fed from the boy's sack lunch—a crowd which may have numbered as many as 10,000 men, women, and children—went looking for Jesus on the eastern shore. They had seen the disciples leave in the only available boat, and they knew that Jesus had not been with them. But when they looked for Jesus, they couldn't find Him.

Figuring He had joined His disciples somewhere along the way, they entered some boats which had just arrived from Tiberias, and they went looking for Jesus. Finally, they found Him in Capernaum—but they were baffled as to how He could have possibly arrived there so quickly. Naturally, their question to Him was, "Rabbi, when did you come here?" It is clear that their question not only meant *when,* but *how* had He gotten there!

In reply, Jesus ignores their superficial wondering and proceeds to get to the heart of the matter: the crowd's own motivation for seeking Him out.

6:26 *Jesus answered, "I tell you the truth, you are looking for me, not because you saw miraculous signs but because you ate the loaves and had your fill."*

Notice that Jesus again uses "the formula of focused attention"—that phrase "I tell you the truth," which other translations render as "Verily, verily," or, "Truly, truly," but which literally and emphatically reads, "Amen, amen." Jesus is making a very pointed and pungent statement here, and He wants to make sure He is heard. He has read the motives of these people, and He tells them plainly, "You didn't come because you understood the signs I performed—the signs predicted in the Old Testament as the credentials of the Messiah. You didn't come because you want to follow Me as your Lord. You came because you want to exploit Me. All you want is more free meals."

Jesus didn't come to give handouts or to be anybody's free meal ticket. He came to give the people something far more enduring and valuable than mere bread. He came to give *Himself.*

Food That Endures

6:27–29 *"Do not work for food that spoils, but for food that endures to eternal* *life, which the Son of Man will give you. On him God the Father has placed his seal of approval."*

Then they asked him, "What must we do to do the works God requires?"

Jesus answered, "The work of God is this: to believe in the one he has sent."

Clearly, these people have seriously misunderstood Jesus and His purpose among them. They are misguided and confused. I'm reminded of the man who wore a lapel button that read in big letters, "BAIK." When someone asked him what BAIK meant, he said, "Boy, Am I Konfused." The other person responded, "But *confused* is spelled with a C, not a K!" And the fellow with the button replied, "Boy, you don't know how konfused I am!" The crowd that Jesus confronted was similarly confused. Notice how Jesus attempts to correct their confusion.

First, He says to them, "Do not work for food that spoils." He is not saying, "Do not work for a living." Many might take these words literally, quit their jobs, and go on the dole! But Jesus is not advocating that. He acknowledged the importance of food when He provided food by miraculous means. Food is necessary for life, and it must be earned. Jesus' point is that food should not be our focus; we should lift our eyes to eternal things and focus on what truly lasts. "Work . . . for food," He says, "that endures to eternal life, which the Son of Man will give you."

Food is a source of survival and life. Good food is also a source of pleasure. Like many people today, these people were focused on a substance that is important to biological survival, health, and strength, as well as on a substance that brings pleasure to the palate. They thought that food—representing survival and pleasure—is what life is all about. And this is the majority view in our world today: People devote their entire lives to working, accumulating, existing, and seeking pleasure.

The Scriptures are always up to date. The words that Jesus spoke to the crowd in Capernaum could just as easily be delivered to the world over Cable News Network today! Our world is still confused. Our values are still misplaced. People still spend their lives in pursuit of bread that goes stale and moldy after a while, instead of pursuing the food that endures to eternal life.

Nothing But Your Soul

Jesus asks the same question of you and me today: "What are you working for?" Are you working merely to make a living, to have a nice home, to be comfortable? Are you one of those who says, "The spirit is willing but the flesh is ready for the weekend"? If so, then your focus is on food that perishes, not on food that endures. If that is your attitude, then these words of our Lord are directed at you as surely as they were directed at the crowd in Capernaum.

Barbara Walters once interviewed three celebrities on one of her ABC television specials: Johnny Carson, Johnny Cash, and Walter Cronkite. In his interview, Johnny Carson came across as a stereotypical playboy, a jaded hedonist. Everything he said communicated the fact that he was living for pleasure—and yet, having done everything and traveled everywhere, he was still unfulfilled.

Walter Cronkite was the avuncular humanist, the worldly-wise philosopher. Retired and wealthy, spending a lot of time on his sailboat, he was making every attempt to enjoy life. Yet there was a wistfulness, even a world-weariness about him, as if the sum total of his life could be expressed in his famous broadcasting tag-line, "That's the way it is"—because there is no more than this.

Johnny Cash, on the other hand, talked about a very rough life, filled with bad choices, alcoholism, drug addiction, and prison. He had come to the brink of destroying his marriage and his life. But then he told Barbara Walters how he had found Jesus. There was a peace in his eyes and the steadiness of contentment in his voice. He spoke of a hope for the future which neither Carson nor Cronkite seemed to have. Johnny Cash made very clear that he had found what Jesus is talking about right here: The bread of life, bread that lasts beyond the mere satisfaction of physical hunger, bread that endures.

Jesus corrects our confused view of life, just as He had to correct the confused view of life of His hearers in that day. The popular view today is that the only reason to work is to get enough money to be secure and comfortable. This is not just the view of "yuppies"—the Young Upwardly-mobile Professionals; it is the prevailing view of our culture. Indeed, this viewpoint seems to succeed for a while, as people are able to amass their IRAs, their $300,000 homes in gated communities, their BMWs and big-screen TVs.

But all of these glitzy possessions ultimately lose their value. They corrode. They decay. They cease to satisfy. And when the time comes to leave it all behind, you take nothing into eternity but your own soul.

Sealed By God

Not only were the people in Capernaum confused about what is truly important in life, they were mistaken about Jesus himself. They thought He was just another prophet. They saw Jesus as the leader who would deliver them from political oppression, feed their bellies, and keep them happy. But they were not ready to crown Him Lord of their lives.

But Jesus corrects this misimpression: "Do not work for food that spoils, but for food that endures to eternal life," says Jesus, "which the Son of Man will give you. On him God the Father has placed"—now, notice this!—"his seal of approval."

What does He mean by God's "seal of approval"?

Whenever you read in the New Testament about being "sealed of God," it is always a reference to the presence of the Holy Spirit. Believers today are said to be "sealed by the Spirit." As Christians, we have the Spirit living in us, and the Spirit controls us to the degree that we consciously and continually turn our will over to Him. But Jesus had the Holy Spirit in full measure, and the Holy Spirit had Jesus in full measure. There was never a moment in Jesus' life when He did not manifest the dynamic of the Spirit. That is why His words had such tremendous impact and power in human lives. That is why His deeds were beyond the ordinary deeds of men.

Jesus was sealed of the Father and fully in tune with the Spirit of God. There has never been anyone like Him before or since in all of history. Jesus was unique.

The Works God Requires

These people were also mistaken about God's will for their lives. Many people are equally confused today.

When the crowd realized that Jesus was talking about something other than physical bread, they said to Him, "What must we do to do the works God requires?" This question is frequently asked today, almost always by someone who has begun to realize that life has a spiritual dimension to it. It is a religious question: "What can I do to please God? How can I win God's favor?"

This question invariably marks a person who does not yet understand God's nature and God's character. Usually they answer their own question by saying, "We must do *everything* to please God," or, "We can do *nothing* to please God."

People who say "We must do *everything*" seem to feel that God is lucky to have them on His side. They have the resources, the money, the brains, the technological ability, the know-how to make God's cause flourish. "Just step aside, God," they seem to say, "I'll handle everything."

I once received a letter from an earnest young Christian who wanted to transform the entire church in America. He wanted to call a national conference of senior pastors of the largest churches in the country. According to this young man, these pastors would pool their ideas, share the secrets of their successes, and devise a master model for every church in America to follow. He reasoned that if these large churches were so successful, there must be a secret to success. If every church in the country learned that secret and followed the same plan, then every church in the country could be just as successful! Even the smallest struggling church could become a megachurch by implementing the master plan!

My eager young friend was an inventive thinker, but there was a fatal flaw in his outlook: His was a man-centered approach that relied entirely on human wisdom, human power, and human insight. He didn't take into account the words of Jesus: "What is highly valued among men is detestable in God's sight."[1]

God doesn't want every church in America to look like Peninsula Bible Church, or Willow Creek Community Church in Illinois, or University Presbyterian Church in Seattle, or First Evangelical Free Church in Fullerton. He chooses to do some of His greatest and most effective work through little white clapboard country churches and small inner-city storefront churches, through individuals and groups of individuals who never get the limelight, but who have made themselves totally available as God's channels of ministry and blessing.

Those who believe, "We must do *everything*," are religious people who seem to be as unaware of God's true workings and intents as nonreligious people are. So they end up trying to do everything for God.

Then there are those who say, "We can do *nothing* for God." There are many pious, well-intentioned Christians who say, "God must do it all." They quote the words of Jesus to His disciples, "Apart from me you can do nothing."[2] "Our job," they say, "is to just sit quietly, wait, and watch for the Spirit to move. Don't initiate. Don't plan. Don't act. God will work it all out."

Our Lord indicates that both of these answers are wrong. They are extremes. They are equally of the flesh. Jesus says there *is* something we can do: "The work of God is this: to believe in the one he has sent."

Jesus wants our active faith. He wants us to recognize that He is present and active in our lives. He lived, died, and rose again, then ascended into heaven and sent the Spirit into this world in order to make Himself and His power available to us. That is the full gospel, the truly good news.

The gospel is so much more than the mere hope of heaven when you die. That's only half of the gospel. The full gospel is that Jesus is alive *now,* He's available to us *now,* He gives us His power *now* for whatever problems and situations we are facing. When Jesus says to believe in the One God has sent, He means we are to believe that it is available to us in every moment of our lives.

"Believe in the one he has sent" also means we must learn to view our situations through God's eyes. We must gain God's perspective on life. That means we must listen to what God has to say. We should trust God's understanding, as it is expressed in Scripture, not our own limited understanding. "Believe in me," Jesus says, in effect. "Believe that I know what I'm talking about. Believe that I can work."

The Works God Requires

The crowd was also mistaken about the signs Jesus performed.

6:30–33 *So they asked him, "What miraculous sign then will you give that we may see it and believe you? What will you do? Our forefathers ate manna in the desert; as it is written: 'He gave them bread from heaven to eat.' "*

Jesus said to them, "I tell you the truth, it is not Moses who has given you the bread from heaven, but it is my Father who gives you the true bread from heaven and gives life to the world."

Imagine the sheer *chutzpah* of demanding a sign after the free miracle-meal Jesus already provided! These people are not satisfied with the sign of the loaves and fishes. They do not accept that miracle as a messianic sign, so they demand another sign. "You gave us ordinary bread and fish," they are saying, in effect. "We can get tuna sandwiches for lunch anytime, anywhere. But if you would wave your hands and produce some *heavenly* food—now *that* would be a *miracle!*"

But Jesus answers, in effect, "Wrong again! It isn't Moses who gives you manna! God gives you manna!"

I have always been amazed at the Jews' fascination with manna. According to the best Bible research available, manna probably tasted like ground coriander seed mixed with honey. The first few bites were probably quite exotic and fascinating. But any food—whether chateaubriand or chipped beef—would become tiresome as a steady diet. The word *manna* literally means, "What is it?" Just imagine the poor Israelites having to eat "What is it?" for breakfast, "What is it?" for lunch, and "What is it?" for dinner, every day for forty years! How can anyone think *that* was wonderful?

Jesus tells the people that they are missing an even greater miracle than manna in the desert. The manna that God provided through Moses was not true bread from heaven. It was only a symbol, a faint shadow of the real thing. What Jesus was trying to get across to them was the message, "The real bread from heaven is me! I came down from heaven, sent by the Father, to feed your restless hunger for meaning and fulfillment and satisfaction!"

More Than Physical Bread

To this the crowd responds with a plea which prompts Jesus to declare plainly the truth He wants them to know.

6:34–40 *"Sir," they said, "from now on give us this bread."*
Then Jesus declared, "I am the bread of life. He who comes to me will never go hungry, and he who believes in me will never be thirsty. But as I told you, you have seen me and still you do not believe. All that the Father gives me will come to me, and whoever comes to me I will never drive away. For I have come down from heaven not to do my will but to do the will of him who sent me. And this is the will of him who sent me, that I shall lose none of all that he has given me, but raise them up at the last day. For my Father's will is that everyone who looks to the Son and believes in him shall have eternal life, and I will raise him up at the last day."

I could spend many pages on those wonderful, gracious words. But let us focus just on a few of the major themes Jesus discloses.

First, Jesus recognizes the universal hunger for "bread"—a "food" that far transcends mere physical bread. "Sir," the crowd said, "from now on give us this bread." This was a mixed crowd, made up of both believers and unbelievers. But when they caught a sense that Jesus was talking about something beyond mere physical food, they immediately wanted it.

I find this principle to be true all over the world: people are hungry—and their hunger goes far deeper than a yearning for a full belly and a comfortable home. There is a restlessness within us that cries for something more, something real. Jesus recognized this in people. Everyone in this crowd wanted what He had to offer. They didn't understand what it was, but they wanted it. They sensed there was more to life than bread.

I once spent an evening talking with a young man who professed to be an agnostic and a pagan. Religion, he said, was nothing more than an aberration of human psychology. At the end of our conversation, I said to him, "You know, John, I believe every man ought to have something bigger than himself to believe in." He looked me right in the eye and said very soberly, "My friend, how right you are." This was just another way of saying, "Give me this bread that is more than physical bread."

Never Hunger, Never Thirst

Second, in verse 35, Jesus tells the crowd plainly how they can partake of this eternal bread of life. He uses two simple concepts that everyone understands in order to make His point: Hunger and Thirst. "I am the bread of life," says Jesus. "He who comes to me will never go hungry, and he who believes in me will never be thirsty."

What do you do when you are hungry? You eat, and if you continue to eat on a regular basis, you will never hunger. What do you do when you are thirsty? You drink, and if you continue drinking on a regular basis, you will never thirst. Jesus is telling the people that when they come to Him, presenting their lives to Him and expecting Him to act in their lives, they partake of Him, the bread of life.

If you keep partaking of Jesus, believing in Him and trusting Him to act, committing yourself to Him on a regular, on-going basis, you will never hunger or thirst. That is how to lay hold of the gift of bread from heaven. That is how to find life that is real life indeed.

Third, Jesus unfolds to these people the mystery of conversion. There are many things no one can explain about conversion, but Jesus makes four profound truths very clear in this passage:

1. Not all who see will come.

Jesus says, "As I told you, you have seen me and still you do not believe." They understood a good deal about Jesus. They recognized Him as a significant person, perhaps even a prophet—but still they did not come to Him in belief. They had an intellectual apprehension of who Jesus was—but intellectual understanding falls short of true trust and commitment of one's entire life and being to Jesus. Many of the people saw Jesus—but they did not come.

2. All who are chosen will come.

If God is at work, people will respond. The Spirit leads them, the Father draws them, and all who are chosen will come. When you truly come to Jesus, you reveal that you have been chosen. You do not have to struggle with it and ask yourself, "Am I chosen?" Just come. If you are willing to come to Jesus, then you have been chosen.

3. All who come are welcomed.

"All that the Father gives me," says Jesus, "will come to me, and whoever comes to me I will never drive away." No matter what you have done or where you have been, when you come you will be welcomed. You will not be cast out. There is no sin that Jesus cannot forgive—so come!

4. All who come are safe forever.

You can never lose what Jesus gives you. He says, "For I have come down from heaven not to do my will but to do the will of him who sent me. And this is the will of him who sent me, that I shall lose none of all that he has given me, but raise them up at the last day. For my Father's will is that everyone who looks to the Son and believes in him shall have eternal life, and I will raise him up at the last day." Jesus says that all who come are safe forever because: (1) that is the work He came to do; (2) it fulfills the Father's will that He should lose no one who comes to Him; (3) it involves the resurrection of the body, the defeat of decay and corruption; and (4) it involves the gift of eternal life.

How reassuring are those wonderful words!

Let me leave you with the essential question of the Lord's discourse: "What are you working for?"

Why are you going back to work tomorrow? Is it merely to earn a living, to put some food on the table, to pay your rent or buy a TV? If that is all you are living for, then you are missing out on the best that God intends for you.

Yes, you should go to work and earn your living—but go with the expectation that the people you meet, the situations you face, and the decisions you make are part of a larger plan—God's plan—and that as you go, Jesus himself goes with you. Every day of your life, you can feast on the bread of life, the bread that has come down from heaven.

There is no more exciting way to live than that.

Chapter Nineteen

Life With God

John 6:41–59

Once while I was teaching a church seminar on prophecy, a young man came up out of the audience and stood beside me on the platform. Then, to the amazement of all, he leaned over to the microphone and announced that he was the prophet Elijah, returned from heaven. I was a bit startled, to say the least. The young man was absolutely serious about his claim, and he told the group that God had instructed him to take over the meeting and teach us the truth about prophetic Scripture.

My reaction, of course, as well as the reaction of every other person in that room, was to disregard this young man's claims. We recognized that he was a troubled and disturbed young man who needed help. With the assistance of a couple of our elders, the man was talked into leaving the platform and the seminar continued without incident.

I think that experience gives me an inkling of what the crowd at the synagogue at Capernaum must have felt when Jesus announced that He Himself was the "bread" which had come down from heaven. Maybe some were puzzled and startled. Others, perhaps, might have thought that Jesus was disturbed or even crazy. You might think that the miracle of the feeding of the 5,000 would be proof enough of His claims—but remember that the people discounted that miracle and wanted another sign. They wanted to set the terms of the miracle: They demanded manna from heaven.

So there was an air of incredulity as Jesus announced Himself to be the "bread of life."

Who Does He Think He Is?

6:41–42 *At this the Jews began to grumble about him because he said, "I am the bread that came down from heaven." They said, "Is this not Jesus, the son of Joseph, whose father and mother we know? How can he now say, 'I came down from heaven'?"*

You can easily imagine their reaction: They must have turned to each other with cynical, disbelieving looks on their faces, and said, "What is He talking about? Come on! We know this guy! We know where He came from! He didn't come down from heaven! He's Joseph and Mary's kid from over in the next town!" They immediately forgot all the wonderful things they had seen Jesus do and say. They forgot the healings. They forgot the miracle of loaves and fishes they had seen just the previous day. Most of all, they had forgotten His penetrating wisdom, His words of grace.

To them, Jesus was once again just an ordinary man.

Many people today react this way to Jesus. Many nonbelievers today are willing to concede that Jesus was a significant figure, an insightful teacher—but nothing more than an ordinary man.

Why were the people in Capernaum so quick to discount His claims? Because their facts were incomplete? Yes, in part. But even more importantly, because they were not looking for the evidence. We don't know whether these people knew about the circumstances of Jesus' birth—the announcements of the angels, the visit of the wise men, the great star that shone over the city of Bethlehem. But if they did know about the wonders that accompanied His birth, they had forgotten all about them.

They knew that Jesus had grown up in Nazareth, and it is clear that Jesus had a fairly normal boyhood. There are various apocryphal "gospels" which tell bizarre and assuredly false stories about the many miracles Jesus supposedly did as a boy. These "gospels" have such names as "The First Gospel of the Infancy of Jesus" or "Thomas's Gospel of the Infancy of Jesus." Some ancient religious cults, such as the Gnostics, accepted these writings as Scripture. But if the boy Jesus had really done all the fanciful miracles described in those so-called "gospels," He would have been the sensation of the nation as an adolescent and in His twenties, and this crowd in Capernaum would not have doubted His claims.

In truth, there is no reliable account of any miracle of Jesus prior to the miracle of Cana, which He performed when He was about thirty years old. And that is why these people doubt His claim to have come from heaven. It is clear from their reaction that Jesus grew up in Nazareth just like anyone else. That's all they knew. They didn't know the whole story, just as many people today don't know the whole story about Jesus. They refuse to examine the evidence, they refuse to listen to the eyewitness accounts of what Jesus did and said, and then—armed with an arsenal of ignorance—they feel smugly justified in rejecting Him.

Drawn by the Father

6:43–47 *"Stop grumbling among yourselves," Jesus answered. "No one can come to me unless the Father who sent me draws him, and I will raise him up*

at the last day. It is written in the Prophets: 'They will all be taught by God.'
Everyone who listens to the Father and learns from him comes to me. No one
has seen the Father except the one who is from God; only he has seen the Fa-
ther. I tell you the truth, he who believes has everlasting life."

Notice how patiently our Lord repeats himself. Again and again He tries
to break through the confusion, the murkiness, the willfulness of the people's
hearts. But Jesus also says a very remarkable thing in these verses: He says
there must be an inner enlightenment of the Father. Belief is not based merely
on hearing the facts about Jesus or hearing the story of His life.

No figure in history has been so widely portrayed in film, in drama, in
story, or in books as Jesus. But hearing about Him is not enough. The inner
eyes of the soul must be opened and flooded with light in order for us to truly
grasp the implications of His life for *our* lives. The inner ears of our souls
must be opened so we can hear and understand that everything Jesus did and
said personally involves us.

I once met a woman from Sacramento, California, who was raised in a
nonreligious family and had never gone to church. As a high school student in
the 1960s, she was invited by a friend to attend the first Billy Graham crusade
in Sacramento. She decided to go—just out of curiosity. She sat there, determined not to be influenced by Dr. Graham. She listened to the choir, to the testimonies and the special music, all the while promising herself not to be
"manipulated" into responding to the invitation to receive Christ.

"I was sure he was psychologically preparing the audience to respond to
an invitation," she told me. "I knew I could withstand any kind of manipulation because I knew exactly what he was doing. But then Billy Graham gave
the invitation—and suddenly I felt I just had to respond! I jumped out of my
seat and went down the aisle immediately. I was embarrassed as I looked
around and saw I was the very first person to respond! But I'm so glad I did
respond."

This woman was born again that night. Why? Because she was drawn to
Jesus by the Father.

We think we choose Jesus, but He Himself said to His own disciples,
"You did not choose me, but I chose you."[1] We think that our choices determine our destiny, but the truth is that our choices are the result of God's
attraction and compulsion, His movement of our souls toward Him.

If you look back to the moment when you first chose Jesus as your Lord
and Savior, it probably seemed to be a natural event, centered on your own
will and desire. But the Scriptures reveal so much more about our humanity
that we ourselves understand. The Scriptures show us that God *must* draw us

to Himself—otherwise we would never come. No one would respond if they were not "drawn" of the Father. And this word for "drawn," in the original Greek, is a very strong word. Every time it is used in Scripture, it means to be "compelled" or "dragged along."

In verse 45, Jesus quotes Isaiah 54:13 and calls this being "taught of God." It is a process whereby our understanding is opened. It may happen suddenly or slowly. It may happen very painfully. It not only happens to non-believers in order to draw them to the point of faith and conversion. It also happens to Christians who need to be continually taught of God. Many have had the experience (and perhaps you know from your own experience) of hearing some truth again and again for years, but never really understanding and internalizing that truth until something suddenly opened their eyes and showed them what it meant.

In each of our lives there come many times, many points of decision, where we must consciously renew our commitment to God, where we must willingly hand back the reins of our life after we have been trying to go our own way. At that point, we are choosing God—and yet, our act of choosing Him is nothing more than a response to His teaching and His leading in our lives because He has already chosen us.

Our Response Is Our Responsibility

Some years ago, I was driving through a small town in the South and I saw a large billboard on the front lawn of a church. The billboard proclaimed in huge letters, "This church is the only authorized spokesman for Jesus Christ on earth." I don't recall what kind of church it was, but I vividly remember being impressed and astounded by the arrogance of that claim! After all, this church was taking upon itself a role that Jesus said was His alone: The role of speaking for and revealing God!

"No one has seen the Father," Jesus declares in verse 46, "except the one who is from God; only he has seen the Father." Jesus is emphatic and unambiguous on this point: There is only one authorized spokesman for the God, and that is Jesus. We must believe in Him because He is the only mediator between God and man.

Then in verse 47 Jesus adds these wonderful words: "I tell you the truth, he who believes has everlasting life." Here we see a two-step process by which God brings us to Himself. Having been drawn, says Jesus, we must believe. Sometimes He draws us through painful experiences, through hurt, loss, and disappointment. But He also draws us through joys, through unexpected blessings and pleasures, through the still, small voice of the Holy Spirit.

Some are drawn through the process of years, while others are spiritually awakened suddenly and dramatically, like Paul on the Damascus Road. It is all in the control of God, but once we have been awakened, our responsibility is to respond and believe. And we must not just believe once, not just commit ourselves once, we must keep on believing and continually commit ourselves to His Lordship, continually feasting on the bread of life.

The Lesson of Death

Jesus makes another statement guaranteed to startle His hearers.

6:48–51 *"I am the bread of life. Your forefathers ate the manna in the desert, yet they died. But here is the bread that comes down from heaven, which a man may eat and not die. I am the living bread that came down from heaven. If a man eats of this bread, he will live forever. This bread is my flesh, which I will give for the life of the world."*

The problem with these people, says Jesus, is that they were focused on the symbol of manna in the wilderness rather than on the reality of Jesus, the living bread from heaven. Although the manna kept the people alive physically, it could do nothing for them eternally, because it was only a symbol of the living bread that was to come.

Many people today make the same mistake as these people in Capernaum: They trust in symbols rather than the reality. They trust the fact that they were baptized, that they joined a church, that they were confirmed in some religious ceremony. Jesus says these symbols have no power to bring life—only the reality, Jesus Himself, can bring life.

He follows this statement with a remarkable claim regarding life—and death. He says that if someone dies apart from Him, that person experiences eternal separation from God, true eternal death. But for the person who has come to Jesus, physical death is merely the gateway to eternal life!

Perhaps this is one reason why God has never allowed human science to truly prevent death. Scientists have discovered cures for many diseases and perfected techniques for extending life, and the average lifespan today is much longer than it was centuries or even decades ago. But even with all our amazing medical technology, the death rate remains exactly what it has always been: 100 per cent.

No one gets out of this life alive! And I think God intends it to remain that way. He is teaching us something through the fact that all people eventually die. He is teaching us that we must all come to terms with our mortality. We must all make a decision as to what our lives are going to mean. Everyone is "taught by God," and death itself is part of that teaching.

When I was a young man in my late teens and early twenties, I couldn't believe I would ever get old. When I looked at the feeble old people around me, with their gray hair and their failing eyesight and their arthritic joints, I thought to myself, "I have so many years ahead of me, I just can't believe that will ever happen to me!" But it has.

What bothers me is that when I go to a restaurant, I always get the senior citizen discount without even asking for it! Why? Because people can tell just by looking at me that I'm getting old! This old body of mine is headed for death and corruption.

Physical death is a symbol that God wants to use to teach us an important truth about the human spirit: The spirit in man is headed for death and corruption, too—unless the Lord of Life intervenes. The Lord of Life is Jesus, the bread from heaven. Only those who receive His life can overcome the effect of death upon the spirit and soul of man.

Notice, too, that it is here, in this passage, that Jesus first hints at the terrible price to be paid for eternal life. In order for us to have life, the Son of God will have to die. He says in verse 51, "If a man eats of this bread, he will live forever. This bread is my flesh, which I will give for the life of the world."

Flesh and Blood

The people were shocked by Jesus' words.

6:52–57 *Then the Jews began to argue sharply among themselves, "How can this man give us his flesh to eat?"*

Jesus said to them, "I tell you the truth, unless you eat the flesh of the Son of Man and drink his blood, you have no life in you. Whoever eats my flesh and drinks my blood has eternal life, and I will raise him up at the last day. For my flesh is real food and my blood is real drink. Whoever eats my flesh and drinks my blood remains in me, and I in him. Just as the living Father sent me and I live because of the Father, so the one who feeds on me will live because of me."

These words were an outrage to the Jews who first heard them. They even sound offensive to our ears. Talk of eating human flesh and drinking human blood is disgusting! And that's how the people reacted to Jesus. You can hear their voices dripping with scorn as they say, in effect, "How can this man give us His flesh to eat and His blood to drink? What does He think we are? Cannibals and vampires? What kind of ghoulish talk is this? Why, we're all Orthodox Jews! This kind of talk isn't even kosher!"

For centuries, the Jews had lived by strict dietary rules. All food had to be "kosher," approved according to Jewish dietary laws. The word kosher means "cleansed," and it had special reference to the preparation of meat. The Jews cannot eat any meat that has not had all the blood drained from it. I once visited a factory in Israel where chickens were killed and canned for food. Every one of those chickens—thousands every day!—had to be killed and its blood drained by a rabbi. If not, it could not be sold on the Israeli market. Clearly, the thought of consuming any kind of blood—let alone *human* blood!—was most offensive to the Jews.

It is possible, however, that these people are being deliberately obtuse, denying what Jesus has already made quite plain: He is talking about His own death. Flesh and blood are symbols of the sacrifice He must make. He has already answered their question, "How can this man give us his flesh to eat?" He has told them that He will give His flesh for the life of the world. That can only mean *death*—His own death—and they are troubled by that.

Behind the protest of these Jews is a kind of defensiveness, the feeling that their sins are not that bad, that it should not require anyone's death to resolve the question of their sins. Again we see an attitude that is as relevant to our own age as the computer chip. People today, just like people then, do not want to believe that their problems come from something so bad within themselves that it requires death to cure it. We're good people! Not perfect, certainly, but all we need is a little adjustment here and there, and maybe a New Year's resolution or two—but we don't need someone to die for us!

The words of Jesus, however, are relentless and uncompromising: "I tell you the truth, unless you eat the flesh of the Son of Man and drink his blood, you have no life in you." He leaves no room for doubt: His death is essential to real life for you and me. Moreover, the life He brings is *real* life, beyond that of mere physical existence: "For my flesh is real food and my blood is real drink." God intends us to have the most real and meaningful life in the universe—a life that transcends mere human existence.

In verse 56, Jesus goes on to tell us that this new, eternal kind of life is the answer to our desire for intimacy, to know and to truly be known by another: "Whoever eats my flesh and drinks my blood remains in me, and I in him." Jesus is sharing His life and His fellowship with us in the most intimate form of communion possible. It is a relationship that is more mysterious, yet more exalted, than any human relationship ever known.

This is the same mysterious concept with which He will later comfort His disciples in the Upper Room, just before His death: "You are in me, and I am in you."[2] Those are very simple words, mere monosyllables—yet to understand what they mean is to grasp the very core of truth itself!

The most intimate physical act in human experience is the act of sex. In God's plan, two people who share their lives together share their bodies and the secret of themselves with each other. That is why sex has accurately been described as "the urge to merge."

The yearning for intimacy is not merely a physical urge, but an emotional and psychological desire. Friendship is a form of intimacy. When you are with a friend, what do you do? You share your secrets, your dreams, your desires, your hurts, your inner self. That is the urge to merge at the psychological and emotional level.

But there is also a *spiritual* urge to merge. True worship is the desire to merge with God, for Him to possess us and for us to possess Him. When we eat and drink the life that Jesus gives us, we experience spiritual union with Him. That is true intimacy.

"You are in me, and I am in you." These words penetrate to the very core of our hunger for intimacy, for love, for fellowship. They reach us in our loneliness and comfort us with the knowledge that we need never be lonely again!

Our model of spiritual intimacy is the relationship between the Father and the Son. "Just as the living Father sent me," Jesus says in verse 57, "and I live because of the Father, so the one who feeds on me will live because of me." Jesus derived His life from the Father, and we are to derive our life from Jesus—in everything we do.

His Death Is Our Life

Verses 58 and 59 give us the Lord's summation of His discourse.

6:58–59 *"This is the bread that came down from heaven. Our forefathers ate manna and died, but he who feeds on this bread will live forever." He said this while teaching in the synagogue in Capernaum.*

Are you learning how to feed on the bread from heaven? Are you learning to conduct every aspect of your life—your work, your family relationships, your friendships, your church relationships, and your inner thought life—in total dependence upon Jesus? Are you learning how to feed on this bread day by day, hour by hour? Are you learning to grow in an awareness of Jesus' constant friendship and fellowship with you, even when you are feeling alone?

That is what the Lord desires in your life and mine.

His death is our life. His blood washes away the stain of what we once were in Adam. We are in Christ now, and we are free to be what we ought to be. The bread of life has come down from heaven to nourish us every day—to give us the strength and power to live our lives as we ought to live, to meet our deaths with courage and peace, secure in the knowledge that if we eat this bread, we will live forever, and He will raise us up in the last day.

Chapter Twenty

To Whom Shall We Go?

John 6:60–71

Have you ever heard the term "evangelical numbers"? "Evangelical numbers" are the figures many pastors use to estimate the size of their congregations. For example, if the official rolls show 1,200 members and Sunday morning attendance averages 1,400 people, a pastor using "evangelical numbers" would "round it off" and say he pastored a church of 2,000!

Some churches will do almost anything to inflate their numbers. Some years ago, a pastor in a California church announced that when Sunday school attendance reached 1,000, he would preach from the belfry of the church! Well, that was a challenge his congregation couldn't resist. Everyone went out and scrounged the neighborhood, bringing in any warm body that could be found. The count was taken, the magic number was reached—and the pastor kept his word.

People put a lot of stock in numbers. But as I look through the Bible, I find that God places His emphasis elsewhere. He is not nearly as impressed with numbers as we are—and He proves that over and over.

For example, in Judges 7, when Gideon summoned the men of Israel to battle against the Midianites, 32,000 answered the call. But the Lord told Gideon that 32,000 was too many. Gideon would have to "down-size" his army. So Gideon sent home 22,000 men—but the Lord said 10,000 was still too many for Him to work with. So Gideon tested his men until he had whittled the number down to 300. And God said, in effect, "Great! That's a number I can work with." God was more interested in quality than quantity.

Here, at the end of John chapter 6, we see this principle again. Prior to this point in His ministry, Jesus has attracted scores of disciples with His startling new message and His miracles. But now many of these disciples begin to discover that He will not do miracles on demand, and that His message is not the promise of prosperity and political liberation they want to hear. And so they fall away.

But here again, as in the story of Gideon, we will see that God is not interested in quantity but in quality. Many desert Jesus—but those who stay will be the ones whom Jesus will train and pour His life into. And they will be the ones who, after His death and resurrection, will turn the world upside-down for God.

A Thinning of the Ranks

The context of this section of John's gospel is that Jesus has concluded His great message on the bread of life in the synagogue at Capernaum—but He has finished on a note that is very offensive to His hearers, talking about eating His flesh and drinking His blood. Many were disturbed by His words.

6:60–66 *On hearing it, many of his disciples said, "This is a hard teaching. Who can accept it?"*

Aware that his disciples were grumbling about this, Jesus said to them, "Does this offend you? What if you see the Son of Man ascend to where he was before! The Spirit gives life; the flesh counts for nothing. The words I have spoken to you are spirit and they are life. Yet there are some of you who do not believe." For Jesus had known from the beginning which of them did not believe and who would betray him. He went on to say, "This is why I told you that no one can come to me unless the Father has enabled him."

From this time many of his disciples turned back and no longer followed him.

We see from this last verse that a period of time is involved here. Over the course of several weeks many of the disciples draw back and abandon the Lord. This incident probably corresponds with the event recorded in the other gospels that took place at Caesarea Philippi, where Peter confessed that Jesus is the Christ. Here is the first thinning of the ranks in our Lord's ministry.

Notice the characteristics of those who desert Jesus. First, they take offense at difficult truth. "This is a hard teaching," they said. "Who can accept it?" By this statement, they implied that they did not want to be troubled with difficult teaching.

I have often found this to be true when people drop out of the church: They are bothered or even offended when difficult doctrines are taught. For example, some feel uneasy about the doctrine of election or predestination. How can God draw us and yet give us free will? Others struggle with the doctrine that God providentially allows difficult experiences—hardships, disasters, suffering, and so forth. "What kind of a God would allow this kind of suffering?" they ask. "These teachings are too hard to understand. Who can

accept these teachings?" If you become bothered or offended by difficult doctrines in the Bible, then the odds are that, sooner or later, you too will drop out
of the Christian cause, just as these disciples did.

In His response, Jesus points out the problem that these people had:
"Does this offend you? What if you see the Son of Man ascend to where He
was before! The Spirit gives life; the flesh counts for nothing. The words I
have spoken to you are spirit and they are life." Read that way, Jesus seems to
be saying, "Are you offended by what I said about eating flesh and drinking
blood? Well, that's nothing to the offense you are going to feel when you see
me ascending into the heavens!"

If we read it that way, however, we have not understood at all what Jesus
is saying. Unfortunately, it is a mistranslation that makes it sound that way.
The translators have inserted these words, "What if . . ."—but in the original
Greek it does not really say that. There is no "what" at all.

The text actually says, "If you were to see the Son of Man ascending
where he was before"—and at this point we would have to supply English
words which the Greek anticipates but which do not directly translate—"then
you would know that it is the spirit that gives life, the flesh counts for nothing." These people were hung up on symbols. When Jesus talked about flesh
and blood, they took Him literally, as if He were suggesting cannibalism! But
He was saying to them, "If you continue following me to the end, and you see
me ascending into the heavens, after my death and resurrection, then you will
understand that I am not talking about flesh and blood, but about what those
things symbolize: That it is the spirit that gives life, and the flesh counts for
nothing."

People often miss the thrust of Jesus' words because they put too much
literal emphasis on the symbols He employs. In John 2, Jesus said to the Jews,
"Destroy this temple, and I will raise it again in three days."[1] They immedi-
ately thought He was talking about the beautiful building on top of Mt.
Moriah. But John hastens to explain that Jesus was speaking of the temple of
His body, which was symbolized by the building.

And in chapter 3, when Jesus told Nicodemus, "You must be born
again,"[2] Nicodemus gaped at Him in amazement and said, "How can a man
be born when he is old?"[3] Nicodemus was thinking literally and obstetrically,
whereas Jesus was speaking symbolically about the gift of eternal life, which
is pictured for us by the gift of physical life that physical birth brings.

So when Jesus speaks here of eating flesh and drinking blood, He is using
symbols to describe an eternal reality. Those who focus solely on the symbols
of Christianity usually become disillusioned sooner or later—and often fall
away. Thousands of churches across our country today are almost empty
because of this kind of disillusionment. All these churches offer are the sym-

bols, the sacraments: baptism, the Lord's supper, ceremonial prayers, ritual music. There is no reality, only symbols.

The affirmation of Jesus is reserved for those who seek the truth wherever it leads, no matter how uncomfortable, unpalatable, or difficult to understand. Our challenge is to feed on the promises and the warnings of God's Word, to accept the truth, to hear what Jesus actually says to us—not just hear what we want to hear.

"People stumble over the truth from time to time," said Winston Churchill, "but most pick themselves up and hurry on as if nothing happened." May that never be said of you and me.

So Close to the Truth—Yet So Far

Jesus is clear on this: Those who draw back are those who really do not believe. He knew from the beginning who would believe in Him and who would betray Him. That is why He says, "This is why I told you that no one can come to me unless the Father has enabled him." The purpose of God's teaching is always to open our eyes to truth—not just religious truth, but *any* kind of truth, for all truth is from God.

It is a spiritual principle that when people obey the truth they know, then they will be taught more truth. But those who resist the truth will lose their capacity to see and to hear the truth anymore. That is the problem Jesus addresses here. He is saying, in effect: "Instead of allowing the Father to draw you to me, you are resisting." Or as Jesus put it on another occasion, "Whoever has will be given more, and he will have an abundance. Whoever does not have, even what he has will be taken from him."[4]

What a tragedy! And it happens all the time. It happened to many of the Lord's disciples. They were so close to the truth—but ultimately they could not accept all that Jesus had to teach them. So they rejected Jesus and lost even the glimmering of truth that they had. That is why we read these sad words in verse 66: "From this time many of his disciples turned back and no longer followed him."

They had gone as far as they would go—and then they turned back. Hebrews 11:6 says, "Without faith it is impossible to please God, because anyone who comes to him must believe that he exists and that he rewards those who earnestly seek him." These who drew back had stopped seeking Jesus—and they lost an opportunity to gain God's reward.

I'm not suggesting that the opportunity was lost forever. I believe some of those who pulled back probably returned again, after the death and resurrection of Jesus. But they missed an opportunity to walk alongside Jesus and learn from Him during His earthly ministry.

The Mark of a True Believer

You can sense the deep disappointment, even a sense of betrayal, in the next words of Jesus.

6:67 *"You do not want to leave too, do you?" Jesus asked the Twelve.*

But note the strong, passionate words of Peter.

6:68–69 *Simon Peter answered him, "Lord, to whom shall we go? You have the words of eternal life. We believe and know that you are the Holy One of God."*

When Jesus asked if the remaining disciples would leave Him too, it was clear that He was not trying to control them. They were free to go. Jesus never holds anyone by force, against his or her will. The few who remain are there by choice, not by force. And here we see the mark of the true believer: He cannot quit Jesus, because his heart has been captured! Responding to our Lord's words, Peter says three things, two of which are profound truths and one of which is a profoundly ironic error.

First: "Lord, to whom shall we go? You have the words of eternal life." In other words, "Lord, we have been thinking about it. We have investigated the alternatives. Now, you're not easy to live with or understand. But Lord, there is no one else who seems to have the truth. Your words are hard words, but those words have gripped our hearts. Only you have the words that lead to eternal life." This statement is one of the marks of a true believer. Peter cannot quit Jesus because he knows that only Jesus has the words of eternal life.

Second: "We believe and know that you are the Holy One of God." In the original Greek, the tense of these words implies a process that has been going on for weeks and months: "We have believed, and have come to know . . . ." Peter is saying, in effect, "We have watched you, and we have come to see that there is nothing wrong in you. You are the Holy One of God, the One without sin. You fit the prophecies. You fulfill the predictions. You have drawn us and compelled us. You are the incomparable Christ, the Messiah." This statement is another mark of a true believer. Peter cannot quit Jesus because he believes that Jesus is the Messiah, the Holy One sent by God.

If you have found Jesus to be (1) the Source of eternal life and (2) the Holy One of God, then where else can you go? Who else can measure up? That is the testimony of all those who walk with Him and follow Him.

I once received a phone call from a young man, a relatively new Christian. "I just can't make it," he said. "I can't continue to be a Christian. It's too hard. I blow it all the time. I'm going to hang it up."

I have heard such statements of discouragement before from other Christians. I said to him, "That's a good idea. Why don't you do that? Life will be a lot easier for you if you just hang it up."

There was a long, stunned silence on the line. Finally, in shocked tones, he said, "You know I can't do that!"

I said, "I know it. Of course you can't quit. Where else can you go? Where can you find the answers and resources you need to get you through your life?" This is what Peter is saying to Jesus. That is the mark of a true Christian: A true Christian can't quit!

The Traitor

The third implication we find in Peter's statement is a mistaken assumption: "Lord, to whom shall *we* go? . . . *We* believe . . . ." Peter is wrong when he says "we," meaning the Twelve. And Jesus corrects Peter's mistaken assumption in the last two verses of the chapter.

6:70–71 *Then Jesus replied, "Have I not chosen you, the Twelve? Yet one of you is a devil!" (He meant Judas, the son of Simon Iscariot, who, though one of the Twelve, was later to betray him.)*

There are three kinds of disciples in this passage: (1) Those who follow Jesus for awhile, then fall away; (2) Those who cannot quit, because their hearts have been captured; (3) One who has never really come, but who will not leave—and that is the problem. Three remarkable things are said here about the one who will stay and betray Jesus: Judas Iscariot.

First, Jesus states that He has chosen all of the Twelve, including Judas. In Luke 6, we see that Jesus spent an entire night in prayer before choosing His disciples. Out of the hundreds who were following Jesus, these Twelve were the ones which, according to the wisdom of the Father, would be alongside Jesus throughout His earthly ministry. These are the Twelve that He would train, mentor, and pour His own life into. Jesus knew the character of Judas, and he was not chosen by accident or mistake. It was the will of the Father that one among that twelve-member apostolic band would betray Him.

Second, Jesus gave power to Judas. On one occasion, Jesus sent the Twelve out before Him into the cities of Galilee and gave them power to cast out devils and heal the sick. The Twelve came back—including Judas!—reporting that they had done all these things. Don't ever forget that: God can give power to do miracles even to those who are not His, if He so chooses.

Our Lord also gave Judas the trusted position of treasurer within the apostolic band. Jesus gave him the bag to keep, from which Judas stole on a regular basis. As the story of Judas develops, it is clear that Judas was never really with Jesus, he was always against Him. Jesus said all along that Judas was a "devil." That is a strong word, and it suggests a lot about Judas—that he was always opposed, always out for himself, always subversive. Judas traveled, lived, ate, and slept with the other disciples, but he was not one of them. He was *never* one of them.

Thirdly, John tells us that Judas is branded forever as the traitor above all others. There are other names that have gone down in history as symbols of betrayal—names such as Benedict Arnold and Quisling—but the name of Judas Iscariot tops the list. Outwardly a disciple, a man who loves Jesus—remember, he betrayed Jesus with a kiss!—yet inwardly a traitor, an enemy, a devil.

I believe that in almost every church congregation, there are probably representatives of all three kinds of disciples. There are those who start out well, who follow Jesus for a while, and then they drop out, they quit. There are those who won't quit, who can't quit, because their hearts have been captured.

And there are the Judases. There are some who want to stay in the church for their own purposes. They want to appear to be Christians but they are not. They are only out for themselves. They do not follow God; they want to use God. And they are the ones who will betray Jesus and His church!

Which group do you belong to?

All of us who claim to be Christians fall into one of these three groups. This passage of Scripture challenges us to renew our commitment to Jesus, to cling to His words of eternal life, to search our own hearts and make sure that we are the kind of disciples that never quit, because our hearts have been captured by God. To whom shall we go? Indeed, only Jesus has the words of eternal life.

Chapter Twenty-One

Is Jesus for Real?

John 7:1–24

The story of Jesus is a story of amazing paradoxes.

Born almost 2,000 years ago in poverty, reared in obscurity, He possessed neither wealth nor influence. Except for one journey to Egypt during His infancy, He never traveled beyond the borders of His own small country.

As a newborn baby, He troubled the soul of a king and attracted the attention of wise men. As a child, He puzzled and amazed the religious teachers of Jerusalem. In manhood, He commanded Nature and walked on the face of a stormy sea and hushed the winds and waves with a word.

He had no formal education, and He never wrote a book, yet even the Library of Congress could not contain all the books that have been written about Him. He never marshalled an army or ruled a nation, yet no military or civil leader ever had a greater impact on the history of the world.

Centuries before the sciences of psychiatry and psychology ever existed, He was the Great Physician of the Soul, binding up broken hearts and healing fragile minds. And without ever administering a medicine or charging a fee, He was the Great Physician of the Human Body, healing the blind and the lame and the paralyzed by the hundreds—and even raising people from the dead.

We date our calendars from the year of His birth. Once each week, the wheels of commerce stop turning, and people stream into houses of worship to honor Him.

The names of the great statesmen, soldiers, scientists, philosophers, and theologians of the past fade into obscurity, but His name increases. And yet, while He was alive, doing the works and speaking the words that have indelibly etched Him into our history and our hearts, His own nation sought His death, and His own family did not understand and believe who He really was.

If we spent the rest of our lives studying the story of Jesus, we would never be able to fully grasp or encompass the mystery and paradox of this great life!

Mounting Hostility

In John chapter 7, we come to the paradoxical story in which Jesus confronts the unbelief of His brothers and the hostility of His own nation. John sets the scene for us.

7:1–5 *After this, Jesus went around in Galilee, purposely staying away from Judea because the Jews there were waiting to take his life. But when the Jewish Feast of Tabernacles was near, Jesus' brothers said to him, "You ought to leave here and go to Judea, so that your disciples may see the miracles you do. No one who wants to become a public figure acts in secret. Since you are doing these things, show yourself to the world." For even his own brothers did not believe in him.*

The events described here took place six months after the feeding of the 5,000 and the discourse on the "bread of life" in the synagogue at Capernaum. If you would like to know some of the events that took place during those intervening months, you can trace them in the gospels of Matthew, Mark, and Luke. The synoptic gospels dwell at great length on the Galilean ministry of Jesus and fill in some of the gaps that John leaps over.

The opening words of chapter 7 have an ominous tone. There is murder in the air. Our Lord is aware of growing hostility against Him. The religious leaders in Judea are plotting His death.

The Feast of Tabernacles is at hand—the great feast of Israel, which occurs annually in early October. During this time, the people of Jerusalem build wooden booths with thatched roofs, and whole families actually move out of their houses and into these tiny, makeshift booths. This is to remind them of the forty years the nation spent wandering in the wilderness, living in tents.

As this feast approaches, the four brothers of Jesus come to Him. In Matthew 13:55, we find the names of these brothers: James and Jude (who, after they came to faith, later wrote the two New Testament letters which bear their names), and Joseph and Simon. Jesus also had sisters, but their names are not given in the New Testament.

Worldly Advice

These four brothers came as a kind of self-appointed Political Action Committee, giving advice to Jesus. Their advice to Him was four-fold and worldly in its tone. To put it in today's terms, they told Him:

(1) "Find a larger arena. Galilee is the sticks. Get down to Judea, to Jerusalem. That's where the action is."

(2) "Let your disciples see your miracles again. You need to keep in touch with your people and keep them charged up."

(3) "If you want to be a public figure, think about public relations! Advertise! Keep your name in front of the people!"

(4) "Give the people what they want. Keep up the miracles. That's what the people want to see, and that's what's going to get you noticed by the world."

Does this kind of advice sound familiar? These brothers were born 2,000 years too early. They could have made a fortune on Madison Avenue! Their advice sounds quite natural and practical to the twentieth century ear. In fact, these four brothers were very savvy by the world's standards.

You often hear this same kind of advice in many churches today. Faced with the command of Jesus to be witnesses and reach the whole world in our generation, many churches, Christian organizations, and Christian leaders say, "We have to go about this in a systematic, businesslike way. Let's hire some consultants. Let's do a survey. Let's do some demographic studies. Let's see what the people really want, and then let's tailor our message to their wants. Let's hire some publicists and an advertising agency to help us market our program. The gospel is no different from any other product; you just have to know how to sell it to the consumers!" That's the kind of advice Jesus got from His brothers.

But there is one other component of this picture that needs to be understood. John provides this missing component in verse 5: "For even his own brothers did not believe in him." Did Jesus' brothers love and respect Him? It's difficult to say for sure. Perhaps the advice they gave Him was couched in sarcasm and indicated a measure of scorn or jealousy. But I think that these brothers were sincere in advising Him to take His ministry in a more visible and public direction. I think they loved Him. But they didn't understand Him and they didn't believe His claims.

These brothers had never seen Jesus do miracles as a child. They didn't understand what He was doing as a Man. They didn't believe He was the promised Messiah. If they had believed, they never would have argued as they did. If they had viewed their brother as the Messiah, they wouldn't have advised Him in such a worldly way. They didn't see Him as any different from themselves. They couldn't figure Jesus out, they couldn't explain His miracles—but neither could they accept His claim to be the Messiah. That is the meaning of these words, "His own brothers did not believe in him."

If they had understood Jesus, they would have realized that God had already outlined a complete program for achieving the messianic objectives.

They could have read God's plan in Isaiah and the other prophets. All through the Old Testament, a carefully outlined plan for the Messiah's life and ministry was laid out, including His suffering and death. That plan would have silenced their worldly advice.

Jesus Responds

In response, Jesus describes the difference between His brothers and Himself, between their worldview and His. This is really the difference between God's way and man's ways.

7:6–10 *Therefore Jesus told them, "The right time for me has not yet come; for you any time is right. The world cannot hate you, but it hates me because I testify that what it does is evil. You go to the Feast. I am not yet going up to this Feast, because for me the right time has not yet come." Having said this, he stayed in Galilee.*

However, after his brothers had left for the Feast, he went also, not publicly, but in secret.

When He says, "For me the right time has not yet come," Jesus means the time has not come for Him to give Himself as the Messiah for the sins of the nation. The Feast of Tabernacles was not the place for the Messiah to be revealed. He was saying, in effect, "You're asking me to go up to the Feast of Tabernacles and make myself known as the Messiah. But that's not God's plan, it would never work, and so I'm not going to do it."

Jesus understood the Scriptures. He knew that God had appointed a pathway, a program, and a timetable for these events to occur. He knew that He would not be offered at the Feast of Tabernacles but at the Feast of Passover. The Feast of Tabernacles is in October, while Passover is in March or April, so He had six months left before His time was to come.

The reason He had to wait until Passover is that Passover was the ceremony that symbolized His own role as the Savior and the sacrifice for human sin. The Passover was instituted in Exodus, and it is the ceremony in which the blood of a sacrificial lamb is sprinkled over the doorposts as a symbol of Messiah's sacrificial death. That is why John the Baptist announced Jesus as "the Lamb of God who takes away the sin of the world."

It must have been a deep heartache for Jesus to know that His own family did not understand and did not believe in Him. There is nothing more hurtful than to be misunderstood by those closest to you. Yet this is what our Lord had to live with all the time.

Hated by the World

When Jesus said, "For you, any time is right," He meant that if His brothers went up to the feast they would only be fulfilling what everybody expected of them. They would be acting as normal religious Jews, fulfilling a religious duty which would not irritate anybody, raise any questions, or challenge any beliefs. That is why He goes on to say, "The world cannot hate you," because His brothers are living in sync with the world. They were not challenging or questioning the world. They were a part of the world.

But Jesus Himself was an offense to the world. He challenged sin and religious corruption. He exposed the hidden filth in the hearts of men. He called evil by its rightful name. He made people uncomfortable. He made people angry. He incurred the hatred—the *murderous* hatred!—of the world.

Jesus certainly would have had very little use for the polite euphemisms of our age—those sanitized, deodorized, "non-judgmental" little terms we have invented so that people don't have to feel guilty over such ugly words as "sin." We change the label on the bottle of poison and think we have changed the poison. Instead, we have made the poison even more dangerous by removing the warning label, by rubbing out the skull and crossbones!

In his book *Uncommon Sense,* columnist Cal Thomas observes,

> "Thief" is [a] word in danger of disappearing. Those accused and convicted of insider trading on Wall Street, of cheating on their income tax, or of padding their expense accounts view themselves as practitioners of "creative accounting," not as thieves. . . .
>
> Government officials "misspeak" themselves. Often a better word to describe their pronouncements is "lying," but hardly anyone admits to being a liar anymore. . . .
>
> Sex has produced a small glossary of words specially crafted to relieve all sense of guilt and personal responsibility for the way people behave. . . . "Sexual preference" may be the least judgmental words ever created. "Sexually active" are two others. . . . Fornication is defined as "human sexual intercourse other than between a man and his wife, or sexual intercourse between a spouse and an unmarried person." Isn't *this* what we mean by "sexually active"? Then why not say so?[1]

Jesus will not play word games with us. Euphemisms are designed to cloud thinking and conceal truth. Jesus came to open our eyes and expose the truth. He arouses the instinctive antagonism of the heart that wants to conceal the true nature of evil. That is why the world hated Him and murdered Him. That is why the world continues to oppose Him today.

So Jesus says to His brothers, "You go. I'm staying awhile." Some have accused Jesus of lying to them. But Jesus did not say, "I am not going," but "I am not *yet* going." He will stay awhile in Galilee because His time is not yet fully come. But after His brothers leave for the Feast, as John records in verse 10, He will also go down to Jerusalem—not publicly, but privately; not as the Messiah, but as just another Jewish pilgrim.

Now we see why Jesus did not want to go to the Feast with His brothers. He did not want to go in the company of His disciples or His brothers, because that would have attracted attention to Him. So He sent His brothers ahead. But He Himself went alone, incognito, so as not to draw attention to Himself.

Whispered Rumors

Arriving at the Feast, Jesus found Jerusalem abuzz with rumors about Him. In the intervening months He had become a national sensation. Reports of His miracles and His teaching had preceded Him.

7:11–13 *Now at the Feast the Jews were watching for him and asking, "Where is that man?"*

Among the crowds there was widespread whispering about him. Some said, "He is a good man."

Others replied, "No, he deceives the people." But no one would say anything publicly about him for fear of the Jews.

Those words capture the atmosphere of the feast. It is an atmosphere of polarization. Some said, "He's a good man! Why, He healed my aunt Lizzie! He opened the eyes of a blind beggar I know!" Others said, "No, He's a deceiver! He teaches people to break the law of Moses by violating the Sabbath. Haven't you heard what our leaders say about Him? You'll stay clear of this man if you know what's good for you!"

So the word had spread about Jesus—not openly, but as whispered rumors. There was fear in that place. The Jewish leaders controlled the people. They were like thought police, or the Gestapo (that's a bitter irony, but true!). Everyone was afraid of being hauled up before the religious leaders of the Jews, so all talk of Jesus was guarded talk.

Teaching That Comes From God

Here we learn why Jesus went to this Feast. He didn't go publicly as the Messiah. He went because this Feast would give Him yet another opportunity to teach the crowds, and call men and women to Himself.

7:14–18 *Not until halfway through the Feast did Jesus go up to the temple courts and begin to teach. The Jews were amazed and asked, "How did this man get such learning without having studied?"*

Jesus answered, "My teaching is not my own. It comes from him who sent me. If any one chooses to do God's will, he will find out whether my teaching comes from God or whether I speak on my own. He who speaks on his own does so to gain honor for himself, but he who works for the honor of the one who sent him is a man of truth; there is nothing false about him.

As we read these words, we have to marvel at the teaching of Jesus! I've often wished I could have heard His words as He spoke so powerfully that even His enemies were amazed at His ability. We clearly see the *authority* of Jesus' teaching: He did not speak like the other teachers of Israel.

According to the text, the Jews ask themselves, "How did this man get such learning without having studied?" In the original language, the text literally says, "How does this man know His letters so well?" The "letters" in the text refer to the Scriptures. Jesus was teaching from the Scriptures. He was taking the ancient prophecies and other passages and expounding them and explaining them.

But He did not teach like the rabbis did. In that day (and this is still true today), every Jewish rabbi began his teaching with words such as, "the sages say . . ." or, "the Talmud teaches . . ." or, "the Mishnah explains . . . ." But Jesus never quoted any authority other than Scripture. He would say, as is repeatedly recorded in John's gospel, "Truly, truly, I say unto you." When He talked like that, people listened. They were completely riveted by what He said.

And when the people asked Jesus to reveal the origin of His teaching, He didn't say, "I'm self-educated. I studied and worked hard to learn the Scriptures on my own." He did not claim to be a self-made man. Rather, He gave all the glory to God the Father. "My teaching is not my own," He said in verse 16. "It comes from him who sent me."

There is a beautiful passage in Isaiah 50 where the prophet predicts the very words of the Messiah:

The Sovereign Lord has given me an instructed tongue,
to know the word that sustains the weary.
He wakens me morning by morning,
wakens my ear to listen like one being taught.[2]

That is the source of Jesus' teaching. That is why His teaching has power. That is why His teaching accords completely with reality.

A friend once wrote me a letter in which he expressed what he wanted in a preacher: "I want to hear a man who knows God and has seen Him recently. I don't want to listen to His press agent." That is how most people feel: They want to hear from somebody who has truly been taught by God.

Jesus was that kind of preacher and teacher.

The Key to Understanding

In verse 17, we find one of the most remarkable passages of our Lord's teaching. Here He gives us the key to understanding His words: "If any one chooses to do God's will, he will find out whether my teaching comes from God or whether I speak on my own." Do you ever wonder if Jesus actually was what He claimed to be? Do you have trouble at times understanding what He is saying in these passages? If so, His answer is: Practice what He says. Obey His words. Repent of your sins. Come to Him. Model your life after His. Treat people as He treated people. Then you will know—not just intellectually, but in your will, emotions, and experience—that Jesus is who He claims to be and His words are truth. That is a knowledge no one can take away from you, because you will have proved it in the toughest, most demanding laboratory of all: The laboratory of life!

This is a principle that runs all through life: You learn by doing. A surgeon may learn all that the medical books can teach him, but until he takes scalpel in hand and makes his first incision, he never really knows what surgery is all about. The same is true in any field: We must experience the reality. We must learn by doing. When you do what Jesus says, you learn what life is truly all about.

Some years ago I met a hard-bitten old Marine general, one of those tough, self-sufficient characters, accustomed to giving orders and having them carried out immediately. After he had retired, he became a Christian and grew in his faith and in Christian character with astonishing rapidity. Everyone who knew him saw the change. Certainly, they had always respected him as a leader. But with his conversion they saw a compassion, an understanding, a new spirit of patience develop in him that was never there before. He became warm and genial toward old bitter enemies.

When I asked one of this general's friends what had happened in his life, he replied, "When the General reads something in the Scriptures, he obeys it immediately." That is why he grew so fast.

Yet some people who have been exposed to the gospel for years and years *never* seem to grow! They may have a lot of Bible knowledge or a little—yet their character is not changed, and their faith seems shallow. Why? Because they do not take that teaching and turn it into real-life experience. They do not learn by doing.

Verse 18 reveals the mark of an authentic learner: "He who speaks on his own does so to gain honor for himself, but he who works for the honor of the one who sent him is a man of truth; there is nothing false about him." That was true, of course, of Jesus. He did not seek His own glory. He did not care whether He spoke to one person or a great crowd in the temple courts. What He said was always true and always compassionate, and He did not care whether anybody praised Him or not.

I have learned that if somebody is obviously seeking a reputation as a Bible teacher and seeing to it that he is recognized and publicized, then much of what he says is fraudulent. Such people may teach some of the truth, but their hearts are wrong. So even though much of what they say is true, it will not have God's power behind it. It will not accomplish much.

But those teachers who are intent on the message and on obedience, and who care nothing about publicity, are the ones you can trust as a teacher. They may not have a lot of flash. They may not have a dynamic preaching style or a huge following. But when they speak, God's own power is embedded in every word. It is God, not the man, who gets the glory every time.

Judge With Right Judgment

In the next section, we see our Lord's skill in public debate.

7:19–24 *[Jesus said:] "Has not Moses given you the law? Yet not one of you keeps the law. Why are you trying to kill me?"*

"You are demon-possessed," the crowd answered. "Who is trying to kill you?"

Jesus said to them, "I did one miracle and you are all astonished. Yet, because Moses gave you circumcision (though actually it did not come from Moses, but from the patriarchs), you circumcise a child on the Sabbath. Now if a child can be circumcised on the Sabbath so that the law of Moses may not be broken, why are you angry with me for healing the whole man on the Sabbath? Stop judging by mere appearances, and make a right judgment."

This interaction, of course, is based on Jesus' healing of the invalid at the pool of Bethesda on the Sabbath. The leaders of the Jews were accusing Jesus of being a lawbreaker because He did that. Jesus' argument is, "Why are you so hostile to me? Why are you seeking to murder me? You are all law-breakers, yet you accuse me of breaking the law!"

The crowd interrupts, "You're crazy! What are you talking about? Nobody's trying to kill you!" They are obviously ignorant of the intrigue of their leaders and the plots to destroy Jesus.

But knowing the intent of the leaders, Jesus continues His argument. He says, in effect, "I made a man well on the Sabbath and your leaders found it shocking! But in obedience to the law of Moses, your leaders circumcise infant boys on the Sabbath day!" What was His point? Circumcision, remember, is an act of ceremonial mutilation, in which the foreskin is cut away and removed as a sign of putting away the evil of the flesh. He is saying, in other words, "If, in obedience to the law, you can mutilate a little boy on the Sabbath, is it not better for me to *heal* on the Sabbath and restore a man to wholeness?"

It is a powerful, unassailable argument. There is apparently no response anyone can make to this reasoning, so the Lord closes the dialogue with a warning: "Stop judging by mere appearances, and make a right judgment." That is, don't just judge by external, superficial, legalistic rules. Get your values straight. Try to understand the reality behind the symbols. Look at matters from God's point of view. Only then can you make a righteous judgment. This message is as clear and applicable today as it ever was.

As a society, we have our values upside down. Our government creates entire bureaucracies to monitor minute amounts of suspected carcinogens in our food, air, and water—yet it also pays subsidies to farmers for producing one of the worst, most highly cancer-causing substances around: tobacco. We are told we must save the whales, yet we allow unborn babies to be slaughtered at a rate of 3,000 abortions per day. School teachers are allowed to teach witchcraft and New Age philosophy in our public schools, yet the Bible, prayer, and the Ten Commandments are banned. We sentence peaceful pro-life activists to prison and we turn convicted repeat killers and rapists loose on society.

And we deceive ourselves. The words of Jesus come home to our generation as strongly as they did to His: "Do not judge by appearance, but judge with right judgment."

The central question of this passage of John's gospel is this: *Is Jesus for real?* That is a question you can only truly answer after you have put Him to the test, after you have experienced Him. His words are strong and confrontational. His life is a paradox and a challenge.

But if you test His words in the laboratory of life, you will find the truth— guaranteed! Yes, Jesus is for real. He is the greatest reality you can ever know.

Chapter Twenty-Two

For Those Who Thirst

John 7:25–52

Owen Roberts, the Welsh social reformer, became concerned about the pathetic child-labor conditions in England during the nineteenth century. To research an anti-child-labor pamphlet he was writing, he went into the coal mines. There he found boys—some as young as nine or ten years old—covered with coal-dust, working in dangerous and rugged conditions deep in the earth.

Roberts found one boy, about twelve years old, coughing and wheezing in the dark tunnel of the mine. The boy was breaking big chunks of coal into smaller chunks, then separating the shale from the coal. "How're you doing, son?" he called to the boy.

"I pull my weight, sir."

Roberts produced a water jug he had tied to his belt and uncorked it, offering it to the boy. "Thirsty?"

"Some," said the boy, taking the jug and tilting it to his blackened lips. He drank deeply, then passed the jug back to Roberts. "Thank you, sir," he said.

"Tell me, son," said the Welshman, "do you know Jesus?"

"No," the boy said, dead serious. "Nobody by that name works around here. Try asking around the north shaft."

Owen Roberts' heart was broken that day. Down in the darkness, deep under the earth, he had found a thirsty boy—thirsty for water, but even more thirsty for *living* water, for the one who alone brings eternal life. This young boy, who spent most of his rugged existence in darkness, grimed with coal-dust, had never before heard the name of Jesus.

As we approach the last half of John chapter 7, we find a message of hope—a message of cool, refreshing streams of living water—for those who thirst.

Confusion

Jesus is teaching in the temple courts, and it is a striking scene. The most impressive aspect of this scene is the boldness and courage of Jesus. We have already seen the mounting hostility and opposition toward Jesus, and the threats of murder leveled against Him by the Jewish authorities. Yet Jesus openly preaches in the courts of the temple. In fact, He almost seems to challenge the authorities to do anything about it!

7:25–27 *At that point some of the people of Jerusalem began to ask, "Isn't this the man they are trying to kill? Here he is, speaking publicly, and they are not saying a word to him. Have the authorities really concluded that he is the Christ? But we know where this man is from; when the Christ comes, no one will know where he is from."*

Notice the expression "the Christ" which appears twice in these verses. To be honest, I wish that term "the Christ" were not used in the translation. "Christ" is a Greek word that means "the Anointed," and it is the Greek form of the Hebrew term, "Messiah." Many people think that Jesus' "last name" is "Christ" in the same way that my last name is "Stedman." But no, "Christ" is not Jesus' *name;* it is His *title.* He is not named "Jesus Christ"; rather, He is Jesus the Messiah, the Christ, the Anointed One of God. When you see the term "the Christ" throughout the rest of this passage, I would encourage you to mentally substitute the words "the Messiah" instead.

As we examine this passage, we find that Jesus is speaking to the people boldly and courageously—and He has stirred up a great deal of confusion in the minds of His listeners. The people are amazed at this teaching—and they are even more amazed that the leaders of the people haven't moved against Him. "Isn't this the man they are trying to kill?" they ask.

In fact, many of the people are so impressed by Jesus that they half-believe that the authorities are convinced that Jesus really is the Messiah. But others in the crowd are quick to point out that the legend of Messiah states that He would appear suddenly, and no one would know where He came from. Malachi 3:1 predicts that God's Messenger (that is, the Messiah) would suddenly appear in the temple. The rabbis took this verse to mean that no one would know His background.

So these people say, "How could Jesus be the Messiah? We know that He comes from Nazareth, in Galilee. He cannot be the Messiah. The Messiah is supposed to arise out of nowhere!" So the people were confused as to what to believe about Jesus.

The Truth-Teller

As always, Jesus cuts through the confusion and gets right to the heart of the matter.

7:28–29 *Then Jesus, still teaching in the temple courts, cried out, "Yes, you know me, and you know where I am from. I am not here on my own, but he who sent me is true. You do not know him, but I know him because I am from him and he sent me."*

The NIV translation renders Jesus' first line in this response as a statement. But I am convinced it is actually a question: "Do you really know me? Do you really know where I am from?" It is a rhetorical question which leaves unspoken the true answer: "No, you do not, for my true origin is not Nazareth. It is not even Bethlehem, where I was born. My true origin is heaven. I come from the Father." This is what Jesus has been saying all along—that He is the true bread from heaven, that He came from God. This is our Lord's argument throughout the gospel.

The great American statesman Henry Clay once attempted to give a speech, but found it difficult to talk over the heckling of his opponents. The hecklers were Southern slave owners, angry with his attempts to take away their right to own human beings as property. So they hissed, loudly and continuously, throughout his speech. Finally, Clay stopped his speech and directed the audience's attention to the slave owners who were trying to drown him out with their hissing. "Gentlemen," Clay announced, "that hissing is the sound you hear when the waters of truth fall upon the fires of hell!"

Jesus is in an even more volatile situation than Henry Clay. He is speaking the truth, boldly and clearly—but His truth isn't so much like a sprinkling of water, but a bucket of gasoline falling on the fires of hell! The result is not hissing, but an explosion!

The Jewish leaders understand that when Jesus says, "He who sent me is true," He is talking about God. And when Jesus says, "You do not know him," He is accusing them of not knowing God! He is indicting the highest religious leaders of Israel for godlessness! Jesus spoke these words deliberately, with precision, knowing exactly what reaction they would evoke.

Is Jesus a troublemaker who delights in taunting these Jewish leaders? Does He take pleasure in overturning the apple cart, so to speak, and forcing His opponents to hear the very words that will enrage them even more? No. Jesus is not that kind of person. He is not a troublemaker, not a mere rebel and rabblerouser. Jesus is a truth-teller in a world of self-delusion. He is an overthrower of lies. He is the personification of truth.

There are few better ways to get yourself in trouble than by telling the truth. Jesus proves the validity of an old Arab proverb which says, "He who tells the truth should keep one foot in the stirrup." Jesus is exposing religious evil, which is homicidal in its fury. There will be a backlash. Those who cannot stand to hear the truth will soon rise up with hammer and nails, and they will crucify the truth on a cross of wood.

On God's Timetable

The reaction to Jesus' words is predictable—and potentially violent. The backlash has begun.

7:30–31 *At this they tried to seize him, but no one laid a hand on him, because his time had not yet come. Still, many in the crowd put their faith in him. They said, "When the Christ [the Messiah] comes, will he do more miraculous signs than this man?"*

That is an accurate description of what always happens when the good news of Jesus is preached, truly and with authority and power. If the truth is proclaimed, a two-fold reaction always results: (1) Some people get upset and angry. (2) Some believe.

When Jesus preached, many responded positively. Here at last was Someone who stripped away the illusions, tore down the facades, and shone the light of truth on the reality of their condition. Jesus forced them to see and understand their sinfulness—but He also showed them how much God loved them and how much God wanted to heal and restore them.

What did Jesus do when these two reactions emerged? He kept right on preaching!

7:32–36 *The Pharisees heard the crowd whispering such things about him. Then the chief priests and the Pharisees sent temple guards to arrest him.*

Jesus said, "I am with you for only a short time, and then I go to the one who sent me. You will look for me, but you will not find me; and where I am, you cannot come."

The Jews said to one another, "Where does this man intend to go that we cannot find him? Will he go where our people live scattered among the Greeks, and teach the Greeks? What did he mean when he said, 'You will look for me, but you will not find me,' and 'Where I am, you cannot come'?"

Notice how clearly and strongly Jesus understands God's timetable, and how assuredly He carries out that timetable. He knows that His time has not yet come, and therefore no one can touch Him or deflect Him from His course. He speaks boldly and courageously—yet the unseen protecting hand of God protects Him from the hostility that His words arouse.

We see this principle at work throughout the Scriptures. For example, in the book of Acts, when the apostle Paul first preached in Corinth, he experienced daunting opposition that threatened to deflect him from his course. But Jesus appeared to him in a vision and said, "Do not be afraid; keep on speaking, do not be silent. For I am with you, and no one is going to attack and harm you."[1] God was invisibly protecting His messenger.

We see the same principle in the Old Testament. That is why Daniel was so comfortable and unafraid in the lion's den. Can you imagine ordering a lion to lie down to be your pillow? Daniel could do so, knowing that God had shut the mouths of the lions and they would not hurt him.

Here, in John 7, our Lord senses this same protection. He is confident that no one can touch Him, and He continues His ministry with the awareness that all the opposition against Him can go no further than God's mighty hand will permit.

This is a great encouragement to us today. If we are walking in the will of God and the strength of God we can be confident that nothing can happen to us except what God allows. And when He allows it—even if it means suffering, even it if means death—then it is the right time for it to happen. That is one of the great lessons of the Christian life.

Does this mean we should be presumptuous and take chances with the life God has given us? Of course not. Someone once said to the great radio Bible teacher Dr. J. Vernon McGee, "I have been studying the Bible, and I believe I am absolutely safe in God's hand. No matter what I do or how dangerous it may be, God will protect me. Even if I step out into a busy street against a red light, I will be perfectly safe if my time has not yet come." But Dr. McGee replied, "If you're foolish enough to step out into traffic against a red light in rush hour—brother, your time has come!"

We learned this truth when Jesus was tempted in the wilderness: We are not to tempt God. Just as He refused to fling Himself from the pinnacle of the temple, we should not be so foolish as to fling ourselves into oncoming traffic! God honors our boldness in speaking and acting for Him. But He does not honor our foolishness or recklessness.

Now, observe our Lord's boldness at this point. He announces what He is going to do: He is going to die. He says, "I am with you for only a short time, and then I go to the one who sent me. You will look for me, but you will not find me; and where I am, you cannot come."

This statement throws His hearers into confusion. "What is He talking about?" they wonder. "Is He going to go out among the Dispersion, the Jews living in foreign lands? Is He going to teach the Gentiles? What does He mean?"

Jesus reserves His answer until the final day of the Feast. In the next section, He will preach one last time at the Feast, and He will talk about the process by which all that He has promised will be fulfilled. And again, His words will divide the opinions of the people.

Living Water

7:37–39 *On the last and greatest day of the Feast, Jesus stood and said in a loud voice, "If a man is thirsty, let him come to me and drink. Whoever believes in me, as the Scripture has said, streams of living water will flow from within him." By this he meant the Spirit, whom those who believed in him were later to receive. Up to that time the Spirit had not been given, since Jesus had not yet been glorified.*

John writes these words years after the day of Pentecost, when the Spirit was given to live in the hearts of believers. But when Jesus was still on earth the Spirit had not yet been given to people as an indwelling presence. Yes, the Spirit of God has always been present everywhere in the world, both before and after Pentecost—but not as an indwelling presence. But here Jesus gives a hint as to how God's timetable is going to be fulfilled. Later, in the great Upper Room Discourse in John 13 through 17, Jesus will teach plainly about the coming of the Holy Spirit, but for now He teaches it by means of a beautiful symbol—the symbol of living water.

Jesus uses the occasion of the last day of the Feast to connect the symbolism of the Feast to the truths He wants to teach. Traditionally, the Feast had been a seven-day celebration. During each of those seven days, one of the chief priests would lead a procession through the Kidron Valley to the Pool of Siloam. He filled a golden pitcher from the waters of the pool and carried it back to the temple and poured it over the altar. This ceremony served to remind the people of the days in the wilderness when God, through Moses, gave them water out of a rock.

But this last day, the greatest day of the Feast, was actually an eighth day which had been tacked onto the original seven-day Feast. On this day, there was no ceremony of pouring water over the altar. So Jesus seized this opportunity to present Himself as a symbol. "If a man is thirsty, let him come to me and drink," He said. "Whoever believes in me, as the Scripture has said, streams of living water will flow from within him."

Jesus is drawing upon the symbolism of the Feast to make a point about Himself. He is saying, in effect, "For seven days, you have seen a ceremony which looks back to when God, through Moses, gave you water from a rock in the wilderness. Well, I am the Rock. Today I announce that if you are thirsty, if you are in the dry wilderness, come to me and I will give you living water to drink!"

The apostle Paul affirms the meaning of these symbols when he writes that the Israelites who followed Moses in the desert all "drank the same spiritual drink; for they drank from the spiritual rock that accompanied them, and that rock was Christ."[2] God was teaching the same truth to the Israelites in the wilderness that He teaches us today: Jesus is the Rock from which we can drink and satisfy the thirst of our hearts.

What does Jesus mean by the word "thirst"? Notice that He places no limits on the meaning of that word! He simply says, "If a [person] is thirsty . . . ." People thirst for many things. Some thirst for meaning, significance, a sense of belonging, a sense that they are *somebody.* To those, Jesus says, "Come to me; I will give you the significance you thirst for." Some thirst for the power to accomplish things. To them, Jesus says, "Come to me, drink of me, listen to my words, and I will empower you to do great things for God."

Thirst is a powerful symbol. Physical thirst is the most powerful drive known to man. Human beings can go for days and weeks without the satisfaction of other drives. We can go without food, without comfort, without sex, without happiness for weeks, and still survive. But no one can live very long without water. When you are thirsty—truly, searingly thirsty—that drive to find water becomes a singleminded, desperate, driving obsession. You can think of nothing but how to satisfy that thirst.

That is the symbol Jesus uses here. If you feel driven, restless, thirsty, desperate for satisfaction in your life, then He invites you: "Come unto me and drink, and I will give you the Spirit, I will empower you and give you significance, I will satisfy your thirst."

Streams of Blessing

It is important to notice what Jesus says—and does not say—in this passage. He does not say, "If anyone comes to me and drinks, I will satisfy his wants." That is what many people today think Christianity is all about. There is a distorted version of the Christian message which says, "Come to Jesus, and He will give you everything you want. He will keep you healthy and make you rich and give you that Cadillac and that big house you want. He will meet all the selfish, material desires of your heart."

But that is not what Jesus says. There are other passages in the gospels where Jesus says that God cares about our lives and will meet our basic human needs. But even that is not what Jesus is talking about here. He says,

"Whoever believes in me . . . streams of living water will flow from within him." Jesus is saying that a sign that the Spirit is at work in you is that *rivers of blessing will flow out of you to others!* If the Spirit is truly flowing through you, then your concern is to reach out and help others in need. When you do, you will find the satisfaction of your thirst—a deep satisfaction of the heart.

Three Results

John traces three results that follow these gracious words of Jesus. First, we again see a clash of opinions among His hearers.

7:40–43 *On hearing his words, some of the people said, "Surely this man is the Prophet."*

[Note: The Prophet is the one Moses predicted in Deuteronomy 18:15, when he said, "The Lord your God will raise up for you a prophet like me from among your own brothers."]

Others said, "He is the Christ [the Messiah]."

Still others asked, "How can the Christ [the Messiah] come from Galilee? Does not the Scripture say that the Christ will come from David's family and from Bethlehem, the town where David lived?" Thus the people were divided because of Jesus.

Second, we see a strange, almost laughable impotence among Jesus' enemies. They don't know what to do with this amazing Man!

7:44–46 *Some wanted to seize him, but no one laid a hand on him.*

Finally the temple guards went back to the chief priests and Pharisees, who asked them, "Why didn't you bring him in?"

"No one ever spoke the way this man does," the guards declared.

It is hard to read this story without seeing the almost slapstick humor of it. The chief priests send out the temple guards to arrest Jesus—and they are flabbergasted when those same guards return emptyhanded. "You knew where He was!" the priests exclaim. "Why didn't you bring Him?" The guards' stammering reply leaves them looking as ridiculous as the Keystone Cops! "Well," they say, "it's kind of hard to explain, but as we were listening to Him, He somehow got through to us. We got so wrapped up in what He was saying that we forgot to arrest Him! We've never heard anybody speak like this man!"

This is an astounding scene: Men who are sent out to arrest Jesus find themselves arrested *by* Jesus! Here is a powerful statement of the kind of Person Jesus is. Have you ever encountered this Jesus before? Do you know Jesus in this way? Have you ever *really* listened to His powerful, upsetting, challenging words before? What is this arresting Man saying to you right now?

In Chapter 3: "The *Real* Jesus," I said that John's gospel is a lens that will help us see Jesus in a whole new way. By returning to this eyewitness account of the life of Jesus, we can remove many of the misconceptions about Jesus that we have unconsciously absorbed over the years. This passage provides one of those startling images of Christ I was thinking of when I wrote those words. Here, in John 7, we find the depth of Jesus' character and the power of His personality drawn for us in bold lines and rich colors. We see the power of His personality not only in the words He said, but in the way people reacted to Him. Perhaps you have never met *this* Jesus before! But this depiction of Jesus—which is so unlike the stained glass distortions and the insipid, almost effeminate images of Jesus that so many people have accepted—*this* is the *real Jesus!*

The third result of Jesus' speech is the bitter hatred of His enemies. After the temple guards return without Jesus, the Pharisees give them the third degree.

7:47–49 *"You mean he has deceived you also?" the Pharisees retorted. "Has any of the rulers or of the Pharisees believed in him? No! But this mob that knows nothing of the law—there is a curse on them."*

For the guards, the Pharisees express anger and derision. For themselves, they express arrogance and pompous superiority. And as for the people they have been appointed to rule and lead and care for—they call the people an ignorant mob and they put a curse on them! These are bitter, snobbish elitists of the very worst kind!

Enter Nicodemus

But now notice that a character from John chapter 3 re-enters the drama: Nicodemus, a Pharisee, a man whose life has already been impacted by Jesus. John records this exchange among the Pharisees.

7:50–52 Nicodemus, who had gone to Jesus earlier and who was one of their own number [that is, a Pharisee], asked, "Does our law condemn a man without first hearing him to find out what he is doing?"

They replied, "Are you from Galilee, too? Look into it, and you will find that a prophet does not come out of Galilee."

Nicodemus raises a word of caution: "In condemning this man, aren't you all in danger of violating the law which you claim to uphold?" Notice: It is a question, not an accusation. Nicodemus is being very careful. He sees how angry and murderous his fellow Pharisees are, and he does not want to come out and actually defend Jesus. Instead, he gently raises a procedural point, hoping to cool the wrath of the religious leaders.

Nicodemus is no fool. He knows the evil and vindictiveness these fanatics are capable of. That is why he went to Jesus secretly by night in John 3. And that is why he speaks very cautiously and noncommittally in John 7. And the response of his fellow Pharisees shows his caution is well-justified, for they instantly turn on him: "Are you from Galilee, too?" they sneer, their words dripping with sarcasm. "Look into it, and you will find that a prophet does not come out of Galilee."

It is important to note that, if you take these words at face value, the Pharisees have made a big mistake. Three prophets had already arisen from Galilee. Jonah was clearly from Galilee, and the prophets Nahum and Hosea were very likely from this region as well. The Pharisees knew their Old Testament; I doubt they would have made such an erroneous statement of fact, even in a state of irrational anger.

One of the oldest manuscripts of John's gospel indicates that they did not say "a prophet" but "the prophet." In other words, I believe they are referring to the Prophet predicted by Moses in Deuteronomy 18. But that is not a major matter. The primary thrust of this passage is what it reveals about the character of the opponents of Jesus: They were sarcastic, arrogant, and contemptuous even of the people they were supposed to lead and serve. Clearly, the stinging condemnation Jesus has leveled at their hearts is well-targeted and well-deserved. He has told the truth about these men, and the truth has struck an exposed nerve—and that is why they wanted to kill Him.

The Promise of Jesus

I want to close this chapter, however, not on the negative note where John leaves us, but on those gracious words of Jesus: "If a man is thirsty, let him come to me and drink." What are you thirsting for? Satisfaction? Meaning? A sense of belonging? You won't find it in any of the things this world prizes so highly—material success, a faster car, a bigger house.

True satisfaction for a thirsty heart is found only by drinking deeply of Jesus, by drawing upon His presence, by leaning on His strength. As you seek your satisfaction in Him, a change will take place within you. You will find yourself reaching out to those around you who are hurting. The living water of the Holy Spirit will spring up in your life and flow out to others as a river of blessing. In return, meaning, significance, empowerment, and a true sense of love will flow back into your life.

That is the promise of Jesus to all those who thirst.

Chapter Twenty-Three

Judging the Judges

John 8:1–11

In his book *Mere Christianity*, C. S. Lewis writes,

> If anyone thinks that Christians regard unchastity [sexual sin] as the supreme vice, he is quite wrong. The sins of the flesh are bad, but they are the least bad of all sins. All the worst pleasures are purely spiritual: the pleasure of putting other people in the wrong, of bossing and patronizing and spoiling sport, and backbiting; the pleasures of power, of hatred. For there are two things inside me, competing with the human self which I must try to become. They are the Animal self and the Diabolical self. The Diabolical self is the worst of the two. That is why a cold, self-righteous prig who goes regularly to church may be far nearer to hell than a prostitute. But, of course, it is better to be neither.[1]

In John 8, Jesus confronts a group of "cold, self-righteous prigs" and a woman who is guilty of open sexual sin. He deals so wisely and graciously with each that this story has become a favorite of many.

We need to make an observation at the outset: There is some controversy among Bible scholars regarding this passage. Some feel that it has been inserted into the gospel of John at this point, that it is not truly part of John's original gospel. It's true that various ancient manuscripts place this portion of Scripture at different places in John's gospel. In fact, some ancient manuscripts actually place it after the 21st chapter of Luke! And some omit it altogether.

While some Bible scholars have expressed doubt as to the authenticity of this story, most scholars agree that this event did occur. It certainly is consistent with John's writing style, and with the style and substance of our Lord's teaching and character. I believe it is placed here at this point in John's gospel because it so beautifully illustrates the statement of Jesus in John 7:24: "Stop judging by mere appearances, and make a right judgment." This passage also connects with the end of chapter 7 by illustrating the efforts of the Pharisees to entrap and corner Jesus—efforts which, as we shall see, fail miserably.

A Story of Contrasts

7:53–8:11 Then each went to his own home.

But Jesus went to the Mount of Olives. At dawn he appeared again in the temple courts, where all the people gathered around him, and he sat down to teach them. The teachers of the law and the Pharisees brought in a woman caught in adultery. They made her stand before the group and said to Jesus, "Teacher, this woman was caught in the act of adultery. In the Law Moses commanded us to stone such women. Now what do you say?" They were using this question as a trap, in order to have a basis for accusing him.

But Jesus bent down and started to write on the ground with his finger. When they kept on questioning him, he straightened up and said to them, "If any one of you is without sin, let him be the first to throw a stone at her." Again he stooped down and wrote on the ground.

At this, those who heard began to go away one at a time, the older ones first, until only Jesus was left, with the woman still standing there. Jesus straightened up and asked her, "Woman, where are they? Has no one condemned you?"

"No one, sir," she said.

"Then neither do I condemn you," Jesus declared. "Go now and leave your life of sin."

This is a powerful, unforgettable story, filled with striking contrasts. The first contrast we note is the contrast between Jesus and the people. He is a great Teacher with an enormous following among the people—yet when everyone else goes home at the end of the discourse in chapter 7, He has no home to go to. He lives out in the open on the slopes of the Mount of Olives. This and other passages confirm that He spent many nights alone on this mountainside. Even His disciples had homes to stay in, but Jesus was quite literally homeless.

If this event is accurately, chronologically positioned in John's gospel, immediately following the Feast of Tabernacles, then it must have occurred in early October. I have been in Jerusalem at that time of the year and have found the nights to be very cold at that altitude. You may remember that once, when a young man told Jesus he would follow Him wherever He went, Jesus said, "Foxes have holes and birds of the air have nests, but the Son of Man has no place to lay his head."[2]

There is a poignancy in this image that stirs our emotions: The Savior of the world, huddled under an olive tree, sleeping alone on a cold October night on the Mount of Olives.

Another contrast we note in this passage is the contradiction between the initial self-righteous attitude of these self-appointed judges and the verdict of guilt which they later pronounce upon themselves. The scribes and Pharisees bring a woman before Jesus and they say, "Teacher, this woman was caught in the act of adultery. In the Law Moses commanded us to stone such women. Now what do you say?"

They think they have Jesus cornered. It's an airtight case. You cannot read this story, however, without wondering, "Where is the *man* who was caught in adultery?" These religious leaders had caught the woman, says verse 4, *"in the act."* There had to be two people involved in this act; only one is brought before Jesus. Why?

Some Bible commentators suggest that perhaps the scribes and Pharisees knew the man—he might have even been one of them!—so they let him go. We have no way of knowing. But we do know that this story indicates that a double standard existed. The woman was condemned; the man was nowhere in sight.

The scribes and Pharisees referred to the law in the book of Leviticus, where God, speaking through Moses, said that adultery was punishable by stoning. They knew that Jesus was the Friend of Sinners, and that He associated with publicans and sinners rather than the religious and the respectable, the rich and famous. They expected Jesus to turn this woman loose—and that would be a contradiction of the law of Moses. Then they would have Him! Not one of them even remotely anticipated how Jesus would solve this seeming dilemma.

Written in the Dust

He began by stooping down and writing with His finger in the dust. What would you give to know what He wrote? This question has intrigued scholars and students through the ages. Once, while reading in the book of Jeremiah, I came across a passage that struck me as a possible indication of what Jesus wrote:

> O Lord, the hope of Israel,
> all who forsake you will be put to shame.
> Those who turn away from you will be written

in the dust
because they have forsaken the Lord,
the spring of living water.[3]

This prophetic passage suggests that Jesus wrote the names of the woman's accusers in the dust. Whatever He wrote, the scribes and Pharisees apparently misunderstood Him. They thought He was stalling for time, and they kept pressing Him, asking Him again and again to answer them and tell them what He would do.

Jesus Upholds the Law

Finally, Jesus stood, looked them right in the eye, and spoke those famous, heart-piercing words, "If any of you is without sin, let him be the first to throw a stone at her." These words stab them in the conscience. They are stunned, they are speechless. He didn't let the woman go, as they expected. In fact, He completely upheld the law of Moses. He said, in effect, "Yes, she must be stoned. Now—let us appoint a qualified executioner. Which of you is qualified? Are you? Or you? Or you? All it takes is one sinless person and we can carry out the penalty of the law."

Let's be very clear on one thing: Adultery is no minor matter. It is a very serious sin. It destroys relationships that have been bonded by the holy sacrament of marriage. It involves the worst and most sordid kinds of lies. It involves betrayal. It defiles the marriage bed. It hurts spouses, it injures children, it brings spiritual and emotional damage to those who engage in it, and it leads to a breakdown of the fabric of our society. There is a very good reason God has outlawed the act of adultery in His law.

Jesus is very clear in upholding God's injunction against adultery. He is not winking at sin. Sexual sin is no minor faux pas that God merely overlooks. It is a serious, damaging sin, and we see that clearly when we examine what Jesus says to this woman and her accusers. In the eyes of justice, apart from grace, the sin of adultery is worthy of death—and Jesus upholds this truth, much to the surprise of the scribes and Pharisees.

But that is not all Jesus does. He also pierced the hearts and consciences of the woman's accusers. He says to them, in effect, "You accuse this woman of sin—and you are right. But you are no better than she is. Your hearts are filled with murder and hatred." Her life meant nothing to these men. They were willing to exploit this woman and her sin, even see her stoned to death, in order to get to Jesus.

But Jesus read their hearts, and what He saw was worse even than her sin. Someone has well said, "If the secret thoughts of a man were written on his forehead, he would never remove his hat!" It should shake us and disturb us to the marrow to know that God, the eternal judge, reads our hearts and knows our secret thoughts from moment to moment.

One by One

As these scribes and Pharisees stood in stunned silence, Jesus stooped down and again began to write. As before, we are not told what He wrote. When you realize that these words, etched by the Lord's finger in the dust of the earth, are the only known writings of Jesus, you cannot help but wish that someone had preserved what He wrote. Did He write their names, as the prophet Jeremiah suggests? Did He write the names of their secret sins?

Or did He write the four words written once before in Israel's history by the moving finger of God: MENE, MENE, TEKEL, UPARSIN. We find those words from the Persian language in the story of King Belshazzar in the book of Daniel. The king had committed the ultimate blasphemy—using the sacred vessels from God's temple during a drunken, profane party. The revelry came to an abrupt halt when a great hand appeared and wrote those four ominous words on the wall. The king turned ashen, and all the lords and courtiers were stunned and silent. The words meant, "You are weighed in the balance and found wanting."

If that is what Jesus wrote, we can understand the actions of these men. Verse 9 says, "Those who heard began to go away one at a time. . . ." They could see what Jesus wrote, and the words rang in their minds as if they had been spoken aloud. When they heard those words, they departed. The oldest ones left first—the ones with the longest record of sin. One by one, they melted away until no one was left but Jesus and the woman alone.

Case Dismissed!

This brings us to another contrast in the story: A guilty woman finds herself forgiven. Jesus looks up from His writing and asks the woman where her accusers are. Did no one stay to condemn her?

"No one, sir," she replies.

"Then neither do I condemn you," says Jesus. "Go now and leave your life of sin."

What a beautiful picture of how God deals with sinners, with you and me. Jesus calls her attention to the fact that she has no human accusers. He has dismissed the jury. Their own sin disqualified them to serve. In a court of law, you can be arrested for a crime and brought before the bench of justice—but if no one appears in court to accuse you, the judge will set you free. Case dismissed!

That is what happens here.

But then come these amazing words: "Neither do I condemn you." Jesus alone has the right to condemn this woman. He alone was without sin. He alone was qualified to stone her. But He did not do so.

Why?

Because He *forgave* her sin. Without forgiveness, justice must be satisfied. God never waves His hand and dismisses sin as if sin is unimportant. His own truth, His law, and His holy character demand that any deviation from righteousness be punished. Justice must be satisfied—unless sin is forgiven. So it is clear that some mechanism is at work here which allows our Lord to forgive this woman's sin.

A legalist may protest at this point, "How can He do this? There is no basis for it! She didn't confess her sin! She didn't express repentance! She didn't even say she was sorry! How can Jesus just let this woman go scot-free?"

And the legalist is right, in that there must be repentance in order for the woman to experience God's forgiveness. God is not some doddering, indulgent old man who says, "Ah, well! Boys will be boys, girls will be girls! Just go on and never mind! We'll just forget it ever happened." Many people have such an image of God, but you never find such an image in Scripture, I assure you! Yes, the God of the Bible is a God of love and mercy, but He is also a God of truth and justice. If we leave out one dimension or the other of His character, we have distorted the truth of God.

So if God requires repentance, why did Jesus set this woman free without a single word of repentance on her part? The answer is so obvious that it is easy for us to miss: Her repentance took place within her heart! Just as Jesus could read the malice and murder in the hearts of her accusers, He could read the true sorrow and repentance within this woman's heart.

When did this repentance take place within her?

Picture with me the scene when she is brought before Jesus: She has been dragged away from a sexual liaison. She is humiliated, angry, rebellious, afraid. Perhaps she strikes out at her accusers. Perhaps she spits at them.

They bring her before a Stranger. Perhaps she has heard of this Man, we do not know. He regards her strangely, with those penetrating eyes. He writes with His finger in the dust. At first she is bewildered by Him. And then she senses that Jesus is more concerned with the sin and hypocrisy of her accusers than with the accusation they have lodged against her! She realizes that His sympathies are with her, that there is mercy in His eyes, that there is compassion in His voice. The rebellion, the anger, the denial begin to drain out of her.

Suddenly she realizes: It's true. She is a sinner. Her sin does deserve the death penalty—yet by some miracle, the penalty has been lifted. Her accusers are drifting away, one by one. And she realizes she is left alone with this Man—this strange but merciful Man who seems to see right through her.

And He accepts her.

And forgives her.

Somewhere in the course of this experience, this woman's heart has been changed. And Jesus—anticipating His sacrificial death on the cross for her sake—accepted the inner evidence of her changed heart and forgave her.

The cross is an eternal event in the mind of God. The sins of those who died in Old Testament times are forgiven on the same basis as your sins and mine: the substitutionary death of Jesus on the cross. There is no other way that God can forgive sin. In anticipation of the cross, Jesus forgave her sin. The proof of this fact is in His words: "Go now and leave your life of sin."

And Jesus says the same words to you and me right now. If we have acknowledged our guilt, then His message to us is, "Neither do I condemn you. Go now and leave your life of sin."

Does this mean we can now go on to live a sinless life? No. We all are born to a fallen nature. But God never asks us to do something that we cannot do. He knows that we will always be prone to sin as long as we are in our human flesh. When He says, "Leave your life of sin," He doesn't mean He expects absolute perfection from us from now on. But He does expect us to set ourselves on a *goal* of sinlessness. We can no longer be content to accept sin as a way of life. Our goal must be to root out every character flaw, every evil habit, every evil thought, every evil deed. And when we fall short of that goal, we are to bring our sin to God, confess it, repent of it, and receive His cleansing forgiveness once more.

Like the woman caught in adultery, you and I have been set free to begin a new and different lifestyle. Our response to the grace of God must be to turn our back on the habits and acts that once enslaved us. We must make a decision never to go back to what we have left behind. That is repentance, and it is a response to the grace and love and forgiveness of God.

"Leave Your Life of Sin"

Perhaps no story better illustrates a repentant response to God's grace than the story of John Newton. Newton was once a sea captain and a slave trader, a cruel and sinful man who obeyed no rules but his own. God reached the heart of John Newton during a voyage from Africa to England, when a fierce Atlantic storm threatened to sink his ship.

Upon his conversion, Newton was a completely transformed man. He became a great preacher and hymn writer. His most famous hymn begins with these penetrating lines:

> Amazing grace! how sweet the sound,
> That saved a wretch like me!
> I once was lost, but now am found,
> Was blind, but now I see.

But there is another hymn of Newton's which is far less famous—which, in fact, you hardly ever hear sung, yet which conveys an equally powerful truth:

> In evil, long I took delight,
> Unawed by shame or fear,
> 'Til a new object met my sight,
> And stopped my wild career.
>
> I saw One hanging on a tree,
> In agony and blood,
> Who fixed His languid eyes on me,
> As near His cross I stood.
>
> Sure, never to my latest breath
> Shall I forget that look.
> It seemed to charge me with His death,
> Though not a word He spoke.
>
> A second look He gave, which said,
> "I freely all forgive,
> My blood was for thy ransom paid,
> I died that thou mayest live."

Those are surely the sentiments of the woman Jesus set free in John 8. He freed her from her accusers. He freed her from her sin. He died, paying the ransom for her sin with His own blood, so that she might live.

Her story is really not so different from yours and mine. We are no more qualified to cast stones than her accusers were. We are all under the same condemnation—and we have all been offered the same gift of forgiveness. If you have accepted that gift, then Jesus speaks the same words to you that He spoke to this woman so many years ago:

"Go now and leave your life of sin."

Chapter Twenty-Four

The Breakthrough to Faith

John 8:12–30

Years ago, while driving alone from Dallas to Southern California, I picked up a couple of young hitchhikers. As we neared the entrance to the Grand Canyon, I asked them if they had ever seen the canyon. They said no, so we decided to spend the night there. It was late on a moonless night when we turned off the road. We parked and found an open space to lay out our sleeping bags, though we could hardly see our hands before our eyes. We went to sleep under the stars.

When I awoke in the morning, the sun was up. I yawned and stretched and threw out my arms—only to find that my left arm dropped down in the void! In the darkness, we had made our beds right on the edge of a cliff that dropped hundreds of feet down into the Grand Canyon! If we had gone two steps further we would have fallen over the edge.

I gave grateful thanks for the light that morning. And I learned an important lesson—a spiritual as well as a literal lesson: It is very dangerous indeed to wander about in the dark!

All around us, people are walking in darkness. They don't know where they are going. They have no idea where the edge of life is, or how deep the precipice beyond. But Jesus has come to light our way. He is the light of the world.

Light on the Path

Beginning with verses 12 and 13 of chapter 8, we come to another dramatic dialogue between Jesus and the religious leaders who oppose Him and seek to destroy Him.

8:12–13 *When Jesus spoke again to the people, he said, "I am the light of the world. Whoever follows me will never walk in darkness, but will have the light of life."*

> *The Pharisees challenged him, "Here you are, appearing as your own witness; your testimony is not valid."*

Jesus opens with an image based on the nightly ceremony in the temple courts, in which two giant candelabra—menorahs, the many-branched candlesticks used by the Jews—were lighted. These menorahs illuminated the whole temple court. It is in reference to this ceremony that Jesus declares, "I am the light of the world. Whoever follows me will never walk in darkness, but will have the light of life." Notice: Jesus does not declare Himself merely the light of Israel, but the light of the entire world.

This is a wonderful promise. There is nothing we need more in this world than light for our path. There are so many people we know—friends, co-workers, neighbors, relatives—who are wandering in darkness. They have no idea what is ahead. They are running straight into disaster and they don't even realize it. They need someone to shine a light and show them the path at their feet—before it is too late.

Jesus sheds His light not only on the world to come—on death and the afterlife—but on this world, on our everyday lives. This is a crazy, turbulent, mixed-up world, where every event has a thousand possible explanations. Who can understand it? Only the person who can see this world by the light of understanding that comes from Jesus.

Jesus is the One who knows life, who explains it, who tells the truth. Through Him, we learn to distinguish what is true from what is false, what is life from what is death, what is light from what is darkness.

And because Jesus gives light to us, we now can share our light with others. The life He gives us becomes a light for other people, so that we can help them also. The image of light that Jesus talks about here is a beautiful picture of the way He gives truth to us, and we pass that truth along to others.

Corroborated Testimony

The Pharisees immediately challenged Jesus. "You are appearing as your own witness," they said. "Your testimony is not valid." At first glance, this would seem to be a reasonable argument. "Where is your proof, your corroboration?" they demand. "Do you expect us to believe you are the Messiah just because you say so?"

And, of course, it is true that we must be constantly on guard not to be taken in by someone who claims to be what he is not. There were many false messiahs in Jesus' time, just as there are many false messiahs in our world today. So claims—especially such lofty claims as messiahhood!—must be carefully evaluated. That is the basis of the argument of the Pharisees.

Now, notice the irrefutable answer that Jesus flings back at His opponents.

8:14–18 *Jesus answered, "Even if I testify on my own behalf, my testimony is valid, for I know where I came from and where I am going. But you have no idea where I come from or where I am going. You judge by human standards; I pass judgment on no one. But if I do judge, my decisions are right, because I am not alone. I stand with the Father who sent me. In your own Law it is written that the testimony of two men is valid. I am one who testifies for myself; my other witness is the Father, who sent me."*

These men have decided to reject Jesus on the basis of a very thin slice of evidence. All they want to see is enough evidence to find fault with and discount. As with many people today, these Pharisees don't want to look at all the evidence. They have no interest in being objective or in discovering the truth. They have their minds set on destroying Jesus. Facts would just get in the way of their goal. So the Pharisees said to Him, "Why should we take your word for it?"

Jesus' reply is three-fold. First, He says, in effect, "You have rejected my claims simply because I make them myself. You don't know anything about me, where I came from or where I'm going. You have no basis for rejecting me. It may be reasonable to say, 'I will suspend judgment while I gather more evidence.' But you have rejected me out of hand, without any evidence against my claims—and that is irrational! My claims may be true or false, but you will never know for sure until you have tested my claims objectively."

Second, He says, in effect, "You reject my claims because you look only at superficial appearances. You judge according to the flesh. You regard me as nothing but a trouble-maker, a threat to your power and influence. You look at me and see a man with no political influence, no wealth, no credentials. You even think I came from Nazareth in Galilee, and for that reason you say I am not the Messiah. But you never investigated and found that I was born in Bethlehem, according to the word of the prophet. You do not know me at all."

Many people today are like those Pharisees. They reject Jesus because they are too lazy or biased to look at the evidence. They judge by superficial appearances. They reject Jesus because they don't want to be bothered with the facts.

Third, Jesus says, in effect, "If you would bother to read your own Scriptures and listen to the testimony of the Father, you would discover that I *do* fulfill the law. My testimony *is* corroborated. The evidence *is* there for your inspection. The law of Moses says that testimony must be established by two witnesses—and my testimony *is* established! I have two witnesses. I myself am one, and God the Father is the other."

What Jesus says is perfectly proper. A man is always free to give testimony on his own behalf in a court of law. But if what He says is corroborated by another witness, then it is more credible. Jesus declares, "The Father testifies in his Word of me, just as I have testified of myself. And the Father testifies of me in the signs that have been done through me. The Father and I have fulfilled the demand of the law. You ought to accept that."

Ignorance of the Father

Jesus has validated His testimony—but the Pharisees are still unconvinced. Why? Because their understanding is completely darkened. They are ignorant of the Father and the corroborating testimony He has given in His Word and in the signs that Jesus did. So they continued to oppose Him.

8:19–20 *Then they asked him, "Where is your Father?"*

"You do not know me or my Father," Jesus replied. "If you knew me, you would know my Father also." He spoke these words while teaching in the temple area near the place where the offerings were put. Yet no one seized him, because his time had not yet come.

Why didn't they arrest Him? Because the invisible hand of the Father restrained them. Despite their ignorance, their hatred, and their murderous intent, they could not stop Him—*because His time had not yet come.* Even though He spoke out in public, right in the temple courts where the offering was collected, where scores of people had to pass every hour, no one could harm Jesus or arrest Him because the Father was with Him.

It is amazing: These men claimed to know God, to study and keep His Word, to teach and lead the people in their understanding of God—yet they could not have been further from God. They could not have been more diametrically opposed to God's purposes. I find this is the problem with many people today—including some of the most "religious" people of all. They say they know God, but the "God" they describe is a "God" of their own creation. They preach and worship a figment of their own imaginations.

Piercing the Pride of the Pharisees

In verses 21 and 22, the dialogue between Jesus and the Pharisees illuminates one of the principle reasons men and women remain in darkness: *pride.*

8:21–22 *Once more Jesus said to them, "I am going away, and you will look for me, and you will die in your sin. Where I go, you cannot come."*

This made the Jews ask, "Will he kill himself? Is that why he says, 'Where I go, you cannot come'?"

Jesus again predicts His death, and the response of the Pharisees drips with sarcasm, scorn, and self-righteous pride. "Will he kill himself?" they ask—and it is not a question, but a verbal twist of the knife. The Pharisees believed that those who commit suicide go to the deepest place in hell, where there is a special torment reserved for them. So their gallows-humor response to Jesus' words is, "He says, 'Where I go, you cannot come'—and of course we can't! He's going to hell and we wonderful, righteous, religious people could never go to hell!"

But Jesus presses His assault upon their pride and arrogance.

8:23–27 *But he continued, "You are from below; I am from above. You are of this world; I am not of this world. I told you that you would die in your sins; if you do not believe that I am the one I claim to be, you will indeed die in your sins."*

"Who are you?" they asked.

"Just what I have been claiming all along," Jesus replied. "I have much to say in judgment of you. But he who sent me is reliable, and what I have heard from him I tell the world."

They did not understand that he was telling them about his Father.

Jesus was saying, in effect, "Your thinking is limited by the narrow confines of this life. You don't have any conception of what is going on in the invisible realms of reality. You do not see the hand of God or the schemes of Satan. You don't have the slightest inkling of my purposes or who I am. And if you do not discover who I am and place your trust in me, your own lives will end in death and eternal separation from God."

Blunt words—but they were *loving* words as well! Only blunt words about the reality of hell could possibly shake these self-satisfied men out of their arrogance and complacency. True, they did not want to hear about hell. Few people do, even today. But Jesus did not come to tell people what they want to hear. He came to tell them what they *need* to hear. He came to tell the truth. Only the truth could hope to set them free and save them from their own sin and folly.

I am amazed and awed at how earnestly Jesus perseveres with these men as He tries to remove their blindness and shine the light of truth on their lives. His words are not words of anger or rejection or condemnation. He is *pleading* with them to open their eyes and live! But in their pride they willfully choose blindness.

I once heard a pastor give his testimony at a conference. He said, "I know people who have been drawn to God by His love and grace, by the 'warm fuzzies' of the gospel. But that is not the way I came to God. I came because my heart was frightened by the prospect of hell and the wrath of God." We Christians are often hesitant to mention such unpleasant subjects as hell and wrath when we witness to others about our faith. But do we really do anyone a favor by so sugar-coating and diluting the gospel that people have no inducement to accept it?

The blunt words of Jesus may seem harsh and impolite and unpleasant— but those words are the *grace* of God to these stubborn, prideful men. God's love for us is relentless, and if we will not respond to the "warm fuzzy" side of the gospel—His love and grace and forgiveness—then He will shout to us and shake us and throw cold water in our faces. He will do what He must in an effort to save us from our own sinfulness and pride.

The Pharisees are startled by the intensity and seriousness of Jesus' answers. What right does He have to tell them they will die in their sins? Just who does He think He is? And so they ask Him: "Who are you?"

His reply, however, is not the bland statement we read in this translation: "Just what I have been claiming all along." There is an emphatic tone in the original language that few English translations manage to convey. Jesus' reply should actually be translated, "I am *absolutely and fundamentally* what I have told you all along." Jesus underscores and drives home the point that He is absolutely who He claims to be. "I have much more to say about you," He adds, in effect, "and it is all true, because it comes from the One who sent me."

Then John records this sad observation: "They did not understand that he was telling them about his Father."

It looks hopeless, doesn't it? The Light of the World stands before them in full radiance—yet ignorance and pride have darkened the minds of these men. But the next section of this passage will show that what seems hopeless with us is always possible with God!

The Breakthrough

Knowing their blindness, pride, and ignorance, Jesus makes one more attempt to reach these Pharisees.

8:28–29 *So Jesus said, "When you have lifted up the Son of Man, then you will know who I am and that I do nothing on my own but speak just what the Father has taught me. The one who sent me is with me; he has not left me alone, for I always do what pleases him."*

And note this . . . !

8:30 *Even as he spoke, many put their faith in him.*

There is no mistake here. Jesus has finally achieved a great breakthrough in His dialogue with the Pharisees. Many of these very men who had rejected and opposed and scorned Jesus have suddenly put their faith in Him!

What made the difference? What changed their hearts? Answer: *The cross!* When Jesus says, "When you have lifted up the Son of Man," He is talking about His coming death upon the cross. He is predicting the hour when He will be lifted up on the cross and give Himself for the sins of the world. When that happens, many will see who Jesus truly is: the Messiah, the Redeemer, the Lamb of God who takes away the sin of the world.

Sometimes we take the cross for granted. We become used to seeing it as a symbol, and we forget what the reality of the cross really meant. It is important, from time to time, for us to contemplate in detail all that the cross entailed for Jesus:

His deep sorrow in the Upper Room.
His loneliness in Gethsemane.
The frightful intensity of His prayers.
The defection of His disciples.
The mingled sweat and blood that fell from His brow.
The traitor's kiss.
The binding and beating; the scourging and spitting.
The mocking and the crown of thorns.
The heavy weight of the cross as He carried it on His back
	through the city streets.
The exhaustion and the collapse.
The humiliation of being stripped.
The impaling of His hands and feet.
The pounding of the hammers on the nails.
The tearing of flesh and tendons; the dislocation of bones;
	the screaming of nerve endings.

The jarring thud of the cross as it was dropped into the hole.

The jeers of His executioners.

The grief and tears of His mother, who stood at the foot of the
cross and watched.

The hours on the cross.

The darkness.

The pain.

The loneliness.

The thirst.

The abandonment.

The terrible cry from His parched lips, "My God, my God!
Why have you forsaken me?"

The consummation: "It is finished."

All of these horrors were in His mind when He said, "When you have lifted up the Son of Man, then you will know who I am."

When I was a boy of eleven, I came to Christ in an old Methodist Brush Arbor meeting. It was literally a "sawdust trail" camp-meeting conversion. I answered the invitation of the evangelist, and I went down front and received the Lord. It was a very real and powerful experience in my life. I had a tremendous sense of fellowship with the Lord for months and months after that.

One of the things I loved to do, even as an eleven-year-old boy, was to sing to myself some of the great hymns of the faith. I learned those hymns from Sunday to Sunday in church, and I sang them during the week as I went about my chores and my play. Those hymns reminded me of who my Savior was and what He had done for me. I used to get up in a hay rack on a Sunday afternoon all by myself and sing these hymns until the tears ran down my cheeks.

I especially recall sitting by myself in the park and singing these words:

> Jesus, keep me near the cross,
> There a precious fountain
> Free to all a healing stream,
> Flows from Calvary's mountain.
>
> Near the cross I'll watch and wait,
> Hoping, trusting ever,
> Till I reach the golden strand,
> Just beyond the river.

I love those words. They speak to me of the power of the cross to change lives and strip away illusion. It was the cross of Christ that spoke to the hearts of those hardened Pharisees—and their hearts were melted and softened, and many came to believe in Him.

And what about you? Are you watching and waiting near the cross of Jesus? Are you hoping and trusting in the power of the cross to bring you safely to the end of your journey?

He is the light of the world. He has penetrated our darkness. He illuminates our path. May His light flow through us and warm us, and may we spend our lives giving that light away to others.

Chapter Twenty-Five

Straight Talk From Jesus

John 8:31–47

A s a boy in grammar school, I was required to learn Patrick Henry's powerful address, delivered at the House of Burgesses in Williamsburg before the Revolution. I still feel a chill up my spine when I remember his words:

> Is life so dear and peace so sweet as to be purchased at the price of chains and slavery? Forbid it, Almighty God! I care not what course others may take, but as for me, give me liberty or give me death!

I find that many people today do not really understand freedom. Most people define freedom as being able to do whatever they feel like doing. We cannot read the Parable of the Prodigal Son without realizing that this is exactly how the Prodigal Son defined freedom. He thought that if he could stuff his pockets full of money, leave home, and seek pleasure and receive instant gratification—Ah, that would be freedom!

He soon found that this kind of "freedom" was just another form of slavery.

The true definition of freedom is "the opportunity to be all that you were meant to be." Don't you long for that? The ability to feel fulfilled, able to achieve and grow and express yourself to the best of your ability—that is true freedom.

In this passage of John's gospel, we come to some of the most famous words Jesus ever spoke. He delivered these words at the close of the Feast of Tabernacles, in the temple courts in Jerusalem. They are powerful words.

They are words of freedom.

Steps to Freedom

8:31–32 *To the Jews who had believed him, Jesus said, "If you hold to my* *teaching, you are really my disciples. Then you will know the truth, and the truth will set you free."*

Here we have a short course in Christian discipleship! But it is also much more. Jesus declares that discipleship—following Jesus and holding to His teaching—is the true pathway to freedom, to being all you were meant to be.

We can break this statement down into four steps—four steps to freedom:

Step 1: Believe

John writes, "To the Jews who had *believed* him . . . ." There is a slight difference between the words John uses in verse 30 and those of verse 31. Verse 30 says, "Even as he spoke, many put their faith *in him."* In the original language, that last phrase is literally "onto him." They stood on Jesus, they clambered onto Him and made their stand on Him. This is language which suggests in visual terms how completely they trusted Him. It is as if they had faith that He could hold them up.

But verse 31 uses a different phrase: "To the Jews who had *believed* him, Jesus said . . . ." This is a different group of people than those in verse 30. These are people who had not yet trusted Jesus as the people in verse 30 had, but they had *believed* Him. They had been intellectually captivated by His arguments and His words, but they had not yet committed themselves to Him. It is to these people that Jesus says, "If you hold to my teaching, you are really my disciples. Then you will know the truth, and the truth will set you free."

Discipleship begins with belief—even if only intellectual belief. These people were at the door. They had taken the first step. But Jesus wanted them to know how to continue on, all the way into complete fellowship with—and reliance upon—Himself.

Belief comes through being convinced by the evidence. You will never find freedom until you examine and are satisfied with the evidence that Jesus is who He claims to be. Hundreds of thousands of people reject Jesus without ever really examining the evidence for the claims of Christ. That is why the gospel of John was written: to provide the evidence for belief. In John 20:30–31, John writes, "Jesus did many other miraculous signs in the presence of his disciples, which are not recorded in this book. But these [signs] are written that you may believe that Jesus is the Christ, the Son of God, and that by believing you may have life in his name."

Obviously, then, if you want to be free, to be all you were meant to be, then you must begin by examining the evidence about Jesus. Read the four gospels for yourself. Read the words of Jesus. Read the Old Testament prophecies that foretold His coming.

Don't reject Jesus just because some atheistic university professor sneers at Christianity in a classroom. Don't reject Jesus because some bizarre cult has distorted and misrepresented Him. Don't reject Jesus because some prominent evangelist was toppled by a sordid scandal. Don't judge Jesus on the basis of what other people do or say. Judge the claims of Jesus on the basis of Jesus Himself, on the basis of His life and His words, and on the basis of Scripture. This is the most important judgment you will ever make; don't let some other person make it for you. Examine the evidence and make up your own mind.

Step 2: Cling to His Word

Jesus said, *"If you hold to my teaching,* you are really my disciples." Meditate on the teaching of Jesus. Ponder His words. Compare what He says with your own experience—and apply it to your daily life. Live the teaching of Jesus every day.

That is the test of any teaching: Is it true? Does it work in the laboratory of my everyday life? Does it explain what happens to me in life? Is it reliable? Hold to the teaching of Jesus and test-drive it on the freeway of life.

Jesus suggests here that when you hold to His teaching, something will take place: "If you hold to my teaching, *you are really my disciples."* What this indicates is that there are two kinds of disciples. There are those who seem to be disciples—outwardly. They conform, they may join the organization, but inwardly they are not fully committed.

But there is another kind of disciple: The disciple who hears Jesus' word and continues in it, thinks about it, dwells in it, lives it, and applies it to every aspect of his or her life. That kind of disciple is the kind described in verse 30, the kind of disciple who has put full faith and reliance upon Jesus—not just intellectual belief.

Step 3: Know the Truth

Jesus said, "If you hold to my teaching . . . then you will know the truth . . . ." Everybody wants to know the truth. Nobody likes to be flimflammed or fooled. Nobody likes to be taken in by a con artist.

What, then, is the truth? Truth is the nature of things as they really are. Truth is seeing through all the illusions, the dreams, the wishful thinking, the facades, and the phoniness. Truth is getting down to the underlying reality, the heart of the matter—to that which really is.

There is no more attractive promise in the Scripture than this! If you hold to the Lord's teaching, you will be able to discern lies and avoid being manipulated. You will be able to resist the false teaching of those religious con artists and cult leaders who want to draw disciples to themselves. You will

recognize the lies, distortions, and half-truths in the news media, the entertainment media, and the advertising media that continually shout at us, trying
to tear down our values and beliefs. You will be able to resist the pressure,
cajoling, and temptation of the people around you who want to lure you into
their own sinful and self-destructive way of life.

Understand, however, that coming to the truth is not an instant, one-
magic-moment event. It is a process. As you daily read, study, and obey the
word of Jesus, as you gradually learn to see life through the perspective of
Jesus, you will begin to see yourself and other people differently. You will
read your newspaper and watch television differently. Your whole system of
values and attitudes and perceiving reality will undergo a gradual yet fundamental transformation.

You will come to know more and more of the truth. And you will gradually, progressively become more and more free, more and more of what God
wants you to be.

First John 5:20 tells us, "The Son of God has come and has given us
understanding, so that we may know him who is true." And Proverbs 2:1–5
agrees that there is nothing more important in life than knowing God, holding
to His Word, and receiving from Him the benefits of His wisdom and truth:

> My son, if you accept my words
> and store up my commands within you,
> turning your ear to wisdom
> and applying your heart to understanding,
> and if you call out for insight
> and cry aloud for understanding,
> and if you look for it as for silver
> and search for it as for hidden treasure,
> then you will understand the fear of the Lord
> and find the knowledge of God.

What a tremendous promise! These words ought to send us all to praying,
searching, listening, thinking, and studying the mind of God in His Word.

Step 4: Freedom!

Jesus promises that as you persevere in the truth, progressively acquiring
deeper and deeper understanding of the things of God, something wonderful
will happen: "The truth will set you free." The truth will deliver you, permit
you to be all that you were meant to be.

What does the truth free us from? It frees us from all those external and
internal hindrances that prevent us from being all we are meant to be in
Christ. Some examples:

Freedom From Fear

The truth frees us from fear and anxiety. It gives us the freedom to act boldly and courageously. I know people who are so timid and fearful they cannot even go outside their homes. They cannot walk along a public street. People who are slaves to their phobias are extreme examples, but they show how fear is a kind of slavery from which we need liberation. Your fears and mine may be of a different kind, but they are just as limiting and confining.

Many Christians are afraid to open their mouths and tell their friends and neighbors about Jesus. They think, "What will they think of me? Will I alienate them? Will I make a fool of myself? I'd better just keep my mouth shut." Fear keeps us from fulfilling the Lord's command to be witnesses, to be salt and light in the world. Fear keeps us from being all we are meant to be in Christ.

Many Christians are afraid to step out in faith and take on a new challenge. Others are afraid to share their own issues and hurts with other Christians, such as in a small group Bible study. Others are afraid to seek help and counseling for painful emotional or relationship issues, so they limp along in a troubled marriage or with crippling emotions and memories from the past. Their fears prevent them and the people closest to them from becoming all they are meant to be.

Freedom From Anger

The truth sets us free from anger, bitterness, and other toxic emotions. Many people, including Christians, live out their lives in a welter of resentment over some injury that was inflicted on them—even injuries they suffered years or decades earlier. Some people are bound by bitterness toward an abusive parent, a spiteful ex-spouse, or a nasty boss. Some are unable to let go of their anger, even though the persons who offended them are long dead.

But as we hold to the Lord's word, the truth of His healing and His forgiving nature begins to take root in our lives. We see Jesus forgiving His torturers even as He hangs upon the cross, and we realize that if Jesus can forgive that, then we can forgive whatever anyone else has done to us. We learn to let go of our bitterness and release our anger. That is the truth that sets us free, so that we can truly become all we were meant to be.

Freedom From Guilt

The truth sets us free from guilt. Millions of people suffer from an oppressive load of shame, regret, and a sense of failure. But as we hold to Jesus' word, we learn to see our past from God's perspective. His grace saturates our memories. We learn how to make amends and heal relationships. We seek forgiveness. We confess our sins. And the chains of guilt gradually slip off of us, leaving us free to live in the Now, free of Satan's accusations against us from the past. Living in a state of continually renewed repentance, we hear, again and again, the same words the Lord said to the woman caught in adultery: "Neither do I condemn you. Go now and leave your life of sin."

And the list goes on and on: Issues and emotions and sins which day by day lose their power over us as we dwell in His truth, as the truth gradually and progressively sets us free. You can see now that this message of Jesus is enormously practical and applicable to our daily lives.

Sons of Abraham—or Slaves to Sin

But for many people, there is a hindrance to finding the truth and freedom that Jesus wants us to experience. We see this problem in the response of the people.

8:33 *They answered him, "We are Abraham's descendants and have never been slaves of anyone. How can you say that we shall be set free?"*

The hindrance to freedom in the lives of these people is clear: *self-sufficiency.* "We are Jews," they say. "We belong to the chosen race. We are descendants of Abraham and we have never been in bondage to any one." Many Bible scholars have scoffed at the obvious fallacy of this claim. How, they ask, could these Jews say such a thing when they were at that time under the heel of Rome? And had they forgotten the various captivities they had experienced under Egypt, Babylon, and Assyria? How could they claim they never were in bondage to anyone?

But these questions miss the thrust of what the people are saying. They are not stupid people, and they know their history and their status under the Roman Empire. They know their nation is in bondage. But they are not talking about political bondage. They understand what kind of freedom Jesus means, and that He is talking about spiritual bondage. Their response to Jesus is actually, "Nobody tells us how to worship. Even though we have been in bondage to other nations, we have never allowed anyone to tell us how to worship God. We will fight to the death for the freedom to worship as we please."

To this day, the Jews remain a fiercely independent and unconquerable people where worship is concerned. They do not allow any oppressor or invader to dictate their relationship with God.

But the Jews in Jesus' audience committed a major error in their response to Jesus. They extended their fierce independence in worship to mean that they, as individuals, were acceptable to God because they were descended from Abraham. They had a misplaced confidence in their own genetic heritage as the guarantor of God's approval.

Once when I was in Dallas, Texas, I drove past Texas Stadium, where the Dallas Cowboys play. Texas Stadium is a unique sports arena. It is not like the Astrodome, the Kingdome, the Superdome, or any of the other enclosed stadia where football is played. Those arenas are completely enclosed and roofed over. Texas Stadium, on the other hand, is only partially roofed over. The spectators are protected, but there is a huge hole over the football field, leaving the players exposed to the elements.

I asked my hosts in Dallas why Texas Stadium was designed with that big hole in the roof. The answer, expressed with typical "Texas humility": "So God can watch His favorite team!" That's how the Cowboys view themselves—"God's Favorite Team"! And that's how these Jews in John 8 viewed themselves: "God's Favorite People."

And that's a problem. There is a sense of self-sufficiency and spiritual pride in these people. They think they are okay the way they are. They may need a few minor adjustments here and there, but they certainly do not need radical transformation. They do not need liberation. They are free because they can trace their genealogy back to Abraham!

Yet it is this attitude which actually perpetuates their enslavement. They cannot bring themselves to the truth, because they feel no need of the truth.

Sin Starts Small—and Grows

Jesus cuts through the self-sufficiency and pride of these people.

8:34–35 *Jesus replied, "I tell you the truth, everyone who sins is a slave to sin. Now a slave has no permanent place in the family, but a son belongs to it forever."*

This is one of the most profound statements ever uttered by Jesus. When you give yourself to sin, whether in attitude or in action, you become a slave to sin. You gradually slip under its control. Later, when you want to break it, the power of sin over your life, you find you cannot. You are a slave to sin.

If freedom is the ability to be all you are meant to be, then slavery is the loss of that potential. There is an enormous potential for destruction in sinful

thoughts and sinful actions that is rarely apparent in the beginning. Sins usually start small, gaining a toe-hold in our lives. Like cancer, sin spreads slowly
and gradually from that single, small toe-hold, until it has infected our entire
lives. Only in hindsight can we see how a pervasive, destructive pattern of
sinful habits began with a single lustful thought, a single unkind act, a single
filthy word, a single indulgence in gossip, a single breach of honesty.

Such small sins never seem dangerous at first. "Everybody does it," we
say. And we begin to take pleasure in sin. And the sin forms a habit within us
that soon becomes unbreakable. And we are enslaved.

If you think alcohol, smoking, and drugs are the only habits that are hard
to break, you are mistaken. Anger and rage are habit-forming. Sexual immorality is addictive, as are pornography and lustful thoughts. Pride is a very
insidious form of addiction. So is prejudice. All of these sins can easily take
root in our lives and enslave us.

Jesus points out the danger when this kind of slavery overtakes us: "A
slave has no permanent place in the family, but a son belongs to it forever."
These Jews had claimed to be free because they were descendants of Abraham. To this claim, Jesus replies, "No. It is true you are in Abraham's house,
but you are not there as sons, you are there as slaves. And slaves do not live in
the house forever. Only the son has a permanent place in the house."

A house is a symbol of privileges and belonging. Jesus is saying that
those who do not hold to His Word, and choose instead a life of slavery, will
lose the privileges and the place of belonging they believe they have as
descendants of Abraham.

A Question of Fatherhood

Jesus next "takes the gloves off" and speaks very bluntly.

8:36–41 *"So if the Son sets you free, you will be free indeed. I know you are
Abraham's descendants. Yet you are ready to kill me, because you have no
room for my word. I am telling you what I have seen in the Father's presence,
and you do what you have heard from your father."*

"Abraham is our father," they answered.

*"If you were Abraham's children," said Jesus, "then you would do the
things Abraham did. As it is, you are determined to kill me, a man who has told
you the truth that I heard from God. Abraham did not do such things. You are
doing the things your own father does."*

*"We are not illegitimate children," they protested. "The only Father we
have is God himself."*

Here, Jesus takes a decisive step toward the unpleasant, unpalatable truth about these people. He explains the source of their evil: It is a question of fatherhood. Jesus is drawing a clear distinction between His Father and their father. He says, in effect, "I talk with my Father all the time, and I have told you what He says. You, however, want to kill me. That reveals what kind of father you have. You have a murderer for a father."

Understandably, this statement did not sit well with Jesus' listeners! They continued to insist, "Abraham is our father." So Jesus pressed even harder: "If you were Abraham's children, then you would do the things Abraham did. Instead, you have your hearts set on killing me, just because I told you God's truth!"

What kinds of things did Abraham do? In Genesis, God sent a heavenly visitor to Abraham and the patriarch welcomed Him. He set a feast for the visitor, listened to the visitor's words, and obeyed the truth. Jesus is pointing out a parallel: God has sent a heavenly visitor to these Jews—Jesus Himself. But instead of welcoming Him, listening to Him, and obeying the truth, they reject Him and plot His death.

The Jews continue arguing: "We are not illegitimate children," they say. "The only Father we have is God himself." Some Bible commentators suggest that this is a sly dig at Jesus' own birth. Presumably, rumors of the virgin birth of Jesus were circulating, and these people were implying that Jesus was born not of a virgin, but of an out-of-wedlock union. If this is true, and if Jesus' audience hoped to silence Him with such insinuations, they were very much mistaken.

Children of the Devil

Now comes the most shocking indictment of all.

8:42–47 *Jesus said to them, "If God were your Father, you would love me, for I came from God and now am here. I have not come on my own; but he sent me. Why is my language not clear to you? Because you are unable to hear what I say. You belong to your father, the devil, and you want to carry out your father's desire. He was a murderer from the beginning, not holding to the truth, for there is no truth in him. When he lies, he speaks his native language, for he is a liar and the father of lies. Yet because I tell the truth, you do not believe me! Can any of you prove me guilty of sin? If I am telling the truth, why don't you believe me? He who belongs to God hears what God says. The reason you do not hear is that you do not belong to God."*

Here are strong words indeed! Jesus is telling them, "What you do reveals to whom you belong. All your proud claims are worthless if your hearts are filled with murder, lust, and hatred. You are not God's children. You belong to your father, the devil!" This is the dramatic climax of His dialogue with these Jewish leaders, and He concludes with three penetrating questions.

First question: "Why is my language not clear to you? Why do you not understand what I say?" He awaits their response. Hearing none, He answers His own question: "Because you are unable to hear what I say. You cannot bear it. You are in denial. You feel threatened by my words. You willfully resist my message. You have stopped up your ears so that the truth will not penetrate and illuminate the true wretchedness of your sinful condition."

And why do they feel threatened by the Lord's message? "Because," He says in effect, "you belong to your father, the devil, and your will is to carry out the desires of your father. And his desires are to murder, to lie, to destroy. There is no truth in him. He is a liar and the father of lies. Because I tell the truth, you want to shut me up."

Jesus has stripped away the facade. It is as if He has turned over a rock, exposing all the creepy, crawly, slimy things that live underneath. The invisible powers which pull men's strings and manipulate their actions like evil puppetmasters are now made visible.

But Jesus has also opened the door to another invisible kingdom—a kingdom of love and power, the kingdom of God. Here we see in stark terms the two realms of invisible reality which govern and control human life. Jesus lived with a continual awareness of the invisible control centers where the great battles of ultimate reality were fought.

Jesus has come to reveal the message and intents of His Father, God the Creator. But in the face of opposition, He must also point out that there is a malevolent being, a hater of men, working behind the scenes. This being is a liar and a murderer who is set on deceiving and destroying human beings. He is engaged in a plan to make human beings believe and spread a great lie. That is what had happened to Jesus' opponents: They have been tricked into serving the satanic plan. In their own pride and willfulness, they had handed themselves over as slaves to Satan's purposes.

"Can You Convict Me?"

Second question: "Can any of you prove me guilty of sin?"

Here, Jesus issues a strong challenge to His hearers. He is certainly the only individual in history who could stand up in public before murderous enemies and throw down such a gauntlet! "Which of you has any evidence against me? Come on! Speak up!" Would you dare your enemies to come up with the dirt on you? They just might do it! But when Jesus makes that challenge, His enemies are speechless—because He is sinless. There is no one who can say, "Jesus, you cheated me," or, "Jesus, you stole from me," or, "Jesus, I caught you in a compromising position," or, "Jesus, you lied." The evidence did not exist. The purity of His life completely silenced His opponents.

Third question: "If I am telling the truth, why don't you believe me?"

There is a relentless logic in His words. He has laid bare the evil of their hearts. He has revealed the reality of these men and shown that they are not the good and decent people they pretend to be. They are slaves to sin and children of the devil.

Does that mean these people are without hope? Are they so completely given over to evil that God cannot help them. No. The choice is still theirs, and that is why Jesus perseveres in His dialogue with them. They desperately need the help of a Redeemer. Jesus is trying to shake them out of their willfulness and bring them to their God-given senses.

There is hope—but only one hope—for these prideful religious leaders. It is the same hope Jesus expressed in verses 31 and 32: "If you hold to my teaching, you are really my disciples. Then you will know the truth, and the truth will set you free." That is the only path to freedom for those who are victims of Satan's lies. As in the words of the great hymn,

> He breaks the power of cancelled sin
> He sets the prisoner free;
> His blood can make the foulest clean;
> His blood availed for me.

These Jewish leaders have heard some very blunt, straight, uncompromising talk from Jesus. It was meant not to hurt them or humiliate them, but to bring them to reality, to save their souls. You and I have also heard the same straight talk from Jesus.

What is our response?

Chapter Twenty-Six

The Choice

John 8:48–59

Thwarted by the great Bible commentator William Barclay called the eighth chapter of John "a chapter which passes from lightning flash to lightning flash of astonishment." As we come to the closing section of John 8—and the conclusion of the dialogue between Jesus and the Jewish leaders in the temple courts at the end of the Feast of Tabernacles—we clearly see what Barclay meant. Truly, this has been an electrical storm of a chapter, with flash after flash of astonishing brilliance—every flash illuminating the dark night of human understanding.

Throughout this chapter, Jesus makes claim after claim about Himself, while pressing the indictment that His accusers are children of the devil, hoping to shake them to their senses. The entire dialogue crackles with electricity and drama, and each thunderous exchange between Jesus and His opponents raises the voltage of this drama. Each statement Jesus makes is more astonishing than the one before—and each exchange raises the stakes: By this point in the dialogue, the Jewish religious leaders have been forced into a definitive, black-and-white decision—either to fall down and worship Jesus as the Son of God or to bend down and take up stones to kill Him!

Jesus Responds to Attack

In verse 47, at the end of the previous section, we saw Jesus tell these religious leaders, "The reason you do not hear [my words] is that you do not belong to God." Hardly a tactful, Dale Carnegie-style message! Apparently, Jesus never read *How to Win Friends and Influence People!* For in verses 48 through 50, we again see the lightning bolts flash between Jesus and His angry critics.

8:48–50 *The Jews answered him, "Aren't we right in saying that you are a Samaritan and demon-possessed?"*

"I am not possessed by a demon," said Jesus, "but I honor my Father and you dishonor me. I am not seeking glory for myself; but there is one who seeks it, and he is the judge."

As often happens when people have been debated into a corner and run out of logical arguments, these Jewish leaders resorted to name-calling, personal attack, and bigotry. "You demon-possessed Samaritan!" they jeer. They were reaching deep into the well of their race-hatred and their religious chauvinism to find the worst insult they could think of!

By contrast, our Lord responds with calm self-possession and self-assurance. "I am not possessed by a demon," Jesus replies, "but I honor my Father and you dishonor me." He goes on to commit His reputation to the Father, saying He doesn't seek His own glory, but the Father seeks glory and He is the judge. Jesus has no need to resort to retaliation or name-calling, because both the truth and God the Father are completely on His side. As the apostle Peter said, "When they hurled their insults at [Jesus], he did not retaliate; when he suffered, he made no threats. Instead, he entrusted himself to him who judges justly."[1]

This is a powerful, instructive example of how you and I should handle personal attack. Jesus makes the claim, "I honor my Father." And how does He honor God the Father? He refuses to respond on His own behalf, leaving all vengeance to the Father. I don't know how that strikes you, but it shames me to realize how quick I am to defend myself when attacked.

Eternal Life—and "The Second Death"

Jesus goes on to make another one of His astounding, thunderous claims.

8:51 *"I tell you the truth, if a man keeps my word, he will never see death."*

Again, Jesus billboards His statement with the phrase, "I tell you the truth," or, "Verily, verily, amen, amen," indicating that He is about to utter a fundamental truth. Having underscored His next words, Jesus goes on to say, "If a [person] keeps my word, [that person] will never see death." Imagine the shock value of that statement! Is there anything in life more certain than death? Yet Jesus claims to have conquered death! In fact, in the original language you can see that Jesus emphasizes this claim with a double negative: "he will *never, never* see death."

The Jewish leaders are going to either misunderstand or deliberately twist His words, saying that Jesus is claiming to have conquered *physical* death.

But Jesus does not claim that Christians—those who keep His word—will never die. He says that when they die physically, they will never *see death.* In other words, when Christians die, they do not pass through coldness and darkness, but they are instantly transported into glory and instant joy.

On his death bed, the great evangelist Dwight L. Moody exclaimed, "Earth is receding! Heaven is approaching! This is my crowning day!" I have seen this same attitude as I've sat beside the deathbeds of other Christians in my congregation. They knew that they were not going into a cold, dark grave along with their mortal bodies. They knew they would not experience decay. They were just moments from instant happiness and glory.

In my many years as a pastor, I have learned to *look forward* to Christian funerals and memorial services. They are usually very pleasant and even *triumphant* experiences. Yes, there are tears and a sense of loss. We grieve over those to whom we must bid at least a temporary goodbye. But underlying everything is a sense that the departed loved one has finished the course of life and entered into a rest and reward which God has prepared. I have stood at the edge of many a grave and felt in my heart the full impact of Paul's words, "O grave, where is thy victory? O death where is thy sting?" There is no sting in the death of the believer.

Christians do not pass from life to death. They pass from this life to an even greater and more wonderfully realized life. But there is a flip-side to this truth: Clearly, if those who keep the Lord's word pass from life to a transcendent form of life, then those who die apart from Christ must, by implication, pass from life to a form of death that transcends mere physical death. This is what the book of Revelation calls "the Second Death."

People today do not like to hear about "the Second Death" any more than Jesus' accusers liked hearing about it 2,000 years ago. As a pastor, I have often heard people say, "Pastor, you're not going to preach hellfire and brimstone to us, are you?" If the Scriptures warn about it, then I must also. The good news, of course, is that there is a way to escape this death. This is what our Lord speaks of here.

Abraham Saw Jesus and Rejoiced

The Jewish leaders are staggered by the Lord's claim. Next we read their bitter response.

8:52–53 *At this the Jews exclaimed, "Now we know that you are demon-possessed! Abraham died and so did the prophets, yet you say that if a man keeps your word, he will never taste death. Are you greater than our father Abraham? He died, and so did the prophets. Who do you think you are?"*

The Jewish leaders treated Jesus' claim as an empty boast, challenging Him with the question, "Who do you think you are anyway? Abraham died! All the great names of the past died! Isaiah, Jeremiah and all the prophets are dead! Do you think you are greater than all of them? Who do you think you are?"

Of course, the answer is yes! Jesus *is* greater than the patriarchs and prophets! In His response He hints at the coming proof of His greatness.

8:54–56 *Jesus replied, "If I glorify myself, my glory means nothing. My Father, whom you claim as your God, is the one who glorifies me. Though you do not know him, I know him. If I said I did not, I would be a liar like you, but I do know him and keep his word. Your father Abraham rejoiced at the thought of seeing my day; he saw it and was glad."*

When Jesus says, "My Father . . . is the one who glorifies me," He is hinting at the resurrection to come. In John 12:23, Jesus states this fact plainly when He realizes that His time has come: "The hour has come," He says, "for the Son of Man to be gloried." The Jewish leaders did not understand that. Perhaps even His disciples did not understand at this point. But it is clear that Jesus understood His own destiny and purpose at this point. He is supremely confident that He is carrying out the Father's purpose in the world, and that the Father will take Him triumphantly through the process of death and on into His resurrection glory. In anticipation of the miracle of His resurrection, Jesus declares himself to be the One who has conquered death. Through the centuries, that declaration has been the hope of life and glory for all who have followed Him.

Jesus goes on to claim intimacy with God. "Your father Abraham is my credential," He says, in effect. "By faith, Abraham looked forward, saw my day, and rejoiced to know that I would come and conquer death. He understood who I am and what I have come to do—and He was glad." Imagine the startling impact of this claim! Jesus' opponents must have looked at Jesus in absolute astonishment!

This greatly helps us understand how to read the Old Testament. Many Christians feel sorry for those who lived before Christ and the cross, because they did not have the Good News of salvation by grace through faith. But Jesus indicates that Old Testament believers saw the Lord very clearly indeed. The symbols of the Old Testament law and prophecies pointed forward to Jesus Christ. Jesus is prefigured in every prophet who spoke. He is pictured in every sacrifice on every Jewish altar. He is represented in every ritual, and in the very form and structure of the tabernacle and the temple.

In this dialogue in John 8, we can see that Jesus fulfills the entire Old Testament. He is the only One who fully knows and understands both God and man. He is the Intimate of God. What a remarkable claim!

The Climax

8:57–59 *"You are not yet fifty years old," the Jews said to him, "and you have seen Abraham!"*

"I tell you the truth," Jesus answered, "before Abraham was born, I am!" At this, they picked up stones to stone him, but Jesus hid himself, slipping away from the temple grounds.

There are many people who contend that Jesus never claimed to be God, that this is a claim that was superimposed on Him by later Christian tradition. But no one who has ever truly read the New Testament could make such an ignorant statement—and additional proof that Jesus did indeed make such a claim is right here in this passage. He says, "I tell you the truth, before Abraham was born, I am!"

Jesus uses two distinct verbs in this statement that are very different forms of the verb "to be." It is a fine but very important distinction. A more precise translation of Jesus' words would read, "Abraham 'became,' but I was already there." Now this is a very strong statement of Jesus' eternal nature. He is not just saying that He existed before Abraham; many cults take the position that Jesus was *created* before Abraham. But no, Jesus is saying here that He has *always* existed. He is God.

In fact, when Jesus says "I am," He is using the name used throughout the Old Testament to describe the ultimate character of God. When God sent Moses to plead the case for Israel's release before Pharaoh, God told Moses to say "I AM WHO I AM" had sent Him. It is no accident or coincidence that Jesus applies the same description to Himself: "Before Abraham was born, *I am."* His words can be interpreted in no other way: Jesus has laid a unique and unambiguous claim to deity!

Jesus is forcing this issue upon these men. He does not placate. He does not soft-sell. He does not compromise. He speaks the unvarnished truth, knowing that He is enraging His opponents, again and again. He knows, in fact, that they are reaching the boiling point—the point of murder! Yet He does not temper His language. On the contrary, He hits harder and harder. Each claim is more staggering than the last.

So the climax comes. These fine upstanding citizens, these men who claim to have superior moral and religious understanding, and who claim to represent God, now stoop to the ground and take stones in their hands. They have run out of arguments. They have run out of insults. They have reached the brink of murder.

The stones they find are probably brick-like cut stones for the construction of the temple—hard-edged, sharp-cornered weapons of torture and death. They lift the stones, ready to hurl them at Jesus—

And Jesus disappears into the crowd.

Notice that there are no Hollywood-style special effects. There are no heroics. Jesus just steps into the crowd and melts from view. This hardly seems possible! Certainly, Jesus would have been recognized. Certainly, someone would shout, "There He is!" and the chase would be on. But no. Here again, we see the invisible hand of God at work, protecting Jesus until His time is come. Jesus knows that a time will arrive when He will be delivered into the hands of these murderous men, but for now He is safe. No one can lay a hand on Him until the Father decrees.

We should take encouragement from our Lord's example. When we walk in the Lord's will, we are supported by this same invisible hand. Nothing can hurt us until God's hour strikes—and when it does, when the moment of pain or death comes, we can accept it, knowing that God can use even pain and death to achieve His eternal purpose. He did so in the life of His Son. He can do so in your life and mine as well.

Figurehead—or Lord?

What shall we make of this Man?

Who are we, in relationship to Jesus?

A. W. Tozer once drew a comparison between the way Christians treat Jesus and the way the British treat their monarchs. The kings and queens of Britain, he observed, are called the rulers of the nation. But they do not rule, they only reign. They do not have power; they are mere symbols of power—figureheads who are addressed as "Your Majesty."

I am afraid there is a great deal of truth in that comparison. This is how we often treat Jesus in our daily lives. We address Him as "Lord," but we give Him no power over our lives. He reigns, but He does not rule over our business life, our sexual life, our recreational life, our thought life, our family life, or even our church life. He is a figurehead, nothing more.

But when we see Jesus as this section describes Him, claiming to be the One who honors the Father by the way He lives, the One who removes the sting of death from those who follow Him, the One who is the Intimate of God and the Object of all the Father's plans and purposes for all ages of time, and the One who is above and beyond time as the Eternal One—

Then we have a choice to make.

We must either worship Him or ignore Him.

We must make Him Lord *in fact,* not merely in symbol. Or else we must admit He is not our Lord at all.

That is the clear choice which confronts us here at the climax of John chapter 8. It is the same choice Jesus flung at His opponents in the temple courts in Jerusalem. They understood with crystal clarity the choice He offered them—and they made their choice with equal clarity, with eyes filled with hatred, and with stones in their hands.

The same choice confronts you and me today. What is *your* choice?

Chapter Twenty-Seven

Believing Is Seeing

John 9:1–41

Georgie Shearing, the British-American jazz pianist, was born blind. He once stood on a New York City street corner during rush hour. With his dark glasses and white cane, he could always count on someone, sooner or later, to offer to assist him across the street. While waiting, he felt a tap on his shoulder. "Excuse me, sir," said a voice, "but I'm blind. Could you help me across the street?"

"Certainly, I'll help you," said Shearing. He reached out, found the arm of the other blind man, and strained his ears to decipher the sound of the traffic. After a few moments, he said, "It's safe to cross. Let's go!" Together, the two blind men set off across the intersection. As they walked, Shearing heard a great deal of horn-honking and yelling, but he was never sure if it was directed at him or not.

Moments later, the two men were safely on the other side of the street. The other blind man thanked Shearing for his help, and went on his way.

Shearing later related the incident to an astonished friend who asked, "George! Why on earth did you do such a dangerous thing?!"

Shearing smiled. "Oh, I couldn't resist the irony of it! The blind leading the blind and all that! And you know, that was the biggest thrill of my whole life!"

When the apostle Paul said we should "live by faith, not by sight," I don't think that's what he had in mind! Faith, however, can result in sight, as the blind man in John chapter 9 is about to discover. There is an old axiom which says, "Seeing is believing." But in this passage of John's gospel, Jesus will disprove that axiom. He will demonstrate to the blind man, to the Jewish leaders, and to you and me that *believing is seeing!*

The Link Between Sin and Suffering

Jesus now encounters the man born blind. In these verses, Jesus addresses one of the oldest questions asked by believers and nonbelievers alike.

9:1–3 *As he went along, [Jesus] saw a man blind from birth. His disciples asked him, "Rabbi, who sinned, this man or his parents, that he was born blind?"*

"Neither this man nor his parents sinned," said Jesus, "but this happened so that the work of God might be displayed in his life."

Perhaps you have known a handicapped child—a child born with physical deformities or mental limitations, with Down's Syndrome or spinabifida. Perhaps you have such a child in your own family. Or perhaps you have a child afflicted with leukemia or some other serious illness. Perhaps, like the man we encounter in John 9, you have a child who was afflicted with blindness from birth. If so, then the question at the outset of this chapter is no mere theoretical exercise. It is the question which throbs at the very core of your own grief and pain. It is not just an intellectual question, but a deeply emotional and spiritual question:

Why would an all-loving, all-powerful God allow people to suffer?

There is no easy answer to that question. But as we walk alongside Jesus and watch Him as He deals with a man who is blind from birth, we may catch a glimpse of God's eternal purposes in the pain of human existence.

As Jesus and His disciples pass this man, the disciples question Jesus. "Rabbi," they ask, "who sinned, this man or his parents, that he was born blind?" The disciples had evidently been taught, through their Judaic upbringing, that suffering was a direct result of human sin.

Notice that Jesus does not deny that concept in His answer: "Neither this man nor his parents sinned," said Jesus, "but this happened so that the work of God might be displayed in his life." He does not say, "You've got it all wrong. Suffering is just a random event that has nothing to do with sin." No, Jesus only addresses the specifics of this case: "Neither this man nor his parents sinned." As we shall see, there is a link between sin and suffering—but it is not the simple "commit-sin-A-and-consequence-B-follows" sort of linkage. The relationship between sin and suffering is real—but it is subtle.

We live in a world that is fallen and imperfect. As a result, specific sins often seem to go unpunished, and suffering often falls on those who are innocent. In this broken and fragmented world, we often suffer unjustly. In fact, one of the most unjust ironies of all in this world is that much of the suffering we endure as Christians comes not as a result of sin, but as a result of doing good! As some cynic once observed, "No good deed goes unpunished."

Where, then, does this subtle cause/effect relationship between sin and suffering come in? It comes in at the fall of man, in the opening chapters of Genesis. Because sin entered the world through Adam, the entire moral sphere is wobbling drunkenly on its axis. This world, which was created to function justly and perfectly, is now a dysfunctional planet, filled with misery, natural disaster, disease, and death. God did not create the world this way; sin corrupted it.

The Scriptures affirm the fact that we are all affected by this principle of human evil. Whether they are visible or not, we all have handicaps. Someone once said, "When you look at a beautiful, powerful athlete, you are looking at the ruin of an Adam." The finest physical, mental, and emotional specimen in the world is second-best to humanity before the Fall. Our minds and bodies don't function as they were perfectly designed to. Our emotions, which God created in us as a source of joy, have become a source of pain and hindrance to us. Everywhere humanity reflects the weakness of the Fall.

But Jesus, in verse 3, makes it clear that suffering is not always directly traceable to personal sin. Sometimes it is, but often it is not. And in the case of this man born blind, Jesus is emphatic: His blindness is not a result of his sin or his parents' sin.

Why did the disciples ask if the man's own sin could have caused his blindness, since he was *born* blind? The disciples were probably thinking of the Jewish rabbinical tradition which states that it is possible for an unborn fetus to sin. Whatever led the disciples to ask that question, Jesus replies, "No, it was not his sin, nor his parents' sin, that caused him to be blind from birth."

Why, then, was he born blind? "So that the work of God might be displayed in his life," says the Lord.

The Work of God

Jesus gives a positive reason, not a negative one, for this man's blindness. He says, in effect, "This man's blindness is not a meaningless disaster. It is an *opportunity*. God is going to manifest His power and His character through the suffering of this man."

There are many examples of this principle outside of the Bible—people who allow God to display His work through their suffering and through their lives. The famous hymn writer, Fanny Crosby, was one such person. Blind from her earliest babyhood as a result of an accident, she wrote many of the most cherished and enduring hymns of our faith, including "Blessed Assurance, Jesus Is Mine." When she was only eight years old she wrote this little rhyme,

> Oh, what a happy child I am,
> Although I can not see.
> I am resolved that in this world,
> Contented I will be.

How many blessings I enjoy
That other people don't.
To weep and sigh
Because I'm blind,
I cannot and I won't!

Fanny Crosby lived to be over 90, and that beautiful, rejoicing spirit characterized her life all her days. It was a manifestation of the work of God in her life, and it was no less a miracle of God than if He had reached down from heaven and instantly restored her sight!

A Parable in Action

Jesus goes on to say that God's chosen hour has struck in the life of this man born blind. He has lived with his affliction for years. Now the culmination of his suffering is at hand—and the work of God is about to be displayed.

9:4–7 *"As long as it is day, we must do the work of him who sent me. Night is coming, when no one can work. While I am in the world, I am the light of the world."*

Having said this, he spit on the ground, made some mud with the saliva, and put it on the man's eyes. "Go," he told him, "wash in the pool of Siloam" (this word means Sent). So the man went and washed, and came home seeing.

As Jesus looked upon this blind man, He received in His heart a signal from the Father, telling Him it was time to act. In chapter 5, Jesus said that this is how He knew what to do and when to do it. He was given an inner vision of the Father at work, and He did only what He saw the Father doing. So, seeing this blind man, Jesus immediately felt a sense of urgency. That is why Jesus said, "As long as it is day, we must do the work of him who sent me. Night is coming, when no one can work." Time is short, He says. The cross looms, and then there will be no more time for Him to work. With this clear sense of urgency, Jesus moves to do what must be done in this blind man's life.

Then He adds a statement that is laden with powerful symbolism: "While I am in the world, I am the light of the world." In other words, "I was sent to bring light into the world. That is my function. Here is a man in darkness, and it is time to bring light into his world."

Then Jesus proceeds to do the work of healing the man of his blindness. John describes the work that Jesus does in simple, straightforward terms.

Jesus spits on the ground, makes clay of the spittle, and anoints the man's eyes with the clay. Then He sends the man to bathe in the pool of Siloam.

The moment when the miracle is revealed is also described by John with a remarkable economy of words, without any razzle-dazzle or smoke and thunder. He writes, "So the man went and washed, and came home seeing." Clearly, it is not the miracle itself that interests John. It is the deeper significance that he reports.

This act of healing is clearly a *parable in action*. Our Lord is not merely interested in restoring the man's physical sight. Yes, He cares about the man and wants him to be physically whole, but there is a deeper insight to be gained here if we will examine what Jesus does in the performance of this miracle. The deeper significance is to be found in the symbols that Jesus uses to accomplish His miracle.

The primary symbol Jesus uses in this living parable is *clay*. What does clay symbolize in Scripture? In Genesis we are told that God formed man from the dust of the ground, from the clay of the earth. That symbolism is used many times in Scripture. Jeremiah says that God is the Potter, we are the clay. He molds us and shapes us into what He wants us to be. And the apostle Paul likens believers to earthen vessels—clay pots—in which God stores His treasure. Clay is not a very powerful substance. It is malleable and fragile. Throughout Scripture, clay is used as a symbol of human weakness.

When our Lord smears clay over this man's eyes, He is saying that something is hindering the man's sight—both his *physical sight* and his *spiritual sight*. It is the clay of his humanity. The blind man's fallen human nature is a hindrance to seeing spiritual truth and reality. Not that Jesus is singling this man out as spiritually blind. In fact, this man is a symbol for all of us; he represents you and me. We are all spiritually blinded by our fallen human nature.

Notice that Jesus does not take the man by the hand and lead him to the pool of Siloam—a word that means "Sent." Jesus *sends* the man on a journey, blind and alone, to the pool. As he picks his way in the dark, he may stumble, he may lose his way, he may encounter unseen obstacles. There is a difficult journey ahead of him. Only when he gets to the pool will his inner sight be granted him.

I have walked this blind man's route from the temple area, down the deep declivity of the Kidron ravine to the pool of Siloam. It was a rugged walk even for a sighted man, and there were many obstacles along the way. For a blind man to traverse this would be very difficult. He would have to ask for directions and for help, and he might easily fall into some of the ruts along the road. It was a difficult journey the Lord sent him on in search of his sight.

This obstacle-strewn journey is a metaphor, an object lesson of the way we gain our own spiritual sight. Physical eyes can easily be opened by His power, but to open spiritual eyes takes a process of overcoming obstacles that lie in the way. After his physical healing, this man must still gain his *spiritual sight*—and the resistance and obstacles in his path to spiritual vision are many times greater than the obstacles and pitfalls in his path in the Kidron ravine! But as we shall see, this man will overcome these obstacles as well, and he will ultimately find himself at the feet of Jesus, with his spiritual eyes wide open, drinking in the light of the world!

A Spiritual Obstacle Course

The narrative is self-explanatory and requires little comment.

9:8–13 *His neighbors and those who had formerly seen him begging asked, "Isn't this the same man who used to sit and beg?" Some claimed that he was.*
Others said, "No, he only looks like him."
But he himself insisted, "I am the man."
"How then were your eyes opened?" they demanded.
He replied, "The man they call Jesus made some mud and put it on my eyes. He told me to go to Siloam and wash. So I went and washed, and then I could see."
"Where is this man?" they asked him.
"I don't know," he said.
They brought to the Pharisees the man who had been blind.

Notice that all this man knows about Jesus is His name. "The man called Jesus," he says, "made some mud and put it on my eyes." He has heard Jesus' name, but he knows nothing more about Him. That is where he begins. That is the sum total of his knowledge and his faith.

Then a new difficulty arises.

9:14–16 *Now the day on which Jesus had made the mud and opened the man's eyes was a Sabbath. Therefore the Pharisees also asked him how he had received his sight. "He put mud on my eyes," the man replied, "and I washed, and now I see."*
Some of the Pharisees said, "This man is not from God, for he does not keep the Sabbath."
But others asked, "How can a sinner do such miraculous signs?" So they were divided.

I love the simplicity and directness of the man born blind. He never complicates anything. "He put mud on my eyes," the man says, "and I washed, and now I see." There is not one flowery adjective in that sentence. There is not one embellishment or superlative. Whenever he is asked, he simply tells his story—then he shuts his mouth.

Here we see the resistance mounting. Led by the Father, Jesus has again deliberately run afoul of the petty Sabbath regulations of the Jewish leaders. In their eyes, He has broken the Sabbath in three separate ways:

First, He spat on the ground and made mud on the Sabbath. The rabbis held that it was all right to spit on a rock on the Sabbath day because that would not make mud. But spitting on the dirt violated the Sabbath because that made mud, and making mud is work, and work is forbidden on the Sabbath day! That is how ridiculous their regulations were.

Second, Jesus healed on the Sabbath—and the rabbis said it was forbidden to heal on the Sabbath day. They specifically said, "If you find somebody with a broken leg, you can keep it from getting worse, but you cannot make it any better. That would be work."

Third, He used spit as a medicine on the Sabbath. There was a specific instruction in the rabbinical literature that spit could not be used on the Sabbath because, in their culture, spit was considered a medicine. The use of medicine was forbidden on the Sabbath day because that too was a form of work.

The religious leaders had so surrounded the Sabbath with narrow, intricately interpreted, petty regulations that one could hardly breathe without breaking the law! And these regulations were the Pharisees' excuse to reject Jesus. Some said, "How can he be from God? He doesn't keep the rules!" But others were more cautious. "Look at the signs," they said. "How can a sinner do such miracles? God seems to endorse what he does!" So there was division among the Pharisees.

Throughout this divisive debate, the formerly blind man sits and listens quietly. Now we see the effect that these events are having on the man's level of faith.

9:17 *Finally they turned again to the blind man, "What have you to say about him? It was your eyes he opened."*
The man replied, "He is a prophet."

This man has grown spiritually. He still regards Jesus as a man, but he sees Him as God's man, a gifted man, a man with insight and understanding, a prophet. All of the Pharisees' resistance to accepting this remarkable miracle has actually deepened his insight and understanding!

Involving the Parents

The Pharisees cannot accept this man's assessment of Jesus. It sets their teeth on edge! So they try another plan of attack. Somehow they need to undermine the man's credibility as a real blind man if they want to assail Jesus' credibility as a healer. So, in verses 18 to 23, they involve the man's parents in the issue.

9:18–23 *The Jews still did not believe that he had been blind and had received his sight until they sent for the man's parents. "Is this your son?" they asked. "Is this the one you say was born blind? How is it that now he can see?"*

"We know he is our son," the parents answered, "and we know he was born blind. But how he can see now, or who opened his eyes, we don't know. Ask him. He is of age; he will speak for himself." His parents said this because they were afraid of the Jews, for already the Jews had decided that anyone who acknowledged that Jesus was the Christ would be put out of the synagogue. That was why his parents said, "He is of age; ask him."

Notice that the man's parents were not ready to go very far in helping him. They admitted he was their son, they confirmed that he had been born blind, but they would go no further. They knew that the religious leaders had already threatened that anyone believing in Jesus was to be put out of the synagogue—that is, excommunicated from the Jewish faith! To these deeply religious people, this was a frightening possibility. So his parents hesitated to take a stand. Instead, they replied, "He is of age; ask him."

The man's parents knew who had opened their son's eyes, but they lied and refused to say because they were afraid. The clay of fallen, fearful, weak humanity continued to blind the eyes of those who were involved in this story.

A Lesson in Witnessing

Now the resistance grows even more intense. The spiritual obstacles multiply. Next the Pharisees call the man who had been blind to the witness stand.

9:24–25 *A second time they summoned the man who had been blind. "Give glory to God," they said. "We know this man is a sinner."*

He replied, "Whether he is a sinner or not, I don't know. One thing I do know. I was blind but now I see!"

When the Pharisees told the man, "Give glory to God," they were putting him under oath. It's the equivalent of putting a person on the witness stand and saying, "Do you solemnly swear to tell the truth, the whole truth, and nothing but the truth, so help you God?" Of course, the Pharisees don't really want the truth. They want the man to confirm their preconceived conclusions.

But he refuses to be drawn into their theological arguments. "Whether he is a sinner or not," he says, "I don't know. One thing I do know. I was blind but now I see!"

Here is a man who knows how to witness! He knows how to share the gospel—and we should take lessons from him. Many people are afraid to say anything about the Lord because they think they will be dragged into a theological argument that will be over their heads. But "witnessing" simply means saying what God has done for you. You don't have to understand theology to be a witness. All you have to do is what this man did: Tell what God has done in your life.

You may not be an authority on theology, but you *are* the world's greatest authority on what has happened to you. As someone once said, "A man with an experience is never at the mercy of a man with only an argument." When you stand on your own experience, no one can argue with that. No one can deny what the Lord has done in your life.

The Pharisees' Blunder

The Pharisees are now about to dig a pit for themselves. Here they fall into their own trap.

9:26–29 *Then they asked him, "What did he do to you? How did he open your eyes?"*

He answered, "I have told you already and you did not listen. Why do you want to hear it again? Do you want to become his disciples, too?"

Then they hurled insults at him and said, "You are this fellow's disciple! We are disciples of Moses! We know that God spoke to Moses, but as for this fellow, we don't even know where he comes from."

The Pharisees have made a fatal mistake! They have admitted there is something they don't know—"as for this fellow, we don't even know where he comes from"—and the man who was blind seizes upon it.

9:30–33 *The man answered, "Now that is remarkable! You don't know where he comes from, yet he opened my eyes. We know that God does not listen to* *sinners. He listens to the godly man who does his will. Nobody has ever heard of opening the eyes of a man born blind. If this man were not from God, he could do nothing."*

Now he has them! With this simple, logical argument, the man who was healed of blindness has pinned the Pharisees to the wall. Note the man's powerful and unassailable argument: "You Pharisees don't know where this man came from, you admit your ignorance—yet He opened my eyes! Obviously, I can now see more clearly than you! You religious leaders are missing the truth that's right in front of your eyes! You are facing the greatest miracle anyone has ever seen—the opening of the eyes of a man born blind! How do you explain this miracle if this man did not come from God?"

Observe, also, how this man has grown in his faith and his understanding. At first, he only knew the man who healed him as "the man they call Jesus." As his understanding grew, the man saw Jesus as "a prophet." Now he says Jesus is the man "from God." In other words, He is not just a prophet, but the One whom God has sent: the Messiah! His insight has grown progressively and tremendously. He has now come to a place of understanding who Jesus is. Spiritually, he has reached the pool of Siloam.

Excommunicated!

As they did earlier in their dialogue with Jesus, the Pharisees have run out of logical argument, so they resort to personal invective and violence.

9:34 *To this they replied, "You were steeped in sin at birth; how dare you lecture us!" And they threw him out.*

When the Pharisees say, "You were steeped in sin at birth," they are referring to his blindness. His physical condition marked him as a sinner in their eyes—someone cursed by God. This attitude gave them the right to feel smugly superior to the "physically challenged" people of their age.

The man's logical and irrefutable replies to their irrational and biased accusations have whipped them into a froth of fury. So, instead of dealing with the logic of his arguments, they call him a cursed sinner, then they lay hands on him and physically throw him out into the street. He is excommunicated from the synagogue—literally out on his ear!

"Lord, I Believe!"

In verse 35 through 38, Jesus and the blind man are brought back together for an important dialogue.

9:35–38 *Jesus heard that they had thrown him out, and when he found him, he said, "Do you believe in the Son of Man?"*

"Who is he, sir?" the man asked. "Tell me so that I may believe in him."

"Jesus said, "You have now seen him; in fact, he is the one speaking with you."

Then the man said, "Lord, I believe," and he worshiped him.

Notice that the man did not have to find Jesus. Jesus found him! After the clay had been washed away from the spiritual eyes of this man, he could see Jesus. But Jesus had one more operation to perform on this man's spiritual eyesight. He asked the man if he believed in the Son of Man, and the man said, "Who is he, sir? Tell me so that I may believe in him."

Then, in a scene that is made powerful by its very simplicity, Jesus says, in effect, "You are looking at him! I am the Son of Man." And the man who was blind fell instantly to his knees in worship!

Jesus adds a closing commentary to this "parable in action" next.

9:39–41 *Jesus said, "For judgment I have come into this world, so that the blind will see and those who see will become blind."*

Some Pharisees who were with him heard him say this and asked, "What? Are we blind too?"

Jesus said, "If you were blind, you would not be guilty of sin; but now that you claim you can see, your guilt remains."

One of the characteristics of human clay is that it begins to fancy itself wise and powerful. We begin to think we are strong and knowledgeable. One of the chief tragedies of any age is the arrogance of men of knowledge who claim to know, but who cannot see their hand before their eyes. Jesus has described them as "blind guides of the blind." Their fate, He said, is that both will fall into the ditch.

In Matthew 11, Jesus prayed, "I praise you, Father, Lord of heaven and earth, because you have hidden these things from the wise and learned, and revealed them to little children."[1] As we read the Scriptures, we should do so with a recognition of our own desperate ignorance, and of our need to be taught by God. He is able to open our eyes if we admit we do not see. But if we think we know, then we are stumbling about in blindness. And walking blind is a good way to end up in a pit.

In verse 40 and 42, there is a brief dialogue between Jesus and some of the Pharisees who were walking along with Him. They ask Him, "Are we blind too?" Jesus replies, in effect, "You are responsible for the light you have, for the truth you know. If you were blind, then you would not be held accountable for truth you were unable to see. But if you, being Pharisees, claim that you can see, yet you willfully ignore the truth of my word, then you will be held accountable and guilty for seeing the light yet choosing to live in darkness." A sobering warning to all of us who have heard the truth, who have seen the light.

The Lord of Light has revealed Himself to us in our darkness. Perhaps you have come to Christ through difficulty, through hardship, through trial, through resistance, but that is all part of God's way to show us the full spectrum, all the rainbow colors, of God's light. As we look to Jesus, the light of the world, our vision may be clouded by tears. It may be difficult to see Him clearly in all His beauty, glory, and majesty.

We may find it hard to see Jesus because of our suffering or the suffering of someone close to us—a spouse or a parent or a child. We may say, "How can a loving, all-powerful God allow such suffering in the life of this innocent person?" And it is true: Very often, suffering comes into our lives that has no direct relationship to sin. Suffering is not always God's discipline or a result of being punished for sin. Suffering is often simply a result of this broken, fallen world into which we have been born.

But Jesus stands ready to break through the darkness of our sin, our ignorance, and even our suffering. He is the light of the world.

Chapter Twenty-Eight

The Shepherd and His Sheep

John 10:1–21

I grew up in Montana, where there are lots of sheep. In those days, sheepherders were considered the lowest form of life in Montana society. Sheepherders were hired hands, unskilled labor. If you couldn't find any other way to make a living, then you became a sheepherder. Not that sheepherders were bad people. There were good, conscientious sheepherders, and there were shiftless, lazy, unreliable sheepherders. Some did a good job, some did not.

But I have learned that there is a great deal of difference between a modern sheepherder and the kind of shepherd that we find pictured for us in John chapter 10. In this chapter, Jesus is pictured for us as the Good Shepherd—not the sheepherder—of the sheep.

The Marks of the True Shepherd

In this chapter, our Lord builds His teaching around the image of a shepherd. He clearly sets Himself apart as the True Shepherd of the sheep in contrast to the false shepherds. Who are the false shepherds? In the context of preceding events—Jesus' debate with the Pharisees in the temple court and the uproar over His healing of the man born blind—it is clear that Jesus sees the Pharisaical rulers of the Jews as false shepherds who twist and distort the law of God.

10:1–6 *"I tell you the truth, the man who does not enter the sheep pen by the gate, but climbs in by some other way, is a thief and robber. The man who enters by the gate is the shepherd of his sheep. The watchman opens the gate for him, and the sheep listen to his voice. He calls his own sheep by name and leads them out. When he has brought out all his own, he goes on ahead of them, and his sheep follow him because they know his voice. But they will never follow a stranger; in fact, they will run away from him because they do not recognize a stranger's voice." Jesus used this figure of speech, but they did not understand what he was telling them.*

In the Middle East, shepherds brought their flocks into one central sheep-fold every evening. There, as many as a half dozen flocks were gathered together and guarded by a gatekeeper behind locked doors. In the morning, the shepherds returned and each called his own sheep. Although the flocks had been mingled together, each flock knew its own shepherd's voice. The sheep of each flock would follow their own shepherd and no other. This is the picture Jesus uses to explain the encounter in chapter 9 between the man who had been born blind and the false shepherds, the Pharisees.

In this section we learn the distinguishing marks of the True Shepherd of the sheep. Through the centuries there have been many false shepherds. Even today there are many false teachers presenting false views of Jesus. Many people ask, "Who is the true Jesus? Who is the true Shepherd of the sheep?" There is the Jesus of the Moonies, the Jesus of the Jehovah's Witnesses, the Jesus of the Christian Scientists, the Jesus of the Mormons, the Jesus of the New Age, the Jesus of a thousand bizarre cults and philosophies. Which Jesus is the True Shepherd? There are five distinguishing marks, Jesus declares, by which we can know which is the True Shepherd.

First mark: "The man who does not enter the sheep pen by the gate, but climbs in by some other way, is a thief and robber. The man who enters by the gate is the shepherd of his sheep." What does He mean, "the gate?" He is referring, of course, to the normal, proper entrance to a sheepfold.

Jesus entered by the proper gate of Old Testament prophecy: He was born in Bethlehem, in accord with the prophecy of Micah. He was born of a virgin, as predicted in Isaiah 7:14. The prophets predicted the special nature of His birth, how He would appear to the nation, how He would be introduced, where He would live, what He would say, and what He would do when He came. Jesus fulfilled all of those prophecies. He came through the gate, exactly as predicted and expected. No other person ever came to Israel this way. If anyone comes any other way, declares Jesus, he "is a thief and rob-ber." But Jesus is the true Shepherd of the sheep.

Second mark: "The watchman opens the gate for him." The watchman or gatekeeper is, of course, John the Baptist. He opened the door. He was the "voice of one calling in the desert, 'Make straight the way for the Lord.' "[1] John the Baptist identified Jesus with the words, "Look, the Lamb of God, who takes away the sin of the world!"[2] The gatekeeper—John the Baptist— opened the gate for the Lamb.

Third mark: "The sheep listen to his voice. He calls his own sheep by name." Every encounter Jesus had in this gospel was a personal encounter with a unique human individual, a person with a name and a face. He met Nicodemus by night. He met the woman at the well of Samaria. He met an invalid man at the pool of Bethesda. He met the man born blind. In each of these encounters, He related to that person as a unique individual with a name and a face. That is the way He relates to you and me. He calls us by name. He meets us in a one-to-one relationship.

Fourth mark: "He . . . leads them out. . . . He goes on ahead of them." When Jesus calls us by name, He leads us out of the blindness and darkness of the world. He goes before us as our example and our guide. In every trial, temptation, sorrow, hurt—even through death itself—Jesus has already gone ahead of us. That is the great truth of Scripture that encourages us to face the pressures, dangers, and pitfalls of life: The Shepherd goes before us. In the words of the 23rd Psalm, "Even though I walk through the valley of the shadow of death, I will fear no evil, for you are with me; your rod and your staff, they comfort me."[3]

Fifth mark: "His sheep follow him because they know his voice. But they will never follow a stranger; in fact, they will run away from a stranger, because they do not recognize his voice." A Christian friend once sent me an article about the teaching of a television evangelist who promised that if people gave money to his ministry, God would make them rich. My friend wrote across the top of the article, "There's something wrong with this!" How right he was! He recognized that this false teaching was not the voice of the Shepherd.

The Gate

Jesus has given us a beautiful picture of the Good Shepherd's relationship to us, His sheep. But verse 6 says that the people did not understand what He was telling them, so in verses 7 through 10, Jesus takes a different tack.

10:7–10 *Therefore Jesus said again, "I tell you the truth, I am the gate for the sheep. All who ever came before me were thieves and robbers, but the sheep did not listen to them. I am the gate; whoever enters through me will be saved. He will come in and go out, and find pasture. The thief comes only to steal and kill and destroy; I have come that they may have life, and have it to the full."*

Now Jesus changes the figure of speech: In this passage, He is not the Shepherd but the gate for the sheep. This is an image taken from the middle of the work day of an ancient Middle Eastern shepherd. In those days, the shepherd would lead his flock out of the sheepfold to the hillsides where they grazed through the morning hours. Then in the early afternoon, he provided a temporary shelter built of shrubs where they could rest. It was a corral-type structure within which the sheep could lie, safe and protected from wild beasts. This corral had an opening, and the shepherd himself would lie across it as a gate, so that no predator could go in, no sheep could go out, without crossing over him. This is the image Jesus uses when He says, "I am the gate for the sheep."

How does Jesus serve this protective role in our lives? By being the gateway to truth. As we enter into Him, we come into an understanding of truth. The Pharisees—whom Jesus called "thieves and robbers"—had stolen the truth. In the case of the man born blind, they had robbed him of the true meaning of the Sabbath, the true meaning of the law, and the meaning of the Shepherd. Jesus is saying, "I am the doorway to understanding the truth about life. And I am the barrier against the error of those false teachers, the thieves and robbers who would snatch away your faith. I bring you understanding, so you will not follow error."

Abundant Life

Jesus goes on to say that whoever enters through Him, through the gate, "will come in and go out, and find pasture." To go into the fold means to find security—something we all deeply desire, especially in this troubled and anxious world. If we enter into Jesus, we do not have to worry about the nuclear threat or the crime rate or the zigs and zags of an uncertain economy. Jesus is our security. He is in charge of all things. "All authority in heaven and on earth has been given to me," Jesus declared to His disciples following His resurrection.[4]

Jesus also says that whoever enters through Him will "go out, and find pasture." To go out means to find liberty. Jesus sends us out into the world again. As He said to His disciples, "I am sending you out like sheep among wolves."[5] You probably know that feeling. You may have felt like a sheep among wolves in your workplace, in your neighborhood—even in your family, if you come from a non-Christian family. Jesus sends you out into the world, but He doesn't send you alone. He is with you, alongside you, and that gives you the liberty to move out into life in any dimension. You can go in and go out. You have both security and liberty.

In verse 10 we find one of the most familiar quotations of Jesus: "The thief comes only to steal and kill and destroy; I have come that they may have life, and have it to the full." Or, as it is more commonly quoted in the King James Version, "I am come that they might have life, and that they might have it more abundantly." Abundant life! Not just surviving, not just existing, but truly *living life to the fullest!*

An abundant life, of course, means a life filled with excitement and adventure. I look back now on almost sixty years of walking with the Lord, and I want to tell you I could not have chosen a more exciting life than the one God has given me! It is filled with constant expectation of what is coming next. Sometimes it is dangerous, sometimes it is difficult, but it is always filled with a sense of adventure. That is what Jesus means by "the abundant life."

He Shares His Life With Us

In the next section, Jesus returns to the metaphor of the Shepherd.

10:11–15 *"I am the good shepherd. The good shepherd lays down his life for the sheep. The hired hand is not the shepherd who owns the sheep. So when he sees the wolf coming, he abandons the sheep and runs away. Then the wolf attacks the flock and scatters it. The man runs away because he is a hired hand and cares nothing for the sheep.*

"I am the good shepherd; I know my sheep and my sheep know me—just as the Father knows me and I know the Father—and I lay down my life for the sheep."

The primary characteristic of the Good Shepherd is that He loves and loves and loves—all the way to the point of death. He is willing to die for the sheep. After the crucifixion and the resurrection, Jesus' followers could never get over the fact that Jesus loved them so much He was willing to die for them. Many of the epistles of Paul, John, James, and Peter contain awestruck references to the great, self-sacrificing love of the Savior. They are continually amazed that the sinless Son of God would give Himself to die for sinful men and women. But that is the mark of the Good Shepherd!

In verses 12 and 13, Jesus contrasts the Good Shepherd with the hired hand. The hired hand doesn't own the sheep, doesn't care about the sheep, and won't risk himself for the sheep. He's just there to collect his paycheck. If danger comes, he's the first one to run. But Jesus is the Good Shepherd. He lays down His life for the sheep.

Notice, too, that Jesus not only lays down His life, but He *shares His* life with the sheep. He says in verse 14, "I am the good shepherd; I know my sheep and my sheep know me—just as the Father knows me and I know the Father." This is a picture of intimacy and intense fellowship between the Shepherd and the sheep.

My own father left home when I was ten years old. Throughout my boyhood and adolescence, I longed to have a father. I saw him from time to time, but in all those years I cannot remember one time he ever showed me any affection. He was not cruel; he just ignored me. That is probably why as a boy I was always moved by the sight of a father and son enjoying each other's company. Since I have grown to adulthood, God in His grace has given me four precious daughters to love. And as a pastor, I have also had the privilege of knowing many young men who have been like sons to me. It has been a rich experience to know and to share my life with these young men and with my own daughters, and for them to share their lives with me.

That is what Jesus speaks of here: An intimacy of fellowship, a beautiful relationship between Jesus and His own, a relationship which mirrors the relationship between the Father and the Son. This relationship, says Jesus, is a result of the sacrifice of His life for us. He lays down His life for us, He shares His life with us, and we share ours with Him.

The Great Shepherd

In the final section of the Lord's discourse on the Shepherd and the sheep, Jesus employs a figure of speech that we can properly call "the *Great* Shepherd."

10:16–18 *"I have other sheep that are not of this sheep pen. I must bring them also. They too will listen to my voice, and there shall be one flock and one shepherd. The reason my Father loves me is that I lay down my life—only to take it up again. No one takes it from me, but I lay it down of my own accord. I have authority to lay it down and authority to take it up again. This command I received from my Father."*

The gracious benediction at the end of the letter to the Hebrews says, "May the God of peace, who through the blood of the eternal covenant brought back from the dead our Lord Jesus, that great Shepherd of the sheep, equip you with everything good for doing His will, and may he work in us what is pleasing to him, through Jesus Christ, to whom be glory for ever and ever. Amen."[6] This benediction points to Jesus as the Great Shepherd.

The first thing Jesus says about His role as the Great Shepherd is that "I have other sheep that are not of this sheep pen." When He says "this sheep pen," He is referring to the nation Israel. Here Jesus is lifting His eyes beyond the cross, beyond the resurrection, and He foresees the gospel going forth to all the nations of the earth. When the Great Shepherd laid down His life for the sheep, He laid it down for both Jews and Gentiles. After His death and resurrection, the gospel broke down those boundaries between Jew and Gentile, and the church of the Great Shepherd spread out beyond the borders of Israel and out into every corner of the earth.

There are still separate sheep pens, and God has a special plan for the sheep pen of Israel, much of which is disclosed in the Old Testament and the book of Revelation. But these separate sheep pens still make up one flock, not two. As Paul says, "There is one body and one Spirit . . . one Lord, one faith, one baptism; one God and Father of all, who is over all and through all and in all."[7] And that one great flock is cared for and loved by one Great Shepherd.

Jesus goes on to say that He lays down His life only to take it up again. He looks forward to the cross—and to the resurrection.

Even though He will be executed like a criminal, even though His life will be fastened to a wooden cross with bloody nails, He makes it clear that He and He alone has the authority to lay down His life and take it up again. Jesus was not hounded to death. He was not crucified against His will. He could have prevented His death and suffering. That is the meaning of the bloody sweat that rolled off of Him in the Garden of Gethsemane. That is the meaning of His plea in the Garden, "My Father, if it is possible, may this cup be taken from me. Yet not as I will, but as you will."[8] He willingly, decisively obeyed the Father to the end.

Divided Opinion

In the end, the work of the Great Shepherd creates a division among men. The response of the Jewish leaders to His message is recorded in the following verses.

10:19–21 *At these words the Jews were again divided. Many of them said, "He is demon-possessed and raving mad. Why listen to him?"*

But others said, "These are not the sayings of a man possessed by a demon. Can a demon open the eyes of the blind?"

People are still divided over Jesus today. "Why pay any attention to Him? This the twentieth century—almost the twenty-first! We don't need a Savior today. Jesus is irrelevant. How can one man's death on a cross 2,000 years ago have any meaning in my life today? Why listen to Him?"

Others say, "Jesus is the ultimate reality. He has changed my life. He has opened my eyes and removed my blindness. Jesus is everything to me."

Opinion on Jesus must divide and divide sharply, because He has left us no middle ground. And once you examine the evidence, once you hear His words, the only reasonable conclusion is that Jesus is who He says He is: the Good Shepherd, who gives His life for the flock, who shares His life with you and me. No one else can satisfy your heart, no one else can resolve the issues of your life, no one can answer the questions about life, death, and the eternal life to come like Jesus can. No one can touch human blindness and human pain and human conflict like Jesus can, because no one can bring healing with a touch like Jesus can.

He is our Shepherd and we are His sheep.

Chapter Twenty-Nine

A Mere Man—or the God-Man?

John 10:22–42

Thee congressman had struggled for weeks over a decision as to how to vote in a highly-charged, controversial issue. His vote turned out to be the swing vote in a legislative body that was evenly divided over the issue. No matter which way he voted, he was going to make a lot of enemies—but he had no idea how soon his enemies would be at his throat.

As he walked out of the House chamber, he was immediately surrounded by angry lobbyists, angry constituents, angry politicians, and reporters shouting questions. They completely encircled him so that he couldn't even walk down the hall. So he stopped and shouted over the babble of voices, "Sorry, I didn't get that! Would you mind screaming that again?"

Jesus knew what it felt like to be encircled and hemmed in by a mob of screaming, angry opponents. As we enter the last half of John 10, we again find Jesus in a dramatic encounter with the leaders of the Jews—and this time they have Him surrounded!

Three Missing Months

Last chapter, we left off at verse 21, with the Pharisees divided and in disarray over Jesus' powerful message about the Good Shepherd and the sheep. That dialogue took place in connection with the Feast of Tabernacles in Jerusalem in early October.

As we come to verse 22, we find that there is a silent lapse of about three months between verses 21 and 22. John sets the stage here.

10:21–23 *Then came the Feast of Dedication at Jerusalem. It was winter, and Jesus was in the temple area walking in Solomon's Colonnade.*

The Feast of Dedication mentioned here is the familiar Jewish holiday called Hanukkah, which takes place in late December—about three months after the Feast of Tabernacles. Jesus has returned to Jerusalem and is walking in the temple area called Solomon's Colonnade, a roofed-in enclosure supported by beautiful decorated columns.

Where was Jesus during the silent three months between verses 21 and 22? The most likely answer is that He had returned to Galilee to minister there. The gospel of Luke records many incidents in the life of Jesus that took place in Galilee. It seems likely that these events occurred in this interim period when, following the Feast of Tabernacles, Jesus went back to Galilee and there sent out the seventy disciples to the various cities in Galilee.

Jesus did many miracles during that time which John chose not to record. As John himself notes in the last verse of his gospel, "Jesus did many other things as well. If every one of them were written down, I suppose that even the whole world would not have room for the books that would be written." John was selective in the editing of his material, and chose not to duplicate much of what was already written in the other gospels—hence the silent three months in the middle of John 10.

John notes that this story takes place in winter, which is the rainy season in Israel. As Jesus walked in Solomon's Colonnade, He was probably sheltered from the rain. There in the stately surroundings of the temple of Jerusalem, during the Feast of Hanukkah, Jesus resumed His teaching.

Hanukkah celebrates the purification and rededication of the temple after it was defiled by the Syrian king Antiochus Epiphanes in the year 165 B.C. The feast looks back on that dramatic period in Israel's history when the Maccabee family revolted against the Syrian overlords. After a terrible time of slaughter and oppression, in which the Syrians sacrificed pigs to idols on the altars of God's temple, Judas Maccabeus and his sons drove out the Syrians, reclaimed the temple for the Lord, and dedicated it anew. That event is celebrated to this day in the Feast of Hanukkah.

There are two likely reasons Jesus returned to Jerusalem. First, He wanted to resume His teaching about His role as the Shepherd of Israel. All of chapter 10 is built around the theme, "The Lord is my Shepherd." Second, He wanted to make arrangements for His final return to Jerusalem on Palm Sunday, when He would enter the city and offer Himself as the Lamb of God, who would be slain for the sins of the world.

"Are You or Aren't You?"

Next we see the beginning of yet another confrontation between Jesus and His opponents.

10:24–26 *The Jews gathered around him, saying, "How long will you keep us in suspense? If you are the Christ [the Messiah], tell us plainly."*

Jesus answered, "I did tell you, but you do not believe. The miracles I do in my Father's name speak for me, but you do not believe because you are not my sheep."

Notice that phrase, "The Jews gathered around him." The original language indicates that the Jewish leaders completely encircled Jesus. He was completely ringed by His enemies—a picture of intense confrontation and threat. In the modern vernacular, they were "in His face." They forced Him to confront their question—and they were determined not to let Him melt away into the crowd as He had done before.

Their question: "Are you the Messiah, or aren't you? If you are, tell us plainly."

The Lord's answer: "I have already told you, but you still do not believe."

If you read John's account very carefully, you will see that there is no place where He has directly stated to the Pharisees, "I am the Christ, I am the Messiah." He did declare Himself as the Messiah to the woman at the well in John 4. And to the man born blind in John 9, He revealed Himself as "the Son of Man." But to these Jewish leaders, He never said, "I am the Messiah." Why?

Because their idea of the Messiah was light-years from the truth. Their own Scriptures predicted what the Messiah would be like and what He would do, but they had completely misread those Scriptures. If He had said, "I am the Messiah," that would have conjured up the image in their minds of a conquering hero who, like the family of Judas Maccabeus, would drive out the Romans, free the temple, and enable the Jews to once again control their own land and their own destiny. That was not the messianic plan that the Father was working out in the earthly life and ministry of Jesus, and He had no wish to mislead the Jews or raise false political hopes in their minds.

So Jesus used other means to demonstrate the fact that He was the Messiah.

Why People Reject the Shepherd

Many Christians wonder, "Why don't people believe in Jesus? Why do they resist the gospel? If He fulfilled the Scriptures so completely, why don't people believe?" Here, the Pharisees have demanded a clear answer as to His identity—is He or is He not the Messiah?—and Jesus, in His reply, gives three reasons why people reject Him.

First, Jesus says that it is not for lack of information! They have plenty of evidence as to His identity—but they have chosen to ignore it. When they demanded that He tell them plainly if He is the Messiah, He replies, "I've already told you." He had not told them in words. He had told them in a language that speaks so much louder than words: Deeds. The old maxim applies here: "Actions speak louder than words." Or, as Ralph Waldo Emerson said, "What you do speaks so loudly I can't hear what you say." But these Pharisees were so willfully hard of hearing and hard of seeing that they could neither see His deeds nor hear His words.

The prophet Isaiah had predicted that when the Messiah came, the ears of the deaf would be unstopped, the eyes of the blind would be opened, the lame would leap as the hart, and the tongue of the dumb would sing.[1] All of these things had taken place under Jesus' ministry. So Jesus clearly indicated by His deeds that He was the Messiah. But the Pharisees refused to "listen" to the loud and clear message of His deeds.

I am reminded of an incident in the life of a pastor friend of mine. This pastor ministered in a large church in an affluent community. One morning he decided to drive down the hill from his home to the newsstand to pick up a paper. He was dressed in dingy gray sweatpants, old tennis shoes, and he wore no shirt. In short, he looked like a bum! He got in the car, drove down the hill, and parked by the newsstand. He bought a paper, then got back into the car and turned the key. It wouldn't start.

It was about two miles back to the house, so he decided to call his wife and have her come down and pick him up in the other car. There was a pay-phone nearby—but he had spent all of his change on the newspaper.

So, ill-dressed as he was, he went to a nearby house and rang the doorbell. A woman opened the door and eyed him warily as he explained that he was the pastor of that large, well-known church in her community. At that moment, he looked more like a prison escapee than a pastor, so it took a lot of explaining. Somehow he managed to convince her that he was who he said he was, and she let him use her phone.

It's not easy to convince people you are who you are when you don't match their expectations! That is the problem Jesus faced. The Jews expected a military leader who would free them from the yoke of Rome, but He came as a Suffering Servant to give Himself for the sins of humanity, and to break Satan's stranglehold of evil on the human race. Jesus completely confounded their expectations. That is why He didn't say to them bluntly, "I am the Messiah."

The second reason people reject Jesus is that they do not want to examine the evidence He has presented. "The miracles I do in my Father's name speak for me," He says in verses 25 and 26, "but you do not believe. . . ." Just as in

Jesus' time, people today have an enormous tendency to select only the evidence that supports their point of view. Anything that might contradict their biases is quickly swept under the rug.

The third reason people reject Jesus as their Shepherd is the most significant of all: "You do not believe because you are not my sheep." Jesus is saying, "You have never come to me. You have never gotten close to me. You have never really found out who I am. You have never asked me to do anything in your life. You have no personal experience of what I can do. You are not part of the flock of which I am the Good Shepherd." That is the third reason many people never find God.

The Great Assurance

Jesus has just set the stage for one of the greatest passages in the Bible. This next passage contains some of my favorite verses of Scripture.

10:27–29 *"My sheep listen to my voice; I know them, and they follow me. I give them eternal life, and they shall never perish; no one can snatch them out of my hand. My Father, who has given them to me, is greater than all; no one can snatch them out of my Father's hand."*

This is one of the most precious assurances in all of Scripture. In these verses, Jesus answers two questions which, at one time or another, trouble the mind of every Christian:

(1) How can you tell a true Christian from one who merely claims to be a Christian?

(2) Can a born-again follower of Christ ever lose his or her salvation?

Verse 27 answers the first question. Jesus says, "My sheep listen to my voice." That is, they are attracted to what Jesus has to say. They believe that what He says is the truth, and they long to hear more.

One of the most encouraging aspects of my forty-plus years of ministry has been seeing the hunger of God's people for His Word. What brings hundreds of people to church every Sunday morning when they could be at the mountains, at the beach, or sleeping in late? They are attracted by the voice of Jesus. Not the preacher's voice or the voice of the choir, but the voice of the Shepherd Himself. They seek His insight, His understanding of the secrets of life, His solutions to the problems of life. That is a prime characteristic of a true sheep of the Shepherd: They long to hear the word of God. "My sheep listen to my voice."

Jesus goes on to say, "I know them, and they follow me." The true sheep of the Good Shepherd are personally, individually welcomed by Him. They feel His acceptance. They know they belong. They feel the Shepherd's strong arms around them as He lifts them and carries them over the rugged terrain of life.

And because they are known by Him, they follow Him. They obey the Good Shepherd and do what He commands. Oh, they will be wayward and willful at times, and they will occasionally lose their way. But the Good Shepherd will seek them and find them, and they will follow. True sheep do not follow the way of the world but the way of the Shepherd.

Why do the true sheep listen to the Shepherd's voice and follow Him? What has made the difference in their lives? The answer is in verse 28: "I give them eternal life, and they shall never perish; no one can snatch them out of my hand." We are drawn to Him because He gives us eternal life—not just once, but continuously. In the original language, Jesus' statement, "I give them eternal life," is made in the present indicative tense, which means He is saying, "I keep on giving to them eternal life, continuously, again and again, never stopping." We are attracted to Him because He is the source of our life.

"They shall never perish," adds Jesus. Eternal life is a quality of life that has no end—and that is an assurance which attracts us to God. We live in a world of corruption and death, a world that is perishing—yet we know that we will never perish, and that is the truth which attracts us to Jesus.

In verses 28 and 29, Jesus answers the question that so many Christians ask: Can a born-again follower of Christ ever lose his or her salvation? And the answer Jesus gives is *no.* Eternal life is a quality of life that is assured, guarded, protected, and guaranteed by God Himself. "No one can snatch them out of my hand," says the Lord. "My Father, who has given them to me, is greater than all; no one can snatch them out of my Father's hand." No one, not even we ourselves, can take us out of the Father's hand.

The man I call my "patron saint," Dr. H. A. Ironside, once preached on the subject of the security of the believer. A woman came up to him afterwards and said, "I don't agree with your doctrine."

"What don't you agree with?" he asked her.

"Well, this doctrine of once saved, always saved," she replied.

"Let me read you a verse which supports this doctrine," he said.

"Oh, I know what you are going to read. You're going to read John 10:28, aren't you?"

"As a matter of fact, that is the verse I was going to read." So he read the words: "I give them eternal life, and they shall never perish; no one can snatch them out of my hand." Then he looked her in the eye and asked her, "Do you believe those words?"

"Not as you interpret them," she replied.

"But I didn't interpret them at all! I just read them to you."

"Well," she replied, "I don't believe those words mean what you say they mean."

"Then let me read the verse this way," he said. "Supposing Jesus said, 'I give them life for twenty years, and they shall never perish for twenty years and no one can snatch them out of my hand for twenty years.' What would you think that means?"

"I think that means they would be safe for twenty years."

"Let us say we changed twenty years to forty years. Would they be safe for forty years?"

"Yes," she said, "I think they would be safe for forty years."

"But it doesn't say twenty years or forty years, it says forever: 'and they shall *never* perish.' The Greek text is very strong at that point. What it literally says is, 'They shall not ever perish forever.' Let's read it that way: 'I give unto them life forever and they shall never perish forever.' Do you believe that?"

"Not the way you interpret it," she replied.

At this point, Dr. Ironside could only throw up his hands. There is an old saying: "A man convinced against his will is of the same opinion still." Or in this case, a woman convinced against her will is of the same opinion still.

But to those who are willing to take this verse at face value, who are not looking to wring some hidden and esoteric meaning out of it that is just not there, this verse is one of the greatest sources of assurance in the entire Bible. We are kept by the sovereign power and the eternal love of God. We may struggle, we may hurt, we may go through times of depression. Our feelings may go up and down, but God's promise to us never changes: If we come to Jesus and become part of His flock, He is our Great Shepherd and we can never perish or be taken out of His hand.

A Shocking Claim

Now we come to another staggering claim of Jesus, one which must have left His opponents' jaws dropping open. In verses 30 through 33, we find this exchange, beginning with the words of Jesus.

10:30–33 *"I and the Father are one."*

Again the Jews picked up stones to stone him, but Jesus said to them, "I have shown you many great miracles from the Father. For which of these do you stone me?"

"We are not stoning you for any of these," replied the Jews, "but for blasphemy, because you, a mere man, claim to be God."

Just as we saw in John 8:58—where Jesus said, "Before Abraham was born, I am!"—we have a scene in which Jesus makes a clear and unmistakable claim to be God. And just as we saw before, we see again that the Jewish leaders respond by taking up stones to stone Him. Though there are some who contend that Jesus never claimed to be God, it is impossible for anyone who has honestly and objectively read the New Testament to say such a thing. Here, in these verses, is additional proof.

The Jews clearly understood that Jesus was claiming deity for Himself. Just as they did in John 8, these Jewish leaders again reach for stones with which to put Jesus to death. They did so because the Law directed that if a man claimed to be God, he was a blasphemer and a dangerous influence on society.

Of course, to these Jews, a charge of blasphemy is just a pretext. They do not want to destroy Jesus out of a pure zeal for God's law. They want to shut Him up because He says things that are uncomfortable to hear, and which pierce their religious facade. When Jesus finally makes a statement that can be used against Him as blasphemy, they think, "Aha, we've got Him now! He made a claim that is so clear we don't even have to wait for the Romans to rule on this! We'll stone Him right here in the temple courts and put Him to death according to the Law because of what He said!"

Now notice how quietly and imperturbably Jesus forces them to establish the ground of their accusations: "Which of my good works are you stoning me for?" He asks. It was a question that skewered them through and through.

These religious leaders could not deny His miracles—yet they couldn't admit that the real reason they were going to kill Him was that He made them look bad and feel bad. "No, no!" they said, "we're not stoning you for your good works. We're stoning you because you claimed to be God, and that is blasphemy!"

The "Gods" and the Son of God

The men who have encircled our Lord have now taken up stones with which to murder Him. In verses 34 through 36, Jesus responds in a most remarkable way—by quoting the 82nd Psalm.

10:34–35 *Jesus answered them, "Is it not written in your Law, 'I have said you are gods'? If he called them 'gods,' to whom the word of God came—and the Scripture cannot be broken—"*

Before we continue, notice that point: "Scripture cannot be broken." God's Word can never be wrong. It cannot be set aside. It cannot be broken.

This is our Lord's view of the whole Old Testament. It cannot be wrong, so if it calls men "gods," then they must, in some sense, be gods. Jesus continues.

10:36 *"what about the one whom the Father set apart as his very own and sent into the world? Why then do you accuse me of blasphemy because I said, 'I am God's Son'?"*

Notice the force of His argument. The 82nd Psalm begins,

> God presides in the great assembly;
> he gives judgment among the "gods."

This psalm deals with the judges of Israel, the human judges who settled the disputes of Israel. The psalmist says that these men act as agents of God. God is in their midst. The judgment they pronounce is the judgment of God. The psalm clearly calls them "gods." Verse 6 of this psalm—the verse Jesus quoted—says,

> I said, "You are 'gods';
> you are all sons of the Most High."
> But you will die like mere men;
> you will fall like every other ruler.

The argument of Jesus is, "If ordinary men can be called 'gods' for serving as judges and doing God's work, and this is not called blasphemy (for the Scriptures say it and the Scriptures cannot be broken and cannot be wrong), then how can you accuse me of blasphemy when I claim to be a Son of God and to do the work of God?"

Some people suggest that this is all Jesus meant to claim, that He is just saying, "I am just like these other men in the Old Testament who were judges. They could be called gods and weren't stoned for blasphemy. So why stone me when I say I am a Son of God?" But Jesus is not saying He is only *a* son of God. He has clearly identified Himself as *the* Son of God. He uses this argument from the Psalms not to weaken His claim to deity, but to expose the weak legal basis for the Jewish leaders' murderous intentions. He is removing the pretext they are using—blasphemy against God—as an excuse for stoning Him.

But Jesus goes much further than this. *Much* further.

Lunatic, Liar, or . . . ?

10:37–38 *"Do not believe in me unless I do what my Father does. But if I do it, even though you do not believe me, believe the miracles, that you may learn and understand that the Father is in me, and I in the Father."*

Some scholars claim that Jesus only claims to be a man doing the work of God. But the claim of Jesus in these verses goes much deeper than that. He says, in effect, "I came from God, I was sent of God, I was one with God. He is in me and I am in the Father. We are one." That is a claim which no mere mortal dare make.

I was once driving with my youngest grandson, Luke, who was then four years old. We were driving through a part of Palo Alto where my wife and I first lived when we came to the Bay Area of California. I told Luke, "I used to live on this street a long time ago, before you were born, and even before your mother was born."

He looked at me curiously and said, "Where was I then?"

"I don't know where you were," I replied. "Your mother wasn't even born yet. I don't even know where she was."

No one can rightfully claim to have pre-existed—no one, that is, except Jesus. And when He makes this claim, He is claiming to share the nature of God.

Jesus rests His case on the unshakable evidence of the work that the Father does through Him—the miracles. "Do not believe me unless I do what my Father does," He says. "But if I do it, even though you do not believe me, believe the miracles, that you may learn and understand that the Father is in me, and I in the Father."

Jesus tells them not just to believe His claims, but to believe the work that God does through Him—and if they learn the truth from those miracles, then they will have to conclude that Jesus is one with God the Father! This is an absolutely shocking claim—unless it is true. In Jesus' day, a person making such a claim was considered a blasphemer; today, we consider such a person mentally ill. As C. S. Lewis has said, Jesus is either totally insane—on par with a person who claims to be a poached egg—or He is a pathological liar or He is telling the truth. What other options are there in the face of such claims?

It is interesting that nobody ever seriously suggests that Jesus was insane! His works were so true, so pure, so powerful, and such a blessing and a deliverance to people in need that they have to be of God. Nobody claims He is mad. The only conclusion left is that He is telling the truth.

And if Jesus is telling the truth, then He is the most important Being in the universe. He is at the center of everything. To ignore Him is to grope in darkness, to live in rebellion, to miss out on joy, peace, and love. Worst of all, to ignore Him is to end up a partaker in the fiery judgment of the world.

A Paradox

But not everyone who heard Jesus rejected Him.

10:39–42 *Again they tried to seize him, but he escaped their grasp.*

Then Jesus went back across the Jordan to the place where John had been baptizing in the early days. Here he stayed and many people came to him. They said, "Though John never performed a miraculous sign, all that John said about this man was true." And in that place many believed in Jesus.

Many people had heard John the Baptist as he prepared the way for Jesus. These people saw the miracles of Jesus as a confirmation of the message of John the Baptist. Here is where the true verdict is made upon the claims of Jesus: "In that place," says the closing phrase of chapter 10, "many believed in Jesus."

That is the only reasonable, just, and logical verdict that can be imposed on the claims and the evidence of Jesus.

The religious leaders could not grasp the mystery of Jesus' existence. To them He was a mere man claiming to be God. But the mystery of His existence is this: He is God poured into human form—a paradox beyond our comprehension, but not beyond our acceptance. He is fully God. And He is the most complete Man who ever lived. He deserves our trust, our worship, our love, and our awe.

He is the God-Man.

Chapter Thirty

The Strange Ways of God

John 11:1–16

Whatis the greatest challenge to your faith? What is the one thing you face in life that presents an obstacle to your ability to completely trust God?

For me there is only one answer. And as I've talked to other Christians over the years, I've discovered that many people would give the same answer I would give. For me and for many Christians, the hardest problem to handle in the Christian life is the fact that God often does not act as we expect Him to. God "gets out of line." He disappoints us. He takes too long.

As Philip Yancey observes, "Some people lose their faith because of a sharp sense of disappointment with God. They expect God to act a certain way, and God 'lets them down.' Others may not lose their faith, but they too experience a form of disappointment. They believe God will intervene, they pray for a miracle, and their prayers come back unanswered."[1]

To many, it sounds faintly blasphemous to say such things about God. Many people are afraid to admit that they have such feelings toward God. They guiltily wonder, "What would other Christians think of me if they knew I felt disappointed by God or angry with Him? Worse yet, what must God think of me?"

The fact is that God has already raised this problem in His Word. It is a problem He wants to help us with, so that we can grow in our faith and in our reliance upon Him. It's a problem He wants us to face squarely and courageously. It is the problem which lies at the throbbing emotional core of the first section of John 11.

The Smell of Death, the Fragrance of Life

John 11:1–16 is an introduction or prologue to one of the most famous events in the life of Christ: the raising of Lazarus. Without question, the raising of Lazarus is the greatest of all the Lord's miracles, apart from His own resurrection.

At this point, it is good to gain a structural overview of the gospel of John. By now, we can see that John's testimony in this book is built around the great miracles of our Lord. In John 2, Jesus' authority over Nature was introduced when He turned water into wine. In John 5, His authority over human illness and weakness was demonstrated when He healed the paralytic at the pool of Bethesda. In John 6 we saw the twin miracles of the feeding of the 5,000, in which He symbolically presented Himself as the bread of life, and walking on water, in which He prefigured the startling nature of the coming New Creation. In John 9, we witnessed the opening of the eyes of the man born blind, which symbolized the removal of the clay of our humanity from our eyes so that we can behold the light of the world.

Now, in John 11, we approach the raising of Lazarus from the dead. This miracle will be the climaxing sign of His identity, establishing His claim to be the Lord of Life, the Conqueror of Death.

It is significant that in the miracles which most reveal the Lord's compassion—His healing miracles, the healing of the paralytic, and the man born blind—two remarkable things happen. First, John observes that when each of these "signs" (as John calls them) takes place, many "believe on Jesus." Many are convinced that He does indeed fulfill the predictions regarding the long-awaited Messiah. People can see that these are not merely parlor tricks or special effects. These healing miracles are the result of God Himself reaching out and touching people with His restoring power and with His love. Many people respond to that power and that love, placing their faith in Jesus.

Second, John notes that these miracles have also inspired mounting, intensifying opposition against Jesus. With each confrontation between Jesus and His opponents, the attacks have become more venomous, more murderous.

This, of course, is what always happens when the gospel invades the enemy-held territory of human pride and self-will. As the apostle Paul himself said, the Christian gospel and the Christian way of life are to some "the smell of death" and to others "the fragrance of life." Some people are healed and set free from destructive habits by the gospel.

But others are resentful, angry, and resistant. They oppose and fight the gospel every inch of the way. They fight to suppress the truth with every ounce of strength they possess, because it is the truth that exposes the corruption and sin at the core of their existence. We see this taking place in the lives of Jesus' opponents, and we see it in our society today.

As we shall discover later in John 11, the raising of Lazarus—this climactic and greatest of all of Jesus' miracles of healing!—is going to bring great and climactic division of opinion. More than ever before, crowds of people will be attracted to Jesus. And more than ever before, those who have opposed Jesus will be intent on destroying Him.

Mary and Martha

John introduces the last of the great miracles of Jesus with these words.

11:1–4 *Now a man named Lazarus was sick. He was from Bethany, the village of Mary and her sister Martha. This Mary, whose brother Lazarus now lay sick, was the same one who poured perfume on the Lord and wiped his feet with her hair. So the sisters sent word to Jesus, "Lord, the one you love is sick."*

When he heard this, Jesus said, "This sickness will not end in death. No, it is for God's glory so that God's Son may be glorified through it."

In these opening words, John gives us insight into a family which means very much in the life of Jesus: the sisters Mary and Martha, and their brother Lazarus. In Luke 10:38–42, we learn a great deal about the very different personalities of these two sisters of Lazarus:

> As Jesus and his disciples were on their way, he came to a village where a woman named Martha opened her home to him. She had a sister called Mary, who sat at the Lord's feet listening to what he said. But Martha was distracted by all the preparations that had to be made. She came to him and asked, "Lord, don't you care that my sister has left me to do the work by myself? Tell her to help me!"
>
> "Martha, Martha," the Lord answered, "you are worried and upset about many things, but only one thing is needed. Mary has chosen what is better, and it will not be taken away from her."

This passage tells us a great deal about these women. Martha was the quintessential hostess. She was a fastidious detail person. She excelled at domestic work and she had the "Good Housekeeping Seal of Approval." Moreover, she was a forthright, frank woman who readily spoke her mind.

Mary, by contrast, was a shy and retiring woman who was more interested in the big picture, the larger questions of life. She didn't care about details or about surface appearances. She wanted to understand deep truths and the meaning of life.

I suspect that this incident was just one among many in which the very different personalities of these two sisters clashed. It is clear that Mary and Martha loved each other, but it is equally clear that they were two very different people.

As John tells us in verse 2, this is the same Mary who anointed the feet of Jesus and dried them with her hair. Although that incident is not described until chapter 12, John anticipates that incident here because he wants us to understand which of the various Marys in Jesus' life he is talking about. John wants us to know that Mary, the sister of Martha and Lazarus, is the Mary who deeply loved Jesus and who expressed her love in this beautiful way.

While we see evidence of Mary's love for Jesus in this chapter, we see even stronger evidence here of Jesus' love for Lazarus. When the sisters send word to Jesus of Lazarus' illness, they say, "Lord, *the one you love* is sick." In fact, the dominant chord in this scene is a chord of love—the love within this family, their love for Jesus, and His love for them. I believe that this home was such a welcome haven for Jesus during His earthly ministry precisely because it was such a love-filled home. There is nothing more beautiful on earth than a home that is filled with love. That is what John presents to us here.

God's Plan for Sickness

As the events of this story are set in motion, Jesus has left Jerusalem and has traveled about a two-day journey to the Jordan River. That was where John the Baptist first began his ministry. You can visit the exact place in modern Israel, just about where the Allenby Bridge is located, which joins Jordan and Israel together.

The message from Mary and Martha reaches Him—and His response is amazing: "This sickness will not end in death. No, it is for God's glory so that God's Son may be glorified through it." What is remarkable about Jesus' words is that, if you examine the schedule of events, Lazarus is already dead as He speaks them! It took two days for the messenger to get to the Jordan, so when Jesus returned to Bethany, Lazarus had been dead for four days. Undoubtedly, Jesus knew that Lazarus was dead, just as He had received insight from the Spirit of God on numerous other occasions. He sees this event as a signal from the Father that something tremendous is going to result from it, and the response He makes is, "This sickness will not end in death."

The sickness, Jesus goes on to say, "is for God's glory so that God's Son may be glorified through it." This is a crucial point to notice, especially in this present age, when so many preachers are selling a "gospel" which claims that sickness is never the will of God for the believer. According to this false health and prosperity "gospel," if you are sick or struggling, then it is due to a lack of faith or to some hidden sin or judgment from God. I have personally stood by the sickbeds of people who were dying, and who were tortured in their dying moments by this false doctrine. Some Christian with misplaced zeal had inflicted on those people the idea that their sickness was a sign of their lack of faith or hidden sin.

But Jesus rebukes that false doctrine. He shows us that sometimes our sickness has a purpose. God can use it and transform it. He can take our sickness and turn it into glory for His Son, Jesus. The fact that Lazarus was sick was not proof that he had sinned or that Mary and Martha had sinned.

It's true that sickness does sometimes result from moral choices we make. Gluttony can produce diseases ranging from diabetes to heart attacks. The abusive, addictive habit of smoking can lead to cancer. And sexual sin can lead to sexually transmitted diseases, from herpes to gonorrhea to AIDS. But we must also acknowledge that diseases ranging from the common cold to cancer can enter the lives of the most saintly and sanctified of God's people. To preach otherwise is unbiblical and dangerous.

Jesus Waits!

In the following verses we are going to see the strange ways of God in action. We are going to learn—through the actions of Jesus and from the perspective of Jesus—how He answers our prayers in strange, puzzling, sometimes exasperating ways, yet always in the most loving and wise way possible.

11:5–6 *Jesus loved Martha and her sister and Lazarus. Yet when he heard that Lazarus was sick, he stayed where he was two more days.*

That is incredible, isn't it? Jesus *waits!* He *deliberately* waits! Verse 5 specifically reiterates Jesus' love for Lazarus and his two sisters, yet verse 6 tells us He simply waits for two days and does nothing!

If someone you loved was sick and dying, would you wait like Jesus did? Of course not! You would call a doctor, an ambulance—if it was a *real* emergency, you would even call 911! But the one thing you would *never* do is *wait!* Yet that is exactly what Jesus does: He waits.

You might say, "Well, why should He hurry? Lazarus is already dead." Yes, but Mary and Martha's hearts were breaking. This is a dearly beloved brother, probably a younger brother, and his death at a young age is a shattering loss to them. Jesus could have been a great comfort to them, even if He didn't have the power to raise Lazarus. Yet even though He knows they need Him, He deliberately remains two days longer. He waits.

Why?

That is the question we all ask. We all know the feelings that Mary and Martha must have felt. We have all prayed, asking God to act and intervene in a difficult situation. We wait for Him to act—and the heavens are silent. There is no word at all. And that hurts. And our tendency is to interpret God's delays as God's denials. We say, "What's the use? He didn't answer my prayer. Prayer doesn't work." I have had this reaction myself a number of times. I'm sure you have, too.

Yet the delay that Jesus displays here is just like the delays we experience in our relationship with God. Clearly, Jesus loves Mary, Martha, and Lazarus, but He just as clearly delays answering their prayer. What God wants to teach us through this story is that God's delay in answering our prayers is not a sign of God's indifference or His failure to hear. It is a sign of His love. That delay may be painful, but God intends it to help us. It makes us stronger. Jesus deliberately delayed because He loved Mary, Martha, and Lazarus, and knew that this delay would strengthen their faith as they saw God work.

Walking by Day

Imagine how Mary and Martha must have felt when the messenger returned with the news of Jesus' reaction: "This sickness will not end in death." It already had resulted in death! Lazarus was already dead for two days! Imagine the disappointment and disillusionment of these two sisters. Added to the pain of their loss was the apparent discovery that Jesus was not what He had seemed to be. So many miracles! So many wise words! Yet He had been completely mistaken in His response to the illness of their brother—and now their brother was dead!

The Son of God would make no such mistake. The true Messiah would not have bungled so badly. Their faith must have been shaken and their minds must have been clouded by the way Jesus responded to their prayer.

After two days of waiting, Jesus acts—and now it is His disciples' turn to be surprised.

11:7–10 *Then he said to his disciples, "Let us go back to Judea."*

"But Rabbi," they said, "a short while ago the Jews tried to stone you, and yet you are going back there?"

Jesus answered, "Are there not twelve hours of daylight? A man who walks by day will not stumble, for he sees by this world's light. It is when he walks by night that he stumbles for he has no light."

Over the objections of His disciples, Jesus now decides to return to Judea—and to danger.

What does Jesus mean when He says, "Are there not twelve hours in the day?" He is referring to the appointed timetable of God, comparing God's plan to the twelve hours of broad daylight in each day. He was determined to walk in the daylight of God's will. To step out of that timetable—even if doing so would *seem* safer by human reasoning—would be tantamount to walking by night. It would lead to stumbling.

The disciples express concern for Jesus' safety if He returns to Jerusalem: "But Rabbi," they say, "a short while ago the Jews tried to stone you, and yet you are going back there?" Jesus, however, tells them that the real danger is not from the murder-minded Jewish leaders in Judea. The only real danger comes from walking by night, walking outside of the Father's will and His timetable.

The metaphor of daylight and night applies not only to Jesus, but to you and me as well. God has appointed a time for each of us, and if we are walking in the sunlight of God's will, there is nothing anyone else can do to shorten it, nor is there anything we can do to lengthen it. Our times are in God's hands. As the psalmist prays, "Teach us to number our days aright, that we may gain a heart of wisdom."

The disciples could not have been more baffled by the Lord's decision to return to Judea! They had just left Judea—probably only a week or so earlier—because the Jewish leaders wanted to put Jesus to death. They must have felt a great sense of relief to get out of the city, with all of its intrigue and danger. The whole time they had been in Jerusalem, they had probably been looking worriedly over their shoulders, wondering when they would all be seized, dragged before the authorities, and condemned to death. They had just barely escaped with their lives—and suddenly Jesus turns around and says, "Let's go back to Judea"!

This is just one of many times Jesus totally confounds His disciples. They simply can't understand His actions. I can identify with these disciples, and perhaps you can, too. There are many times when the ways of God are baffling, when we simply cannot understand what God is doing, why He is allowing this or that to take place in our lives. We are baffled—and we are discouraged.

The irony is that when the ways of God seem baffling, it is not He who is acting strangely, it is we who do not understand. It is God who is the realist. He always acts in perfect accord with what the situation demands. He does not suffer from illusions and limited understanding as we do. All of His acts are carried out in accord with reality.

As we look at Jesus' words here in His dialogue with His disciples, several facts become clear:

First: When Jesus left Judea, He did so out of obedience to God, not out of fear of the Pharisees. How can we know that? Because He now decides to return to Judea—even though conditions have become *more* dangerous, not less. He is walking right into the jaws of death.

When Jesus left Jerusalem before, He was not running in fear from His enemies. He was keeping to God's timetable. Inexorable, inevitably, the moment of the cross was approaching—yet Jesus Himself was in charge of every event, every detail, which led to His death. The Father had composed the score, and Jesus was conducting the symphony of events.

Or, let's take another analogy: If you are a backyard barbecuer, you know what has to be done when you have steaks on the grill. You put the steaks on over the coals for a while until the fat begins to melt off the steaks. As the fat hits the coals, the flames leap up and you have to move the steaks back a bit to let the flames die down.

Whenever Jesus made an appearance in Jerusalem, He stirred up the flames of antagonism. The fat was figuratively in the fire whenever He confronted the Jewish leaders. Then, from time to time, He would remove Himself from Jerusalem and the situation would simmer down a bit.

Jesus knew that He was going to die in Jerusalem, but He also knew that God the Father had appointed the hour for His death, and that hour had not come yet. The hour of His sacrifice on the cross would be the Passover, the great feast of Israel, when He would be offered as "the Lamb that was slain from the creation of the world."[2] Jesus was carefully engaging, then disengaging, His enemies, keeping the coals hot. He was motivated not by fear but by obedience to the plan of God. It was all a question of timing.

A Form of Sleep

Next we see a deep gulf between the attitude of Jesus and the attitude of His disciples. The subject: Death.

11:11–15 *After he had said this, he went on to tell them, "Our friend Lazarus has fallen asleep; but I am going there to wake him up."*

His disciples replied, "Lord, if he sleeps, he will get better." Jesus had been speaking of his death, but his disciples thought he meant natural sleep.

So then he told them plainly, "Lazarus is dead, and for your sake I am glad I was not there, so that you may believe. But let us go to him."

Notice what Jesus is saying here: When we stand beside a loved one's grave and our heart cries out, "Why?", heaven's answer is, "What is death?

Just a form of sleep." Death is not final for the one who knows Jesus. It is merely an introduction to another, greater experience of life. From our limited human perspective, we view death as a final farewell, a leap into mystery and darkness and silence. The death of a loved one leaves us feeling lonely and bereft, wandering alone through life. But Jesus says, "No, death is sleep."

When Peter Marshall was Chaplain to the United States Senate, he told of a twelve-year-old boy who knew he was dying. The boy asked his father, "What is it like to die?" The father hugged his son to himself and said, "Son, do you remember when you were little and you used to come and sit on my lap in the big chair in the living room? I would tell you a story, read you a book, or sing you a song and you would go to sleep in my arms. Later, you would wake up in your own bed. That is what it's like to die. When you wake up from death, you are in a place of security and safety and beauty."

That, Jesus declares, is what death is like. And throughout the gospels, and indeed throughout the entire New Testament, death is pictured as sleep. "Brothers," Paul writes to the Thessalonians, "we do not want you to be ignorant about those who fall asleep, or to grieve like the rest of men, who have no hope. We believe that Jesus died and rose again and so we believe that God will bring with Jesus those who have fallen asleep in him."[3]

A Hard Lesson to Learn

The disciples misunderstand when Jesus says that Lazarus sleeps. So Jesus proceeds to tell them plainly: "Lazarus is dead."

After dropping that bombshell, Jesus makes a statement that is shocking at first glance: "and for your sake I am glad I was not there, so that you may believe." Jesus was *glad He* was not there when Lazarus died? Why was He glad? For the sake of the disciples! So that their faith would be strengthened! He delayed going for the sake of His followers—for the sake of those who were with Him and also for the sake of Mary and Martha, so that their faith might be strengthened when they see the full, amazing power of God in action. That is the lesson of the opening verses of John 11.

This is a hard lesson for all of us to learn. It has been a hard lesson for me. There have been many times when I have cried out to God for help, times when I thought a situation was so bad it couldn't get any worse. "Lord," I prayed, "Please act! Don't delay any longer!" That is hard. It's hard to keep believing while we are forced to wait.

There is only one answer to our questions when God chooses to delay. It is the answer God Himself gives us in Isaiah 55:8, "For my thoughts are not your thoughts, neither are your ways my ways." There are dimensions to our problems which we cannot imagine, but which God sees clearly. There are possibilities and opportunities in every situation that we cannot conceive of. So we must wait and learn and trust, knowing that God loves us and is working out His plan, even while our own faith and patience are being stretched to the breaking point.

God Is Going to Amaze You!

In verse 16, we catch a glimpse of the character of one of the most intriguing members of Jesus' band of disciples: Thomas. Here, sketched in by a single line of dialogue, we see both the intense loyalty and the deep pessimism of Thomas.

11:16 *Then Thomas (called Didymus) said to the rest of the disciples, "Let us also go, that we may die with him."*

Thomas is referred to as "Thomas (called Didymus)." *Didymus* is a Hebrew word meaning "the twin." Evidently Thomas was one of a pair of twins. Interestingly, the other twin never appears in Scripture. To the question, "Where is the other twin?," one wise Bible commentator replied, "Look in the mirror." Indeed, many of us can identify with the gloomy outlook of Thomas.

Is that the level of your faith right now? When faced with peril and discouragement, many of us easily fall into an emotional and spiritual slump. We examine our circumstances and we say, "God cannot work in this situation. There is no hope. It's time to throw in the towel."

In his book *The Light Within You,* John Claypool sheds this light on the character of Thomas, a disciple we can all identify with from time to time:

> Some time ago, in my own devotions, I worked through the gospel of John again and had occasion to ponder anew this man Thomas. This time yet another facet of his being, one that somehow I had never seen before, came home to me, and that was Thomas' chronic pessimism. Even in the face of his obvious loyalty and honesty and flexibility, I could not ignore the fact that Thomas invariably seemed to expect the worst out of the future. He continually faced the Great Not Yet with very little positive openness to what might happen, and with a lot of negative presumptions about what was going to be.
>
> For example, his words about accompanying Jesus back to Jerusalem have a bitter, fatalistic ring to them: "Let us also

go, that we may die with him" (John 11:16, KJV). The spirit here seems to be more one of exasperation and despair rather than deep commitment and companionship. Thomas was not saying, "I see what you are attempting and, dangerous as it is, I want to risk it with you." He rather seems to have been say- ing, "The whole thing is suicidal. Nothing good can possibly come of it. We might as well face facts; this movement has had it. Let's resign ourselves to the worst."[4]

Perhaps as you look at your own circumstances, you can identify with the pessimism of Thomas. If so, there is one lesson you can take from this story and apply right now to your life—whatever your circumstances, whatever your unanswered prayer, whatever you are having to patiently endure right now. That lesson is this: *God is going to amaze you!* He is not going to let you down. On every page, Scripture drives us back to the realization that we can trust Him, we can believe Him. God's word is His bond.

We pray and we ask God to act—and He doesn't act. At least, not yet. So what should we conclude?

Perhaps a more relevant question is: What is the purpose of prayer? Is it to bend God's will to our own? Or should we pray in order to conform our will to His? We human beings are an arrogant species—and I readily include myself in this indictment. We think that our finite minds understand reality better than the mighty, infinite mind of almighty God! We say, "God! You're taking so long! What's wrong with you?"

But true Christian humility says, "God, I don't understand you and your ways. What do you want to teach me through this experience of waiting? How can I learn to better rely on your wisdom and your love for me through this difficult experience?" God's word to us will never fail. His love toward us will never falter. We cannot always understand His delays. But if we are open to learning and growing through these times of waiting, we can expect to be amazed at the truth that He will someday reveal to us, at the perfect hour of His own choosing.

If Jesus had been at the side of Lazarus as he lay dying, Jesus would doubtless have intervened and healed him—and that would have been a tre- mendous answer to prayer! A miraculous healing! A sign of God's love and power!

But it would have been nothing compared to the miracle that God in His infinite wisdom wanted to do, the miracle that came about because Jesus waited:

The raising of Lazarus from the dead!

Chapter Thirty-One

The Conquest of Death

John 11:17–44

C harles had spent most of his life avoiding the subject of death. He refused to go to the doctor for fear of a terminal diagnosis. He put off such decisions as making a will or buying life insurance or purchasing a burial plot, because to do so would be to admit his own mortality.

After he passed his seventieth birthday, however, a change came over Charles. He began to accommodate himself to the fact that he would not live forever. He made his peace with God, and he made his final arrangements for his exit from this life.

One day, while attending the funeral of a business acquaintance, he sat in the church pew, contemplating his own future. At the end of the funeral, as the other mourners were filing out, he leaned over to the friend seated next to him and said, without any fear or reluctance, "The next one of these parties they throw, I'll be the guest of honor!"

And he was right.

Many of us, like Charles, live our lives in a state of denial when it comes to the subject of death. But death lies ahead for all of us. While the Christian can face death with an eternal hope, we have to acknowledge that death is not our friend. Death is our enemy.

As we come to John chapter 11, we find that death lay in the future of a man named Lazarus. But we will also see that Jesus has been given authority over even this great enemy. Jesus has conquered the enemy called Death.

Act I: The Resurrection and the Life

As we come to John 11:17–44, we find that Lazarus has been dead for four days. Jesus is going to miraculously reverse this situation in an event that is structured like a three-act play. Each act involves one of the three members of this special family which Jesus knows and loves so well: Mary, Martha, and Lazarus. In the first act, verses 17 through 27, Jesus challenges Martha's faith.

In the second act, verses 28 through 37, Jesus shares Mary's grief. In the third act, verses 38 through 44, Jesus restores Lazarus's life.

This miracle—like every other miracle of Christ that is recorded in this gospel—is enacted with a quiet dignity and majesty. There is no magic incantation, no shouting, no thunder or lightning. There is just a simple word of command. The fact that Jesus raises this man back to life with a single command is powerfully significant. This story certifies Jesus' claim to be Master over life and death.

And now, the curtain rises. The scene opens in the sleepy village of Bethany.

11:17–27 *On his arrival, Jesus found that Lazarus had already been in the tomb for four days. Bethany was less than two miles from Jerusalem, and many Jews had come to Martha and Mary to comfort them in the loss of their brother. When Martha heard that Jesus was coming, she went out to meet him, but Mary stayed at home.*

"Lord," Martha said to Jesus, "if you had been here, my brother would not have died. But I know that even now God will give you whatever you ask."

Jesus said to her, "Your brother will rise again."

Martha answered, "I know he will rise again in the resurrection at the last day."

Jesus said to her, "I am the resurrection and the life. He who believes in me will live, even though he dies; and whoever lives and believes in me will never die. Do you believe this?"

"Yes, Lord," she told him, "I believe that you are the Christ, the Son of God, who was to come into the world."

In these verses, John first shines his spotlight upon Martha. Many of Mary and Martha's friends have come out from Jerusalem to the "suburb" of Bethany to give them comfort—evidence, perhaps, of how prominent and well-known these women were in Jerusalem society. When Martha hears that Jesus is coming, she leaves her guests and her sister Mary and goes out to meet Jesus on the road. This is very characteristic of her. Martha is a woman of action. Mary, on the other hand—consistent with her shy, retiring nature—waits at home.

During her brother's illness, Martha must have often thought, "Oh, if Jesus were only here!" Now, as she runs to meet Jesus on the road to Bethany, those words seem to come automatically to her lips: "Lord, if you had been here, my brother would not have died." I don't believe Martha is reproaching her Lord, demanding to know why He didn't come sooner. It is clear in this account that she knows her message did not reach Jesus until after Lazarus was dead. There was no way Jesus could have responded before Lazarus died. Martha is simply expressing to Jesus, "Lord, I wish you could have been here, because if you had, my brother would not have died."

And notice what she says next: "But I know that even now God will give you whatever you ask." What does Martha mean? What does she expect from Jesus? Did she really expect Jesus to raise Lazarus from the dead? Is that why she says "even now"? Is she saying, "Even now that my brother is dead, I know God can do a great miracle through you"?

Clearly not. Notice that Jesus replies, "Your brother will rise again," and Martha answers, "I know he will rise again in the resurrection of the last day." She does not say, "Well, of course he will rise again! He'll walk right out of that grave today! That's exactly what I expected you to do!" No, she mistakes His meaning and says, "Yes, I know he will be resurrected at some distant, future time." Clearly, a physical raising from the dead is the *last* thing Martha expects.

What, then, is she looking for from Jesus? I believe she is looking for comfort, a release from the terrible, crushing grief she feels. I believe she is saying, "Lord, even though my brother is dead and gone, I know that you can heal the grief that I am feeling. I know you can heal the pain that my sister and all of my brother's friends are feeling."

I'm sure we can all identify with the level of Martha's faith. She has a little faith—enough faith to believe that God will act at some future time. But she does not reckon with who Jesus is. She has forgotten that God is active in the Here and Now, not just the past, not just the future.

How often have you thought to yourself, "I know God has worked in the past, and I know He will work again in the future, but I expect no miracles today"? In the daily grind of life, our world seems to be so barren of miracles that we think, "The days of miracles are gone. God can't work now." That is the level of Martha's faith. She believes in an ultimate resurrection and in the ultimate program of God. Her theology is sound, but she has forgotten that God is active in the Here and Now.

That is the lesson Jesus wants to impress upon Martha. Notice how He shifts Martha's focus away from a fixation on the long-range *program* of God to the *Person* of Jesus. He says, "I am the resurrection and the life. He who believes in me will live, even though he dies; and whoever lives and believes in me will never die. Do you believe this?" Even in the grammar of this passage, the focus is on that first personal pronoun: "I"—"I am the resurrection and the life." Jesus is teaching Martha that when He himself is present, God can work. Everything God ever did in the past, everything He has promised to do in the future, He can do in the Here and Now! He is telling her to fasten her faith upon Him, because He is the focus and source of all life, including the new life of the resurrection!

In His next words, Jesus addresses the fears we all have about death: "He who believes in me will live, even though he dies." He addresses our fears for those who have already died, our relatives and friends who have gone before us. We wonder, Are my loved ones in the ground, experiencing corruption? Jesus says, No, they are experiencing an even greater form of life! As Dwight Moody once said, "One day you will hear that D. L. Moody of Northfield, Massachusetts, is dead. Don't you believe it! In that day I will be more alive than I have ever been before." That is what Jesus is saying here: Your loved one who has died, who believed in me, will live forever. What a tremendous hope!

And Jesus addresses the fears we have regarding our own approaching death: "And whoever lives and believes in me will never die." The sense of this statement in the original language is very strong. Jesus literally says, "Whoever lives and believes in me will *never, ever die forever.*" This is the great hope that prompts the apostle Paul to exult,

> "Where, O death, is your victory?
> Where, O death, is your sting?"[1]

Paul can jeer and taunt the Grim Reaper, the dreaded master of all human destinies, because that enemy has been overcome by Jesus on behalf of all who believe in Him!

Notice that Jesus twice states the condition, "He who believes in me." Jesus underscores the fact that faith in Himself is the prerequisite to eternal life. God has opened only one avenue to eternal life, and that is Jesus Christ. To those who have heard His word and received His offer of grace, Jesus extends the marvelous promise of everlasting life. But to those who refuse Jesus, there is nothing ahead but darkness.

Notice Martha's three-fold response: "Yes, Lord, I believe that you are the Christ, the Son of God, who was to come into the world." She expresses belief that Jesus is (1) the Christ (that is, the promised Messiah); (2) the Son of God (that is, Deity Himself); and (3) the One "who was to come into the world," the One predicted by the prophets. Jesus had told her to focus not on the long-range program, but on His Person—and she says, in effect, "Yes, Lord, I will focus on your Person. You are what you claim to be."

Act II: The Grief of Jesus

Now John turns to the second act of this three-act drama: the story of Mary and her relationship with Jesus.

11:28–37 *And after she [Martha] had said this, she went back and called her sister Mary aside. "The Teacher is here," she said, "and is asking for you." When Mary heard this, she got up quickly and went to him. Now Jesus had not yet entered the village, but was still at the place where Martha had met him. When the Jews who had been with Mary in the house, comforting her, noticed how quickly she got up and went out, they followed her, supposing she was going to the tomb to mourn there.*

When Mary reached the place where Jesus was and saw him, she fell at his feet and said, "Lord, if you had been here, my brother would not have died."

When Jesus saw her weeping, and the Jews who had come along with her also weeping, he was deeply moved in spirit and troubled. "Where have you laid him?" he asked.

"Come and see, Lord," they replied.

Jesus wept.

Then the Jews said, "See how he loved him!"

But some of them said, "Could not he who opened the eyes of the blind man have kept this man from dying?"

Here, Mary greets Jesus with the same words as Martha—yet she does so in a totally different atmosphere. John underscores the fact that when Jesus saw Mary she was weeping, and all those who came with her were weeping. When Martha came to Jesus, she spoke the same words—"Lord, if you had been here, my brother would not have died"—but she said it in a much more stoic and resigned way than Mary does here. Martha is practical, pragmatic; she holds her emotions in. Mary is a woman of strong feelings, and she openly displays her grief. Here are two very different personalities, and Jesus dealt very differently with each of these women.

Jesus dealt with Martha by focusing on her need for increased faith. His dialogue with her was intended to stretch and enlarge her faith, and center it in the source of all life: the Person of Jesus Himself.

But here Jesus sees Mary grieving and weeping openly, so He focuses on her need for comfort and consolation. Mary's heart is broken, her soul is shattered. Jesus responds by sharing her emotions, by empathizing deeply with her pain—and this is not hard for Him to do, because He, like Mary, has a great love for Lazarus.

In verse 33, we read, "When Jesus saw her weeping, and the Jews who had come along with her also weeping, he was deeply moved in spirit and troubled." It is very difficult to capture in English what the original language of the text conveys here. The word for "deeply moved in spirit" is a word that occurs only three or four times in the New Testament, and in each place it is associated with a sense of indignation, of anger. It is a word the Greeks used to describe a horse snorting with anger. Jesus is not merely sad in this passage. He is indignant! He is moved with anger, and it showed in His face! John emphasizes that His reaction to the deep grief of Mary and her friends is one of sharp anger.

Why? With whom or with what is Jesus angry? Certainly not at Mary and the other mourners! Jesus is angry with the Grim Reaper! He is angry with Death!

I remember when I first visited the Berlin Wall, not long after the close of World War II. The city was still very much in ruins from the war, and the Wall had just been erected. My spirit boiled with anger as I walked up and down that grim, offensive dividing line between East and West Berlin. I saw the little shrines which grieving people had left in memory of loved ones who had been shot and killed trying to escape the bondage of Communism. I seethed with anger against the horrible injustice of Marxist slavery. I was "deeply moved in spirit and troubled"—though my anger at the injustice of that Wall was nothing compared to the holy anger of Jesus against the injustice of Death.

We *should* feel "deeply moved in spirit and troubled" against injustice and death. It is right to be angry when we see the needless starvation and suffering that occurs in various places around the world. It is right to feel angry at the terrible results of evil that we see around us—pornography (especially child pornography), abortion, racism, murder, and rape. It is right to be angry when a drunken driver runs a traffic light or crosses a freeway divider and destroys an entire family. It is right to feel offended when a child is molested or beaten by a trusted adult. We should be angry whenever that Liar, that great Murderer of mankind, strikes and wreaks pain and death and destruction.

"Jesus Wept"

Now we come to verse 35—"Jesus wept"—famed as the shortest verse in the Bible. But what a profound verse!

Jesus asks where they have laid His friend Lazarus, and as He starts out to the tomb, he weeps. It is important to note that the word "wept" used here is a different word from that used to describe the weeping of Mary and the other Jews in verse 33. It is a word which literally means that He "burst into tears." While walking to the tomb His grief overwhelmed Him, so much so that the Jews saw Him and said, "See how he loved him!"

I think the Jews misunderstood the grief of Jesus. Yes, Jesus loved Lazarus, but I don't believe He was weeping over the loss of His friend. Jesus knew that He was on His way to restore Lazarus to life! He knew that in a few moments, all weeping would be changed to rejoicing! He knew as a certainty what Mary and Martha could not even imagine: Their dear brother would soon be back again in their arms.

Why, then, did Jesus weep? Because He was sharing their heartache!

Could there be any more beautiful expression of the nature of God than this? Jesus weeps with us! He mingles His tears with our own!

The apostle Paul tells us to "rejoice with those who rejoice; mourn with those who mourn."[2] Here, in these two words, "Jesus wept," we see that our Lord Himself set the example for us all. Knowing that death and grief were about to be reversed, He nevertheless felt the sorrow of the hearts of Lazarus' sisters and friends—and He wept!

Act III: The Defeat of Death

In the third act of this drama, the miracle is about to begin.

11:38–41a *Jesus, once more deeply moved, came to the tomb. It was a cave with a stone laid across the entrance. "Take away the stone," he said.*

"But, Lord," said Martha, the sister of the dead man, "by this time there is a bad odor, for he has been there four days."

Then Jesus said, "Did I not tell you that if you believed, you would see the glory of God?"

So they took away the stone.

Lazarus is about to be raised—but before the miracle can take place, two obstacles must be removed. One of these obstacles is the stone—that is, the *physical* obstacle. According to John's account, the tomb was a cave. If it is the traditional site which you can visit in Bethany today, then the tomb of Lazarus was not a horizontal cave set into the side of a hill, but a vertical cave—a dungeon-like hole into which you descend by steps. To seal the tomb, a stone is placed flat on the surface, completely covering the hole. While I question the authenticity of many of the traditional sites that are revered in the Holy Land (there are, for example, at least five sites which claim to be the birthplace of the virgin Mary!), the tomb of Lazarus may indeed have been the kind of tomb exemplified by the traditional site. In any case, the mouth of the tomb was sealed by a heavy stone.

In preparation for the miracle, Jesus orders the removal of the stone. As in the miracle at Cana and the miracle of the feeding of the multitude, there is a combination of human and divine effort at work in this miracle. God supplies the restorative, creative, life-giving power—but it is *people* who remove the stone.

Now notice the protest of pragmatic Martha: "Lord, don't do this! We will all be offended by the odor!"

But Jesus does not rebuke her. He encourages her to remember His earlier words: "Did I not tell you that if you believed, you would see the glory of God?" He urges her to trust Him, to stretch her faith, to not falter. Sometimes our faith needs that little extra spark to enable us to go on with God. That is what Martha needed.

"Lazarus, Come Out!"

The mourners obediently roll the stone aside, and Jesus now turns to the great task at hand, beginning with a simple prayer.

11:41b–42 *Then Jesus looked up and said, "Father, I thank you that you have heard me. I knew that you always hear me, but I said this for the benefit of the people standing here, that they may believe that you sent me."*

Throughout this account, we see that the things Jesus says and does are said and done for the sake of those who watch. Earlier in John 11, He said to the disciples, "For your sake I am glad I was not there, so that you may believe."[3] He delayed coming to Bethany for two days because He loved Mary and Martha. Now He prays aloud for the sake of the people who are watching to see what He does. He wants them to know that God the Father is involved with Him in this. He wants them to see that He is not a mere magician seeking to astonish them, but the Son of God come to make an active difference in their lives. He calls upon God Himself to act. It is a simple prayer of gratitude, spoken to prove that what happens next is the work of Almighty God.

11:43–44a *When he had said this, Jesus called in a loud voice, "Lazarus, come out!" The dead man came out, his hands and feet wrapped with strips of linen, and a cloth around his face.*

The sight of a mummified dead man coming out of the tomb must have brought the crowd of onlookers to their trembling knees!

Why did He speak the name of Lazarus in that loud voice? Someone has suggested that if He had only said, "Come out!" without naming Lazarus specifically, Jesus might have emptied the entire cemetery! Remember that in John 5, Jesus said, "A time is coming when all who are in their graves will hear" the voice of the Son of Man "and come out."[4] One day that voice will summon *all* the dead to rise—but for now, Jesus singles out Lazarus to be raised.

How did this miracle occur? How was life returned to a body that had been ravaged and killed by disease? No one knows. No one can explain it. We only know that, as the onlookers breathlessly observed, a figure appeared in the mouth of the tomb, bound in grave clothes, staggering toward the light.

Unbinding One Another

We see again that in order for this miracle to be consummated, human and divine effort must once again be joined.

11:44b *Jesus said to them, "Take off the grave clothes and let him go."*

Only God can give life—but we, as human beings, can help to unbind one another. This is a beautiful image of the way we minister to one another in the body of Christ.

Jesus understood that Lazarus needed more than life: He needed liberty, he needed to be set free. That is the power that God places in our hands. We cannot regenerate people, but we can help to free other people from the chains and bonds of the past. We can teach them the Word that frees. We can welcome them into true Christian fellowship. We can encourage them. We can listen to their stories and give them a new family in which they can be affirmed, surrounded by love, and freed of painful memories and emotions.

This is not just a story of a miracle that happened long ago. If we do not grasp the powerful implications of this story for our own lives, for the Here and Now, then we have missed the point altogether! Like Martha, you and I need to see that God's program is active not only in the past and the future, but in the present.

Perhaps God seems to be delaying in answering your prayers. Perhaps you, like Martha, are having your faith stretched. Wait. Watch. Expect God to act. He is working in your situation even now, as you read these words. He is active in the Here and Now.

Perhaps you are grieving some deep loss. The loss of a loved one. The loss of a marriage or other relationship. The loss of a career. The loss of your reputation. The loss of your health. If so, then you can know, from this story, that Jesus mingles His tears with yours, just as He wept with Mary. Jesus has been touched by all the emotions that you and I feel—even the misery of grief.

Jesus is alongside you to lead you through whatever you are facing right now. He has the power, if necessary, to raise the dead or set aside the laws of nature to bring you through your circumstances. But what's more, He has the power not only to take you out of your circumstances, but to take you *through* them.

So don't focus your attention on the problem, but on the Person. Don't focus on the darkness of the grave, but on the One who is the Resurrection and the Life. The Master has come! And He has called us out of death and bondage, and into life and liberty!

Chapter Thirty-Two

God's Will or Our Will?

John 11:45–54

One of the great historic controversies of the church is the disagreement between Christians who believe in free will versus Christians who believe in predestination. To put the question as a theological paradox, "Are we predestinated to believe in free will or do we have the God-given choice to believe in predestination?" Now, *that* is a puzzling conundrum!

Here, in the wake of the raising of Lazarus, we see a series of events which give us insight into the question of whether we really have free will, or whether we are completely bound by the deterministic will of God.

Unbelief Beyond Belief!

Next we see a clear example of people exercising their free will, both for good and for evil.

11:45–46 *Therefore many of the Jews who had come to visit Mary, and had seen what Jesus did, put their faith in him. But some of them went to the Pharisees and told them what Jesus had done.*

Some of the Jews used their God-given free will to place their faith and trust in the Lord of Life. But not all.

The Jews who went to the Pharisees were the ones who opposed Jesus. When you think about it, this is absolutely amazing! These people have just seen a dead man brought back to life by the power of God—and they have chosen to make themselves the enemies of that power! How could any thinking person make such a choice? How could anyone choose to oppose a Man who has the power of life in His hands—and even in His voice? Yet human unbelief is so stubborn that it will persist even in the face of such overwhelming evidence as the raising of a man from the dead!

In Luke 16, Jesus tells a story that reinforces this fact: The story of the rich man and the beggar. In that story, the rich man and the beggar both die and go to their respective rewards—the rich man to hell and the beggar to heaven, to Abraham's bosom. The rich man, in his torment, saw the beggar (whose name, by the way was Lazarus!) standing by the side of Abraham. The rich man called out, "Father Abraham, have pity on me . . . and send Lazarus to my father's house, for I have five brothers. Let him warn them, so that they will not also come to this place of torment."

Abraham responds, "They have Moses and the Prophets; let them listen to them."

The rich man pleads, "No, father Abraham, but if someone from the dead goes to them, they will repent."

But Abraham replies, "If they do not listen to Moses and the Prophets, they will not be convinced even if someone rises from the dead."[1]

In John 11, a man named Lazarus does indeed rise from the dead—and just as Jesus predicted in Luke 16, there are some among those who witness this event who continue in stubborn unbelief. It never ceases to astound me that people will believe what they choose to believe—even when a mountain of evidence contradicts them! Truly, this is unbelief beyond belief!

Two Human Viewpoints

In this story, some believe and some do not. In each case, a choice is made without force or coercion of any kind.

Those who believe do so because they are convinced by the evidence that Jesus is the Messiah, that He has power over life and death. That conviction compels them to commit themselves to Him.

Those who do not believe make a willful choice in direct contradiction of the evidence. Logically, rationally, they *should* accept the evidence. Instead, they refuse to believe and they set in motion the machinery that will ultimately take His life. They do this of their own free will—but . . . !

Free will always entails consequences. Human beings are always free to choose, but they are not free to choose the consequences. Here is where free will and God's sovereign predestination are harmonized. Each of us has the power to accept or reject Jesus Christ, but we cannot choose the consequences of that choice. The consequences of our choices follow according to the sovereign program of God. In this account, we see the inescapable consequences that follow the choice to oppose Jesus.

11:47–53 *Then the chief priests and the Pharisees called a meeting of the Sanhedrin.*

"What are we accomplishing?" they asked. "Here is this man performing many miraculous signs. If we let him go on like this, everyone will believe in him, and then the Romans will come and take away both our place and our nation."

Then one of them, named Caiaphas, who was high priest that year, spoke up, "You know nothing at all! You do not realize that it is better for you that one man die for the people than that the whole nation perish."

He did not say this on his own, but as high priest that year he prophesied that Jesus would die for the Jewish nation, and not only for that nation but also for the scattered children of God, to bring them together and make them one. So from that day on they plotted to take his life.

A dead man is brought back to life—and the first reaction of the Pharisees is to call an emergency session of the Sanhedrin! This is a 911 situation! Things are getting out of hand! The polls indicate that Jesus has pulled way ahead of the ruling Pharisee party! So the religious leaders have come together in an emergency session to take action.

John records these events from three separate viewpoints: The first is the viewpoint of the Pharisees, a natural, human point of view. The second is the viewpoint of the Sadducees, another natural, human point of view. Both of these viewpoints are fatally flawed. The third viewpoint is that of God Himself, which is always the realistic and redemptive point of view. Let's examine each of these viewpoints in turn.

First, there is the Pharisees' view. The council of the Sanhedrin was composed of two parties, the Pharisees and the Sadducees. The Pharisees were what we would today call "fundamentalists." They were the religionists, the party that took everything in the Law literally. Their number one goal was to live by the letter of the Law. Their point of view comes through in the opening verses of this passage. "What are we accomplishing?" they ask—or more literally, "What are we doing?" There is a note of panic in that question. Things are getting out of their control, and they are losing their composure.

They go on to project their fears into the future: "Here is this man performing many miraculous signs. If we let him go on like this, everyone will believe in him, and then the Romans will come and take away both our place and our nation." In other words, "If we don't stop this man, everyone is going to accept Him as the Messiah! What a tragedy! He'll lead a political uprising, and then the Romans will come down on us like a storm-cloud! They'll take away our temple and our nation!"

With some twenty centuries of hindsight, it is easy for us to see how wrong the Pharisees were about Jesus. In fact, when they opposed Jesus and crucified Him, they brought about the very consequences they were trying to avoid! Their choice to crucify Jesus was the very reason why, some forty years later, the Romans beat down the gates of Jerusalem, overwhelmed the city, and dismantled the temple stone by stone! Many Jews were slaughtered, and many others were led away into captivity. Israel ceased to exist as a nation from that time until it was re-created by the United Nations on May 14, 1948—all because of what the Pharisees and the Sadducees chose to do in these very verses of John 11!

The Pharisees thought that the political existence of Israel was being preserved by their own clever political intrigues and manipulation. They either didn't understand or they forgot that Israel had been preserved throughout its history because of the sovereign hand of God's protection. What kept this nation a nation, and what preserved the temple, was the hand of God. When the leaders of Israel put the Messiah to death, God removed His protection—and the Gentiles, who had been hovering like birds of prey, swooped in and fulfilled the predictions that Jesus Himself made that the city would be destroyed.

Next, John records the viewpoint of the Sadducees, as exemplified in the words of Caiaphas, the high priest. Caiaphas belonged to the party of the Sadducees, and had won the office of high priest by being the highest bidder for the job. During this period, the Romans determined who would be the high priest. They put the office up for sale, so that whoever among the Jews could come up with enough money could have this coveted job. The term of high priest was supposedly only for one year, but history records that Caiaphas held this powerful position for some eighteen years—an indication of just how wealthy and powerful he was.

Caiaphas speaks here as a Sadducee—a religious liberal who does not have a strong, literal belief in God, who does not believe in anything supernatural, who denies the existence of miracles, angels, or life after death. The viewpoint of the Sadducees would not be considered at all unusual in our own secular, materialistic, agnostic age.

The first thing that hits you as you read the words of Caiaphas is an attitude of complete arrogance. He is utterly contemptuous of those around him. "You know nothing at all!" he says—and it is impossible to imagine a more rude and abrasive introduction than this. This is typical of the style of the Sadducees. Josephus, the Jewish historian of this period, observes, "The manners of the Sadducees are far rougher than the Pharisees, both to each other and to their equals, whom they treat as strangers."

The philosophy of Caiaphas is that of a Mafia don: "If this guy gets in our way, there's only one thing to do: Terminate Him. Rub Him out. Waste Him. It's better that one man die than that we lose control of the rackets." It is an utterly ruthless and pragmatic philosophy. There's not a hint of idealism or ethics to taint his utilitarian, Machiavellian world-view. There are many people who operate by the same selfish, unprincipled philosophy today.

But like the viewpoint of the Pharisees, the viewpoint of the Sadducees is fatally flawed. Caiaphas does not reckon with all the factors in this situation. As the apostle Paul observes, "We speak of God's secret wisdom, a wisdom that has been hidden and that God destined for our glory before time began. None of the rulers of this age understood it, for if they had, they would not have crucified the Lord of glory."[2] There is a wisdom which secular wisdom does not know and cannot see because it lacks essential knowledge of the facts. Men continually make decisions which look right to them, but which are disastrously wrong and which bring tragic effects upon themselves and upon society.

God's Viewpoint

In verse 51, John reveals to us the divine view of this situation. After Caiaphas says, "It is better for you that one man die for the people than that the whole nation perish," John observes, "He did not say this on his own, but as high priest that year he prophesied that Jesus would die for the Jewish nation, and not only for that nation but also for the scattered children of God, to bring them together and make them one."

Here is a confirmation of the prophecy of Isaiah, who promised that One would come who would bear the sins of the nation: "We all, like sheep, have gone astray, each of us has turned to his own way; and the Lord has laid on him the iniquity of us all."[3] The priests, of course, did not believe this prophecy. Yet, in his office of high priest, this corrupt man uttered a true and reliable prophecy that he himself did not understand, and would not have accepted if he did understand it!

Here we can see clearly the sovereign hand of God at work—an unseen yet inexorable hand which turns the pages of human history, one by one. In our God-given free will, we human beings can do our worst—yet we cannot alter the divine plan. As Richard Halverson, retired Chaplain of the United States Senate, once said, "Nothing men can do will thwart or alter the sovereign will of God; and nothing God does ever sets aside the free choice of man." That is how these two truths—human free will and divine sovereignty—balance and complement each other. It is not a question of free will *or* predestination, not either/or. It is a case of both/and.

The biblical position is that we human beings have been given free will, yet we are so limited, so ignorant, so blinded, so selfish that even when we are allowed to exercise free will, we generally choose the wrong thing. Yet the will of God is sovereign over all, and even the sinful choices of foolish, self-willed human beings are all ultimately blended into God's plan. His program cannot be thwarted. God can take any effort to subvert His plan and turn it into an avenue for *advancing* that plan. That is what He did in the case of Caiaphas.

Caiaphas himself was a rogue, a crook, a ruthless unbeliever—but he held the office of high priest, so God made him a prophet and spoke through him anyway. Clearly, if God can use Caiaphas, He can use any person, willing or unwilling, and even without their being aware they are being used! In fact, there are other places in John's gospel where we see the enemies of Jesus prophesying God's truth in spite of themselves.

For example, in John 7:34, after Jesus has said, "You will look for me, but you will not find me; and where I am, you cannot come," the Jewish leaders responded by saying, "Where does this man intend to go that we cannot find Him? Will he go where our people live scattered among the Greeks, and teach the Greeks?" Later, in fact, the gospel of Jesus Christ did indeed go out among the dispersed Jews and to the Greeks! In their scorn and derision of Jesus, the Jewish leaders had unintentionally prophesied God's truth.

Men and women ignore the unseen hand of God, and their decision to ignore God's activity in the world leads them to make choices that are—for them—completely disastrous. We see this principle at work in verse 53, in which John tells us where the willful reasoning of the Pharisees and the Sadducees leads: "So from that day on they plotted to take his life." There was no longer any debate as to *whether* Jesus should be killed. The only questions they asked were "When do we kill Him?" and "How do we kill Him?" From that moment on, the only agenda item at every meeting of the Sanhedrin was "Kill Jesus."

These men did not realize that they had set a goal of destroying their own true Messiah. The miracles Jesus had done meant nothing to them—not even the miracle of raising a man from the dead! They didn't want to look at the evidence. They didn't want to be "confused by the facts." They simply wanted to eliminate the Man who threatened their own power and popularity.

This story offers a clear example of the way God works in the world. He does not overrule human free will, and human free will overwhelmingly tends to choose in opposition to God. Yet God, in His sovereignty, will accomplish His purposes, regardless of human choices and even human sin.

Operating on God's Timetable

So the Jewish leaders have made their decision: Jesus must die. In so doing, they have become the unwitting instruments of God's plan to redeem the world through the sacrifice of His Son. Jesus knows what lies ahead for Him, because He has been predicting His own death on numerous occasions. It is not a fate He seeks to avoid. He courageously looks death squarely in the face. But He knows God's timetable, and He knows that the time of His sacrifice has not yet come.

11:54 *Therefore Jesus no longer moved about publicly among the Jews. Instead he withdrew to a region near the desert, to a village called Ephraim, where he stayed with his disciples.*

Jesus understood the plan of God. He had a clear and unerring sense of God's control of history, of the invisible factors which were at work in every human situation—and He adjusted His own behavior accordingly. He withdrew to an obscure village some fourteen miles northeast of Jerusalem. He withdrew because the time of Passover—when He would be offered as the Lamb of God upon the cross—had not come. As near as we can tell from the evidence in the passage, it is now about February, so He still has several weeks to wait and teach His disciples before Passover arrives in early April.

As we know from the other gospels, when the time was right, Jesus joined the other pilgrims who were going down the Jordan Valley to Jerusalem to celebrate Passover. He went precisely on schedule—that is, on *God's* schedule.

There is a message to us in the actions of Jesus in verse 54: The lesson to you and me is that we need to understand the times in which we live, and the fact that God is still moving, still at work, still carrying out His program in our own times. According to His schedule, God is moving in the affairs of human beings, raising up kingdoms, throwing down kingdoms, elevating some to power, removing others from power. God's hand moves invisibly through our world, moving events in ways that no secular mind can comprehend.

The apostle Paul has given us an astounding and revealing statement in his first letter to the Corinthians: "But we have the mind of Christ." Think of it! If we immerse ourselves in the Word of God, we have the mind of Christ! We are able to think—even if on a limited and finite level—the thoughts of God. If we know how God thinks, if we tune our minds to see His hand moving through the events of our times, then we can align our free will with His sovereign will! Instead of becoming unwilling and unwitting instruments in God's hands, as Caiaphas and the other evil leaders were, we can be *God's partners,* helping Him to carry out His eternal plan.

We have the same free will that those Pharisees and Sadducees had—the freedom to choose to follow Christ or to oppose Him. If we saturate our minds with the thoughts of God, then we are thinking biblically. And when we think biblically, we face life realistically. We make decisions that bring us safely through all the toils, struggles, and perils of life. We can experience the highest purpose any human being can know—the purpose of being a part of God's eternal purpose and plan.

Are you seeking the mind of Christ? Are you learning to discern, as Christ discerned, the times in which you live so that you will not waste your days in useless pursuit of foolish things? Imagine the horror those Pharisees and Sadducees experienced at the end of their lives when they discovered they had wasted their years in hardened opposition to the very thing they claimed to uphold: the eternal plan of God! May that never be said of you and me.

May our lives be spent as useful, obedient instruments of God's redemptive purposes in this world. There is no more challenging and satisfying way to live than that.

Chapter Thirty-Three

Worship or Waste?

John 11:55–12:11

In 1950, the year I came to Palo Alto, I spent the summer traveling around the country with Dr. H. A. Ironside. During that time, my wife had to stay in the home of her parents in Great Falls, Montana. I often thought about how Elaine had to work so hard, taking care of our two little girls, while I traveled the country and met interesting people and had exciting experiences. I very much wanted to express my feelings of love and appreciation for her.

One day during this tour, I was walking down a street in Buffalo, New York, when I saw a beautiful fur coat in a store window. The price, however, was way beyond my range—about $100. That may not seem like much money for a fur coat these days, but it was a lot of money in 1950. So I went to Mrs. Ironside, who was quite wealthy and very sympathetic, and told her what I wanted to do. She was very understanding and offered to lend me the money to buy the coat, and I would pay her back a few dollars a week.

When I got home and handed Elaine that incredible gift—a gift we could never have afforded without Mrs. Ironside's help—she was amazed and delighted. To this day, that coat hangs in a closet in our home. I don't think she can bear to part with it, because it represents a gift of love—an extravagance bordering on foolishness! Yet that is the way love behaves. Love doesn't count the cost of expressing itself. It simply delights in giving in order to show what is in the heart.

That is the kind of love and the kind of gift we see in John 12. Mary, the sister of Lazarus, has a heart that is filled to bursting with love for Jesus, and in this passage we will see her pour out that love in a very costly way, in a gift of precious, imported perfume. And as we watch this beautiful act of sacrificial love by Mary, we will learn an important lesson that we can apply to our own lives today.

Countdown to Crisis

Ten . . . nine . . . eight . . . .

As we pick up this story, a countdown has begun in the life of Jesus: a countdown to the crisis of the cross.

As we come to John chapter 12 (and we should note that the last three verses of chapter 11 actually belong with chapter 12), we see again how John is very careful in selecting the events he presents in his personal memoir of the life of Christ. In this chapter, John records a trio of events from the final week of Jesus in Jerusalem—a week that will culminate in His death upon the cross. The three incidents John chooses to relate are:

(1) The dinner given in Jesus' honor in the village of Bethany;

(2) The Lord's triumphal entry into Jerusalem, when He fulfilled the prophecies of Zechariah concerning the King of the Jews; and

(3) His reaction to the visit of a delegation of Greeks who have asked to see Him during the celebration of the Passover feast.

For now, we will examine the first of these three events.

11:55–57 *When it was almost time for the Jewish Passover, many went up from the country to Jerusalem for their ceremonial cleansing before the Passover. They kept looking for Jesus, and as they stood in the temple area they asked one another, "What do you think? Isn't he coming to the Feast at all?" But the chief priests and Pharisees had given orders that if anyone found out where Jesus was, he should report it so that they might arrest him.*

These verses convey the atmosphere that prevailed in Jerusalem just before this Passover. Josephus, the Jewish historian, has written that during the Passover the population of the city frequently rose to more than three million people. There were no hotels or motels to accommodate these vast numbers, so people camped out on hillsides or stayed with friends. They came from all over Palestine, and even from foreign lands, to ceremonially purify themselves for the celebration of Passover.

Many of the people who gathered in Jerusalem were looking for Jesus. "Isn't he coming to the Feast at all?" they asked each other. Jesus had become famous throughout the countryside, and His confrontations with the religious leaders in the temple courts were legendary. He was the sensation of the nation—so much so that the Pharisees had put out a warrant for His arrest. To many of the people, He was a wonder-worker, perhaps even the next king of Israel. But to the Sanhedrin, He was Public Enemy No. 1.

Would He dare show Himself in defiance of the religious authorities? Would He or would He not appear in Jerusalem during Passover, the greatest of all the Hebrew celebrations? These were the questions being buzzed about by the Jerusalem rumor mill.

Twenty centuries later, the remarkable Person of Jesus continues to fascinate the masses. This fact was brought home to me in a conversation I had with Doug Coe. Doug has a dynamic behind-the-scenes ministry of prayer in the corridors of power in Washington, D.C. During our talk, he told me about his travels around the world and the talks he had with people of various countries and faiths. "I've met Buddhists, Hindus, Muslims, people of every imaginable religion," he said, "and if you mention 'Christianity' or 'religion' to any of these groups, the response is invariably cold. But if you mention Jesus Himself, that is a different matter altogether! Regardless of where people come from or what they believe, there is instant respect for the name of Jesus. Everyone is curious about Jesus."

Many Forms of Worship

As chapter 12 opens, Jesus returns to the site of His greatest miracle.

12:1–3 *Six days before the Passover, Jesus arrived at Bethany, where Lazarus lived, whom Jesus had raised from the dead. Here a dinner was given in Jesus' honor. Martha served, while Lazarus was among those reclining at the table with him. Then Mary took about a pint of pure nard, an expensive perfume; she poured it on Jesus' feet and wiped his feet with her hair. And the house was filled with the fragrance of the perfume.*

Here, Jesus is reunited with His friends, Mary, Martha, and Lazarus, in the village of Bethany. They have prepared a special dinner in honor of Jesus. This dinner takes place not in the home of Mary, Martha, and Lazarus, but—as we learn from the other gospels—in the home of Simon the leper. We don't know anything about Simon except that he was once a leper, and was very likely healed by Jesus (if he had not been healed, he could not have hosted this supper). Since there was a warrant for the arrest of Jesus, it certainly took courage for the friends of Jesus to gather in His honor. It was probably a quiet, private dinner, with only Jesus and His closest friends as invited guests.

Why does John include this event in his account? I believe he wants to teach us the true meaning of worship. It is interesting to note that all the participants in this story are acting in line with their character: Martha is serving, Lazarus is fellowshiping with Jesus at the table, and Mary is worshiping Jesus by anointing His feet with an expensive, fragrant ointment.

Some Bible commentators make a point of the way these three friends of Jesus spent their time: Martha served (least importance), Lazarus fellowshiped (middling importance), and Mary worshiped (greatest importance). I cannot agree. I believe each of these three actions is an important form of worship. It's true that Mary worshiped Jesus in a very direct sense, but Martha also worshiped by her service and Lazarus worshiped by spending time in the presence of Jesus.

Worship, the center of Christian life, can take various forms. Martha did what she was most comfortable doing and what she was gifted to do: She served. Perhaps, like many people, she found it difficult to express in words how she felt about the Lord, but Martha loved to serve. Coming from a faithful heart like Martha's, that is eloquent language and true worship!

On another occasion, recorded in Luke 10, Martha tried to put together a spur-of-the-moment meal for Jesus. On that occasion, everything was going wrong. Anxious and pressured, trying to do too much, Martha finally exploded in anger and blamed her problems on Jesus. "Lord, don't you care that my sister has left me to do the work by myself?" she complained. "Tell her to help me!" It was probably Martha who inspired these lines:

> There's a gladness in her gladness when she's glad,
> And a sadness in her sadness when she's sad.
> But the gladness in her gladness
> And the sadness in her sadness
> Are nothing to her madness when she's mad!

That would be an apt description of Martha on that first occasion when she made a supper for Jesus. But here, in John 12, Martha has grown in her character and her faith. Now she's glad, filled with love for Jesus, rejoicing with her sister over the return of their beloved brother from the abyss of death. Martha expresses her love and gladness through service.

Service is legitimate worship. There is no more quintessentially *Christian* way to live than to do everything we do "as unto the Lord."[1] Whether you work in a church, in an office, in a field, in the military, in a man-hole, or in the home as a stay-at-home mom, you can do everything you do "as unto the Lord"—and that is true worship. Nothing transforms work into worship like doing it "as unto the Lord."

There once was a boy who thought he should be paid for the chores he did around the house. So one morning he made out a bill and laid it beside his mother's breakfast plate. It read:

> Washing the car $1.00
> Taking out garbage 50
> Cutting lawn 1.50
>
> Total $3.00

His mother looked at the bill without saying a word. But at lunchtime, when the boy came home from school, he found a note beside his plate. It read:

Washing clothes	$0.00
Ironing shirts	0.00
Cooking food	<u>0.00</u>
Total	$0.00

Love, Mother.

After reading the note, the boy rushed to his mother and hugged her. Nothing more was ever said about the bill. That's the true service of love. That is how Martha served and worshiped.

Lazarus: Worship by Fellowship

Lazarus worshiped the Lord by spending time with the Lord. He enjoyed the mere presence of Jesus—talking with Him, listening to Him, laughing together, sharing their hearts with one another.

It is interesting to transpose this situation to our own day. Suppose Lazarus has just been raised from the dead—and the event was covered live on Cable News Network! Would he be able to enjoy a quiet dinner with Jesus as he does in this account? I doubt it. Lazarus would be in demand as a guest on Good Morning America, Larry King Live, Donohue, and the 700 Club! There would be book offers and movie deal. Lazarus would be so hemmed in by the crowds that he would have no time for a quiet supper with Jesus!

But notice how Lazarus is dealt with in this account: He is scarcely featured at all! He is content just to be with Jesus, basking in His presence, sharing thoughts and feelings and memories. That too is a form of worship.

We can worship just as Lazarus did. We can experience the companionship and fellowship and presence of Jesus. We can meet Him regularly for prayer, and we can talk with Him throughout the day.

Notice, too, the *courage* of Lazarus in associating so closely with Jesus. Later in this account, we will see that the enemies of Jesus also want to kill Lazarus! Despite the threats by the religious leaders against Jesus and anyone who follows Jesus, Lazarus risks their wrath by openly and publicly associating himself with the Man whose arrest they seek. That, too, is worship. We have the opportunity to worship as Lazarus did whenever we take the risk of publicly associating ourselves with Jesus of Nazareth.

The Fragrant Worship of Mary

The next act of worship we see is that of Mary, who took a pound of imported perfume and poured it on Jesus' feet. Nard is a costly perfume derived from the aromatic resin of a special plant, which at that time grew only in India. In today's inflated terms, this ointment would have been worth perhaps $10,000—which is why we will later see Judas complain about Mary's extravagance in pouring out the equivalent of a year's wages to anoint the feet of Jesus.

Where did this perfume come from? Some commentators speculate that Mary belonged to a wealthy family and could easily afford such lavish expenditures. Others suggest that Mary might have received the ointment as a gift, that it was a precious keepsake she had kept for many years, perhaps in anticipation of her wedding day. The nard was sealed in an alabaster jar, and could not be released without breaking the neck of the jar. Mary did so, and poured the entire pound of perfume over Jesus until the fragrance filled the whole house. According to the other gospel accounts, she anointed His head first, and the ointment ran down until it covered His feet. Then she unbound her hair and used it to sponge up the excess ointment.

John is particularly aware of the significance of Mary's act of worship. In the accounts in Matthew 26:6–13 and Mark 14:3–9, Jesus responds to Judas' protest:

> "Leave her alone. . . . Why are you bothering her? She has done a beautiful thing to me. The poor you will always have with you, and you can help them any time you want. But you will not always have me. She did what she could. She poured perfume on my body beforehand to prepare for my burial. I tell you the truth, wherever the gospel is preached throughout the world, what she has done will also be told, in memory of her."[2]

John's account attaches beautiful symbolism to her act of worship, of anointing His body for burial. As the alabaster bottle is broken and the costly perfume is poured out upon Jesus, John notes that the fragrance of the perfume fills the entire house, just as the fragrance of God's love goes out into the entire world when the body of His Son is broken and His costly blood is poured out.

In this action, Mary expresses all the love that is in her heart for Jesus. Some people confuse this action with another account in Luke 7, where an unnamed woman bathes the feet of Jesus with her tears and wipes them with her hair. (That unnamed woman might have been Mary Magdalene, a prostitute out of whom Jesus had cast seven demons.) The incident in Luke 7 occurred in the house of a man named Simon (a common name in ancient Israel), but it was not the same Simon and not the same house. The incident in Luke's gospel took place in Galilee, far to the north of Jerusalem, while this account in John 12 took place in Bethany, just outside of Jerusalem.

The incident in John 12 clearly concerns Mary of Bethany, the sister of Martha and Lazarus, about whom there is never any mention of an unsavory past. John makes it clear that Mary understood the work of Jesus and the change He had made in her heart. She was grateful to Jesus for the richness and blessing He brought to her life—not only in restoring the life of her brother Lazarus, but in the life-transforming teaching she has heard from Him while sitting at His feet. That is why she worships Jesus with an extravagant love. That is why she has spared no expense.

But not only has she been extravagant in sacrificing a precious perfume on her Lord, she has been extravagant in flouting the customs of her times. She entered a supper where women were usually not welcome. She let down her hair in an open setting, where men from outside her family were present—an unthinkable act in that culture. She openly expressed her affection and adoration for Jesus—again, an unthinkable act in that culture.

But that is how love behaves. It cares nothing about expense. It cares nothing about what other people think. It cares only about the object of that love. Worship is what naturally proceeds from a heart that has been transformed by love. It can be expressed in many ways: By sacrificial giving, as in the example of Mary. By service, as in the example of Martha. By fellowship and seeking out the presence of the Lord, as in the example of Lazarus.

True worship is a choice to invest oneself—in whatever way, in giving, in service, or in fellowship—in order to express the love of a grateful, transformed heart.

The Counterfeit Disciple

But not everyone at this dinner was there to worship Jesus. Not everyone was there as His friend. There was a counterfeit follower present. Judas Iscariot reveals what is in his heart—and it isn't worship.

12:4–8 *But one of his disciples, Judas Iscariot, who was later to betray him, objected, "Why wasn't this perfume sold and the money given to the poor? It was worth a year's wages." He did not say this because he cared about the poor but because he was a thief; as keeper of the money bag, he used to help himself to what was put into it.*

"Leave her alone," Jesus replied. "It was meant that she should save this perfume for the day of my burial. You will always have the poor among you, but you will not always have me."

Judas is an example of those who regard true worship of the Lord as a waste of time, effort, and money. There are many such people in the church today. They appear to be part of the church, yet their hearts are far from God's purposes.

John reveals the heart of Judas in these verses: Judas talked about caring for the poor, but he had no real concern for people in need. That was just a cover, an excuse, a disguise. As the treasurer of the disciples, he wanted the money for himself.

It always amazes me to realize that the Lord not only selected Judas but actually appointed him *treasurer*—even though He knew full well what kind of man Judas was! John didn't know the kind of man Judas was at the time, nor did any of the other disciples. But with the benefit of hindsight and experience, John was able to accurately assess the state of this man's heart. He was able to ascertain that Judas was a thief.

By taking together all that has been said about Judas in all four gospels, it is easy to understand what Judas' motivation was in stealing money: He wanted to buy a piece of land! By the time he betrayed Jesus, he lacked only thirty pieces of silver to complete the transaction. That was the amount for which he contracted for to betray our Lord. Perhaps he was cynically milking his relationship with this famous wonder-worker to get what he could get while the ride lasted. Or perhaps he really believed that Jesus would become the king, the political savior that the people expected, and he planned to build a palace for himself on a choice piece of real estate when Jesus came to power.

Whatever his view of Jesus, we know that Judas was planning to invest his stolen loot in a tract of land. That is why he complained over what he thought was a waste of money. No doubt he thought of all the land he could have bought with just the contents of that one alabaster jar. Both then and now, people like Judas view true worship as nothing but a waste.

Why couldn't John or any of the others see through the deception of Judas? Because true evil almost always comes to us in disguise. If you want to find the Judases of our own time, don't look among the atheists or any other group that is openly opposed to Jesus Christ. Look in the church itself! You will find them sitting in pews, or teaching Sunday school, or sitting on church boards, or standing in pulpits, or writing Christian books, or preaching on television or radio. I'm not saying that most or even many of those who do such things are Judases. I'm sure that most who publicly profess to follow Christ are true Christians.

But all it took to betray Jesus was one counterfeit follower among twelve.

We often think that evil is easy to recognize, that evil always wears the black hat and twists its mustache while leering and laughing wickedly. But the truth is that the worst and most anti-Christian evil is deceptive to the core, is hard to recognize, and comes disguised in the false trappings of devotion and good intentions. Their words and actions are subtle and soothing and beguiling. As M. Scott Peck observes in *People of the Lie,*

> Since the primary motive of the evil is disguise, one of the places evil people are most likely to be found is within the church. What better way to conceal one's evil from oneself, as well as from others, than to be a deacon or some other highly visible form of Christian within our culture? . . . I do not mean to imply that the evil are anything other than a small minority among the religious or that religious motives of most people are in any way spurious. I mean only that evil people tend to gravitate toward piety for the disguise and concealment it can offer them.[3]

This description of "evil people" applies, no doubt, to Judas, as it does to many outwardly religious people in our own day. It is a sobering statement to reflect upon—not for the purpose of ferreting out the "evil people" in our own midst, but for the purpose of self-examination. You and I would do well to ask ourselves, "Why do I attend church? Why am I involved in Christian activities? Am I a Christian so that I can worship the Lord in service, giving, and fellowship—and am I making a pretence of following the Lord only for the sake of what I can get out of it? Am I a disciple—or a Judas?"

Examples of True Worship

At the end of this account, John reintroduces the people who have provided the mounting conflict in this powerful drama. They are the people who will soon be crying, "Crucify him! Crucify him!" before Pilate. They are murderers and power-hungry conspirators—and they are outwardly religious. They are the religious leaders of the Sanhedrin, the chief priests who are committed to destroying Jesus.

12:9–11 *Meanwhile a large crowd of Jews found out that Jesus was there and came, not only because of him but also to see Lazarus, whom he had raised*

*from the dead. So the chief priests made plans to kill Lazarus as well, for on
account of him many of the Jews were going over to Jesus and putting their
faith in him.*

A large crowd of the curious have come out to see not only Jesus, but
Lazarus, whom Jesus raised from the dead. This leads the chief priests to target not only Jesus, but Lazarus. As the countdown to the crisis continues, even
those whom Jesus has healed and helped are coming under the same peril that
He is. And the same is true today.

If we would follow Jesus and publicly identify ourselves with Him, there
will be risk, there will be persecution. It goes with the territory.

But the privilege of knowing Jesus and fellowshiping with Him on an
intimate basis is worth any risk, any abuse, any persecution, even death itself.
Lazarus had already experienced the worst that life could do to him, including
the coldness of the grave, so he knew he had nothing to fear. He could boldly,
publicly declare himself to be a friend of Jesus, whatever the cost, because the
privilege of knowing and following Jesus far outweighed the penalties that the
chief priests wanted to impose.

John chapter 12 is our model for true worship in its various dimensions.
Lazarus, Mary, and Martha—who knew Jesus face to face—lived out their
worship in courageous identification with Jesus; in fellowshiping with Jesus;
in giving to Jesus; in serving Jesus. God grant us transformed hearts, filled
with love, adoration, and gratitude, so that our worship might be like theirs.

Chapter Thirty-Four

Triumph or Tragedy?

John 12:12–26

T he horse's name was Bucephalus, and he was the largest, wildest, most majestic-looking animal the king had ever seen. Six ropes were tied to the horse's neck, for it took six men to hold the beast in place as it reared and snorted and struck sparks from the ground with its hooves. King Philip of Macedon walked all around the horse, admiring its strength and spirit. "Have you ever seen a more magnificent animal?" asked the eager Thessalonian merchant who had brought the steed to the king's court.

"Never," admitted the king, "but I can't use such an animal. He is too wild."

The merchant was crestfallen.

"Let me break him, father," said a youthful voice. The king turned and saw his sixteen-year-old son standing with his hands proudly on his hips. "If the horse will let me ride him, then buy him for me," the prince continued. "If I fail to ride him, I will pay you a forfeit equal to his price."

King Philip agreed, and the young man mounted the animal—and the wild horse immediately calmed down and allowed the young prince to put him through his paces. The entire court broke into applause.

King Philip was amazed—and delighted. He ran to his son and embraced him. "My son!" he exclaimed. "Macedonia is too small for you! You are ready to conquer kingdoms! Go—and become king of the world!"

And that young prince did go on to conquer all the Greek states, then Asia, Persia, Syria, Egypt, India, and Babylon—in short, all of the known world—and he did this shortly before his early death at the age of 33. His name was Alexander the Great.

There are interesting parallels between these two kings, Alexander and Jesus. Both died at the age of 33, both were hailed as king of the world, and both established their credentials as conquering kings, in part, by riding a horse or a colt.

But notice the contrasts between this Greek conqueror, Alexander, and the Jewish Messiah, Jesus: Alexander rode a mighty, spirited, kingly steed named

Bucephalus; Jesus rode a humble, lowly foal of a donkey. Alexander conquered political kingdoms; Jesus conquered human hearts, and meekly went to His death at the hands of the religious and political authorities. Alexander was a mere human being who declared himself to be a god; Jesus was fully God, yet humbled Himself and submitted to the indignity of being poured into human form. Alexander wept when he discovered there were no more worlds for him to conquer, and died after a drinking binge; his empire completely disintegrated within a few years of his death. As Jesus hung dying on the cross, He declared triumphantly that His mission on earth was finished; after His death and resurrection, His kingdom grew and grew at an amazing rate.

That is the difference between an earthly king and a heavenly king, between a king who comes on a mighty charger and a king who comes on the foal of a donkey. Someday, Jesus will return to earth riding a majestic white horse (see Revelation 19:11–16), but in John 12 He comes as the most humble and unassuming king in human history!

"Hosanna!"

John gives us a very succinct account of our Lord's entry into Jerusalem—the event we celebrate every spring as Palm Sunday.

12:12–15 *The next day the great crowd that had come for the Feast heard that Jesus was on his way to Jerusalem. They took palm branches and went out to meet him, shouting,*
"Hosanna!"
"Blessed is he who comes in the name of the Lord!"
"Blessed is the King of Israel!"
Jesus found a young donkey and sat upon it, as it is written,
"Do not be afraid, O Daughter of Zion;
see, your king is coming,
seated on a donkey's colt."

The traditional view of this event is that it is a well-deserved recognition of our Lord's Messiahship; that at last He is receiving a proper welcome as King, in fulfillment of the prophecy of Zechariah 9:9, which is quoted here. The crowd shouts, "Hosanna!" which means, "Save us now!" They see Him as a conqueror and acknowledge Him as king of Israel. Most of us have grown up with the traditional image of this event as a moment of joy and triumph for our Lord—but that is not true.

Here, again, we see how important it is to learn about Jesus from Scripture rather than tradition. The gospel of John sweeps away our distorted ideas and misconceptions, replacing them with the simple, pure truth of John's eyewitness account. If you carefully read this and the other gospel accounts of this event (see Matthew 21:1–9; Mark 11:1–10; Luke 19:29–38), it becomes clear that it was not the city of Jerusalem and its inhabitants who welcome Jesus as King. Rather, it was people from outside of Jerusalem—"the great crowd that had come [to Jerusalem] for the Feast," as John says in verse 12— who actually lay down their palm branches and shout hosannas and blessings as Jesus rides into town. These were not the residents of the city, but pilgrims, outsiders, people from around Judea and Galilee and Idumea and Decapolis and even foreign countries.

According to Matthew's account, the whole city was stirred and in an uproar over Jesus' entry as the procession came down the Mount of Olives. Instead of joining in the acclaim and celebration, the Jews of Jerusalem suspiciously asked, "Who is this?" The crowd of the procession—people who had streamed into Jerusalem for the Feast of Passover—had to inform them, "This is Jesus, the prophet from Nazareth in Galilee."[1]

Bewildered and Amazed

John shows us that no one—not even John himself—understood the true meaning and nature of the first Palm Sunday.

12:16–19 *At first his disciples did not understand all this. Only after Jesus was glorified did they realize that these things had been written about him and that they had done these things to him.*

Now the crowd that was with him had continued to spread the word that he had called Lazarus from the tomb, raising him from the dead. Many people, because they had heard that he had given this miraculous sign, went out to meet him. So the Pharisees said to one another, "See, this is getting us nowhere. Look how the whole world has gone after him!"

Even the disciples were bewildered by this turn of events. They had been with Jesus in Galilee when the crowd had tried to crown Him King following the feeding of the multitude—and they had seen Him reject the crowd's acclamation. Here, however, they see He is willing to receive the plaudits of the crowd. This must have been very confusing for them. They must have been amazed by this seeming inconsistency in the behavior of their Lord. As John says in verse 16, they were not able to make sense of these events until after Jesus was glorified, until after the resurrection.

And there were others who were bewildered and amazed by this turn of events: The crowds were buzzing with the incredible news that Jesus had raised a man who had been dead four days, and they all wanted to catch a glimpse of the famous Wonder-Worker. The Pharisees—who had been conspiring for months to kill Jesus—were baffled as to how to proceed against Him. As we learn in the other gospel accounts, they were afraid to take Jesus prisoner during the Passover Feast, fearing a violent reaction from the crowds. Now, as the whole populace seems to be swept up in the excitement over Jesus, they decide that things are getting out of control, and something has to be done to stop Jesus. "See," they grumble, "this is getting us nowhere. Look how the whole world has gone after him." The entrance of Jesus had upset their plans, forcing them to proceed with their murderous conspiracy ahead of schedule.

A Strategic Day

Another common misconception about the first Palm Sunday is the belief that the welcome Jesus received was a spontaneous demonstration. The way most of us picture this event was that Jesus rode into the city on a donkey, and the crowd suddenly appeared out of nowhere and began shouting and breaking branches off of palm trees. But a careful reading of the four gospels gives us a very different picture altogether.

This demonstration was very carefully orchestrated—by none other than Jesus Himself! He was the One who was carefully initiating events according to His schedule. In the other gospel accounts, we see that Jesus made arrangements weeks in advance for a donkey to be available to Him. He had made these arrangements during a quick visit to Jerusalem several weeks earlier. It was during that same visit that He also arranged to rent a room in which He and His disciples would celebrate the Passover together. He knew weeks or months (or perhaps even years) earlier what was going to happen to Him, and when it was going to happen.

Jesus knew that the prophet Zechariah had predicted that Messiah would come, riding into the city on a colt which no man had ever ridden—and that is a remarkable feat in itself. Having grown up in Montana, I know what it's like to ride a colt which has never been ridden before. From time to time I've even broken a horse; I once got aboard a two-year-old colt that had never been ridden—for a total of two-and-a-half seconds! I think it is noteworthy, then, that when Jesus gets on the back of this unridden colt, His authority over Nature is so complete that this unridden colt behaves as meekly as if it was already broken.

But there is another prophecy that Jesus knew, one of the most amazing prophetic passages of the Old Testament: Daniel chapter 9. That passage predicts that a special period of 490 years of Jewish history would run its course, beginning at the time the command was given to rebuild the walls of Jerusalem following the Babylonian captivity. When 483 of those years would elapse, Messiah—"the Anointed One, the ruler"[2]—would be presented to His people. In two fascinating books, *Messiah the Prince,* and *Daniel the Prophet,* Sir Robert Anderson demonstrates that on the very day that Jesus rode into Jerusalem, exactly 483 years had elapsed since the issuing of the commandment to build the walls of Jerusalem!

(You may well ask, "But what about the last seven years—the seven years which, when added to 483, make up the full 490 years of Jewish history prophesied in Daniel 9?" In Daniel 9:26, the prophet says that after the 483 years are fulfilled, "the Anointed One will be cut off"—a clear reference to the death of Jesus of Nazareth. Following that cataclysmic event, there is a break, a silence of an indeterminate number of years. After that long and unknown number of years, suggests Daniel 9:26–27, the final seven years will take place. Those seven years will be a period of worldwide upheaval at the end of the age—a time described in Revelation 6 through 19 as the Great Tribulation. You and I live in that great silent gap between the first 483 years and the last seven years. For a more complete discussion of this subject, see my book *God's Final Word: Understanding Revelation,* especially 140–41.)

Clearly, that first Palm Sunday was a strategic day in the history of Israel. Our Lord was fully aware of this prophecy—and He carried out His messianic role at precisely the appointed time.

The Tears of a King

Another common misconception about the first Palm Sunday was that Jesus' entry into the city of Jerusalem was a triumphal entry. In fact, the New International Version of the Bible inserts a subheading in over this story in each gospel: "The Triumphal Entry." Certainly, this event had the outward trappings of a triumph: Shouts of praise, throngs lining the streets, palm fronds waving, branches and cloaks spread before Him like a royal carpet.

But this was not a triumphal entry in the heart of the Lord. We get a deep and poignant glimpse into the heart of Jesus in the account of this event in Luke 19, verses 41 through 44:

> As he approached Jerusalem and saw the city, he wept
> over it and said, "If you, even you, had only known on this day
> what would bring you peace—but now it is hidden from your

eyes. The days will come upon you when your enemies will build an embankment against you and encircle you and hem you in on every side. They will dash you to the ground, you and the children within your walls. They will not leave one stone on another, because you did not recognize the time of God's coming to you."

Clearly, there is no triumph in this event for Jesus! When He came over the brow of the mountain and saw the city spread before Him, His heart didn't fill with joy. No, His eyes filled with tears! Not only was He unable to enjoy the acclaim of the multitude, He was actually weeping!

And He went on to lament the hardness of heart of this great city. Though the pilgrims from outside Jerusalem were celebrating His entry, the people who lived in the city ignored or resented His entry. They did not recognize the time of God's coming to them—and as a result, they would undergo a severe and terrible judgment. In this passage in Luke, Jesus predicted the coming destruction of Jerusalem and the temple. His fateful prediction was fulfilled forty years later when the city and the temple were destroyed by the Roman army.

I remember watching television in 1951 and witnessing the triumphant return of General Douglas MacArthur to San Francisco. He had just concluded six years as the commander of the occupation forces in Japan. During those years, he was the virtual overlord of Japan, and he used his power to totally restructure the Japanese government, military, and constitution.

As his motorcade rolled along Market Street, streamers and confetti were flung from every window. I particularly remember a closeup shot of MacArthur's profile as he basked in the enthusiasm of this wild and ecstatic welcome. It was an expression of quiet pride and satisfaction. MacArthur's entry into San Francisco was truly a triumphal entry—and it was quite a contrast from our Lord's entry into Jerusalem. Jesus was coming to Jerusalem as King—not in triumph to receive a throne, but in sorrow to pronounce a sentence of judgment upon the nation.

The other gospels show that, following His entry into the city, Jesus went immediately to the temple and cleansed it of the moneychangers. You will remember that in chapter 7 of this book, where we examined the temple cleansing described in John 2:12–25, we noted that there were *two* temple cleansings, not one. He cleansed the temple both at the beginning and the end of His ministry, and in that chapter of this book we examined the significant differences between those two cleansings. The cleansing in John 2 was the one which took place at the beginning of His ministry, and the cleansing described in the synoptics (which John does not mention) takes place here, after His entry into Jerusalem, and just before He offers Himself upon the cross.

"We Wish To See Jesus"

When Jesus came into Jerusalem in fulfillment of the ancient prophecies, He came as King—but not the kind of king the people expected. As He had throughout His ministry, Jesus once again confounded the expectations the Jewish people had of their Messiah. As He approaches the city, He comes not like Alexander the Great or any other conqueror, riding on a mighty war-horse. Rather, He comes on a donkey, a symbol of peace and humility. His only scepter is a broken reed, His only crown a crown of thorns, His only throne a bloody cross.

What does this scene tell us? It tells us that outward appearances mean nothing to God! He doesn't care about symbols of might and power, but about love and purity. He has no use for golden crowns and purple robes if they are draped around hearts that are defiled and unyielded to Him.

That is why John goes immediately from this event to another event which probably occurred a day or two later in the course of this strategic week: The visit of a group of Greeks to the Passover Feast.

12:20–24 *Now there were some Greeks among those who went up to worship at the Feast. They came to Philip, who was from Bethsaida in Galilee, with a request. "Sir," they said, "we would like to see Jesus." Philip went to tell Andrew; Andrew and Philip in turn told Jesus.*

Jesus replied, "The hour has come for the Son of Man to be glorified. I tell you the truth, unless a kernel of wheat falls to the ground and dies, it remains only a single seed. But if it dies, it produces many seeds."

The disciples must have been amazed at this reaction of our Lord. These Greek pilgrims had probably come in contact with the teaching of the Old Testament and were drawn by the pure, monotheistic image of a great, loving Creator-God. Though they had not converted to Judaism, they did come to the Passover Feast to celebrate with the Jews. This was not as unusual a situation as it might seem at first. Remember, the outer courts of the temple were called "the courts of the Gentiles." Many Gentiles would go to the Jewish temple to celebrate the Jewish holidays—even though they were strictly forbidden to go beyond those courts.

Notice that these Greeks picked out the two disciples who had Greek names: Philip and Andrew. Philip, we are told, was from Bethsaida, on the northern side of the lake of Galilee, an area in which many Gentiles had settled. These Greeks were sincere people, not mere curiosity seekers. They said to Philip, "Sir, we wish to see Jesus." These are significant words.

Over the years, I have stood in many pulpits as a guest speaker. Often I have looked down on a pulpit and have seen these words inscribed on a plaque or even written on a 3x5 card and taped to the pulpit:

"SIR, WE WISH TO SEE JESUS."

It is a phrase many preachers use as a reminder that their congregations have not come to see a pastor and to hear his eloquence. They have come with a hunger to see Jesus. Those are challenging, humbling words.

As these Greeks convey these words to Jesus via Philip, they evoke an unusual response from Jesus. He has not been pleased by His reception from the Jews of Jerusalem—yet when He hears that a group of Gentiles want to see Him, He immediately responds, "The hour has come for the Son of Man to be glorified!"

You will recall that, throughout this gospel, there have been several occasions where people have tugged at Jesus or prodded at Jesus, and His response has been, "My hour has not yet come." For example, when His mother came to Him at the wedding in Cana because there was no more wine, He replied, "Woman, my hour has not yet come." He did not mean He would not help her, because He did help her. He meant that what He would do would not accomplish her desire—which was that He reveal Himself as the promised Messiah—because His time had not yet come. That was the first of several occasions where He made it clear that His time had not come.

But the moment He hears that these Gentiles—these unclean, unchosen aliens who were from outside of the house of Israel!—had arrived, he responds, "The hour has come . . . !"

And He goes on to utter a message, which He introduces with "the formula of focused attention": "I tell you the truth," or, "Truly, truly, I say to you." By now, you are well aware that when you see those words, you should pay close attention to what follows. And Jesus says, "Unless a kernel of wheat falls to the ground and dies, it remains only a single seed. But if it dies, it produces many seeds."

What does He mean? He is talking about Himself! Jesus Himself is the kernel of wheat. Unless He is willing to die, unless He goes to the cross—which now towers over Him, overshadowing Him—His whole purpose in coming to earth will have been wasted. "But if it dies, it produces many seeds." He sees these Greeks as the first seeds to be produced from the kernel which is about to fall to the ground and die. These Gentiles symbolize the great harvest that is about to be reaped throughout the earth. Once He had died and risen again, the world—not just the Jewish race, but the entire world!—would see the outcome of His work and His life.

But it could not happen without death. It could not happen without the cross.

If Jesus had not died, we probably would not know any more about Him than we know of any other great religious leader, such as Buddha, Mohammed, or Confucius. Without the cross, we might not have heard of Him at all. Remember how meager the results of His teachings were. He spoke—and so few seemed to understand.

It wasn't His miracles that cause this Man to leave such a lasting and deep imprint upon the world. It was His death. Because of the cross, He did something He never could have done otherwise: He shared His life with millions of people. The only way to true glory is to die.

Living Begins With Dying

Up to now, Jesus has been talking about His own impending death. But now He applies this principle to your death and mine.

12:25–26 *"The man who loves his life will lose it, while the man who hates his life in this world will keep it for eternal life. Whoever serves me must follow me; and where I am, my servant also will be. My Father will honor the one who serves me."*

Here is the great Christian paradox. Here is the unmistakable mark of an authentic gospel: It begins with dying. It begins with a cross. If you hear a gospel proclaimed from a pulpit, or in a book, or on the radio, or on television, and that gospel does not begin with a cross and with the fact that some part of you has to die, then it is not the true gospel. That is the identifying mark.

So many "gospels" today—both secular and religious—preach that you can have it all: you can be rich, you can indulge yourself, you can be and do anything you imagine. But those are false gospels, and Jesus declares that if you follow those gospels, then you will lose everything. Life will slip through your fingers, no matter what you do, no matter how you grasp at it. If you live only to please yourself, you will lose *everything*—even the very *self* you have been trying to please!

"The man who loves his life will lose it," says Jesus, "while the man who hates his life in this world will keep it for eternal life." That doesn't mean you have to hate yourself. It means you must recognize that living for yourself will never supply what you really want out of life. Only when the Lordship of Christ assumes total control over your life, only when God becomes your everything and self becomes nothing, only when your love for God is so great that your self-love becomes as hate by comparison—only then will you truly find and keep yourself for eternal life.

That is why the gospel includes a cross. That is why the cross has become the symbol of Christian faith. That is not just the cross of Jesus. It must become your cross and mine, the cross where our own selves and all our selfishness has been nailed and put to death.

God does not want you to despise yourself and to beat yourself down and to tell yourself what a terrible person you are. He wants you to feel loved and valued. That's why He has offered you His grace and His forgiveness. But God also knows that the only true and accurate sense of self-esteem you can have is a self-esteem that begins with a cross. True, godly self-esteem does not begin with the premise, "I'm okay, you're okay," because we are not okay at all. We are sinners.

Godly self-esteem begins by saying, "I'm not okay, but Jesus is wonderful, and He died for me, to remove my sin and to make me acceptable and sinless and completely okay with God. And now, out of gratitude, I choose to crucify my old self and my old wants and to live completely for Him—and that's okay with me!" As A. W. Tozer once wrote,

> In every Christian's heart there is a cross and a throne, and the
> Christian is on the throne till he puts himself on the cross; if
> he refuses the cross he remains on the throne. . . . We all want
> to be saved but we insist that Christ do all the dying. No cross
> for us, no dethronement, no dying. We remain king within the
> little kingdom of Mansoul and wear our tinsel crowns with all
> the pride of a Caesar; but we doom ourselves to shadows and
> weakness and spiritual sterility.[3]

Jesus goes on to hammer nails of truth right through our flesh and into the cross at our backs. "Whoever serves me must follow me," He says, "and where I am, my servant also will be." In other words, if we are to serve Jesus, we must go the way He went. If we are unwilling to follow Christ wherever He leads, then how can we truly call ourselves His servants? Why should a servant not submit to the same pain and indignity that his Master has endured? Why should a servant not go where his Master has gone?

This is not a matter to be taken lightly. Just look where His steps have led! Up ahead is a hill called Calvary. There are *three* crosses on that hill, not just one. Room enough for Jesus. And for you. And for me.

How the Kingdom Grows

The cross of Christ stands for two things in your life and mine: It stands for a once-and-for-all decision to invite Jesus into our lives as Lord and Savior; and it stands for a daily, continual series of choices. We must not only sur-render to Jesus once; we must surrender repeatedly, moment by moment, day by day. Every minute of every day, we must renew our own commitment to self-crucifixion. We must continually surrender all claim to ourselves, all rights to run our own affairs. And that hurts. It cancels our own plans. It confounds our ambitions. It feels like death. Because it is death. Self-crucifixion is the death of self so that Jesus can come and live in us and through us.

But the amazing thing about crucifying self is that *this* form of death produces an even greater quality of life, along with a peace and a joy that nothing can ever take away. Jesus uses the symbol of a kernel of wheat not only of Himself but as a symbol of everyone who follows Him.

If you belong to Jesus, every day will have its cross, every day will have something you ought to do, but don't feel like doing. That is your cross. "If anyone would come after me," said Jesus, "he must deny himself and take up his cross daily and follow me."[4] Every day we have to die a little (or even a lot!) in order to live for Jesus. Millions of followers of Jesus Christ have proved this to be so. Life comes only out of death—the death of self.

And when we die, when our own kernel of wheat falls to the ground like that of Jesus Himself, we too can produce many new seeds. Others see Jesus through our own death, through the daily choices we make to crucify self and live for Jesus. That is how His kingdom grows. That is how the death of one kernel produces many seeds.

Here is the choice Jesus sets before us: If we choose to die with Him, then we shall live. "I tell you the truth," said our Lord, our Master, our Savior, "unless a kernel of wheat falls to the ground and dies, it remains only a single seed. But if it dies, it produces many seeds."

Chapter Thirty-Five

Faithful Belief—and Fatal Unbelief

John 12:27–50

Ⅰf you go to modern-day Jerusalem, you can visit the Garden of Gethsemane—the very same place where Jesus went through His agony before the cross. In that garden are ancient, gnarled, massive olive trees, some of which are believed to date back to the days of Jesus. It may be that one of those old trees may have stood as a silent witness next to the exact spot where Jesus knelt in prayer and great drops of bloody sweat dropped from His brow.

The agony of Jesus in the Garden is one of the most memorable events associated with the drama of the cross. So it seems strange, as we examine John's account of this drama, that John includes *no mention* of our Lord's struggle in Gethsemane—especially since John was one of the three disciples (along with Peter and James) who were with Jesus that night! Why is this?

We can't know for sure, but it may be that it has to do with the eyewitness nature of John's gospel. Perhaps because John, like Peter and James, fell asleep and missed much of what occurred in the garden, he chooses not to include it in his journal-like gospel.

Yet, even though John does not relate the Gethsemane story in his gospel, he does include an incident which many Bible commentators refer to as "the Little Gethsemane." That is what we come to in this portion of John chapter 12.

"The Little Gethsemane"

12:27–29 *"Now my heart is troubled, and what shall I say? 'Father, save me from this hour'? No, it was for this very reason I came to this hour. Father, glorify your name!"*

Then a voice came from heaven, "I have glorified it, and will glorify it again." The crowd that was there and heard it said it had thundered; others said an angel had spoken to him.

You can see why this segment of John's gospel is called "the Little Gethsemane." It reflects, in condensed form, the same agony of spirit Jesus is seen to express in the Garden of Gethsemane in the synoptic gospels. The incident John describes occurred perhaps two days before the experience in the Garden. Jesus has just declared the great law of the harvest—"I tell you the truth, unless a kernel of wheat falls to the ground and dies, it remains only a single seed. But if it dies, it produces many seeds."

Then He goes on to say, "Now my heart is troubled, and what shall I say? 'Father, save me from this hour'? No, it was for this very reason I came to this hour. Father glorify your name!" The way this reads in the New International Version, it sounds like a Shakespearean soliloquy, an inner dialogue that Jesus has with Himself, spoken aloud. And while I believe it can be read that way, I don't believe that's what John intended.

When Jesus says, "No, it was for this very reason I came to this hour," the word "No" is not in the original text. It is supplied by the English translators. I don't believe Jesus is merely having a dialogue within Himself. I believe He is praying, sincerely and fervently, to the Father, asking to be delivered from the pain and spiritual anguish of the cross, which He sees looming in His immediate future. He was facing a terrible ordeal—an ordeal beyond our ability to imagine. He had no illusions about the horror that lay ahead of Him.

A comparison of this account with the accounts of Gethsemane in the other gospels reveals a close parallel. The words in John 12:27, "Now my heart is troubled," echo His lament in Gethsemane, "My soul is overwhelmed with sorrow to the point of death."[1] Compare also the words in John 12:27, "Father, save me from this hour," with what He said in the Garden, "My Father, if it is possible, may this cup be taken from me."[2]

But there are also contrasts between the agony in Gethsemane and "the Little Gethsemane" which John relates here. In John 12:28, Jesus says, "Father, glorify your name!" And a voice comes from heaven, saying, "I have glorified it, and will glorify it again." A crowd of people is there, and they hear both Jesus and the voice from heaven. It is a public affirmation of Jesus and the work He is about to do on the cross. In Gethsemane, however, "an angel appeared to him and strengthened him" in the solitude of His private anguish.[3]

Clearly, "the Little Gethsemane" account is not intended by John as a parallel version of the Garden of Gethsemane account. These are two separate occasions, and "the Little Gethsemane" account in John 12 does not take place in Gethsemane at all. What this account shows us is that the mental torture our Lord experienced did not begin on the night of the cross. It was something He lived with and which could be witnessed in His life from time to time, especially during that last fateful week in Jerusalem. He knew that He was approaching a climactic moment of agony, shame, and physical pain beyond anyone's ability to absorb or comprehend. And the massive weight of the cross already pressed down upon His soul. It was an agony He experienced not once in the Garden, but several times.

Jesus foresaw the bloody sweat, the traitor's kiss, the mockery, the crown of thorns, the scourging, the nails and the spear, and the terrible torment that wrenched those awful cries from His tortured spirit as He endured shame and humiliation and separation from the Father. He saw the mouth of Hell yawning before Him, and all of that is compressed into those words, "Now my heart is troubled."

Coming Glory

After the voice came from heaven, the people who heard it speculated on the source of the voice. Some thought they had only heard the sound of thunder. Others thought it was the voice of an angel. Jesus answers their speculations here.

12:30–33 *Jesus said, "This voice was for your benefit, not mine. Now is the time for judgment on this world; now the prince of this world will be driven out. But I, when I am lifted up from the earth, will draw all men to myself." He said this to show the kind of death he was going to die.*

This divine voice has been heard two times before. The first time was following His baptism by John the Baptist, when the Spirit of God descended like a dove and a voice from heaven said, "This is my Son, whom I love; with him I am well pleased."[4] The second time was when He was transfigured on Mount Hermon, and His companions, Peter, James, and John saw Moses and Elijah appear and talk with Jesus, and a voice from heaven said, "This is my Son, whom I love; with him I am well pleased. Listen to him!"

Now, for the third time, a voice from heaven is heard, affirming the Father's good pleasure at the faithfulness of His beloved Son. Our Lord's ordeal will be terrible beyond description, and Jesus has no illusions about it. Yet God declares that out of this ordeal will come greater glory for God.

What will that glory consist of? Jesus cites three elements of that glory. First, God will be glorified when the cross brings judgment to the world. "Now is the time for judgment on this world," He says. The cross will expose the evil and falseness of the philosophies of this world. The corruption and selfishness of human values will be laid bare. Jesus will lead the way to the cross—and we must follow Him, and nail our own selves to that cross. "If anyone would come after me," said Jesus, "he must deny himself and take up his cross daily and follow me."[5] Those who take up their cross daily and follow Jesus have judged themselves. Those who do not will be judged by the cross.

Second, Jesus declares that God will be glorified when Satan is overthrown by the cross. "Now the prince of this world will be driven out," He says. Because we are continually being deceived by Satan, we have no concept how completely he controls and manipulates the human race. The human race is blindly led by the demonic delusions that Satan sends into the world. But the cross cancels his power over us, allows us to be delivered from his schemes and enlightened regarding his lies. The cross is our guarantee that Satan will one day be cast into the lake of fire, never to trouble the human race again.

Third, Jesus says that God will be glorified when the human race is drawn to Jesus. "But I," said Jesus, "when I am lifted up from the earth, will draw all men to myself." You may have heard this text used to mean that if a preacher exalts and lifts up Christ in his preaching, people will be attracted to Him. But that is not what Jesus means. The fact is, true Christ-centered preaching tends to drive as many people away as it attracts. Jesus is not talking about preaching. He is talking about something else altogether—and John explains to us exactly what Jesus means.

"He said this," said John, "to show the kind of death he was going to die." When Jesus talks about being "lifted up from the earth," it is a graphic, horrible depiction of His death, when He is nailed to a rough wooden cross, and that cross is swung up into the air, and dropped into a hole in the ground, then pounded into place. Jesus is saying that when He is lifted up on the cross and allowed to dangle by His bleeding wounds, then all of mankind, both men and women, and from every race on earth, will be drawn toward Him, and they will be delivered and saved from their sins. (Note, by the way, that the word "men" is used here in the sense of "humankind," "humanity," without regard to gender.)

When Jesus says that He will "draw all men" to Himself, does He mean that all people will be saved? No. Then in what sense will He draw the entire human race to Himself? In the sense that all will be either judged or saved. No one can escape Jesus of Nazareth. No matter what path you may take in this life, He stands at the final destination. We may neglect Him or ignore Him now, but a day will come when we have to face Him. He will either be our Savior or He will be our Judge. There is no third alternative.

Fateful Unbelief

12:34–36 *The crowd spoke up, "We have heard from the Law that the Christ [Messiah] will remain forever, so how can you say, 'The Son of Man must be* *lifted up'? Who is this 'Son of Man'?"*

Then Jesus told them, "You are going to have the light just a little while longer. Walk while you have the light, before darkness overtakes you. The man who walks in the dark does not know where he is going. Put your trust in the light while you have it, so that you may become sons of light." When he had finished speaking, Jesus left and hid himself from them.

Why did the Jews fail to recognize their Messiah? If He did such wonderful signs, and so completely fulfilled the Old Testament prophecies, why didn't they recognize Him and receive Him?

The answer, given in these verses, is a study in the steps of unbelief. The first step to unbelief is to *exercise a selective faith,* a faith that believes some, but not all, of the Word of God. The crowd said, "We have heard from the Law that the Christ [Messiah] will remain forever, so how can you say, 'The Son of Man must be lifted up'?" There are passages in Isaiah, in Daniel, and in Zechariah and elsewhere which clearly state that once the Messiah appeared He would remain God's chosen forever. Other passages predicted His arrival as a Deliverer who would lead Israel to victory. This crowd had chosen to focus on such passages as Isaiah 9:

> For to us a child is born,
> to us a son is given,
> and the government will be on his shoulders,
> And he will be called
> Wonderful Counselor, Mighty God,
> Everlasting Father, Prince of Peace.
> Of the increase of his government and peace
> there will be no end.[6]

On hearing these words, the Jews of Jesus' day—and, for that matter, the practitioners of the Jewish faith today—say, "That is our Messiah!" But they were selective in the way they heard the Word. They had focused on some passages about the Messiah and neglected others.

It is fascinating to note that this crowd understood exactly what Jesus meant when He said, "when I am lifted up from the earth." They knew He was referring to the cross. The cross offended their preconceived notion of who Messiah would be and what He would do. Their conception of the Messiah would never be lifted on a cross to die; their Messiah was a conqueror and a deliverer. The "Son of Man" that Jesus introduced to them was not the kind of Messiah they wanted.

Many of us fall into the same trap today. We focus on this passage or that passage of Scripture and we say, "This is what God is like. This is what He has promised me. He has promised me healing and peace and joy." And then when trials and problems arise, we say, "I claimed the promises of God, and they didn't work." When that is our position, we are actually saying that God is unfaithful to His word. In short, we are saying that God is a liar!

But the Bible says that God is faithful, that He cannot and does not lie. History confirms that God fulfills His promises to the letter. If we don't see His promises being fulfilled, it's not because God has failed. It's because there is *something wrong with us*. We are not seeing Scripture clearly. We are not seeing God clearly. We are not seeing life clearly. There is a darkness inside us, and our vision is so clouded that we don't even know the darkness is there!

Instead of blaming God, we should ask ourselves where *we* have gone wrong. We should ask God to open our understanding. If we bring our questions to God, He will enlighten us—because that is His business. He is the Light-Giver!

Walk in the Light

The second step to unbelief is to *ignore the present opportunity*. That is what these Jews were doing. Jesus said to them, "You are going to have the light just a little while longer. Walk while you have the light, before darkness overtakes you."

What was the opportunity these people were ignoring? The opportunity to listen to Jesus and learn from His words! Imagine the privilege that was slipping through their fingers—to hear God's words directly from the mouth of God's only Son! As near as we can determine from the evidence in the text, this was the last opportunity these people would have to hear the words of Jesus. After this discourse, He never spoke to the multitudes again. Instead, says verse 36, He hid Himself. The next appearance of Jesus will be a private appearance in the Upper Room.

"Walk while you have the light," Jesus told them. "This is the critical hour! Seize it! Act on it! For soon the opportunity will pass, the light will fade, and you will be left in the dark." If these people failed to act on what they could see in this brief moment of illumination, they would be condemned to stumbling and groping in the dark.

The third step to unbelief is to *deny the need for light*. "The man who walks in the dark does not know where he is going," says Jesus. These people proudly embraced their own darkness as if it was light—and that would be their undoing.

We seldom get the chance to experience total darkness. Turn out your lights, close your doors, pull the shades—and still you will find a little bit of light leaking into the room through cracks. In our civilized society, we are so surrounded by light sources—digital clocks, nightlights, streetlights outside our windows—that few of us ever experience total darkness.

But if you've ever toured one of the major limestone caverns in our national parks, such as Mammoth Cave in Kentucky or Carlsbad Caverns in New Mexico, you may have an idea of what complete darkness is really like. The tour guide takes you deep underground, then turns out the lights in the cave and tells you to hold up your hand in front of your face. Even after waiting for your eyes to adjust, you still can't see your hand in front of your face. Without the light which comes down from above, via electric wires, the darkness in those caves is complete.

Imagine trying to find your way through an underground cave in total darkness. Imagine the dangers that might await you—the low ceilings, the sudden drops, the hidden obstacles, the pits. In a spiritual and moral sense, those are the kinds of dangers that await those who choose to stumble blindly through their lives.

The Light Is Extinguished

This crowd has rejected Jesus' messiahship and His light. Is it too late for them? No, Jesus still invites them, "Put your trust in the light while you have it, so that you may become sons of light." He invites them to embrace the truth and step into the light.

To act on truth changes you. If you act on the truth that you have received—even if your knowledge of the truth is limited—you will become more truthful and more wise. If you face reality as it is, then you will begin to live realistically. That is living and walking in the light.

If you respond to the light, you will become inwardly enlightened. Not only that, you will also *become a light to others.* People will watch you, and by watching you live and walk in the light, they will learn to see reality as well.

Jesus has made His final proclamation, He has issued His final invitation. The light of Jesus is about to go out of their lives. In fact, even as the crowd stands and listens to Jesus, the light of Jesus is being removed from them. It is as if the sun has gone behind a cloud at sunset: "When he had finished speaking," says verse 36, "Jesus left and hid himself from them."

Now the darkness of this crowd is complete.

There will be no more miracles of the Old Creation, no more wine or loaves or fishes. There will be no more miracles of the New Creation, no more miracles of walking on water or dead loved ones raised from the grave. There will be no more wondrous words spoken on hillsides or in the temple courtyard.

The cross casts its shadow. A black darkness covers everything and everyone.

And the people of Jerusalem persist in their fatal unbelief.

God's Patience and God's Wrath

The remainder of John 12 is the apostle's commentary on the unbelief of these people. In fact, says John, the unbelief of these Jews was predicted 700 years earlier by the prophet Isaiah.

12:37–41 *Even after Jesus had done all these miraculous signs in their presence, they still would not believe in him. This was to fulfill the word of Isaiah the prophet:*

"Lord, who has believed our message and to whom has the arm of the Lord been revealed?"

For this reason they could not believe, because, as Isaiah says elsewhere:

"He has blinded their eyes
and deadened their hearts,
so they can neither see with their eyes,
nor understand with their hearts,
nor turn—and I would heal them."

Isaiah said this because he saw Jesus' glory and spoke about him.

In this amazing passage, John quotes two sections from the prophet Isaiah. The first is from the well-known 53rd chapter, which depicts "the Suffering Servant" who was "pierced for our transgressions" and "crushed for our iniquities," who has healed us by His own wounds.[7]

John quotes the opening lines from that chapter in which the prophet Isaiah marvels at the blindness and deafness of the people. "Lord," John quotes, "who has believed our message and to whom has the arm of the Lord been revealed?" God's words were delivered to the people, but the people did not heed them. They ignored the Lord's mighty arm, by which many wonderful signs and miracles were performed. John cites the rejection of Jesus the Messiah as the fulfillment of this ancient prophecy of Isaiah. Just as Isaiah had foreseen, the people had turned a deaf ear to all he had to say.

John goes on to quote another well-known passage, this time from Isaiah 6, which describes the prophet's vision of the glory of Jehovah. After witnessing the Lord seated upon a throne, high and exalted and wreathed with smoke, surrounded by flying seraphs who called out "Holy, holy, holy is the Lord Almighty," Isaiah then hears the Lord say to him, "Go and tell this people: 'Be ever hearing, but never understanding; be ever seeing, but never perceiving.' Make the heart of this people calloused; make their ears dull and close their eyes. Otherwise they might see with their eyes, hear with their ears, understand with their hearts, and turn and be healed."[8]

Many people read this and misunderstand because it sounds as though it is God's fault that the people don't believe. And there's no sense in trying to explain it away: This passage does, in fact, say that God prevents people from believing—*but it is not God's fault that they don't believe!* Does that sound like a contradiction to you? It can be very easily explained.

The fact is, these people had an opportunity to believe. They were invited to believe. They were shown miracle after miracle, evidence upon evidence. It is not that God arbitrarily chooses some to be saved and some to be damned. These people have made a choice to reject the truth, and God simply seals and notarizes a choice they have already made. This is simply a restatement of a spiritual fact of life: What you choose and what you persist in doing is what you will eventually become. If you persist in refusing and rejecting the truth, you will eventually lose your ability to even recognize the truth when it is right before your eyes. As an anonymous poet once observed,

> There is a line by us unseen,
> that crosses every path,
> The hidden boundary between
> God's patience and his wrath.

Jesus = God

In verse 41, after twice quoting from the book of Isaiah, John makes a startling statement: "Isaiah said this because he saw Jesus' glory and spoke about him." Here again is another of the many places in John's gospel which states in no uncertain terms that *Jesus is God.* Here John gives his commentary on those quotations from Isaiah—quotations that describe God in all His glory, seated upon His throne, high and exalted and wreathed with smoke, surrounded by flying seraphs calling out "Holy, holy, holy is the Lord Almighty!" And John's commentary on these passages in Isaiah is that Isaiah was actually looking forward in time and describing the glory of Jesus! In other words, John is stating that the Almighty Jehovah God of the Old Testament is none other than Jesus Himself!

Today there are many cults and religions that claim to be "Christian" but which deny that Jesus is God. Incredibly, many even assert that Jesus never claimed to be God and that the Bible never claims Jesus to be God. In the course of our study in John, however, we have seen numerous passages where Jesus explicitly claims His own deity.

True Belief

How, then, should we respond to Jesus the Christ, the Messiah, the Anointed One, the Son of Man, the Son of God? What kind of faith does this unique Person in human history demand from you and me?

We find the answer to these questions in the closing verses of John 12.

12:42–43 *Yet at the same time many even among the leaders believed in him. But because of the Pharisees they would not confess their faith for fear they would be put out of the synagogue; for they loved praise from men more than praise from God.*

John tells us that many of the religious leaders believed in Jesus—but what kind of belief was it? They believed that Jesus was who He said He was, that He was the Messiah, that He was the Anointed One of God. But they didn't act on that belief. Their belief did not change the way they lived their lives. They believed in their heads; but in their hearts and in every other aspect of their lives, they were in a state of unbelief. They were afraid to commit themselves or stand in opposition to their peers. They wanted the praise of men more than the praise of God.

Here John presents us with people who "believed"—after a fashion. But their love of the praise of men and their fear of the opposition of men misled them into final darkness. Reading this passage, we have to ask ourselves: Is our faith any different, any deeper, any more real than that of these religious leaders who "believed"—but were unchanged by what they believed?

John goes on to record the words of Jesus which summarize the claims He has made throughout His ministry. These are not words Jesus spoke on this occasion—Jesus, remember, has hidden Himself from the crowd at this point—but are meant to sum up the meaning of Jesus' life and ministry.

12:44–50 *Then Jesus cried out, "When a man believes in me, he does not believe in me only, but in the one who sent me. When he looks at me, he sees the one who sent me. I have come into the world as a light, so that no one who believes in me should stay in darkness.*

"As for the person who hears my words but does not keep them, I do not judge him. For I did not come to judge the world, but to save it. There is a judge for the one who rejects me and does not accept my words; that very word which I spoke will condemn him at the last day. For I did not speak of my own accord, but the Father who sent me commanded me what to say and how to say it. I know that his command leads to eternal life. So whatever I say is just what the Father has told me to say."

Look at the claims Jesus makes in this statement. Again, Jesus lays claim to full deity and equality with God the Father. "When a man . . . looks at me," says Jesus, "he sees the one who sent me." Jesus reveals God because Jesus *is* God. When you deal with Jesus, you are dealing with God.

Jesus claims to unveil reality because He *is* Ultimate Reality. "I have come into the world as a light," He says, "so that no one who believes in me should stay in darkness." To know Jesus is to understand the central fact of life.

Jesus comes as a Savior, not as a Punisher. "As for the person who hears my words but does not keep them," He says, "I do not judge him. For I did not come to judge the world, but to save it." Judgment does not fall on us immediately, even though we disbelieve. God is patient. He sent His Son not to chastise us but to save us. He gives us the opportunity to hear, again and again, that we might awaken and respond to Him. But, though judgment does not come immediately, it will come.

It is not Jesus Himself, but His word that is our judge if we reject Jesus. "There is a judge for the one who rejects me and does not accept my words," He says. "That very word which I spoke will condemn him at the last day."

Sometimes people ask, "What about those who have never heard the gospel? Will God really condemn those who have never heard?" But that is not the real issue. God does not condemn us for what we have not heard, but for ignoring what we have heard. The final judge is the word we have heard, the truth of Jesus that we already know. This means that those who are condemned on that day are *self-condemned.* They stand silent before the throne, rendered speechless by their guilty knowledge of truth they have not obeyed.

Jesus' final statement in chapter 12 is a reminder to His hearers of the authority behind all He says: "For I did not speak of my own accord," He declares, "but the Father who sent me commanded me what to say and how to say it. I know that His command leads to eternal life. So whatever I say is just what the Father has told me to say." The issue is life itself—eternal life, the most crucial issue any individual will ever face.

I once had a baffling electrical problem in my house. The circuit breakers kept cutting off the electricity for no apparent reason. At first we thought we had overloaded the circuit, so we unplugged several appliances. Not only did unplugging appliances fail to solve the problem, the circuit breaker actually became worse, until the breaker would trip if just one appliance was plugged in. So I opened the electrical box and carefully examined the wiring and the breakers. Finally, I discovered that two wires were touching. This should have been no problem, since both wires were insulated. But on closer inspection, I discovered that the insulation on those wires had been worn away somehow, so that there was enough of a contact for current to leak from one wire to the next—and that created a short-circuit which tripped the breaker. Once I had discovered the problem, it was a simple matter to fix it.

As I repaired the wires, I was struck by a parallel between that electrical problem and the Christian faith. We all have a capacity for faith. We all have the ability to hear the truth and accept it. But sometimes our faith leaks away. We make a moral compromise. We permit lies to take up residence in our souls. We harbor bitterness and anger. Gradually, almost unnoticed, our faith drains away until the circuit breaker of God's natural law is tripped—and the flow of God's power suddenly stops.

The question John confronts us with at the end of chapter 12 is this: Is something draining your faith? Are you unable to lay hold of the great and glorious promises of the gospel because there is some area where you are deceiving yourself? Some sin or habit or bitterness you are clinging to, even though the Bible clearly says it is wrong?

It is not enough to believe Jesus with our heads. It is not enough to simply agree that Jesus is the Messiah. Jesus does not want us to simply nod our heads and agree with Him. He wants to *change our lives.* If the gospel has convinced us but has not transformed us, then we are just like those Jewish leaders who "believed" but were left in darkness.

The electrifying power of God is available to you and to me and all who truly believe. May we have the courage to commit ourselves to Him, to believe not only with our heads, but with our hearts and our entire lives.

Chapter Thirty-Six

Servant Authority

John 13:1–17

Two men, who had been friends for years, had a weekly habit of meeting in a London restaurant for lunch and a lively philosophical debate. Today's menu: roast beef and Yorkshire pudding. Today's topic of debate: the difference between power and authority.

"Well, I say there is no difference," said the first man. "Power is authority. Having the power to force your will gives you the authority to do so."

"Now, there you are quite mistaken," said the other man, "and I'll give you an example to prove my point. If a rhinoceros were to enter this restaurant right now, there is no denying that he would have great power here. But I would be the first to stand and assure him that he has no authority here whatsoever!"

As we come to the 13th chapter of John, we see another demonstration of the difference between power and authority. In this chapter, we will see Jesus—who was the Creator-God in human form—set aside all His power while exercising the most profound form of authority of all: *servant authority.*

John's Focus

John introduces his study in servant authority with a number of powerful, significant phrases.

13:1–5 *It was just before the Passover Feast. Jesus knew that the time had come for him to leave this world and go to the Father. Having loved his own who were in the world, he now showed them the full extent of his love.*

The evening meal was being served, and the devil had already prompted Judas Iscariot, son of Simon, to betray Jesus. Jesus knew that the Father had put all things under his power, and that he had come from God and was returning to God; so he got up from the meal, took off his outer clothing, and wrapped a towel around his waist. After that, he poured water into a basin and began to wash his disciples' feet, drying them with the towel that was wrapped around him.

As the Lord enters the Upper Room with His disciples it is a somber and crucial hour in His ministry. Jesus knows that the time has come for Him to leave this world and go to the Father. The cross not only overshadows Him at this hour, but its weight presses on His shoulders. The disciples are nervous and tense, having witnessed the growing opposition of the authorities to Jesus. More than once, they have seen these leaders stoop down and take up stones to kill their Master. They have seen the murderous glint of hatred in the eyes of Jesus' powerful enemies. They have no doubt that the religious leaders are plotting to do away with their Lord.

As he relates this story, John chooses to focus on different aspects of this event than the writers of the synoptic gospels. Clearly, John's intention is to supplement, not duplicate, the other three gospel accounts. In Matthew, Mark, and Luke, the central feature of the Upper Room is the establishment of the sacrament of holy communion—the Lord's Supper. It is fascinating that John does not mention this feature of the story at all. Instead, he focuses on an event which the other gospels do not report: The washing of the disciples' feet.

The most important question about any event is not, "What happened?" but, "Why did it happen?" The "Why?" question appears to be John's primary concern as he focuses on Jesus' reasons for washing the feet of His disciples. John supplies six such reasons why Jesus did what He did.

Six Reasons

The first reason Jesus washed the feet of His disciples is evident: "Jesus knew that the time had come for him to leave this world and go to the Father." His time was short, and He knew it all too well. When you know your time is short, you become very focused. You are aware of each tick of the clock. You feel the pressure of accomplishing all your goals and settling all your affairs before the sands of the hourglass run out. This is what Jesus was feeling.

Throughout His ministry, Jesus had known He was to be the Lamb of God who would take away the sin of the world. He also knew that, according to the Father's timetable, He was to be offered as the Lamb of God during the Passover Feast. That Feast was instituted in Egypt when the angel of God's wrath passed over the houses of the Israelites, sparing the firstborn sons of the Jews while the Egyptians were judged by God. The sign that a household belonged to God was the spilled blood of a lamb, painted upon the door-posts—a symbol of the shed blood of Jesus which, centuries later, would drench the rough beams of a Roman cross.

In that rich and redolent symbolism, our Lord sees Himself and knows His time has come. The grain of wheat must fall to the ground and die. But Jesus also foresaw that, after His death—and as a *result* of His death!—a great harvest of Jews and Gentiles would follow. That event was at hand and time was short.

The second reason Jesus washed the feet of His disciples is that He was moved by an overwhelming love for His disciples. Listen to these beautiful words: "Having loved his own who were in the world, he now showed them the full extent of his love." Jesus knew what was coming and He dreaded it— yet for the sake of His disciples, He pressed on. Within twelve hours, He would be hanging upon the cross. Yet, having loved His own to the utter- most—even though He was about to be tortured and to pass into a dark strug- gle that no other human being can comprehend—He didn't think of Himself, but of those friends He loved.

The third reason Jesus washed the feet of His disciples follows: "The evening meal was being served, and the devil had already prompted Judas Iscariot, son of Simon, to betray Jesus." Jesus was always aware of the invisi- ble kingdom that surrounded Him—a kingdom of darkness. He knew that the devil was bringing about a crisis—and that the instrument of His plan was Judas, one of His own disciples.

The wording of the original Greek text is very interesting here: "the devil had put into the heart that Judas would be the one to betray him." Notice, it does not say "into the heart of Judas." Perhaps the editors of the NIV are cor- rect in interpreting this line as meaning that Satan "had already prompted Judas Iscariot. . . ." But many Bible commentators take this as a reference to the devil's own heart. They suggest that Satan had determined in his own heart to use Judas as his victim and his instrument to betray and destroy the Lord. For example, F. F. Bruce translates this passage, "The devil had already resolved that he would use Judas Iscariot to betray him."

By this time, Judas had already given himself over as a servant of the devil because of a willful, continuing pattern of deceit and greed and selfish- ness—and the devil had Judas under his thumb. This statement of John's indi- cates how easily we can be victimized by the devil. As we allow sin to take root in our lives, we progressively give Satan power over our minds and behavior. He can put thoughts into our minds and hearts and, in time, we can find ourselves betraying our highest hopes, values, and ideals.

So the third reason Jesus washed the feet of the disciples was that He knew that His enemy was at work. The devil was closing in on Him.

The fourth reason is that Jesus was in charge of all events surrounding His coming death and resurrection. As John says, "Jesus knew that the Father had put all things under his power." Some years ago, a book called *The Passover*

Plot suggested that Jesus was the helpless victim of a murder conspiracy among the Jewish leaders and Roman authorities. But John makes it clear that Jesus was in complete charge of events. He knew what He had to do, and He was carrying it out on schedule.

The fifth reason was that Jesus knew exactly who He was. He knew "that he had come from God and was returning to God." He knew His origin and His future, and He was completely secure in His own identity. Throughout this account, Jesus never panics. He is always in control, moving with a quiet dignity through the events of His arrest, His trial, His torture, and His death. He is in control because He knows fully and precisely who He is and what His mission is in the world.

The sixth reason Jesus washed the feet of the disciples—and the most urgent and immediate reason—is the motive implied in verses 4 and 5: "So he got up from the meal, took off his outer clothing, and wrapped a towel around His waist. After that, he poured water into a basin and began to wash his disciples' feet, drying them with the towel that was wrapped around him." He is demonstrating the kind of servanthood He wants them to live out in their own lives.

Like Quarrelsome Children

It is clear from this account that Jesus is doing what His disciples ought to have done. In those days it was customary for a servant to wash the feet of anyone entering a house, so that the dust of the roads could be removed. It may well be that Jesus, in order to teach them what it means to be a follower of Christ, had assigned His disciples to "footwashing duty" on a rotating basis. Yet on this occasion, all of the disciples refused to stoop to this menial chore. Why?

In Luke's gospel, we find the answer. Luke says that as Jesus was preparing to institute the Lord's Supper, the disciples argued among themselves as to which among them was the greatest. This may well have involved a debate as to the seating order. Perhaps each felt entitled to a seat of honor next to Jesus. While the famous painting of this scene by Leonardo da Vinci is a beautiful work of art, it fails to convey an accurate image of what really took place. As someone once said, the painting gives the impression that Jesus has just said, "All you fellas who want to get in the picture, come to this side of the table!"

Jesus and His disciples didn't sit in chairs, but on couches. They lay on their left sides, with their right hands available for eating. It is clear from Luke 22 that John was on one side of Jesus while Judas was on the other, which is why Jesus was later able to hand Judas the piece of bread which was to indicate that he was a traitor. Perhaps Jesus Himself chose His closest friend John to be beside Him. Judas, however, probably manipulated his way into a position next to Jesus—perhaps to throw suspicion off of himself.

The image you get from reading Luke 22 and John 13 is not the image of solemn dignity which the da Vinci painting conveys. It is an image of grown men acting like children, refusing to cooperate or behave or do their chores until Jesus, like a wise parent, shames them with His own example. Each disciple seems to be thinking, "Jesus is about to manifest Himself as the Messiah and the Deliverer—and I'm going to be His right-hand man, not a mere servant! I'm not about to be a footwasher in His kingdom!"

100 Per Cent Pure Peter!

During the Revolutionary War, a man in civilian clothes was riding his horse along the brow of a hill when he encountered a group of soldiers. The soldiers were struggling to mount a heavy cannon on a fortified gun emplacement to defend against a British attack. The stranger halted his horse and watched as three soldiers grunted and strained, trying to position the canon. A few feet away, a fourth soldier barked orders and berated the men, but didn't lift a finger to help them.

The stranger nudged his horse over near the man who was shouting orders. "Those men could use some help," the man on horseback said. "Why don't you lend a hand instead of shouting at them?"

The soldier said, "Sir, I'm a corporal!"

"Oh!" said the stranger. "I beg your pardon. Please, let me help." He dismounted, joined the three soldiers, and put his shoulder to the task. Soon the canon was in place.

The stranger returned to the corporal and said, "Mr. Corporal, the next time you have a job like this and not enough men to do it, send a message to me at my headquarters, and I will come and help you again. Just ask for your Commander-in-Chief, George Washington."

Then General Washington remounted his horse and rode away from the speechless corporal.

That is much like the situation we see here in the Upper Room—only instead of one arrogant corporal we have twelve self-important men with quarrelsome voices and dirty feet. Jesus waits until they are all reclining at the table, then, without a word, He arises, removes His garments, and assumes the role of a servant. Notice that when Jesus removes His outer garments, He is left wearing nothing but the loincloth of a slave. He kneels before each disciple in turn—even Judas!—and He washes the feet of each one and dries them with a towel. These twelve men are shocked, stunned, and ashamed—and rightly so.

John goes on to explain the meaning of this act.

13:6–9 *He came to Simon Peter, who said to him, "Lord, are you going to wash my feet?"*

Jesus replied, "You do not realize now what I am doing, but later you will understand."

"No," said Peter, "you shall never wash my feet."

Jesus answered, "Unless I wash you, you have no part with me."

"Then, Lord," Simon Peter replied, "not just my feet but my hands and my head as well!"

I'm so grateful for Peter—"Mr. Every Christian!" He makes all the same mistakes you and I would make if we were in his shoes. John describes three things Peter does. First, in typical Peter-fashion, he displays his utter ignorance: "Lord, are you going to wash my feet?" In the original language, this question is very emphatic. Clearly, Peter is offended by the Lord's actions, because he has totally misunderstood the nature of authority.

Like most of us, Peter was raised to view authority as a hierarchical structure. Authority belongs to the man at the top, and the sign of authority is that other people serve him. When people work *for* you and *under* you, you have authority. That is the universal pecking order, the way things work. Peter was offended because the Lord ignored the natural order of things. Peter knew that Jesus was the Master, and he himself was the servant—and he thought he understood what Jesus was up to: shaming the disciples out of their arrogance and pride, making them feel small for their quarreling. Peter did not want to take part in an object lesson on pride—he was too proud for that!

But Jesus had an even deeper purpose than a mere object lesson on pride—and Peter didn't understand his Master's purpose. Jesus describes Peter's problem and ours when He says, "You do not realize now what I am doing, but later you will understand." Jesus was not merely trying to shame His disciples and quell their argument. He was giving them a powerful lesson in the true meaning and nature of authority. Even though Peter and his disciples didn't grasp the deeper significance of their Master's actions then, Jesus promises that "later you will understand."

Peter's reaction to this promise is 100 per cent pure Peter! "No," he says, "you shall never wash my feet."

Jesus responds to this statement with a warning: "Unless I wash you, you have no part with me." In other words, "Unless you release your pride and let me wash your feet, you will have no fellowship with me. Peter, your pride is getting in the way of our relationship. You must allow me to serve you, or you will never understand what fellowship with me is all about."

That's all Peter needs! Again. in typical Peter-fashion, he swings to the opposite extreme, demonstrating his love for Jesus in these words, "Then, Lord, not just my feet but my hands and my head as well!" That is a beautiful response, coming from a heart that is truly loyal and loving toward Jesus. Yes, Peter is ignorant and impetuous and proud. He fails and sins and stumbles repeatedly. But one thing always shines through Peter's rough exterior: his love for Jesus.

It's an encouragement to me to see that Jesus always deals graciously with Peter, as He does with us. Jesus always looks beyond our flaws and sins, and looks upon our hearts. We Christians don't always have their doctrines straight. We let Jesus down. We stumble. But if we love the Lord and want to have a relationship with Him, He knows that and He deals with us accordingly.

Regenerated—Not Re-Re-Re-Regenerated!

Jesus responds to Peter's impetuousness with a full explanation of what He is doing by washing the feet of His friends. That explanation is the heart of this entire passage, for it is there that He unfolds two great truths, one a theological truth and the other an intensely practical truth.

13:10–11 *Jesus answered, "A person who has had a bath needs only to wash his feet; his whole body is clean. And you are clean, though not every one of you." For he knew who was going to betray him, and that was why he said not every one was clean.*

There is a natural logic in Jesus' words. He is simply restating what was true in the culture of the day. Everybody took baths in the morning, and thus were "clean." But as they went about the dusty streets, their feet became dirty. They didn't need another bath just so that their feet would be clean. This is a beautifully simple and symbolic teaching. To His disciples (except Judas), He says, "You are clean." They have been saved, as Paul says, "through the washing of rebirth and renewal by the Holy Spirit." They have been born again— an event that occurs only once. All but Judas had already experienced this washing.

Jesus is saying that those who have had a complete bath—the washing of regeneration—need only to have their feet washed from time to time in order to be completely clean. Like Peter, many Christians become confused on this point. They think they need a bath when all they need is to have their feet washed. They think that every time sin comes into their lives, they need to be saved all over again! But when we commit ourselves to Jesus and the Holy Spirit regenerates us, we are saved. Once is enough. We only need to be regenerated, not re-re-re-regenerated! As the old hymn tells us,

> There is a fountain filled with blood,
> Drawn from Emmanuel's veins.
> And sinners plunged beneath that flood
> Lose all their guilty stains.

The Symbolism of Foot Washing

The symbolism of the washing of feet suggests the on-going activity of continuous confession and cleansing that we are to experience in our spiritual lives. As John tells us in 1 John 1:9, "If we confess our sins, he is faithful and just and will forgive us our sins and purify us from all unrighteousness." That is our daily walk—a walk of daily cleansing. When we live this daily walk of confession and re-purification and the continual cleansing of our feet, we experience continual fellowship with Jesus.

This means starting and ending every day by acknowledging our need for cleansing from the unkind words, the sinful attitudes, the impure thoughts, the dishonest acts, the rebellious and willful behavior that we are so prone to, even as Christians. It means we live out each day with a desire to expose and obliterate those hidden sins and bad habits that hinder our walk with God. We do not merely accept our defects of character, but we commit ourselves to continual spiritual growth and moral change and purity.

Next, Jesus comes to His second explanation that washing of the disciples' feet symbolizes—and this application is intensely practical.

13:12–17 *When he had finished washing their feet, he put on his clothes and returned to his place. "Do you understand what I have done for you?" he asked them. "You call me 'Teacher' and 'Lord,' and rightly so, for that is what I am. Now that I, your Lord and Teacher, have washed your feet, you also should wash one another's feet. I have set you an example that you should do as I have done for you. I tell you the truth, no servant is greater than his master, nor is a messenger greater than the one who sent him. Now that you know these things, you will be blessed if you do them.*

Jesus introduces this teaching by forcing them to think. He asks them, "Do you understand what I have done for you?" Perhaps, after asking the question, He waited for an answer, like a teacher employing a Socratic dialogue with a class of students. If He did wait for an answer, then it is clear that the response was silence. No one raised a hand or ventured an answer. So Jesus continued.

"You call me 'Teacher' and 'Lord,' " He said, "and rightly so, for that is what I am." And then He gives them the practical lesson: "Now that I, your Lord and Teacher, have washed your feet, you also should wash one another's feet. I have given you an example that you should do as I have done for you."

In other words, "You have accepted me as your Teacher and your Lord—in short, as an Authority. And I am! And do you know what the true basis of authority is? Service! Humble, obedient, loving service to one another!"

Again, we have to remember that this account dovetails with the other gospel accounts of that last evening in the Upper Room, just hours before the crucifixion. During that same evening, according to Luke 22, a dispute had arisen among the disciples over "which of them was considered to be greatest"—a dispute, in other words, over the issue of *authority*. And Jesus rebuked their quarreling with this statement:

> "The kings of the Gentiles lord it over them; and those
> who exercise authority over them call themselves Benefac-
> tors. But you are not to be like that. Instead, the greatest
> among you should be like the youngest, and the one who rules
> like the one who serves. For who is greater, the one who is at
> the table or the one who serves? Is it not the one who is at the
> table? But I am among you as one who serves."[1]

The disciples called Him Teacher and Lord. They recognized a unique authority within Him and they responded to that authority by following Him. But why? What was it about the authority of Jesus that attracted them? Was it that Jesus commanded them, bossed them, and lorded it over them? No! It was because He *served* them! It was the *servant authority* of Jesus that drew them and made them eager to follow Him.

When Jesus talks about worldly authority, about the masters and bosses of the Gentile world, He says, "You are not to be like that." In other words, Christians are not to engage in hierarchical authority, in lording it over one another. Our churches are not to be hierarchies of bosses, but lowerarchies of servants, where Christians compete not to lead and rule, but to love and serve. That is what Jesus showed us when He stooped to serve and wash feet. That is what He means when He says, "I have set you an example that you should do as I have done for you."

The issue of servant authority is one of the greatest challenges the church faces today. We are called to demonstrate a different kind of authority than that which is practiced by the world—yet instead of demonstrating servant authority, the church has adopted the leadership models of the world. We have popes, bishops, priests, reverends, chairmen, superintendents, and authorities of every description. We even have unofficial "church bosses" and "power brokers"—those individuals in the church who are feared and obeyed, even when they have no official title or job description in the church structure. But that is not the kind of authority Jesus modeled and taught to His church. He taught that it is those who quietly, humbly *serve* who earn the mantle of authority in the church.

Two Actions

In the example of Jesus, we see two actions that we, as Christians, should be involved in. First, we should be engaged in service to one another. As the apostle Paul tells us, "Serve one another in love."[2] This is a command and an example for *all* Christians—but most especially to those who are in positions of teaching and authority. In a true Christian fellowship, all genuine authority is directly related to the willingness of those in authority to be foot-washing servants of others.

The second action the Jesus' example encourages us to undertake is a ministry of helping each other in the church keep our "spiritual feet" clean. That is why Jesus says in Matthew 18, "If your brother sins against you, go and show him his fault, just between the two of you. If he listens to you, you have won your brother over."[3] And that is why the apostle Paul tells us, "Brothers, if someone is caught in a sin, you who are spiritual should restore him gently. But watch yourself, or you also may be tempted."[4] And that is why James says, "Confess your sins to each other and pray for each other so that you may be healed."[5]

Again using "the formula of focused attention," Jesus underscores the crucial importance of "spiritual foot washing." In verses 16 and 17, He says, "I tell you the truth, no servant is greater than his master, nor is a messenger greater than the one who sent him. Now that you know these things, you will be blessed if you do them."

As always, the emphasis of our Lord's teaching is not on knowing, but on *doing*. It is not enough to know. It is not enough to agree. It is not enough to teach and preach. We must *do*, even as Jesus did. We must love, even as Jesus loved. We must serve, even as Jesus served.

It is from doing and loving and serving that all true authority descends.

Chapter Thirty-Seven

The One Commandment

John 13:18–38

At times I grow tired of the ugliness of our world. We are all sickened by reports of wars and atrocities, of terrorist bombings and shootings, of urban riots and poverty, of murder and rape, of drug abuse and pornography, of innocent children beaten or sexually exploited. It is impossible for any human being to absorb and emotionally process even a tiny fraction of the misery and horror that takes place on this planet. Most of us shrink from even attempting to process it. When the stories and the pictures scream from our newspapers and TV sets, many of us tune out or turn away.

Many solutions have been proposed for these problems, and most of those solutions are so naive and simplistic it is laughable. "Flying kites for peace" can do little to stop or slow the building of nuclear weapons. Displaying bumper stickers that say "Abolish Hate" or "Visualize Peace" may make some motorists feel more self-righteous than their fellows—but when cut off on the freeway, they're as likely to honk and swear and gesture obscenely as any other road-warrior. We've tried education, legislation, indoctrination, rehabilitation, persuasion, and diplomacy—and whatever we do, whatever we try, the problems of our world just get worse, not better.

So now we turn to Jesus and we ask, "Lord, do you have a solution?"

And He says, "Yes, I have."

But when He tells us what His solution is, it sounds like the same kind of naive advice we have already heard and discarded as too simplistic: "Love one another." As we turn to the last half of John 13, however, we will discover a deep and practical reality in these words of Jesus that we desperately need to discover for our own times. In this passage, we will see Jesus do three things:

(1) He will send the traitor out to commit his crime.

(2) He will give His disciples a new commandment, which will sum up all ten of the old commandments in a single sentence.

(3) He will reveal Peter's own future.

That, in chronological order, is the outline of John 13:18–38. But as we examine this passage together, I am not going to take these events in chronological order. Instead, we will begin with the new commandment of Jesus: "Love one another." And by looking at these events through the lens of this new commandment, we will be able to see more clearly the significance of the actions of Judas and Peter.

The New Commandment

We will begin by jumping to the middle of this passage, just after Judas has left the Upper Room.

13:31–35 *When he [Judas] was gone, Jesus said, "Now is the Son of Man glorified and God is glorified in him. If God is glorified in him, then God will glorify the Son in himself, and will glorify him at once.*

"My children, I will be with you only a little longer. You will look for me, and just as I told the Jews, so I tell you now: Where I am going, you cannot come.

"A new command I give you: Love one another. As I have loved you, so you must love one another. All men will know that you are my disciples if you love one another."

Here is a moment of high drama, introduced by these mysterious words about being "glorified." At the very moment of His betrayal, He says, "Now is the Son of Man glorified." In fact, Jesus refers specifically to His betrayal when He says that He is "glorified"! Judas goes out, the door slams—and Jesus turns to His disciples and says, in effect, "Now, at this very moment, as my fate is being sealed, I am being glorified. Now, as Judas goes about his dirty work, God's purpose is being advanced and fulfilled through Me." Jesus says, further, that not only is the Son being glorified, but so is the Father.

What is this glory that Jesus refers to? It is nothing less than His sacrifice upon the cross!

Notice also that Jesus waits until Judas has made his exit before giving His new commandment. He begins by addressing His disciples as "my children." This is the first time He has ever called them His children. It is a term of affection, of tenderness. Most Bible scholars agree that it is immediately after these words, where Jesus gives His disciples a new commandment, that He instituted what we now call "the Lord's Supper" or communion, immediately following the Passover meal.

At that same moment, throughout the cities of Judea and Galilee and all through the length and breadth of the land of Palestine, Jewish families were gathering to eat the Passover lamb. It was traditional then, as it still is today, for the father to act as the host for the family and to invite the children to ask questions, so that they could understand the meaning of the Passover. Usually, the littlest child would begin by asking, "What do these things mean?" and the father would explain.

Clearly, this is what our Lord is doing in the Upper Room. He sees Himself as the head of a family, and He addresses His disciples as children, as little children in need of understanding.

And He has very sad news for His children: He is leaving them. "Where I am going," He says, "you cannot come." Within twelve hours He will be fastened to a cross. Within twenty hours, His broken body will be cold and sealed inside a dark tomb. There is very little time—only enough for a few last instructions.

"A new command I give you: Love one another," He says. "As I have loved you, so you must love one another."

Simple words. But are they too simple? What good can such a sentiment do against the horrors and evils of our world? Who can even carry out this advice? The world has always agreed that love is what we need to solve our problems. All the ugliness, the crime, the abuse, the violence, the broken relationships, the drug and pornography trafficking, the prostitution, the adultery—all these ills would vanish if we truly learned and practiced what Jesus meant when He said, "Love one another."

But this is not just another hollow, vacuous, well-intentioned sentiment. The words "love one another" have real power to change lives—*if* we will understand the hidden truth, the dramatic secret, at the heart of those words. As we examine those three simple words, we have to ask ourselves, "How do we do this? How do we truly love one another?"

The answer: We have to love even when we do not feel like loving, even when the person we are called to love is an unlovely, unloving person.

"Love one another" is a deceptively simple-sounding formula because it is about the hardest thing we will ever be called upon to do. The love that Jesus talks about—the love which the Bible calls *agape* or unconditional love—is a love that is rooted in the will, not in our emotions. The very fact that Jesus must *command* us to love one another means that this kind of love must be practiced under the most adverse of circumstances.

We don't need to be commanded to love people who are attractive or generous or delightful or kind or helpful. The people Jesus *commands* us to love are those who are unlovely, stingy, nasty, dull, selfish, or downright mean. They are the people in our families, our workplaces, and our churches that we have a hard time liking and getting along with. They are the ones whose personalities clash with ours.

So how are we supposed to stir up warm, fuzzy feelings toward such people? Jesus' answer: We don't have to. In most cases, we probably will never be able to. The fact is, feelings are not the issue. The issue is obedience to a commandment: Love one another. Seek the good of other people, even people you don't like. Be helpful to other people, even if they are nasty in return. Be patient with other people and serve them, even if they never thank you. Agape-love is a choice, not a feeling.

To love as Jesus loved does not mean that you have to be a doormat, and that you allow people to continually wipe their feet on you. Sometimes the best way to love another person is to *confront* their sin and abuse. If, for example, you are in an abusive relationship and your spouse has a habit of violently abusing you, God does not expect you to subject yourself to that abuse in order to "love one another." You need to be protected, and that abuser needs to be confronted with his sin.

This new commandment that Jesus gave is a prescription for empowering His followers to change the world. By teaching His disciples to love one another as He loved them, He was reshaping and remolding them into His own image, so that His character would be lived out through them—even after His departure from the world. And their Christlike love would be the means by which the world would be reached for Jesus: "All men will know that you are my disciples," He told them, "if you love one another."

He also gave His followers a powerful motivation for loving one another: "As I have loved you," He said, "so you must love one another." It is a straightforward case of cause and effect. Jesus loved His disciples in order to stimulate and awaken their capacity to love one another. If they wanted to demonstrate their love for Him, then they could best do so by loving one another.

Henry Drummond, who was an associate of D. L. Moody, used the illustration of a magnet and a piece of steel to illustrate Jesus' command that we love one another as He has loved us. He noted the well-known scientific fact that if you take a piece of steel and attach it to a magnet, in time the magnetic properties of the magnet will be acquired by the piece of steel—and it, too, will be a magnet. In the same way, if we dwell on His love for us—a love beyond our deserving, a love extended to us even while we were rebellious and lost in the ugliness of our sin—then we will gradually acquire that kind of love. The magnetic love of Jesus will become our nature, just as it is His nature—and people will feel the magnetic attraction of our own Christlike love.

Follower on the Outside, Traitor on the Inside

Now let's look at the other two players in this drama. How do the actions of Judas and Peter relate to this new commandment? In the examples of these two disciples, we will gain insight into why people who call themselves Christians—even some who unmistakably *are* Christians—do not always keep this commandment and manifest this kind of love.

Judas and Peter are both disciples of Jesus Christ. Both are close companions of Jesus, having been with Him for three and a half years. Both have something valuable to teach us. Let us first take the case of Judas. In verses 18 through 20, Jesus begins by quoting a passage of Scripture—a passage which predicts an act of betrayal.

13:18–20 *"I am not referring to all of you; I know those I have chosen. But this is to fulfill the scripture: 'He who shares my bread has lifted up his heel against me.'*

"I am telling you now before it happens, so that when it does happen you will believe that I am He. I tell you the truth, whoever accepts anyone I send accepts me; and whoever accepts me accepts the one who sent me."

Here, Jesus quotes Psalm 41:9, which was written a thousand years before these events by David. This line from an ancient psalm predicted that one who ate bread with the Lord would lift up his heel against Him—a powerful and violent image. It suggests the picture of a trusted friend who, in the midst of fellowshiping and sharing a meal with you in your own home, would give you a karate kick in the face without any warning! It is a carefully chosen image, suggesting an act that is contemptible, dastardly, and almost inhuman in its treachery and ferocity. It is the image of a person who, in exchange for love and kindness received, deals out sudden violence—a sneak attack.

Jesus cites this psalm to show what is about to happen to Him: He is about to be betrayed in a despicable way by a trusted and loved disciple, who has only received kindness from the Lord.

Judas did not have to be that traitor. He was not doomed, chosen, or foreordained by God for that role. He, like all human beings, had free choice—the ability to choose either good or evil. Throughout this account there is evidence that Judas could have turned and repented at any point. If Judas had not fulfilled the prophesy of Psalm 41:9, it doubtless would have been fulfilled in some other way—even though it is pointless to speculate how. God has a thousand and one ways to fulfill His purposes. But one fact is clear: Judas was never forced into the role of traitor. It was a role he chose for himself by the daily moral choices he made.

In verse 20, Jesus again introduces and underscores a statement with "the formula of focused attention": "I tell you the truth," He says, "whoever accepts anyone I send accepts me; and whoever accepts me accepts the one who sent me." What does Jesus mean? He is saying that the reason Judas refused to believe was that he never received Jesus as Lord. He never yielded his heart, he never turned over his will to Jesus. Although he walked with the disciples, he always pursued his own course, his own interests, his own purposes.

Outwardly, Judas was a follower of Jesus. He, along with the rest of the Twelve, was sent out by Jesus and empowered to do amazing miracles in His name. The Scriptures report that when the disciples came back, *all twelve* reported that they had seen devils cast out by their word, people healed, and the dead raised. The Lord gave power to all the Twelve, including Judas, even though the Lord knew what was in the heart of Judas.

This is a sobering thought! Your doctrine can be as orthodox as can be. You can be an elder, a deacon, a pastor, or a Sunday school teacher. You can establish a Christian organization which feeds thousands of hungry children. You can be a world-famous evangelist. You can write Christian books that sell in the hundreds of thousands. You can pastor a thriving congregation and preach dynamic sermons which move people to tears. You can personally lead hundreds of people to Christ. And having done all that, it is still possible that God does not have control of your heart, that He is not your Lord and Savior. God can use anyone and anything to accomplish His purposes—even a Judas.

What makes us genuine as Christians is not what we have accomplished for Jesus. After all, Jesus Himself said,

> "Not everyone who says to me, 'Lord, Lord,' will enter the kingdom of heaven, but only he who does the will of my Father who is in heaven. Many will say to me on that day, 'Lord, Lord, did we not prophesy in your name, and in your name drive out demons and perform many miracles? Then I will tell them plainly, 'I never knew you. Away from me, you evildoers!' "[1]

The true test of our genuineness as followers of Christ is whether or not we have yielded our hearts and our lives under His lordship. It doesn't mean that the genuine follower of Christ never sins. Rather, it means that we are not content to allow sin to take up permanent residence in our lives. Even though we will stumble and fail, our goal is always to repent and return and recommit ourselves to Jesus.

Here we begin to see one reason why there are people who call themselves Christians, people who outwardly seem to be Christians and seem to experience God's power working through them, yet who do not keep the great commandment of Jesus to "love one another." In some cases, it may be the

"Judas syndrome" at work. You look at such people, and you see the outward trappings and appearances of a disciple—but inside, there is no love, no Christlikeness, no spiritual reality. That person is a Judas.

Judas was a man who had a reputation as a follower of Christ. He had done great things in the power of Jesus. But in his heart, he had given himself over to sin and self-deception. In the end, his lord was not Jesus, but Satan.

A Piece of Bread

Our Lord goes on to announce the coming betrayal to the disciples.

13:21–27a *After he had said this, Jesus was troubled in spirit and testified, "I tell you the truth, one of you is going to betray me."*

His disciples stared at one another, at a loss to know which of them he meant. One of them, the disciple whom Jesus loved, was reclining next to him. Simon Peter motioned to this disciple and said, "Ask him which one he means."

Leaning back against Jesus, he asked him, "Lord, who is it?"

Jesus answered, "It is the one to whom I will give this piece of bread when I have dipped it in the dish." Then, dipping the piece of bread, he gave it to Judas Iscariot, son of Simon. As soon as Judas took the bread, Satan entered into him.

This is an extremely difficult moment for Jesus. He is described as "troubled in spirit." Jesus doesn't hate Judas for what he is about to do. Jesus hurts for him and grieves for him. He is in great emotional pain for this man who has doomed himself by his own lying, treachery, and greed.

Notice that the disciples do not believe it is Judas. He is so smooth and deceptive that, as Matthew's gospel records, he brazenly attempts to bluff and pretend innocence to Jesus' face:

> Then Judas, the one who would betray him, said, "Surely not I, Rabbi?"
> Jesus answered, "Yes, it is you."[2]

This is a private exchange between Judas and Jesus, out of the hearing of the other disciples. Judas has covered up his motives so well that none of the other disciples has the slightest inkling that it is he. After three and a half years of living with these men, he has never said anything to the other disciples to tip them off that he was a counterfeit disciple, that he had a hidden agenda that was opposed to Jesus' agenda. He had hidden and covered it all.

As this account makes clear, when Jesus identifies Judas as the traitor, He does so only to John. John, "the disciple whom Jesus loved," is lying on his side with his head close to that of Jesus. Simon Peter, across the table from John, says (with typical impetuous curiosity), "Ask him which one he means." John relays Peter's question to Jesus. Quietly, out of earshot of the others, Jesus replies, "It is the one to whom I will give this piece of bread." And He dips the bread in the dish.

It is a mark of friendship and honor for the host of the Passover to dip a piece of bread into a bowl of crushed fruit and wine—one of the dishes of the Passover supper—then hand the dipped bread to the honored person. Since Judas is on the opposite side of Jesus from John, our Lord simply dips the bread and passes it to him.

At this point, the other disciples are still unaware of what this means. But John records that as Judas takes the morsel of bread, something dark and sinister takes place: "As soon as Judas took the bread, Satan entered into him."

"Get it Over With . . ."

John relates the brief but crucial interchange between Jesus and His traitorous disciple.

13:27b–30 *"What you are about to do, do quickly," Jesus told him, but no one at the meal understood why Jesus said this to him. Since Judas had charge of the money, some thought Jesus was telling him to buy what was needed for the Feast, or to give something to the poor. As soon as Judas had taken the bread, he went out. And it was night.*

This is obviously a profound and significant word which John adds at the end of this section: Judas leaves the presence of Jesus and goes out into the night. Darkness has entered into Judas, and Judas has entered into darkness.

This is an amazing scene. Here, in the same Upper Room, are the dynamic personifications of Good and Evil, of Light and Darkness. The Son of God, the Lord of Glory, the Creator of Heaven and Earth, watches knowingly as Satan himself enters into Judas and sets in motion a plan to destroy Jesus—and Jesus does nothing to stop Satan.

There is a teaching going around in Christian circles which says that before Christians do anything—such as a worship service, a prayer meeting, or an act of ministry—they should "bind Satan." I've never seen any indication in Scripture that it is our job to "bind Satan." In fact, we see quite clearly in this passage that our Lord specifically refrains from stopping Satan. Even though Satan is personally present in that same room, and even though Jesus knows that Satan has personally entered into Judas, Jesus allows Satan to carry out his schemes, knowing that even the worst that Satan can do can be woven into the plan of God.

It is amazing to contemplate all that Judas turned his back on—just for the sake of thirty pieces of silver. He walked and talked with Jesus. He repeatedly heard the message of eternal life from the lips of the Savior Himself. He saw the miracles. He even saw Lazarus raised from the dead. After all of that, he still refused to open his life and surrender his will and make Jesus his Lord. Yet Jesus was patient and compassionate right to the end, to the very last moment.

The spirit of Jesus was troubled when He spoke of the betrayal. He was grieved and sorrowful—not for His own sake, but for the loss of Judas' eternal soul. It wasn't until Satan actually entered into Judas that Jesus gave up on Judas. At that moment, John tells us, Jesus ceased all effort to persuade or change Judas, and He told Judas, "What you are about to do, do quickly." In other words, "Get it over with."

And Judas got up and went out into the night. And for Judas, there would never again be a morning.

"Before the Rooster Crows . . ."

Now what about Peter? His story closes John 13.

In the example of Peter, we see another and very different reason why people who call themselves Christians do not keep the great commandment of Jesus to "love one another." Peter's case is very different from that of Judas. Whereas Judas was a counterfeit Christian, Peter was a genuine, loyal, committed follower of Christ. But Peter was defective in this regard: His understanding of Christian love was deficient. He loved Jesus with an inadequate quality of love.

As you read Peter's story, you have to admire the patience of Jesus. In verses 36 through 38, Jesus has just given His new commandment—"love one another"—to the eleven remaining disciples (Judas has already left). Jesus has also told the disciples that He is going away, and that where He is going, they cannot come.

13:36–38 *Simon Peter asked him, "Lord, where are you going?"*

Jesus replied, "Where I am going, you cannot follow now, but you will follow later."

Peter asked, "Lord, why can't I follow you now? I will lay down my life for you."

Then Jesus answered, "Will you really lay down your life for me? I tell you the truth, before the rooster crows, you will disown me three times!"

Peter is a classic example of a person who "just doesn't get it." Like a schoolchild with a short attention span, Peter immediately shoots up his hand and says, "Lord, where are you going?" Where has Peter been?! How has he managed to completely miss what Jesus has been trying to tell him and his fellow disciples—and even the multitudes and the religious leaders—for so long? Jesus has repeatedly told them all that He is going away, He is going to die, He is going home to the Father. Somehow, Peter has not heard and understood what Jesus has been saying over and over.

But Jesus does not rebuke His friend Peter. I believe He is patient with Peter because He knows his impetuous but loyal heart. He knows that the question Peter meant to ask was not, "Where are you going?" but, "Why can't I go with you?" It is a childlike question, and if you're a parent, you have heard it many times: "Why can't I go, Daddy? Why can't I go, Mommy? I wanna go too!"

Jesus answers Peter's question with a statement that is appropriate to Peter's limited level of understanding. It is the kind of answer a parent gives to a child who is not ready to hear the truth in adult terms. "Where I am going, you cannot follow now, but you will follow later."

Tradition says that, long after this dialogue took place in the Upper Room, probably thirty years later or more, Peter did indeed follow where Jesus went before him. He was imprisoned in Rome, the story says, and he was condemned to die by crucifixion. Feeling unworthy to die in exactly the same way that his Lord had died, Peter asked that he be crucified upside down. His request, says the tradition, was granted and the words of the Lord—"you will follow later"—were literally fulfilled.

Jesus tells Peter, in effect, "You cannot follow me now because I have a unique and solitary work to do on the cross. No one else can do it for me or with me. I have been called to suffer and die alone for the sake of the human race."

The Wrong Kind of Love

But there is another reason why Peter cannot follow the Lord now: Peter's love is the wrong kind of love.

Peter was perfectly sincere when he said to Jesus, "Lord, why can't I follow you now? I will lay down my life for you." He was thoroughly committed to Christ and His cause—even though his understanding of that cause was limited. He believed he was truly ready to lay down his life for his Lord. Jesus knows he means it.

But Jesus also knows that Peter has not yet developed the strength of character to follow through on that commitment. So He responds to Peter, "Will you really lay down your life for me? I tell you the truth, before the rooster crows, you will disown me three times!"

Peter loves Jesus. He's loyal to Jesus. He's ready to die for Jesus—at least, he believes he is. But Jesus knows that Peter's love is not *agape* love. It is purely natural, human affection—and mere affection cannot handle the demands that the Christian life and its trials often make upon our love.

In a purely natural and human sense, there were probably any number of people Peter might have been willing to lay down his life for: a mother, a father, a brother, a sister, a close friend, a wife, or children. Natural human affection can lead a man or woman to make the ultimate sacrifice by running into a burning building or jumping onto a live grenade or tackling an armed gunman. Under the right circumstances, Peter was probably capable of such acts.

But even though natural human affection can induce someone to sacrifice oneself for the sake of another, natural human affection cannot make someone a bold witness for Jesus. That takes a special kind of love—a love born of the Spirit living within. Many contemporary Christians are in the same boat with Peter. They do not yet manifest the unique quality of love that Jesus is talking about when He commands us to "love one another." Natural human affection and natural human zeal cannot do God's work.

I have seen many new "baby" Christians, their faces aglow and their hearts aflame with love for the Lord. They often dream up grandiose plans to win the world for Christ. Some have great gifts of organization and they set up programs to carry out their plans. They are sincere. They are loyal to the Lord. They would lay down their lives for Him. They are fired up with zeal as they buttonhole people on the streets or witness door-to-door or try to coerce their own family members into believing in Jesus (and often setting back the very evangelizing process they are trying to advance!). That is what natural zeal does.

People filled with that kind of zeal are always exciting to be around. I imagine that few people were ever bored in Peter's presence. Such people are eager and energetic, but their work for Jesus has a tendency to fall apart because, like Peter, they don't understand the weakness of human flesh. The good news is that God can still use people and teach people at this exciting stage in their spiritual development. That is what He did with Peter. As we shall see in John 21, Jesus can teach us and build us up through the process of pain and hurt, rejection and failure. In fact, I don't know any Christian who has ever been greatly used by God who didn't go through such a process.

The Secret to Power

Jesus has great things in store for Peter. After the Day of Pentecost, when the Spirit of grace comes upon Peter and the other early Christians, and he is able to experience an inner awareness of the love of Jesus, an amazing change will come over Peter. With boldness and with Christlike love, he will preach so powerfully in the strength of the Spirit that 3,000 people will turn their lives over to Jesus in one day.

And Jesus wants to perform that same transformation in our lives that He did in the life of Peter. He wants us to learn the same lesson of love that Peter did.

The lesson of the Upper Room for you and for me is so simple and so profound: "Love one another." That is the secret to power. That is the secret to changing the world. When we manifest that kind of love, as individuals and as a body of believers, then we truly become a loving community. People are attracted to that kind of love. People are convinced and transformed by that kind of love. When the world sees us loving one another by the power of the Holy Spirit, then the world will know that we have been with Jesus—and the world will want to know this Jesus too.

"All men will know that you are my disciples," says Jesus, "if you love one another."

Chapter Thirty-Eight

The Cure for Heart Trouble

John 14:1–14

If there is one affliction that *everybody* feels prone to, it is the affliction called *stress.* I would define stress as our physical, mental, emotional, and spiritual response to the changes, pressures, and demands of our lives. When we are "stressed out," we often experience physical symptoms—digestive disorders, disrupted sleep patterns, nervous tics, high blood pressure, and on and on. Our moods and attitudes become colored by stress. Even our relationship with God can undergo negative changes.

But Jesus has the cure for stress. We find it in the first verse of John 14. I call this verse *The Concise Manual for Stress Management.* If you are feeling "stressed out" right now, have I got news for you!

Stress Is Normal

Jesus continues His discourse in the Upper Room.

14:1 *"Do not let your hearts be troubled. Trust in God; trust also in me."*

Notice that this verse comes right after Jesus' revelation to Peter that he is going to deny his Lord. This came as a shock to Peter. He could not believe himself capable of such a thing. So the words of Jesus cut him to the marrow.

Yet Jesus did not want Peter or any of the other disciples to become discouraged. So He said—not just to Peter but to all eleven remaining disciples, "Do not let your hearts be troubled. Trust in God; trust also in me." The word "your" in this verse is the plural form. When Jesus says, "Do not let your hearts be troubled," He is addressing all the disciples.

It is easy to understand why the disciples' hearts might be greatly troubled. They were aware of the mounting peril to Jesus. They knew that the priests and the rulers of the Jews were determined to put Him to death. Also, they were probably ashamed of their own behavior just minutes earlier, when they had argued about who among them was the greatest. They must have also been troubled to hear Jesus say that one of them was going to betray Him. Most of all, they were afraid of losing Jesus. He was their Lord, their Messiah, their Leader—and if He went away, what would happen to them and to their cause? They didn't understand what Jesus was telling them. And they were afraid.

So Jesus tells them, "Do not let your hearts be troubled. Trust in God; trust also in me." Does this mean that Christians should never feel anxious, pressured, or afraid? Does this mean that such feelings are sinful? Are we supposed to feel cheerful and confident, even when our circumstances point to approaching disaster? Many Christians have taken John 14:1 to mean exactly that.

But those who believe that way forget that Jesus Himself was not immune to deeply troubled feelings in times of hurt or pressure. Several times in the gospel of John and in the other gospels we read that Jesus was "deeply troubled in spirit." From the example of Jesus, we know that we should expect to feel troubled at times, especially in times of pressure and danger. Stress is a normal human response to change and problems in life. So when Jesus says, "Do not let your hearts be troubled," He is telling us that, while we cannot prevent stress, we can overcome it. That is why this passage has such rich meaning for us.

Many Rooms

The first thing Jesus tells us in this verse is, "Trust me." He says to His disciples, "Trust in God; trust also in me." As rendered by the NIV, this seems to be a *command* from Jesus to trust and believe—and this is a valid interpretation. But the original language can also be interpreted as saying, "You already believe in God; now believe in me as well." In other words, "You have already found relief from stress through your faith in God; now I want you to trust me as well." Here again—as He has numerous times before in the gospel of John—Jesus clearly places Himself on a plane of equality with the Father, speaking not only as a man but as God.

Then Jesus goes on to reveal to His disciples a number of secrets which have been kept hidden since the foundation of the world.

14:2–4 *"In my Father's house are many rooms; if it were not so, I would have told you. I am going there to prepare a place for you. And if I go and prepare a place for you, I will come back and take you to be with me that you also may be where I am. You know the way to the place where I am going."*

We are so used to thinking of heaven as an eternal dwelling place for believers that it is probably difficult for us to understand what a radical teaching Jesus was offering to His disciples at that moment. "Heaven" to the first century Jewish mind essentially meant what the word "universe" means to us. In the Hebrew culture, the idea of "heaven" did not so much convey an eternal destination, but the vast dwelling place of God. In this statement, Jesus takes the concept of heaven—which He calls "my Father's house"—and He refines and expands it for our understanding. It is a place of "many rooms," a place in which we will live after we have left this world.

Just consider with me for a moment the size of the Father's "house"—the universe. Start with our own solar system. The earth orbits the sun at a distance of 93 million miles. At that distance, it takes *eight minutes* for light to travel from the sun to the earth (it takes more than *five hours* for sunlight to reach the farthest planet, Pluto). Our own sun is just one among approximately *100 billion suns* in our own Milky Way galaxy—and our galaxy is so vast that it would take a beam of light about *300,000 years* to travel from one side of the galaxy to the other. As unbelievably vast as our own galaxy is, it is just *one out of some 100 billion galaxies* in the known universe, and there are millions of light-years of utter emptiness separating each of those billions of galaxies!

In John 14, we hear Jesus, the One who created all of this immensity with a thought and a word, saying—with remarkable understatement!—"In my Father's house are many rooms." In the place where God dwells, in the heavens and the heaven of the heavens, there are many places to live. I have long taken this statement to suggest that there may be other habitable planets in our universe—perhaps even planets where intelligent beings live. Our Lord's suggestion in John 14:2 opens up whole new vistas of imagination to us.

Since my high school days, I have been intrigued by the great 200-inch Hale Telescope on Mount Palomar in Southern California, which for years was the most powerful telescope ever made. As I write these words, an even more powerful telescope has just turned its eye on the heavens—the Keck Telescope, atop a sleeping volcano in Hawaii. Four times more powerful than the Hale Telescope, Keck is powerful enough to detect a 15-watt nightlight on the surface of the moon! The reason I am so fascinated by telescopes is that I envision them as periscopes which peek through the big front window of the Father's house!

It is truly awesome to contemplate what is suggested in the words, "In my Father's house are many rooms." Whatever the ultimate meaning embedded in these words of Jesus, it is clear that He wants His disciples—not just the eleven men in that Upper Room, but you and me as well—to be comforted by this truth.

"I Will Come Back"

And Jesus has other words of comfort to offer—words that are clearly designed to help the disciples face their fear—especially the fear of death. What would become of Jesus if He died? Would they ever see Him again? What would become of them if all this turmoil in Jerusalem should sweep them up and result in their deaths?

The thought of death has a sobering effect upon all of us. As Samuel Johnson said, "To know you will be hanged in the morning marvelously concentrates the mind." The prospect of death focuses our attention on what is truly important. We realize we have no time to waste on trivialities and non-essentials. Every second takes on immense importance. And yet, *all* of life should be lived out with a sober sense of the importance of every second—not in fear, but with a sense of urgency. We all have much to do for God, and limited time in which to do it!

In these verses, our Lord gives us three comforting facts about death which enable us to put death—and all of life!—in proper spiritual perspective.

First, He is going to prepare a place for us. We do not know where that place is—a physical location in the universe, another universe, another dimension, or something else completely beyond our ability to imagine. I personally believe that heaven does *not* involve a rearrangement of some part of our universe so that we can live there. Rather, I suspect that heaven primarily involves preparing *us* for a whole new dimension of existence!

Paul suggests this possibility when he writes, "Our light and momentary troubles are achieving for us an eternal glory that far outweighs them all. So we fix our eyes not on what is seen, but on what is unseen. For what is seen is temporary, but what is unseen is eternal."[1] What does that mean? I don't know, but it sounds absolutely wonderful! The coming glory is unseen, it's unimaginable, it's beyond our comprehension—and isn't that a marvelous fact to cling to! It is not merely comforting, but elevating and exhilarating! The Lord is working out a whole new dimension of existence for us, and when it is ready (or when *we* are ready!), He will return for us.

Second, Jesus says, "I will come back." This statement parallels many other New Testament passages where Jesus and the writers of the New Testament epistles predict His return. Paul offers this same word of encouragement in 1 Thessalonians: "For the Lord himself will come down from heaven, with a loud command, with the voice of the archangel and with the trumpet call of God, and the dead in Christ will rise first. After that, we who are still alive and are left will be caught up with them in the clouds to meet the Lord in the air. And so we will be with the Lord forever. Therefore encourage each other with these words."[2]

Throughout twenty centuries of Christian history, these verses in John 14 have been used to encourage believers to expect the Lord's coming when they die. At the moment of death, every believer is received into glory by Jesus.

As Stephen was being stoned to death he said, "Look, I see heaven open and the Son of Man standing at the right hand of God."[3] I believe this indicates that these two events—the second coming of Jesus to carry out His prophetic program and the coming of Jesus for each believer at the moment of his or her individual death—are really one and the same.

You might think it absurd to think that the deaths of all believers and the future coming of Christ could all occur at a single universal moment in eternity, outside of time as we understand it. Yet I believe there is good evidence in Scripture to believe that the moment we step out of time, we step into eternity—and in eternity there is never any need to wait for anything. I am convinced that after we draw our last breath, each of us as believers will be caught up in that climactic world-shaking event and we will all enter into glory together. (I deal with these ideas at greater length in my book *Authentic Christianity;* see the chapter entitled "Time in Eternity.")

Third, Jesus says, "I will . . . take you to be with me that you also may be where I am." He will take us to live with him forever! Just to be with Jesus: that is all we want. There is a hymn I used to sing as a young Christian which I never hear anymore. But the words are powerful and comforting to the believer:

> No matter where on earth we dwell.
> On mountaintop or in the dell.
> In cottage or in mansion fair.
> Where Jesus is, 'tis heaven there.
>
> Oh, hallelujah! Yes 'tis heaven!
> 'Tis heaven to know my sins forgiven.
> On land or sea, no matter where.
> Where Jesus is, 'tis heaven there.

To be with Jesus: that is heaven. As someone once said, "You don't go to heaven to find Christ. You go to Christ to find heaven." This is the reassurance Jesus gives His disciples, both then and now.

Jesus' Narrow-Minded Words

In verses 5 through 11, two disciples—Thomas and Philip—engage Jesus in a dialogue that brings out still more marvelous yet mysterious truths. These two disciples are bewildered and confused by what Jesus says, just as many of us contemporary disciples are as we read His words. After Jesus says, "You know the way to the place where I am going," Thomas interrupts with a question.

14:5–7 *Thomas said to him, "Lord, we don't know where you are going, so how can we know the way?"*

Jesus answered, "I am the way and the truth and the life. No one comes to the Father except through me. If you really knew me, you would know my Father as well. From now on, you do know him and have seen him."

This disciple has been called "Doubting Thomas," but I don't think that is a good name for him. I would call him "Honest Thomas." You may have had the experience of explaining an idea to someone who was afraid to say, "I don't understand." You talk, and they nod and say "uh-huh," but later you find out they don't have a clue what you were talking about, and they were afraid to admit it. Thomas is not that kind of person. He's not afraid to say, "I don't get it. Could you run that by me again?"

Thomas reminds me of a gentleman named Cordell Hull, who was Secretary of State under Franklin Roosevelt. Hull once took a train trip through New England with a friend. Looking out the window, he observed a flock of sheep feeding on a hillside. His companion idly remarked, "Those sheep have recently been sheared." Hull stared at them a moment, then said, "Well, sheared on this side anyway." Thomas was that kind of a man. He would go no further than what he could see and understand.

When Thomas asks Jesus, "How can we know the way?", Jesus does not rebuke him. Instead, Jesus takes his question as an opportunity to expand His revelation of Himself. Indeed, this reply of Jesus is one of the most famous and profound statements in all of Scripture: "I am the way and the truth and the life. No one comes to the father except through me." This is an astounding claim! Notice that Jesus does not say, "I show the way, I teach the truth, I lead you to the life." He is not merely a way-shower. He is the Way!

No other religious leader could ever make such a claim. Buddha called himself a guide to the way. Mohammed called himself a prophet and a teacher of the truth. There are many religious teachers and religious writings that offer a portion of the truth. There is some truth in the Koran. There is even some truth in the Book of Mormon. But none of these people or writings are The Truth. None of them are The Way. None are The Life. Only Jesus can make that claim. He is the source of Truth and Life and Ultimate Reality. "No one comes to the Father," He says, "except through me."

Many bristle with indignation when they hear those words. Once, when I quoted those words in a Bible study, a woman objected, "But that's so narrow-minded!"

"Yes, it is," I said at once. "The truth is often very narrow-minded. If you want to reach someone by telephone, you have to dial the right number. 'Almost' isn't close enough. If the number you dial is off by just one digit, you'll reach the wrong number. Does that mean the phone company is narrow-minded?"

"Well," she said, avoiding the point I was making, "I still think you should interpret that verse in a way that is less narrow-minded."

"Oh?" I said. "Well, let's see. Jesus said, 'I am the way and the truth and the life. No one comes to the Father except through me.' How would you interpret those words in a way that is less narrow-minded?"

She stood speechless for a moment, then said, "Well, I never claimed to be a theologian. . . ."

"Jesus wasn't talking to a bunch of theologians when He said those words," I replied. "He was talking to ordinary people, and He was speaking very plainly. He said He Himself was *the* way, *the* truth, and *the* life, and nobody could come to God the Father by any other means than Himself. He underscored it and emphasized it. There's no way He could have made His point any plainer, is there?"

The woman was never able to refute my conclusion—but neither did she accept it. Her arguments ended in a shrug. This statement of Jesus is one which, I believe, we must be very narrow-minded about. To be "broad-minded" where crucial spiritual truth is concerned—especially when the words of Jesus are so clear—is very dangerous indeed!

Jesus goes on to reassure Thomas, saying, "If you really knew me, you would know my Father as well. From now on, you do know him and have seen him." Thomas had seen the Father because he had seen Jesus! Thomas' problem was not that he did not know the Father, but that he didn't realize that he knew the Father. "Thomas," Jesus says, in effect, "I'll let you in on something. You have been on a face-to-face, first-name basis with the God of the universe and you didn't even know it! But now you know—because you have known me."

"Show Us the Father"

Now it is Philip's turn to interrupt.

14:8–11 *Philip said, "Lord, show us the Father and that will be enough for us."*

Jesus answered: "Don't you know me, Philip, even after I have been among you such a long time? Anyone who has seen me has seen the Father. How can you say, 'Show us the Father'? Don't you believe that I am in the Father, and that the Father is in me? The words I say to you are not just my own. Rather, it is the Father, living in me, who is doing his work. Believe me when I say that I am in the Father and the Father is in me; or at least believe on the evidence of the miracles themselves."

I suspect that everyone was surprised when Philip spoke up—almost as if the table itself had spoken! This was quiet, studious Philip—the disciple who rarely said anything. Yet in his plea we hear all the yearning and hunger that humankind feels for God: "Lord, show us the Father and that will be enough for us."

Our Lord's answer is a quiet rebuke: "Don't you know me, Philip, even after I have been among you such a long time? Anyone who has seen me has seen the Father. How can you say, 'Show us the Father'?" Here, Jesus speaks a riddle wrapped in an enigma. Here is the impenetrable core of the mysterious Doctrine of the Trinity—the fact that three distinct Persons can exist together as one God. It is a truth and a paradox beyond our comprehension. There is nothing in our experience with which to compare it.

Then Jesus goes on to compound the mystery: "Don't you believe that I am in the Father, and that the Father is in me?" Later in this chapter, Jesus will again point to this mystery as the model for our relationship with Him: "You will realize that I am in my Father, and you are in me, and I am in you."[4] That is the greatest secret in all of Scripture—the amazing truth that God and human beings can have a relationship with one another and work together to achieve God's eternal purpose.

What could be more amazing and elevating than the fact that God moves in us and through us to achieve His perfect will? As an old country preacher once put it, "God puts the unction in our gumption." We need the gumption, the resolve, the will to act—and we need God to put the unction upon it and the power behind it so that our meagre human efforts can be supernaturally multiplied for eternal results. When we have the faith to allow God to act in us and through us, He satisfies our hungers and calms our fears. As Philip indicates—almost inadvertently—when we see and know the Father and have His power operating in us, that is enough for us. We are satisfied.

We access the presence of the Father through faith in the Son. Faith in the Son is the answer to all our fears—fear of danger, fear of inadequacy, fear of death, fear of the future. As Jesus said at the beginning of this passage, "Trust in God; trust also in me." Faith is trust. Faith is the assurance that whenever we fall, we fall into the arms of a loving God.

The Greatest Promise Ever Made

Jesus goes on to make a promise—what some Bible scholars have called "the greatest promise ever made."

14:12–14 *"I tell you the truth, anyone who has faith in me will do what I have been doing. He will do even greater things than these, because I am going to the Father. And I will do whatever you ask in my name, so that the Son may bring glory to the Father. You may ask me anything in my name, and I will do it."*

Christians, says the apostle Peter, have received "great and precious promises" from Jesus.[5] Surely this is one of them. It is so great a promise that we must read it very carefully. This promise can be broken down into three important parts. First, Jesus says, "anyone who has faith in me"—that is, the person who keeps on believing in Jesus, the person who continues to grow and trust as a Christian—"will do what I have been doing." Remember, these words were first addressed to the apostles. When He spoke of the works that He did, He referred to His miracles: healing the sick, raising the dead, opening the blind eyes, and curing the lame.

This promise was literally fulfilled in the book of Acts, where we see Peter and John heal a man who was lame from birth; where we see Peter raise a young woman named Dorcas from the dead; where the apostle Paul delivers people from demonic oppression and illness. We even see that when Peter walks through the streets and his shadow falls on sick people, they are healed. "Anyone who has faith in me will do what I have been doing," says Jesus—and these words have been fulfilled.

The second part of this promise is even more intriguing: "He will do even greater things than these, because I am going to the Father." Every once in a while, a starry-eyed young Christian will say to me, "God has anointed me to do the greater works that Jesus promised"—meaning greater physical miracles. I submit to you that Jesus cannot possibly mean that our miracles can exceed His. How can we possibly do greater works than commanding a storm to be calm or raising the dead back to life or casting out demons? There are no greater miracles than these! When Jesus speaks of "greater works," He means that they are greater in a spiritual dimension.

Again, this is a promise that has been fulfilled, and it continues to be fulfilled in our own time. On the day of Pentecost, just forty days after Jesus gave this promise to the disciples, the apostle Peter—empowered by the Holy Spirit—preached so mightily that 3,000 people were converted in one day! That never happened during Jesus' ministry.

And that promise continues to be fulfilled again and again in our own era. For example, when Billy Graham preached on the Parable of the Prodigal Son at Wembley Stadium in London in 1955, 3,000 people became Christians. Remember who else told that parable? Jesus did! But if you read Luke 15, where that parable is recorded, you don't find that even one person was converted when Jesus told that story! Dr. Graham was using material that Jesus "wrote," but he got much greater results than Jesus ever did! That is the kind of "greater work" that Jesus predicted.

Just think: In His ministry in Palestine, Jesus probably never spoke to crowds larger than 7,000 people or so. But I myself have spoken to crowds of over 10,000 people. Evangelist Luis Palau once told me how thrilled he was to address a crowd of 700,000 people in a stadium in Guatemala City. And Dr. Billy Graham once preached to over a million people gathered in a great public square in Seoul, Korea!

I don't say this to glorify men at the expense of Jesus. It is still God who provides the power and produces the results, and the human beings who do God's works are merely His instruments. The point is that Jesus predicted that these "greater works" would take place, and they have taken place, and they continue to take place.

Why are mere men and women doing "greater works" than Jesus Himself did? "Because I am going to the Father," explains Jesus. He is saying that, after He is resurrected and ascends to the throne of power, He will send the Spirit to do these works through us.

In the Name of Jesus

And that brings me to the third part of Jesus' promise: prayer. Jesus promises we will do "greater works" than He did, and He links this promise to *prayer*. He says, "And I will do whatever you ask in my name, so that the Son may bring glory to the Father. You may ask me for anything in my name, and I will do it." Notice that He twice uses that phrase "in my name." What does Jesus mean when He says that if we ask anything in His name, He will do it?

As Christians, most of us are used to ending our prayers with words such as, "in the name of Jesus, Amen." It is virtually automatic, a mere verbal appendage, like signing a letter, "Yours truly." Is this what Jesus means? If we sign all our prayers "in Jesus' name, Amen," will He give us a blank check and say yes to everything we pray? Many people think this is what Jesus promises—and then they are disappointed when their prayers are not answered in the way they want. They get angry with God and say, "God doesn't keep His promises."

I submit to you that there is something much deeper and more profound at work when we pray in the name of Jesus. It means that when we pray, we acknowledge that Jesus is the Lord, not we. It means that we are to pray for the advance of His program, His will, His agenda, not our own. It means that the purpose of prayer is to mold our will to conformity with His, not bend God's will to ours. It means that when we pray, we recognize that we are the servants, working in partnership with Jesus, willing to do whatever Jesus asks if it will further His kingdom.

I have heard many people pray in such a way that they seemed to treat God as if He were a genie from the magic lamp. They command Him, as if He were their servant. It is their own will, their own wants, their own agenda that is uppermost. There is no humility, no sense of Christian servanthood in their prayers.

If we want to understand what Jesus means when He says, "I will do whatever you ask in my name," we should look to the prayer life of Jesus Himself. It is in the prayer relationship of Jesus to the Father that we find our example for our own prayer life. And what was His example to us? It was the example He left to us just a short time after He spoke these words.

After leaving the Upper Room, He went out into the Garden of Gethsemane, fell to His knees, and prayed, "Father, if you are willing, take this cup"—the cup of the cross!—"from me; *yet not my will, but yours be done.*"[6] Jesus did not want to go to the cross; in His humanity, it was simply not His will to endure such incomprehensible agony. And He presented His honest petition to the Father: "If there is any way possible, please spare me the agony of the cross." But Jesus recognized that it was not His will but the Father's that He was there to carry out. So He prayed in the name and according to the will of the Father: "Yet not my will, but yours be done." Jesus was praying in the Father's name, just as we are to pray in the name of Jesus.

Our prayers should be like His: honest, yet humble. God gives us the right to spread our petitions before Him, but ultimately our attitude must be, "Lord, I pray this in the name of Jesus, for the sake of Jesus, that His kingdom will be advanced; not in my name, but His; not my will, but His; and if my will gets in the way of His will, may the will of Jesus be done, not mine." That is what it means to pray in the name of Jesus.

And if we listen carefully to the words of Jesus in the Upper Room, we can see that this is exactly what Jesus says: "I will do whatever you ask in my name, *so that the Son may bring glory to the Father.*" The goal of our prayers should not be a sleeker car or a problem-free life or any of the other selfish things we are prone to pray for. Our goal should be that whatever we pray for may ultimately advance the purposes of God and bring glory to God.

When that becomes the way we pray, then we will see God work in a mighty way through us, as His Spirit empowers us and moves in us and inspires us to pray prayers that are pleasing and honoring to God. Then we will see the true meaning of Jesus words—"You in me and I in you"—being lived out to the Nth degree in our daily lives. That is the greatest truth and the greatest promise in the Bible.

God is carrying out His work of reaching, changing, healing, and restoring the world through ordinary people like you and me. That is our task and our agenda—and ultimately, it is our *joy!*

Chapter Thirty-Nine

Another Is Coming

John 14:15–31

One of the most pervasive social phenomena of our times is the vast number of human potential seminars that are offered. For a few hundred dollars, we can learn all about our secret powers and hidden abilities from some New Age guru. In a single weekend, we can discover an entirely new and exciting plane of existence!

I've talked to a number of people who have been to such seminars, and most of them wish they had saved their money. There *is* a path to Power that is open to everyone, but it doesn't cost anything to find it, and there is no secret initiation, no guru, no set of tapes or books to buy. You might say, however, that this path to Power was first unveiled in a first-century weekend retreat! It was a special seminar with a most remarkable curriculum, conducted by Jesus of Nazareth with just eleven selected participants. This seminar took place not in some hotel conference room, but in Jerusalem, in a place called the Upper Room.

A Gift From the Father

In verses 15 through 17, Jesus introduces another Person, whom He calls the "Paraclete"—a Greek word which could be translated Counselor, Advocate, Comforter, Strengthener, or Helper. It literally means "one who comes alongside." In this passage, Jesus introduces a Person we know as the Holy Spirit. Much confusion abounds in Christian circles today regarding the Person and the work of the Holy Spirit. But in this passage, we hear our Lord Himself as He taught about the Spirit. So let's take our seats in the seminar alongside the disciples and hear about this powerful Person in Jesus' own words.

14:15–17 *"If you love me, you will obey what I command. And I will ask the Father, and he will give you another Counselor to be with you forever—the*

Spirit of truth. The world cannot accept him, because it neither sees him nor knows him. But you know him, for he lives with you and will be in you.

Packed into this brief paragraph are six remarkable facts about the person of this Counselor, the Holy Spirit. First, we learn that He will be a *gift* from the Father to true believers. "I will ask the Father," says Jesus, "and he will *give* you another Counselor."

I say *"true* believers" because not every person who calls himself or herself a Christian will receive the gift of the Holy Spirit. A true believer is one who has been drawn to Jesus by His love and is ready to obey what Jesus says. There are many people who merely use Christianity as a disguise or as a label to make themselves feel they are "good people." But to those who are true followers of Jesus Christ, He promises to give His Spirit as a Comforter, a Counselor, and an empowering Presence.

Of course, this discourse in the Upper Room is not the first time Jesus has ever alluded to the Holy Spirit. In John 7, the account of the Feast of Tabernacles, Jesus stands up and says, "If a man is thirsty, let him come to me and drink. Whoever believes in me, as the Scripture has said, streams of living water will flow from within him." And after this statement of Jesus, John adds, "By this he meant the Spirit, whom those who believed in him were later to receive. Up to that time the Spirit had not been given, since Jesus had not yet been glorified." [1]

"Another Counselor"

The second thing Jesus says in this passage is that this Spirit will be "another," a separate but similar Person to Himself. "I will ask the Father," says Jesus, "and he will give you *another* Counselor." This Counselor is not Jesus Himself, but *another* Person. It is important to note that the specific Greek word for "another" which Jesus uses in this statement is a word that means "another of the same kind." Here again is a clear reference to the mystery of the Trinity: three persons—Father, Son, and Spirit, all distinct, yet comprising one God.

The Spirit will take over the work that Jesus had been doing with the disciples. The reason they have held true to their faith for three and a half years was that they have been with Jesus. Jesus upheld them, counseled them, taught them, strengthened them, and ministered to them—but He would soon be going away. So here He promises *another*—another of the same kind as He is, another Person who is fully God—who will come and take over His work and be the Presence of God among them.

"With You Forever"

The third fact Jesus announces is that the Spirit will be a continually abiding presence, He will be with the followers of Jesus forever. "I will ask the Father," says Jesus, "and He will give you another Counselor to be with you *forever.*"

When the Spirit comes into our lives, He does not come and go, come and go. He does not have to be invited in again and again. He comes to dwell in us and He comes forever. The writer of the book of Hebrews puts it this way: "God has said, 'Never will I leave you; never will I forsake you.' "[2] That is the strongest negative in the Greek language. God is saying, in effect, "I will never, under any circumstances, ever leave you nor forsake you."

Some groups teach that we continually need to get "more of the Spirit." But you can't have "more of the Spirit"! Our goal can and should be to allow the Spirit to have more of us—more control of our behavior, more control of our thoughts, more of our time spent in prayer and worship—but as genuine Christians, we have all of the Spirit we are ever going to get! The Spirit is a Person, and He does not come in bits and pieces. He comes as a whole person, He comes complete, and He comes to live in us forever. Throughout the New Testament, we see confirmation that the Spirit comes once and for all and forever.

A Revealer of Truth

The fourth fact is that the Spirit will be a *revealer of truth.* He is, says Jesus, "the Spirit of truth." What He does and says can be relied upon as absolute reality. I know of no aspect of the Spirit's work that is more important than this. The Spirit gives us the Word, and that Word, interpreted by the Spirit, is absolutely dependable.

Moreover, truth is what the Spirit demands from us in our relationship with Him. He will not accept anything but truth from us. If you want to maintain a good relationship with God, then be honest with Him, with yourself, and with others. Admit your need. Admit your feelings. Admit your sin. Don't pretend to be more spiritual or more righteous than you are. There is nothing more disruptive to our relationship with God than lies.

"The World Cannot Accept Him"

The fifth thing Jesus tells us about the Holy Spirit is that this amazing resource is available to Christians, but is *unavailable to the world.* "The world cannot accept him," He says, "because it neither sees him nor knows him."

We see this clearly as we look around at our secular society. We see how the First Amendment guarantee of freedom of religion has been stood on its head and used to eradicate all traces of Christian belief and Christian values from public life, such as our government institutions and our public schools. Secular society refuses to acknowledge God and cannot see Him, and so tries to keep God out of His own world. Though He holds everything in His hands and guides and directs the destinies of people and nations, the world cannot accept Him, cannot see Him, cannot know Him. To the world, the most important and profound reality in all the universe is regarded as a matter of complete irrelevancy.

A Message for the Eleven

The sixth fact Jesus discloses is that the Spirit is a resource that is available from within. "You know him," He says to His disciples, "for he lives with you and will be in you." It's very important to see that these words apply only to these eleven men.

We know from other Scriptures that, since Pentecost, we receive the Spirit the moment we come to Jesus. There is never a moment in a Christian's life today when it can be truly said, "The Spirit lives with you and will be in you." These words apply only to these men because they were in a transition period, before Pentecost, when the Spirit had not yet come as He came on the day of Pentecost.

Jesus was saying that, prior to Pentecost, the Holy Spirit was with these men, alongside them, but not in them. Later, after Pentecost, the Spirit would take up residence inside them. The Spirit would then be an indwelling presence.

This remarkable revelation concerning the Spirit is confirmed to us by 2,000 years of human history. The Spirit did indeed come on the Day of Pentecost. He did impart strength and boldness to these men so that they lost all fear and began to witness boldly in Jerusalem. And He has come to every believer since that time. So we can believe that Jesus knew what He was talking about in this revelation of the Person and work of the Spirit.

Obedience Flows From Love

In verses 18 through 21, Jesus turns his attention to the fears of His eleven faithful friends. The hearts of these disciples were filled with anxiety and foreboding because Jesus told them He was leaving them. It was little comfort to them that another Person—a Person they knew nothing about—was coming in His place. How much comfort would it be for you if your beloved mother or father or spouse said, "I'm leaving you and you will see me no more—but don't worry, I'm sending Uncle Joe to stay with you, and though you've never met him before, you'll like him"? There's not much comfort in that! In these verses, Jesus deals with that concern.

14:18–21 *"I will not leave you as orphans; I will come to you. Before long, the world will not see me anymore, but you will see me. Because I live, you also will live. On that day you will realize that I am in my Father, and you are in me, and I am in you. Whoever has my commands and obeys them, he is the one who loves me. He who loves me will be loved by my Father, and I too will love him and show myself to him."*

The good news for these men is that they would not lose Jesus when the Spirit came. He would still be with them by means of the Spirit, and He would stay with them. He literally says, "I will not leave you as orphans"—and that is surely how they felt, fatherless and abandoned. The One they had learned to love and follow and emulate, the One who seemed so strong and protective, the One they looked up to like a Father was leaving them. But here Jesus promises them, in effect, "When the Holy Spirit comes to you, I will come with him."

Here, Jesus puts His finger on the most wonderful truth about the Spirit: His primary work is to make Jesus known in the world. The Spirit has come to testify not of Himself, but of Jesus Christ. The truest mark of the Spirit-filled life is not signs or wonders or tongues, but an ever-deepening consciousness of the reality of Jesus Christ. That is the Spirit at work.

"Before long," Jesus continues, "the world will not see me anymore, but you will see me." This is a reference to His appearances following the resurrection. Following the crucifixion and resurrection, the disciples saw Him and spoke with Him several times over the course of forty days. But there is an even deeper meaning to His words. He is saying, "You will continue to see me by means of the Spirit. You will know me more richly, more deeply, more truly after the Day of Pentecost than before." As Jesus said to His followers at the close of Matthew's gospel, "And surely I will be with you always, to the very end of the age."[3]

And Jesus goes on to say that there is a new vitality coming as a result of the coming of the Spirit. "Because I live," says Jesus, "you also will live." People whose lives were dull and meaningless will suddenly come alive in the Spirit, as the life of Jesus is released in them. This is the promise of the Spirit.

Then Jesus talks about how that new life will be expressed through believers, beginning on the Day of Pentecost. "On that day," He says, referring to Pentecost, "you will realize that I am in my Father, and you are in me, and I am in you." I never get over the wonder of that phrase. Here Jesus expresses in the simplest words the most profound truth that can ever engage the mind of man: "You are in me, and I am in you." This is our first experience when we come to Christ. Suddenly, we are adopted into a new family, we are children of God. We have been transferred out of darkness into the kingdom of light.

We are in Christ and He is in us. Once we understand what this statement truly means, we realize that we do not have to demonstrate how much we can do for God, but what He can do through us. Many Christians are caught in the rat-race of trying to perform for God, but God doesn't want our performance. He wants our love and obedience. He wants us to open up our lives and allow Him to live His life through us. Once we understand this truth, the pressure is off. We are free to live in Him.

Finally, says Jesus, if we want to have a relationship of progressive obedience with Jesus, the key is *obedience.* If you have Jesus in your heart, the one thing you want more than anything else is to know Him better. As Paul wrote, "I want to know Christ and the power of his resurrection and the fellowship of sharing in his sufferings, becoming like him in his death."[4] What Paul is expressing is his great *love* for Jesus, and out of his love flows a natural desire for obedience. Obedience is not difficult to those who are filled with love. The clue to Christian behavior is not law, not demand, but *love.*

"My Peace I Give You"

At this point in the discourse, one of the disciples interrupts. His name is Judas—not Judas Iscariot, the traitor, who has already left the room, but another disciple whose name was Judas.

14:22–24 *Then Judas (not Judas Iscariot) said, "But, Lord, why do you intend to show yourself to us and not to the world?"*

Jesus replied, "If anyone loves me, he will obey my teaching. My Father will love him, and we will come to him and make our home with him. He who does not love me will not obey my teaching. These words you hear are not my own; they belong to the Father who sent me."

Loving obedience brings a deepening knowledge of Jesus that enhances the beauty of Christian character. As Howard Hendricks puts it, "The opposite of ignorance is not knowledge, but obedience." It is obeying truth, not merely filling your head with facts, that cancels out ignorance and brings true understanding.

Having shown us who the Holy Spirit is, Jesus now tells us what the Spirit will do when He comes.

14:25–27 *"All this I have spoken while still with you. But the Counselor, the Holy Spirit, whom the Father will send in my name, will teach you all things and will remind you of everything I have said to you. Peace I leave with you; my peace I give you. I do not give to you as the world gives. Do not let your hearts be troubled and do not be afraid."*

Here are four further revelations of the work of the Spirit. First, the Spirit comes at Jesus' request and in His place; He represents Jesus to us.

Second, the Spirit teaches us and reminds us of the words of Jesus. The Spirit reminded John of the things Jesus said throughout His ministry and in the Upper Room, so that John could set them down for our encouragement and instruction in this gospel. When John and his fellow New Testament writers set out to record the words and the story of Jesus, they were able to recall everything Jesus said, because the Spirit brought His words back to their minds.

Third, the Spirit teaches us the meaning and implications of the words of Jesus. The Spirit enabled men like Paul, John, Peter, and the other writers of the New Testament epistles to apply the words of Jesus to newly emerging situations in the life of the fledgling church, so that the early church could grow and be established. And as we read the gospels and the rest of the Bible, this same Spirit opens our understanding and helps us to apply God's truth to the daily realities of our own lives.

Fourth, Jesus says that the work of the Spirit is to impart the peace which He alone can give: "My peace I give you," He says. What is the peace of Jesus like? We see it at work in the final week of Jesus' life. You see His serenity in event after event of those final moments of His earthly ministry. He is always in charge, never stampeded or goaded or panicked. Even when He stands as a prisoner before Pilate and Herod and the chief priests, it is clearly evident—even to them!—that they are prisoners of history and of their own sinful selves, and that Jesus is their judge.

As He was entering the most terrible ordeal any human being ever experienced, Jesus made a last bequest to you and me: His peace, His serenity. "My peace I give you." We can have that peace under any circumstance, because, as Jesus says, it is not the kind of peace the world gives or even knows. What is the peace of the world like?

If you go to a doctor and say you have no peace, he will write you a prescription for a tranquilizer. That is chemical peace. It is artificial, it dulls the mind, it eventually wears off, and it can be habit-forming. That is one way this world dispenses its peace.

The world also promotes other kinds of peace, such as escapism: Take a trip to Hawaii. Go skiing at Vail. Go sailing. Play some golf or tennis. Visit Disneyland.

But when you get back from your vacation, your troubles are still there. The world's peace is temporary. Jesus has given us His peace, which lasts forever.

Entering the Battle

At the close of John 14, Jesus answers the question that must have been uppermost in the minds of His disciples: "When will the Spirit come?"

14:28–31 *"You heard me say, 'I am going away and I am coming back to you.' If you loved me, you would be glad that I am going to the Father, for the Father is greater than I. I have told you now before it happens, so that when it does happen you will believe. I will not speak with you much longer, for the prince of this world is coming. He has no hold on me, but the world must learn that I love the Father and that I do exactly what my Father has commanded me. "Come now; let us leave."*

These words seem to close the discourse in the Upper Room. At this point, Jesus and the disciples leave and go out to Gethsemane's darkness. But before they go, Jesus indicates that there will be an intervening period before the Spirit comes. During that intervening time, two things must happen.

First, Jesus must go to the Father. "This news should make you rejoice," He says in effect. "If you really loved me you would rejoice, because it means I am about to be delivered from the pain, weakness, and shame of this existence. My earthly limitations will be past. I am being reunited with my Father in glory." It always strikes me as strange that we grieve so much for those who have died and gone to glory. We forget that they have entered into joy and release, into an experience of beauty and peace beyond our understanding. When we grieve for a Christian who has died, we are truly feeling sorry for ourselves. We need not feel sorry for that loved one. That is what Jesus says here: "If you loved me you would be glad I'm going back."

Second, the Spirit will come after the devil is conquered. Jesus tells His disciples, in effect, "I have told you about the Holy Spirit so that when He comes, you will remember what I've told you and believe. I don't have much time left to talk to you, because Satan, the ruler of this world is coming, and the greatest battle in all of history is about to begin."

Jesus is looking ahead to the next few hours, when He will grapple in the darkness with His enemy, Satan. In that struggle, He will drink to the dregs the cup which the Father has given Him—a cup filled with shame, agony, and incomprehensible loneliness. Perhaps, in these closing moments of the Upper Room discourse, Jesus is thinking of those words from Isaiah 53: "He was pierced for our transgressions, he was crushed for our iniquities; the punishment that brought us peace was upon him, and by his wounds we are healed." The punishment that should have been ours is about to be laid on Him. Because He is entering into this terrible struggle, He can bequeath to us His peace.

And victory is certain, Jesus tells His disciples. "He has no hold on me," He says, referring to Satan. The devil has no foothold of sin in Jesus' life which he can lay hold of and use as leverage against Him. Victory is absolutely certain.

Yet, it is a victory with a terrible cost.

I have often wondered why Jesus would go through such an experience. Why would Jesus endure such suffering for the sake of undeserving and sinful people like me? We cannot understand it, this side of eternity. The only answer we have is the answer Jesus gives in verse 31: "The world must learn that I love the Father and that I do exactly what my Father has commanded me."

Jesus went into the deepest agony and darkness the human soul can ever know *because He loved the Father*. The Father had determined that this was the only way to achieve His plan, so He sent the Son, and the Son obediently went out of love for the Father. Jesus came to earth and went to the cross in complete faithfulness to the Father's command.

And that is the example of loving obedience He leaves to you and me.

Chapter Forty

The Vine and the Fruit

John 15:1–11

C ome now; let us leave."
With these words, Jesus calls His disciples to leave the Upper Room and go with Him up to the Garden of Gethsemane, which is on the Mount of Olives. To get to the Garden, Jesus and His disciples had to leave the southwest corner of the old city of Jerusalem on the side of Mount Zion (where the Upper Room was located) and wend their way across the Tyropoeon Valley, around the outer walls of old Jerusalem, up through the Kidron Valley, and finally up to Gethsemane's Garden. This path took them past the many vineyards that were tended around the outskirts of Jerusalem in that time. In the bright light of the full Passover moon, the vineyards would have been quite visible.

I believe that, as He did so often throughout His earthly ministry, Jesus once again used whatever was at hand to illustrate the truths He wanted to instill in His followers. So as Jesus and His disciples walked together, the vineyards they passed became the basis for some of His most profound and important teaching—the discourse known as "The Vine and the Branches." This is a very important discourse, for Jesus has already turned His steps toward the cross, and He only has a few hours in which to impart a few last words of instruction to His friends.

The True Vine and the Branches

Although John doesn't specifically say so, I imagine that Jesus probably picked up a length of vine in His hands as He said these words.

15:1–3 *"I am the true vine and my Father is the gardener. He cuts off every branch in me that bears no fruit, while every branch that does bear fruit he trims clean so that it will be even more fruitful. You are already clean because of the word I have spoken to you."*

Jesus doesn't want to be misunderstood, so He explains His symbolism in very clear terms. "I am the true vine," He says. With these words, He contrasts Himself with the well-known symbol of the vine that is used in the Old Testment as a symbol for Israel. For example, the psalmist says, "You brought a vine out of Egypt; you drove out the nations and planted it."[1] When Jesus says, "I am the true vine," He is *not* saying that Israel is a false vine. He is saying that He is the reality, the true vine, of which Israel was only a symbol, a picture.

Pruning and Trimming

Jesus goes on to identify God the Father as the gardener (literally, the "earth worker") and believers as the branches of the vine. There are two kinds of branches: fruitless branches and fruitful branches—which means, of course that there are two kinds of believers, the fruitless and the fruitful. The difference between fruitful and fruitless branches is the difference between night and day. The first work of the Father in this great vineyard is to prune the vine so that it will bear fruit.

In Northern California, where I have spent most of my years of pastoral ministry, there are many vineyards. At a certain time of the year, the vinekeepers cut off "sucker shoots" from the vines—branch-like canes of vine which do not bear fruit. Suckers produce many leaves but no fruit. If allowed to remain, suckers sap the life of the vine and reduce the amount of water and nutrient that reaches the fruit. The goal of pruning vines is to direct as much water and nutrient to the fruit as possible, to increase the quality and quantity of fruit.

It is not difficult to understand the meaning of the Lord's analogy—especially in light of what has just taken place within the band of Jesus' disciples. One fruitless branch has already been removed—Judas Iscariot. The pruning of disciples from twelve to eleven in number was the work of God. Within the congregation of the faithful, there appear from time to time men and women who appear to be believers, but who never become fruitful branches. They seem to give evidence of life, just as Judas did when he did miracles in Jesus' name along with the other eleven. But they have never borne true fruit and they never will. It is the Father's task to remove them.

In John's first letter, the apostle talks about such people: "They went out from us, but they did not really belong to us. For if they had belonged to us, they would have remained with us; but their going showed that none of them belonged to us."[2] This "pruning of the vine" has taken place again and again throughout the history of the church, and it continues to take place today.

Notice that the Father not only prunes the unproductive branches off the vine, He also trims the productive branches so they will be even more productive. "Every branch that does bear fruit," says Jesus, "he trims clean so that it will be even more fruitful."

Pruning and trimming are painful processes. Jesus makes it clear that in order for us to be as fruitful as possible, the false believers among us will be cut out from among us, and we ourselves, as genuine believers, will have to face the pain of being trimmed, cleaned up, and cut back. We will be corrected. We will experience hurts and struggles. We will be tried and tested and refined. The dirt and cobwebs of sin that cling to us will be scrubbed away.

The Fruit God Expects

At this point, the key question we must ask ourselves is, "What kind of fruit does God expect from us?" Jesus does not identify the meaning of the symbol of fruit in this passage. Why? Because it was already clearly identified in the Old Testament. For example, in Isaiah 5, the prophet says that God came to the nation of Israel—the vineyard of the Lord of Hosts—looking for fruit. "When I looked for good grapes," says God in verse 4, "why did it yield only bad?" Then in verse 7, the prophet gives us the key to what constitutes good fruit and bad:

> The vineyard of the Lord Almighty
> is the house of Israel,
> and the men of Judah
> are the garden of his delight.
> And he looked for justice,
> but saw bloodshed;
> for righteousness, but heard
> cries of distress.

The fruit that God desires are justice and righteousness, not oppression and misery and mistreatment. When we link the words of Jesus in the New Testament with the words of the prophet Isaiah in the Old Testament, it is clear that the fruit He wants us to produce is Christlike character. That is why Paul, in Galatians 5:22, lists the fruit of the Spirit as "love, joy, peace, patience, kindness, goodness, faithfulness, gentleness, and self-control." Here are nine character qualities, like nine sweet grapes hanging in a single cluster. This is what the Father is now laboring to produce in your life and in mine.

If you truly belong to Jesus, He will produce the fruit of the Spirit in your life. God is not primarily interested in producing happiness in our lives, but true joy. He is not so much interested in giving us lives without problems or sickness; He is interested in our complete wholeness (what we used to call "holiness") regardless of our problems or health. He is not primarily interested in what we can accomplish for Him, but in the kind of people we become. He is not so much interested in our success as in our serenity. These are the qualities He is working to produce in our lives.

Discipline and Dependence: It Takes Both

Jesus describes our role in the process of bearing fruit.

15:4–5 *"Remain in me, and I will remain in you. No branch can bear fruit by itself; it must remain in the vine. Neither can you bear fruit unless you remain in me.*

"I am the vine; you are the branches. If a man remains in me and I in him, he will bear much fruit; apart from me you can do nothing."

Here, Jesus describes a two-sided process—our side and His side. We have a responsibility to remain in Jesus, and He binds Himself with a promise that He will then live in us. For a believer to bear fruit, both sides of this process must operate. We need have no doubt that Jesus will fulfill His side of the bargain. But we must commit ourselves to keep our side. It is not enough for only one side to keep the bargain. Both sides of the process must operate in order for fruit to be produced.

When I was twenty-one, I bought my first car, a used Model A Ford with a rumble seat. I purchased it from my older brother for $15 (he had paid $35 for it a couple years earlier). Being a used car, it had used car problems. For example, it was sometimes very hard to start. On one occasion, when it completely refused to start, I called my brother and asked him to help me get it going.

He came over, lifted the hood, and handed me a screwdriver. "Touch it to the top of that spark plug, Ray," he told me. "Just hold it right there." I did just what he said—and suddenly I felt a terrible jolt run through my arm and almost take the top of my head off. I jumped back with a yowl, but my brother was perfectly calm. "Well," he said, "the spark's okay."

Then he worked on the carburetor. After a few adjustments, he succeeded in getting the car to run. But I learned something that day I never forgot: It takes both gas and spark to run a car. One or the other alone will never accomplish anything. When Jesus says, "Remain in me, and I will remain in you," He is saying that it takes both His operation and our cooperation to produce fruit. Many Christians focus on one or the other, either sitting back and letting

God do all the work or trying to take over and do everything for God. But that makes no more sense than trying to run a car without gasoline or without spark plugs.

Our responsibility is to remain in Jesus. That means following Him, staying close to Him, talking with Him daily, reading His Word, doing His word, obeying His commands, and worshiping Him. These are the disciplines of the Christian life. As Christians, we are called to *discipline our lives.* That means building habits that bring us closer to Jesus, while doing away with those habits and sins that hinder our relationship with Him. The more we practice these disciplines, the closer we grow to Jesus, and the more consistently we remain in Him.

And what happens to us if we do not remain in Jesus? We become fruitless. "Apart from me," says Jesus, "you can do nothing." That does not mean that apart from Jesus, you turn into an inert lump of lifeless matter. Certainly it is possible to be active and to look busy even if we are apart from Christ. You can raise a family without Christ. You can run a business without Christ. You can be an active church-member without Christ. You can even preach sermons and write Christian books without Christ. You can fill your days with tremendous activity and busyness, and you can impress hundreds or even thousands of people with all the things you seemingly have done for God. But in the end, it will count for nothing. In God's sight, you will have been fruitless.

Always remember: The disciplines of the Christian faith are important, but those disciplines alone are ultimately barren. Spiritual disciplines without spiritual dependence cannot produce true fruit. We must remain in Christ, and we must allow Him to remain in us. We must seek His friendship, His presence, His strength, and His wisdom every day. This is a truth I know from my own personal experience—and my own personal failures.

As a young Christian, I devoted myself to memorizing Scripture, studying the Bible, and getting up early each morning to pray and discipline myself. I did this as part of a spiritual discipline program I learned in the Navigators. It was a good program, and the Navigator disciplines had a profound and life-long impact on my spiritual growth. Yet there was a time in my life when I thought the disciplines were enough. I thought I was achieving a great richness in my Christian experience because of all the time I spent praying and all the Bible knowledge I was amassing, but in time I found I was really barren, cold, and empty in my spiritual life!

Discipline is necessary, but so is dependence. We need to talk to God, but we also need to listen for Him to speak to us. We need to read His Word, but we also need to wait for His presence. We need to serve God, but we also need to expect God to work.

Evidence That We Are True Branches

Jesus gathers up His entire teaching on the vine and the branches in the closing verses of this passage.

15:6–11 *"If anyone does not remain in me, he is like a branch that is thrown away and withers; such branches are picked up, thrown into the fire and burned. If you remain in me and my words remain in you, ask whatever you wish, and it will be given you. This is to my Father's glory, that you bear much fruit, showing yourselves to be my disciples.*

"As the Father has loved me, so have I loved you. Now remain in my love. If you obey my commands, you will remain in my love, just as I have obeyed my Father's commands and remain in his love. I have told you this so that my joy may be in you and that your joy may be complete."

Here again, Jesus refers to the work that the Father does as the gardener of the vineyard: He removes the fruitless branches. Those like Judas who mingle awhile with God's people, who appear to be believers, who display the "leaves" of a true branch but not the fruit of a true branch, eventually "wither"—all semblance of life dries up and disappears—and they are fit only to be picked up, thrown into a fire, and burned. This is an apparent reference to the end of the age, when the angels will come and gather out of the Kingdom of God all those who are counterfeits, who are not true followers. They will be thrown into eternal fire and be burned.

These are sobering words. It is hard to read these words without wondering, as the disciples wondered in the Upper Room, "Is it I? Could it be that I am one of these false followers, and that I am self-deceived into thinking I am a true Christian? How can I know that I am one of the true, fruit-bearing branches?" In verses 7 through 11, Jesus gives us four reassuring evidences of fruit.

First evidence: We pray with power. "If you remain in me and my words remain in you," says Jesus, "ask whatever you wish, and it will be given you." The first evidence of a fruitful life is the impact of answered prayer. You become effective. The work you do for God accomplishes something. You ask what you need for that work, and it is granted.

It is important to notice the precise turn of phrase Jesus uses here. He says, "If you remain in me and *my words* remain in you. . . ." The phrase "my words" is *rhema* in the original language, and refers to His specific promises, not His Word, His *logos,* which means the whole of the revealed Word of God, the Bible. Jesus is saying that *prayer* and *promise* are linked together.

Prayer is not a way of getting God to do what we want, but a process of joining God in partnership with Him, so that He can achieve His promises through us. When we pray according to the promises of Jesus, our prayers are effective. So we would do well to read, study, and align our lives with the promises of God and the mind of God. When we pray according to God's will, says Jesus, whatever we ask will be done.

Second evidence: Our witness glorifies God. "This is to my Father's glory," says Jesus, "that you bear much fruit, showing yourselves to be my disciples." I have heard scores and scores of testimonies from people who can affirm that they were converted to Jesus after seeing a life transformed by the power of God. Do we openly glorify God by telling others about what He has done in our lives? Is Jesus a wonderful friend we can't help but introduce others to? Or do we nullify the effect of the gospel by keeping it to ourselves?

One of the fruits God desires in our lives is the glory that we bring to Him as we bear witness to Him by our words and by our lives.

Third evidence: Our lives are marked by love. "As the Father has loved me," says Jesus, "so have I loved you. Now remain in my love. If you obey my commands, you will remain in my love, just as I have obeyed my Father's commands and remain in his love."

Christlike love is the answer to the great problem of our age—the pervasive mood of meaninglessness and worthlessness that afflicts so many in our society. Why do so many people feel insecure and worthless? And why do they try to hide their insecurities by boasting and seeking status symbols and scrambling after success? Because, deep inside, they feel rejected and unloved. They are seeking a kind of love and acceptance they can't understand, and in the words of the old country-western song, they are "looking for love in all the wrong places."

God offers the most complete love anyone could ever know. It is *agape* love, unconditional love, a love which does not demand performance or beauty or intelligence or anything else. It loves without asking anything in return. It loves even the unlovely and the sinful.

When our love is like that of God, people see God through us. They feel loved and accepted. They learn that they no longer have to prove themselves or earn God's love. Our message to the world is, "God loved you so much He sent His Son to die for you. You are precious to Him. He wants to affirm you, make you whole, and give you back your humanity." People respond to that love. When they find that kind of love, they want to know Jesus and love Him back.

The great theologian, Karl Barth, was once asked, "What is the most profound scriptural truth you have ever found?" And this man, who has been called the greatest theologian of the twentieth century, replied simply, " 'Jesus loves me, this I know, for the Bible tells me so.' " There is nothing greater than love. When our lives are marked by God's love, then God is able to harvest the fruit that He desires.

Fourth evidence: We have joy. "I have told you this," says Jesus, "so that my joy may be in you and that your joy may be complete." What was His joy? We catch a glimpse of it in Hebrews 12:2, which says,

> Let us fix our eyes on Jesus, the author and perfecter of our
> faith, who for the joy set before him endured the cross, scorn-
> ing its shame, and sat down at the right hand of the throne of
> God.

His joy was the expectation that He would be the instrument of redemption for the entire world. His joy was the joy of being used by God to further the eternal purposes of God—and that joy belongs to Jesus, to you, or to me—there is no joy in the world that compares to it.

That is the inheritance of every genuine believer—love, joy, and peace. "Peace I leave with you," says Jesus. "Remain in my love. . . . I have told you this so that my joy may be in you and that your joy may be complete." The world does not understand such joy. It does not depend on how much wealth you possess. It does not depend on having a life of leisure or a fleet of Mercedes or a membership at the Pebble Beach Country Club. You can have joy even when your health is slipping away, when your business is failing, when you are facing opposition, when you have lost your job, or when a loved one passes away.

True Christian joy runs deeper than happiness, deeper than sorrow. It does not depend on circumstances. It depends only on God, and God is always faithful.

On that night, as the disciples walked past the vineyards, on the path which led from the Upper Room to Gethsemane, and beyond—all the way to the cross—Jesus led the way through the valley of the shadow of death. And He talked about love. And peace. And joy.

These are the fruit of which the Vine Himself bore as He made His way to the hill of the cross. And we, who are branches of the vine, can produce the same fruit, regardless of what cross we face. That is the promise of our Lord Jesus.

Chapter Forty-One

Love and Hate

John 15:12–16:4

Edith Louisa Clavell was a British Red Cross nurse working behind the German lines during World War I. She enabled a number of English soldiers to escape, until she was captured by the Germans and sentenced to death. She was led before a firing squad and, before being blindfolded, was allowed to make a final statement. She bravely faced the German officers and the six armed soldiers—most of them barely out of their teens—who would soon take her life. Then, in a voice that rang clear and bell-like across the courtyard, she said, "Take away my life, but I shall not hate you. In the name of my Lord Jesus, I forgive you."

Can you love your enemies in the name of the Lord Jesus? Can you love those who hurt you? Can you love those who hate you and abuse you? This very week, you may be called upon to love somebody you do not like or who does not like you. You may even be called upon to love someone who has dealt you a terrible wound. There is nothing theoretical or hypothetical about the issue of Christian love. This is a subject that hits us right where we live.

A Decision, Not a Feeling

Jesus has already revealed the fundamental secret of Christian living, from which everything else flows: "You in me and I in you." In the second half of John 15, we learn how this secret of Christian living is to be lived out in a hostile world through our *love*.

15:12–15 *"My command is this: Love each other as I have loved you. Greater love has no one than this, that one lay down his life for his friends. You are my friends if you do what I command. I no longer call you servants, because a servant does not know his master's business. Instead, I have called you friends, for everything that I learned from my Father I have made known to you."*

Both at the beginning and at the end of this paragraph, Jesus commands us to love one another. If we claim to be Christians, if His life is in us and we are in Him, then we have no option in the matter. Some people read this and say, "How can you command love? Either you love people or you don't. You can't make people love other people."

But the command of our Lord has nothing to do with feelings. When Jesus commands us to love, He does not command us to generate feelings, but to make a decision. Christlike *agape* love is a decision to act for the benefit of another person, no matter how you feel about that person. Until we understand the true nature of Christian love, we cannot begin to obey our Lord's command.

Marilyn is a housewife who was raped at knife-point in her own home. The rapist was later caught, prosecuted, and sentenced to prison. After he was sent to prison, Marilyn felt God calling her to go to the prison and visit the man who had assaulted and terrorized her so that she could express God's love to him. So she and her husband went to the prison, and Marilyn told this man that she forgave him. I would like to say that this man was transformed, and that he immediately gave his heart to Jesus, but that did not happen. He remained unmoved and unchanged.

How did Marilyn feel going to the prison and witnessing to this man about the love of Jesus?

"It was the last thing in the world I wanted to do," she recalls. "I was physically sick at the thought of seeing him again. On an emotional level, I was afraid of him, I was repulsed by him, and—I have to be honest—I hated him. But, with my husband's support and the prayers of many Christian friends, I was able to go to the prison and face him and say what I had to say. My feelings were not the issue. I knew that what God wanted was my obedience. He wanted me to love this man with my will and my words, even though in my emotions I couldn't stand the sight of him."

That is what Christlike love is like: deliberate, decisive, firm, obedient, gracious. This kind of love is not indulgent or weak, as many people mistakenly think. *Agape* love does not just forgive people, it also holds people accountable. As someone once said, love that is too timid to hold wrongdoers accountable for their own good and the good of others is "sloppy agape." Marilyn practiced true *agape* love toward her attacker. She forgave him—but she also testified against him in order to put him in prison. "Love," says the apostle Paul, "does not delight in evil but rejoices with the truth."[1]

The love that Jesus commands is a decision, not a feeling. It is clear-eyed and realistic. The love of God always seeks the highest good of the person being loved, even in the most extreme and unlovely situations.

The Motive for Our Love

What is the benchmark and the motive for all our love? The love of Jesus. We are to love one another, He says, "as I have loved you."

And how did Jesus love His disciples? Well, have you ever considered how difficult it must have been at times for Jesus to love His disciples? Remember, these were stubborn, selfish, quarrelsome, ambitious, often presumptuous men. They were disobedient and lazy at times. They failed Jesus again and again. Most of all, they were dense! Jesus had to explain the same truths to them again and again, and they still didn't get it! You can hear the exasperation in His voice in the many times He says to them, "How long must I be with you?"

These men could be annoying and even infuriating. In short, they were people just like us!

In verse 9, Jesus told us how He loved the disciples: "As the Father has loved me, so have I loved you." That is the key to love. We should not give love only in response to a warm-fuzzy feeling. Our love should flow from a heart that has received love from God. That is how Jesus loved.

When His disciples were quarrelsome or dense or difficult, He didn't simply grit His teeth and try to be nice. He reflected on how the Father loved Him, and how wonderful it was to be approved and loved by God. That is why He went out on the hillside to pray: There He was renewed and strengthened by the Father's love. That was His "filling station" where He "refueled" with the Father's *agape* love so that He could go back to the disciples and put up with their fragilities, futilities, and follies. That is our example.

Who are you struggling with right now? Who is the person who irritates you and strains your patience to the breaking point? Go to God in prayer. Reflect on the love God has extended to you. Think of how His love for you is symbolized by the cross. Remember how He cares for you, supports you, and acknowledges you as His own. Soon, you will discover something amazing happening—something which Paul describes in Romans 5:5: "God has poured out his love into our hearts by the Holy Spirit, whom he has given us," and that love then flows out to other people around you.

Over the years, I have been shocked to learn that not everybody is as loving, patient, gracious, and kind as I am! Have you found that too? People are hard to love at times. I have had to learn to stop *trying* to love people—that is, to stop gritting my teeth and counting to ten and trying to be patient. Instead, I have tried to simply reflect again and again on the amazing truth that God loves me unconditionally, even though He knows all my sins and all my flaws. Out of this realization flows my love for others.

What Christian Love Is Like

Not only does Jesus *command* us to love, and tell us *how* to love, and *exemplify* love, He goes on to say what that love will look like. Certainly, there is more to *agape* love than mere words. There is more to love than joining hands on a Sunday morning and singing, "They will know we are Christians by our love." The love Jesus commands is a love that is manifested not only in words and song, but in *deeds.*

"Greater love has no one than this," says Jesus, "that one lay down his life for his friends." Those words are inscribed on the headstone of Dawson Trotman, founder of the Navigators, who drowned while saving lives after a boating accident in upstate New York. To lay down your life is to love to the uttermost. You cannot demonstrate any deeper love than that.

That kind of love was demonstrated by a British explorer, Lawrence Oates, during Robert Scott's disastrous expedition to the South Pole. As the Scott party was returning from the Pole, they encountered a raging blizzard. Due to the bitter cold, Oates' feet became frostbitten. As they trudged on, his frostbite turned to gangrene.

"Leave me here," he begged his companions. "Save yourselves." But the other men refused to leave him, and they struggled onward for another day.

The party pitched a tent for the night, and the following morning Oates said to his friends, "I'm going outside. I may be some time." He walked out of the tent and never returned.

Oates' act of self-sacrificing love is known only because it is recorded in Robert Scott's diary of the journey. Scott and the rest of his party died before reaching their base camp. Even though Lawrence Oates' sacrifice did not succeed in saving the life of his friends, it was an act of love to the uttermost, the kind of love Jesus talks about when He says, "Greater love has no one than this, that one lay down his life for his friends."

But there is even more to what Jesus is saying than that. He is not only talking about dying on another person's behalf, because death is a once and for all event. Jesus was talking about *love as a lifestyle.* He was talking about laying down one's life as part of a continual process.

Jesus goes on to say, "You are my friends if you do what I command. I no longer call you servants, because a servant does not know his master's business. Instead, I have called you friends, for everything that I learned from my Father I have made known to you." Notice how He elevates these men from the level of mere servants, who must obey in order to avoid punishment, to the level of *friends* who want to obey because they have been admitted into the inner secrets of another person's life.

What is the difference between an acquaintance and a friend? Acquaintances are people who know us on the outside, on the surface. With friends, we share what we are going through—joys, hurts, failures, the secret places of our lives. Jesus has let these eleven men approach Him, closer than the level of servants, closer than the level of acquaintances, all the way to the innermost level of friends. He has shared His secrets with them. He has shared the secrets of the Father's nature and of His plan for the world. More than that, Jesus had shared His own struggles, His pains, His emotions with these disciples. Very soon, as they enter the Garden of Gethsemane, Jesus will say to Peter, James, and John, "My soul is overwhelmed with sorrow to the point of death. . . . Stay here and keep watch."[2] That kind of honesty and openness is love—the sharing of yourself with another human being, the act of removing the facades and exposing the reality of your heart. Jesus loved His disciples with that kind of love.

One way we can express this kind of Christlike love is by being open and honest in sharing ourselves with others. I don't mean that we should tell our secrets to everyone on the street-corner! Rather, we should expose the reality of our hearts with a few trusted believers in a small group setting, just as Jesus shared Himself with the Twelve.

I believe all Christians should be in small groups, studying the Bible together, worshiping God together, fellowshiping together, serving Jesus together, sharing their lives together. Small groups were the essential building blocks of the first-century church, and they are the essential means to transcend the bigness of big churches today. If you have never been involved in a small group Bible study, I urge you to find one or start one right away. Find a few like-minded believers and agree to meet together on a weekly basis, agree to do some ministry together, agree to spend time sharing yourselves with one another, learning about God together, and really loving one another as Jesus commanded.

I liken Christian small groups to a flock of sandhill cranes—those great long-necked birds that fly south every winter in a majestic V-formation. A bird-fancier once told me three remarkable facts about these birds and their aerial migration habits. First, there is always a leader to the V-formation. That leader sets the direction for the entire formation. Second, it is never the same leader! These birds instinctively share the leadership among themselves, taking turns being out in front and setting the course for the group. Third, whenever they fly, the rest of the birds encourage the leader, honking all the way: "*Honk!* Keep it up! *Honk!* Good going! *Honk!* Lead on, MacDuff!"

To me, that's what a great small group ministry is like. That's what our Lord is describing here to His eleven remaining friends. He is telling them that mutual sharing is a form of love.

A Strategy of Love

Jesus shows us how we are strategically linked to God's plan—and how our primary weapon in that strategy is our Christlike love.

15:16–17 *"You did not choose me, but I chose you to go and bear fruit—fruit that will last. Then the Father will give you whatever you ask in my name. This is my command: Love each other."*

"You did not choose me," says our Lord, "but I chose you." When He says He "chose" us, He uses a word that conveys the sense that we have been *strategically placed.* Why? For the express purpose that we should bear fruit, eternal fruit, fruit that will last. "Then the Father will give you whatever you ask in my name," He continues.

He is telling His disciples—and you and me!—that Jesus chooses His followers, He positions them for strategic advantage so that we can conquer hostile enemy territory with our love. If we are facing opposition from our neighbors, or a cantankerous boss, or a difficult family member, or a bossy church member, Jesus wants us to know that the pressure and the pain of that situation is no accident. God wants to use that situation in our lives so that (1) we can be changed and made into more gracious, prayerful, loving, patient, powerful Christians; and so that (2) we can make a difference in the lives of those around us. He wants us to bear fruit—both the fruit of the Spirit, refined Christian character, and the fruit of witness which glories God and attracts people into His kingdom.

Facing the World's Hostility

It should not surprise us that, as Christians, we will encounter the same kind of hostility that Jesus faced. So He prepares us to be hated.

15:18–20 *"If the world hates you, keep in mind that it hated me first. If you belonged to the world, it would love you as its own. As it is, you do not belong to the world, but I have chosen you out of the world. That is why the world hates you. Remember the words I spoke to you: 'No servant is greater than his master.' If they persecuted me, they will persecute you also. If they obeyed my teaching, they will obey yours also."*

I've seen it again and again: A person becomes a Christian and then goes to tell friends and family members—and is shocked and dismayed to run into a wall of hostility. Every other joy that person has shared—a new job, a new house, a new relationship—has been greeted with enthusiasm and affirmation. But if that person goes back to his or her friends or parents or siblings and says, "I've just accepted Jesus Christ as my Lord and Savior! This is the greatest thing that's every happened to me!"—there will be a strange resistance, strange looks, cold indifference, perhaps even open antagonism. Such a hostile reception has confused and bewildered many a new Christian.

Jesus wants to help us understand and face the hostility of the world we live in. So, in this passage, He tells us two things:

First, don't take it personally. This hostility is directed at Jesus, and He experienced it long before we did. Certainly, there are times when we needlessly bring the world's hostility on ourselves by being insensitive, overbearing, or overly aggressive in our witnessing. But in general, the hostility we encounter when we talk about our faith is not directed at us at all (even though it feels very personal indeed!). It is helpful to remember that before the world hated us, it hated Jesus first.

Second, Jesus says the world's hostility will come because we are transformed people. "If you belonged to the world," He says, "it would love you as its own. As it is, you do not belong to the world." We are different (or at least we *should* be!), and the world does not like people who are different, people who by their lifestyle convict the world of sin. Society will pressure us to conform, to shape up, to play the game.

You don't have to be religious to be hated. The world always hates those who are different, those who don't conform. Almost two centuries ago, a man invented the first umbrella and tried it out on a walk through the streets of London. He soon ran into the hostility of people who didn't want some oddball walking their streets with his own personal roof on a stick! They pelted him with stones and rotten vegetables and chased him off the street!

If we are like Christ, then we will be marked as different, and the world will treat us with hostility. So how should we respond to the world's hostility? I like the response of one new Christian who was confronted by his old worldly friends. They said, "Jack, you're just no fun anymore. You don't get drunk or sleep around anymore. You don't gamble or steal cars and go joyriding anymore. You just don't know how to have a good time anymore."

"Hey, you've got it all wrong," he wisely replied. "I can do all those things whenever I want to. I can get drunk or sleep around or any of that stuff anytime I please. The only thing is I don't want to anymore. It's my wants that have changed." This young man went on to explain that he had occasional temptations along these lines, but he had made a commitment to a deeper desire in his life—a desire for change, for purity, for pleasing his Lord. Jesus says that when you commit yourself to Him, your life changes, and your friends may be convicted and angered by those changes. They may treat you cooly—or even harshly. "That is why the world hates you," says Jesus.

Persecution cannot be avoided, Jesus tells us. The servant is not greater than his master, so if Jesus was rejected, we will be, too. If Jesus was not delivered from hostility, we will have to face it, too. It cannot be avoided. It goes with the territory—that is, it goes with the task of being a Christian in hostile, enemy-controlled territory!

Ah, but there is good news, too. Jesus assures us that the hostility of the world will not be universal. Just as some people responded favorably to Jesus and listened to Him, there will be some who respond favorably to us. "If they persecuted me," He says, "they will persecute you also. If they obeyed my teaching, they will obey yours also." So take heart. Some will listen—and be converted.

The Source of Hostility: Godlessness

The world's hatred is deep-rooted and entrenched. Much as we would like to eliminate the world's persecution, it will always be there until Jesus takes us out of the world.

15:21–25 *"They will treat you this way because of my name, for they do not know the One who sent me. If I had not come and spoken to them, they would not be guilty of sin. Now, however, they have no excuse for their sin. He who hates me hates my Father as well. If I had not done among them what no one else did, they would not be guilty of sin. But now they have seen these miracles, and yet they have hated both me and my Father. But this is to fulfill what is written in their Law: 'They hated me without reason.'"*

What is the source of this deep-rooted hostility against Jesus and His followers? Jesus says it is *godlessness*—"they do not know the One who sent me." It is startling to realize that the godless people Jesus was talking about were the *religious* leaders of the day! These were supposedly men of God, men who prided themselves on their knowledge of God. But Jesus said they did not truly know God—the true God, the One who sent Him. They served a false god, a god of their own making.

But, says Jesus, these men were without excuse, because they heard His words and saw His works. When someone is exposed to the truth and still rejects it, his condemnation is multiplied. By rejecting the words and the works of Jesus, they manifested their contempt for the Father. Furthermore, Jesus says that their hatred is a fulfillment of biblical prophecy: "They hated me without reason."

Forewarned Is Forearmed

Finally, Jesus arms His followers for the coming hostility by warning them of what is to come and instructing them in how to respond.

15:26–16:4 *"When the Counselor comes, whom I will send to you from the Father, the Spirit of truth who goes out from the Father, he will testify about me; but you also must testify, for you have been with me from the beginning.*

"All this I have told you so that you will not go astray. They will put you out of the synagogue; in fact, a time is coming when anyone who kills you will think he is offering a service to God. They will do such things because they have not known the Father or me. I have told you this, so that when the time comes, you will remember that I warned you. I did not tell you this at first because I was with you."

In these verses, Jesus prepares us for the world's hostility with four strong statements. First, the Counselor, the Holy Spirit, is coming, Jesus promises. For us, of course, the Spirit has already come, but for these eleven disciples, the coming of the Holy Spirit at Pentecost was still a future event. The Spirit will bear witness within us to the reality of the risen and living and powerful Lord, and the witness of the Spirit within us will empower us to be witnesses to the world.

I have seen many classes offered on how to witness. I wonder if anyone really needs such classes. I don't believe people need to be taught the mechanics of witnessing. I don't see anywhere in the New Testament that the early believers needed to be trained as witnesses. I have found that those who have experienced the reality of Jesus by means of the Holy Spirit do not need to be trained in witnessing techniques. They only have to open their mouths and talk about what God has done for them.

Second, Jesus makes a statement that applies specifically to these eleven men, but which also has application to your life and mine. He says, "But you also must testify, for you have been with me from the beginning." How do you witness? You tell someone what has happened to you. That's all! You review what God has done for you since the beginning of your Christian life. There is no more perfect and effective witness than the testimony of your own personal experience.

Third, don't give up! The persecution will be fierce. It may even be violent. "A time is coming," He says, "when anyone who kills you will think he is offering a service to God." Even so, stand your ground. Jesus will stand by you and steady you, however fierce the persecution.

Fourth, be forewarned, be ready. "I have told you this," He says, "so that when the time comes you will remember that I warned you." Forewarned, as the saying goes, is forearmed. We do not have to be surprised and ambushed when hostility and persecution come our way.

Once and for all, let's get rid of this cherished fantasy that so many Christians have, that we can settle down in this world, be liked by everybody, and have no problems and no hardships. There is a *war* going on, but victory is certain—*if* we are on the right side! And the way we can be sure that we are on the right side in this war is to examine our weapons and make sure we carry the armament of God:

We are on God's side if we go into this war armed not with hate and anger, but with weapons of truth and love.

Chapter Forty-Two

The New Strategy

John 16:5–33

Out of curiosity, I once thumbed through the Yellow Pages and counted up all the churches. There were Apostolic, Assembly of God, Baptist, Brethren, Christian & Missionary Alliance, Church of Christ, Congregational, Episcopal, Evangelical Covenant, Evangelical Free, Foursquare, Free Methodist, Friends, Full Gospel, Independent Bible, Interdenominational, Lutheran, Mennonite, Nazarene, Pentecostal, Presbyterian, Reformed, Salvation Army, and on and on—thirty-six churches in all. And that was just in one modest-size community, Palo Alto, California. I got to thinking how many *thousands* of churches there had to be in the many communities up and down the San Francisco Peninsula, and around the entire Bay Area. And my mind wandered to all of the *hundreds of thousands* of churches up and down the state of California, and the *millions* of churches across the United States and around the world.

And I thought, "If all of those churches were like the church in the book of Acts, how would Palo Alto and California and the nation and the world be different than they are today?" There is no doubt the world would be *tremendously* different! Poor, small, persecuted, yet unbelievably powerful and vigorous, the tiny first century took on the world and shook the mighty Roman empire to its foundations. The early church grew and spread like fire through dry grass. In fact, the early church was so dynamic that when Paul and his missionary companions came to Thessalonica, on the outskirts of the Roman empire, the Jewish leaders complained, "These are the people who have turned the world upside-down!"[1] That was the impact of the early church.

What has happened in the past 2,000 years? We have more churches than ever before, yet society is disintegrating faster than ever before! Why are so many churches today so weak and ineffectual? Why do Christians seem to have so little impact on society? Could it be that we have lost sight of the strategy for the church which our Lord laid down at the beginning of Christian history?

Convicting the World of Sin

Jesus—the Lord and Founder of the church—describes His strategy for the church to the eleven apostles who remain after the defection of Judas.

16:5–11 *"Now I am going to him who sent me, yet none of you asks me, 'Where are you going?' Because I have said these things, you are filled with grief. But I tell you the truth: It is for your good that I am going away. Unless I go away, the Counselor will not come to you; but if I go, I will send him to you. When he comes, he will convict the world of guilt in regard to sin and righteousness and judgment: in regard to sin, because men do not believe in me; in regard to righteousness, because I am going to the Father where you can see me no longer; and in regard to judgment, because the prince of this world now stands condemned."*

The entire strategy for the church, Jesus declares, begins with people who have been *inwardly transformed.* His strategy is for the Holy Spirit to take up residence in and among Christians. As the Spirit transforms Christians from within, the church will convince and convict an unbelieving world of sin, righteousness, and judgment.

Notice, by the way, that God's strategy is not for the Holy Spirit to directly and personally convict the world, but for the Holy Spirit to convict the world *through the church.* Remember, as Jesus has carefully pointed out, the world cannot receive the Holy Spirit because it does not know Him (see John 14:17). It is the transforming work of the Spirit, which He performs in the lives of Christians like you and me, that will ultimately impress the world. That is the first element of our Lord's strategy for the church.

Notice, too, that Jesus does not say that the church will convict the world of its "sins," plural, but of *sin,* of its fundamental sinful nature. Unbelieving society will be shown that it is living in violation of God's intention for humanity. The primary reason God wants to convict the world of sin is His great *love* for the human race. Rebellious human beings refuse to accept His love, and insist that God just wants to limit our freedom and destroy our fun. But God truly wants us to experience the full glory and beauty He intended for humanity—a glory and beauty that is destroyed by sin.

How will the unbelieving world respond when we, as transformed Christians, convict it of sin? Some people will be attracted. They will realize that much of the pain in their lives has been the result of living lives that are out of touch with basic reality. They will be impressed by these Christians who have discovered the secret of life, the secret of inner peace and true Christian love.

But others, as we saw in John 15, will respond with hostility. When the light of truth shines on their evil way of life, they will become angry and vengeful. We already see this happening today. All a Christian has to do is mind his own business and live a Christian lifestyle, and sooner or later, some unbeliever will become angry and offended simply by that Christian's quiet, unassuming example. "No one can tell me how to live my life!" the non-Christian shouts. "I have a right to choose my lifestyle and my behavior, and you narrow-minded Christians have no right to sit in judgment of me!" They will respond like this even if you never say one judgmental word to them. Why? Because the very *example* of a righteous, godly life is enough to make such people feel judged and guilty.

Convicting the World of Righteousness

The next thing the world will be impressed by, as the Spirit performs His transforming work through the church, is *righteousness.* Another word for righteousness is *wholeness,* or what the Old Testament calls *holiness.*

When I was younger, I used to associate the word *holiness* with grim, sour, straight-laced people who never smiled or enjoyed life. I never liked the word *holiness* until I learned to substitute another word for it that says exactly what holiness is—*wholeness.* I have never met anyone who does not want to be a whole person. To be a whole person means to be a person who is balanced and complete. That is what it means when we sing that God is "holy, holy, holy." It means that God is whole, complete, and perfect.

The good news of the gospel is that we do not have to make ourselves whole. In fact, we *can't* make ourselves whole. The only way to wholeness is to come to Jesus. He gives us the Spirit, and the first work of the Spirit is to give us what we could never earn—righteousness, holiness, inner wholeness before God. The Old Testament has a wonderful term for that: "the beauty of holiness." It is an inner beauty—the beauty that comes as a result of the transforming work of the Spirit.

We are talking about *inner beauty.* There is something beautiful about whole people. They attract us, they captivate us, they capture our attention. The truly beautiful people, says Jesus, will be those who—despite all the failure, weakness, and fragility of their lives—have faith in Jesus and are allowing the Spirit to transform them and bring about an inner wholeness and Christlikeness.

Convicting the World of Judgment

Jesus tells us that the Holy Spirit, operating through us, His church, will convict the world of judgment. In verse 11, He tells us exactly what kind of judgment He is talking about: "The prince of this world now stands condemned." This is a judgment that has already taken place: Satan—the ruler of this planet, the invisible spirit which masterminds the psychology of unbelievers, distorting their thinking and seducing them into illusions and self-destructive sin—has been judged!

What is Jesus talking about here? He is saying that the world has been freed from domination by the evil prince named Satan—freed not in a final sense but in a very real sense nevertheless. Although the world continues to groan under the heel of Satan, individual people are finding liberation and freedom from satanic enslavement. They are finding liberation from sinful habits they never believed they could break. They are finding spiritual freedom and a sense of peace. They are finding freedom from loneliness and despair. They are discovering that heaven is theirs—not only in eternity but in the Here and Now.

"He Will Guide You into All Truth"

Jesus gives us the next step in His strategy for the church.

16:12–15 *"I have much more to say to you, more than you can now bear. But when he, the Spirit of truth, comes, he will guide you into all truth. He will not speak on his own; he will speak only what he hears, and he will tell you what is yet to come. He will bring glory to me by taking from what is mine and making it known to you. All that belongs to the Father is mine. That is why I said the Spirit will take from what is mine and make it known to you."*

Here we catch a poignant glimpse of the heart of our Lord. Standing on the threshold of death, in the shadow of the cross, facing the most terrible experience of pain, horror, and abandonment anyone can ever know, Jesus takes pity on His disciples. He has compassion on them for their bewilderment, blindness, and limited understanding. He says, "I have much more to say to you, more than you can now bear." He does not want to overburden these men, knowing the grief and confusion they are about to be thrown into. That is one of the most encouraging words in all of Scripture.

When will these men be able to bear more of the knowledge He wishes them to have? Not during His post-resurrection appearances. He did very little teaching between the time of His resurrection and ascension. Clearly, Jesus was looking forward to the coming of the Spirit on the Day of Pentecost, and the inspired writing of the New Testament. In verse 13, Jesus says, "When he, the Spirit of truth, comes, he will guide you into all truth." Jesus is talking about the entire story of Acts, when the Spirit moved out in power into the world, working through the church. He is talking about the writing of the epistles of the New Testament, the marvelous letters of Peter, James, John, Paul, and others, written under the direct inspiration of the Holy Spirit.

Further, Jesus says, the Spirit "will tell you what is yet to come." That is a reference to the book of Revelation. In this passage, the disciples receive a preview of the New Testament from the lips of Jesus Himself! Jesus promises that the Spirit will come with a guide-book for the church, and indeed for the human race, which reveals all the treasures of God's thoughts and wisdom. That is why it is so important for all of us to study this book, because it is the life-manual given to us by God to increase our understanding.

Sorrow into Joy

Beginning with verse 16, Jesus makes a series of significant statements that the disciples find difficult to understand.

16:16 *"In a little while you will see me no more, and then after a little while you will see me."*

What a strange thing to say: "I will disappear then reappear again!" His disciples were understandably puzzled by these words, and they turned to each other for understanding.

16:17–20 *Some of his disciples said to one another, "What does he mean by saying, 'In a little while you will see me no more, and then after a little while you will see me,' and 'Because I am going to the Father'?" They kept asking, "What does he mean by 'a little while'? We don't understand what he is saying."*

Jesus saw that they wanted to ask him about this, so he said to them, "Are you asking one another what I meant when I said, 'In a little while you will see me no more, and then after a little while you will see me'? I tell you the truth, you will weep and mourn while the world rejoices. You will grieve, but your grief will turn to joy."

Here Jesus gives us a guide to reading the Scriptures. One of the most common objections people have to the Bible (particularly people who have never spent much time reading the Bible!) is, "The Bible contradicts itself. It's full of errors." That's exactly what these disciples are saying. "Jesus is contradicting Himself! We don't understand." But once you understand what Jesus means, it becomes clear that the problem is not that Jesus contradicts Himself but that the disciples are limited in their understanding.

16:21–24 *"A woman giving birth to a child has pain because her time has come; but when her baby is born she forgets the anguish because of her joy that a child is born into the world. So with you: Now is your time of grief, but I will see you again and you will rejoice, and no one will take away your joy. In that day you will no longer ask me anything. I tell you the truth, my Father will give you whatever you ask in my name. Until now you have not asked for anything in my name. Ask and you will receive, and your joy will be complete."*

In this section, verses 16 through 24, Jesus is preparing His disciples for His death—and for His resurrection. We understand the facts of the crucifixion and of the empty tomb, of course, because we have the benefit of hindsight. These disciples did not understand His meaning, even though He had repeatedly predicted His death. Were they dense? Were they in denial? Were they simply displaying the same propensity for wishful thinking that you and I might have shown in the same situation? For whatever reason, despite Jesus' repeated predictions of His own death, His disciples were slow to grasp and accept the full meaning of what He was saying.

Jesus knew that they would not understand His words as He spoke them. But He also knew that in a few days, they will have the benefit of hindsight, just as we do. They will have seen the horror of the cross, and they will have fled from it. They will have seen the empty tomb, and their hearts will rejoice. And *then* they will remember His words to them.

It's important to notice the precise turn of phrase Jesus uses in this passage: "Your grief will turn to joy." He does not say, "You will grieve for a while, and then you will experience joy." He says, in effect, "Your grief and pain and sorrow will be *transformed* into joy. The cross, which is now an instrument of torture and death, will become an object of glory." That is a promise similar to the old alchemists' dream of transmuting lead into gold.

Then Jesus illustrates His teaching with a beautifully apt word-picture. Every mother knows exactly what Jesus means when He talks about a woman in labor. The pain of birth is one of the most intense forms of pain there is—at least, so I am told by those who should know! Yet, when the baby is born, the mother's face is filled with a joy beyond any other joy on earth. But note this:

What caused the woman's pain? The baby. And what caused her joy? The very same baby!

This is an excellent analogy to what the disciples are about to experience. The horror of the cross is about to torture and murder their Lord and Master. Yet it is the sacrifice of Jesus on that same cross that is also going to bring about the resurrection and salvation and joy!

As He has done several times before on the night He was betrayed, Jesus links His teaching to the issue of *prayer.* "In that day," He says in verse 23, referring to the day of Pentecost, the day when the Spirit comes, "you will no longer ask me anything. I tell you the truth, my Father will give you whatever you ask in my name. Until now you have not asked for anything in my name. Ask and you will receive, and your joy will be complete."

Paul affirms the teaching of Jesus when he writes, "Do not be anxious about anything, but in everything, by prayer and petition, with thanksgiving, present your requests to God. And—" And what? What is the next thing Paul says? And all your problems will magically disappear? No. Paul says, "And the peace of God, which transcends all understanding, will guard your hearts and your minds in Christ Jesus."[2] That is the answer to your prayers. Your sorrow will be turned into joy. Perhaps not instantly, perhaps not overnight, but God does give us His peace for our darkest trials when we pray and present our requests to Him. That is the promise of God, and He is faithful to His promises.

"Don't Ever Think God Don't Love You!"

In this next passage Jesus explains the underlying foundation for our prayer relationship with God.

16:25–28 *"Though I have been speaking figuratively, a time is coming when I will no longer use this kind of language but will tell you plainly about my Father. In that day you will ask in my name. I am not saying that I will ask the Father on your behalf. No, the Father himself loves you because you have loved me and have believed that I came from God. I came from the Father and entered the world; now I am leaving the world and going back to the Father."*

Jesus says here that a day is coming—a day in which you and I now live—when those who follow Jesus will no longer have to relay their prayers through Jesus; His followers will have direct access to the Father, if they come in the name of Jesus. Before, Jesus' disciples had to ask Jesus to pray on their behalf, but now, says Jesus, "the Father himself loves you because you have loved me and have believed that I came from God." Because we come in the name of the Son, and we love the Son, we can go to the Father and know that He hears our prayers, because of His love for us, which is rooted in His love for the Son.

What a tremendous, elevating thought! God loves you and me! That great American preacher, Dwight L. Moody, was a backwoods sort of man who had a rather slippery grasp of English pronunciation and grammar. It was said of him that he was the only man who could pronounce the word "Jerusalem" as a single syllable. Once, he went to England to preach at that very nexus of western culture, Cambridge University. When the Cambridge students heard that Moody—this uncouth, unlearned American stem-winder—was coming to their university to speak, many of them were outraged. A delegation of students went to the chapel where Moody was to speak and sat down in the front row (in fact, the person who told me this story many years ago was one of those students). They planned to break up the service with heckling and cat-calls.

When Moody came to the platform, the first thing he did was look down at those young men in the front row. Addressing them directly, he said, "Young gentlemen, don't ever think God don't love you, for He do!" They were so startled by Moody's words they forgot to heckle! They just sat there stunned as Moody went on to preach about the love of God for a broken, hurting world. At the end of his sermon, several of these young men—including the man who told me this story—went forward and accepted Christ as their Lord and Savior.

That is the foundation upon which our lives rest: the love of God—a love which we could never earn or deserve, but which is ours because of Jesus. So, my friend in Christ, "don't ever think God don't love you, for He do!"

A Breakthrough Understanding Belief

Jesus finally gets through to His disciples.

16:29–30 *Then Jesus' disciples said, "Now you are speaking clearly and without figures of speech. Now we can see that you know all things and that you do not even need to have anyone ask you questions. This makes us believe that you came from God."*

Speaking without figures of speech, Jesus has just stated the bare facts of the Incarnation: "I came from the Father. I came into the world. I am leaving the world. I am going back to the Father." On hearing this the disciples brightened, nodded their heads and said, "By George, I think we've got it! You really are who you claim to be, the Son of God. Now we have the truth. Your teaching has finally gotten through to us."

Next we read Jesus' response.

16:31–32 *"You believe at last!" Jesus answered. "But a time is coming, and has come, when you will be scattered, each to his own home. You will leave me all alone. Yet I am not alone, for my Father is with me."*

These disciples have announced that they understand and believe at last—and to a limited extent, they do. But Jesus knows how truly limited their understanding and their faith still is, and how their commitment as disciples is about to be stretched to the breaking point. He says to them, in effect, "So you think you know the truth! Well, you have it in your heads, but it still hasn't penetrated to your hearts. Within an hour, Peter, you are going to be slashing away with your sword in my defense, and then a few hours more and you will claim you never heard of me. And the rest of you are going to run like rabbits and hide behind your doors, leaving me to face my trial alone. That is how dependable your faith is right now."

But Jesus concludes on a note of triumph.

16:33 *"I have told you these things, so that in me you may have peace. In this world you will have trouble. But take heart! I have overcome the world."*

Here are amazing words indeed! Just hours before the cross, Jesus claims victory!

And Jesus shares His victory with His friends. "I know you don't get it," He says to them, in effect. "I know you fellas are going to make a lot of mistakes. Things are going to be hard. The world is going to hate you and persecute you. But be of good cheer! I have overcome the world. The victory is already won. I can use your mistakes and your suffering, as well as your little morsel of faith and your fumbling efforts, in order to advance my cause."

That is an amazing strategy—and even an absurd strategy, from a human perspective. It is not the kind of strategy a man like Patton or MacArthur or Schwarzkopf would ever conceive. The strategies of this world focus on being smart, on being sharp, on being strong. But the strategy of God has a different focus altogether. His strategy is to use the foolish things to confound the plans of the wise. He uses the weak things to pull down the fortresses of the strong.

God's strategy for the church was used by the early church in the book of Acts to turn the world upside-down. It's five essential features are: (1) Christians must experience an inner transformation; (2) Christians must rely upon the guidebook to life which God has given, the Bible; (3) Christians must pray, then wait for God to transform their sorrows into joy; (4) Christians must rest upon the foundation of God's unfailing love; and (5) Christians must believe God, offering up to Him their entire lives—mistakes, failings, suffering, weakness and all—and God can then work, turning our weakness into strength.

If the church could rediscover this mighty strategy in our own age, at the end of the twentieth century, it could once again demonstrate the power it had in the first century, when Christians were a dynamic force for change, turning the world upside down. We don't need better promotion and more clever propaganda and more effective fund-raising and more polished spokesmen.

God just wants *us*. He wants us to come as we are and lay ourselves at the feet of Jesus. Our prayer is, "Lord, I'm a mess. I foul up. I fail. I'm weak. I have a lot of problems. And those are my *best* qualifications! Please take me and use me as part of your strategy to reach others, to heal lives, to further your eternal plan."

Jesus has won the victory over the world—and He has won it through the pain, weakness, and humiliation of the cross. That cross is our symbol and standard of victory as we carry out His strategy—a strategy which relies on frail and fallible human beings like you and me.

The world would laugh and say that such a strategy could never succeed. But we know that it cannot fail, for Jesus has already overcome the world!

Chapter Forty-Three

The Longest Prayer

John 17

It was lunchtime on the farm in a little German Mennonite community in the Midwest, circa 1912. As he did at lunchtime every day except Sunday, Papa came in from the fields, set his work-gloves on the kitchen table next to his plate, then washed his hands and the back of his neck at the pump over the kitchen sink.

Mama already had lunch on the table, and the children were sitting in their places, hungrily eyeing the serving dishes. Papa sat down, folded his hands, and bowed his head. Everyone else at the table did likewise. And Papa began to pray.

He blessed the food. He prayed for the harvest. He asked God's blessing on the church and the missionaries. He prayed for old Mr. Enns, who was sick with the grippe. He prayed on and on.

Meanwhile, Papa's four-year-old son, who was sitting at Papa's elbow, was squirming in his chair, peeking at the food and listening to his stomach growl. Finally, the little boy could stand it no longer. *"Papa, zach amen!"* the little boy whispered in Low German. "Papa, say 'Amen'!"

Mama suppressed a gasp. The other children shot furtive glances of horror at their little brother. No one ever interrupted Papa at prayer!

Yet Papa just kept praying as if he didn't hear. After another minute or so, Papa said, "Amen." Then he picked up one of his work gloves from the table beside his plate, reached over, and whacked the little boy in the back of the head—not hard enough to hurt him, but hard enough to send him a message. Then Papa began to eat. Nothing else was said—and the little boy never said *"Papa, zach amen!"* again.

In John 17, we come to another long prayer. This is, in fact, the longest recorded prayer of Jesus. This prayer closes the discourse of our Lord which begins in the Upper Room and which precedes His agony in the shadows of Gethsemane. In this prayer, we can discern the inner thoughts of His mind and learn much of His relationship with the Father.

But there is another sense in which this prayer is long. It is the longest in *scope,* for in this prayer Jesus prays not just for the disciples who were with Him on that night, but for *all* believers who would put their trust in Him over the next twenty centuries—including you and me.

Glorified by the Cross

Our Lord's prayer in John 17 can be segmented into three themes: (1) Jesus prays for Himself, that He may be glorified, verses 1 through 5; (2) Jesus prays for the eleven remaining disciples, verses 6 through 19; and (3) Jesus prays for the whole church, from the first century down through the centuries, that it may be unified. Let's look first at how Jesus prays that He may be glorified.

17:1–5 *After Jesus said this, he looked toward heaven and prayed:*

"Father, the time has come. Glorify your Son, that your Son may glorify you. For you granted him authority over all people that he might give eternal life to all those you have given him. Now this is eternal life: that they may know you, the only true God, and Jesus Christ, whom you have sent. I have brought you glory on earth by completing the work you gave me to do. And now, Father, glorify me in your presence with the glory I had with you before the world began."

Here, Jesus asks to be glorified by means of the cross. This is what He means by the words, "the time has come." Throughout John's gospel, we have seen Jesus moving resolutely and deliberately toward this hour—an hour of crisis and conflict in which Jesus goes alone into a battle with the powers of darkness. When He prays to be glorified through the cross, this is not a selfish prayer, for He immediately adds that His ultimate goal is that, through His death and glorification, He will bring glory to the Father.

What does Jesus mean by "glory"? To glorify means to reveal hidden riches. When the sun appears from behind the clouds, the gloom lifts from the entire landscape, and a dazzling radiance illuminates everything in sight. That is the effect that is suggested by this word "glorify."

When Jesus was sacrificed on the cross, the hidden riches and radiance of God's love and truth became visible to the world. John began his gospel by saying, "The Word became flesh and lived for a while among us. We have seen his glory." What was His glory like? It was "full of grace and truth."[1] Though once they were hidden, all of God's inner qualities of grace and truth became visible when Jesus came. In John 17, Jesus prays that, through the cross, something that has been hidden from the world will now be manifested.

Jesus goes on to state that the cross gives Him the authority to give eternal life to all whom the Father brings to Him. What is eternal life? Not what most of us might define as eternal life—that is, conscious existence that goes on and on. No, Jesus has a much more elevated and sublime definition of eternal life: "Knowing God." That, says Jesus, is *real* life. Having a personal relationship with the Father through His Son is living life to the full. Certainly it is life that will go on forever, but even more importantly, it is a quality of life that is satisfying and elevating beyond measure.

So in these few words, Jesus conveys that the cross reveals both His Lordship and His Saviorhood. He is the source of life to all who come to Him. That is why we sing, in one of the great hymns of our faith,

> In the cross of Christ I glory,
> Towering o'er the wrecks of time;
> All the light of sacred story
> Gathers 'round its head sublime.

By allowing Himself to be nailed to the cross, Jesus sanctified that ugly Roman instrument of torture and turned it into a symbol of God's love and glory. The cross is the bridge which spans the gulf of sin, allowing us to come to God. The cross is the reason Jesus came into this world. As unthinkably horrible as it was, this death by crucifixion was the capstone and crowning glory of all the work Jesus came to do.

Glorified as the Creator

Next, in verse 5, Jesus prays to be glorified by returning to heaven: "And now, Father, glorify me in your presence with the glory I had with you before the world began." As He looks beyond the cross to His resurrection and ascension, Jesus asks the Father to restore to Him the glory He had as Creator, the glory of the eternal God, the glory He set aside when He was poured into human form at the moment of the Incarnation.

Before He came to earth, the Son of God was the Creator, the One who invented all the marvels of the universe. As we sing in the famous hymn,

> Fairest Lord Jesus,
> Ruler of all nature,
> O Thou of God and man, the Son.

He has always possessed the glory of the Creator, the Ruler of all nature. But now, as He goes to the cross, He takes on the glory not only of Creator but of Redeemer. As He prays, He now asks to take up again His lordly, creative glory, because His redemptive work is about to be finished.

Kept and Preserved

Now Jesus makes a transition from His prayer for Himself to His prayer for His disciples by summarizing the work He has just concluded.

17:6–8 *"I have revealed you to those whom you gave me out of the world. They were yours; you gave them to me and they have obeyed your word. Now they know that everything you have given me comes from you. For I gave them the words you gave me and they accepted them. They knew with certainty that I came from you, and they believed that you sent me."*

In verses 9 through 19, Jesus prays for the eleven friends He is leaving behind. This prayer divides into three sections. First, He prays for them because they belong to Him; then He prays that they may be kept from the enemy—that is, from the world and the devil—and finally He prays that they may be sanctified. He opens with words of tender concern.

17:9–11a *"I pray for them. I am not praying for the world, but for those you have given me, for they are yours. All I have is yours, and all you have is mine. And glory has come to me through them. I will remain in the world no longer, but they are still in the world, and I am coming to you."*

Jesus says in this prayer that these disciples belong to Him as a gift from the Father. He has spent more than three years with them, and they are dear friends of His. We can identify with this prayer, because this is the way we pray: first, for those we love, for family and friends, the ones who are closest to our hearts. This doesn't mean Jesus had no concern for the world, because He came to die for the world. But He knows that He is leaving these men behind, and He is concerned for them, so He prays for them, commending them to the Father's care after He has left them.

A Swiss preacher was once visiting in the home of a friend of his, who was a preacher in Scotland. One morning, the Scotsman served his guest kippered herring for breakfast.

"Ah, this is delicious," said the Swiss clergyman after several bites. "But tell me, what does 'kippered' mean?"

" 'Kippered'? Well, that means 'kept' or 'preserved,' " answered the Scotsman.

The Swiss nodded and finished his breakfast. Afterwards, the two clergymen went into the garden to have morning devotions together. First the Scotsman prayed, and then the Swiss. The Swiss preacher surprised the Scot when he prayed to God that his host might be "kept, preserved, and kippered"!

In verses 11 through 13, Jesus prays that His eleven chosen friends will be kept and preserved by the power and authority of God the Father.

17:11b–13 *"Holy Father, protect them by the power of your name—the name you gave me—so that they may be one as we are one. While I was with them, I protected them and kept them safe by that name you gave me. None has been lost except the one doomed to destruction so that Scripture would be fulfilled.*

"I am coming to you now, but I say these things while I am still in the world, so that they may have the full measure of my joy within them."

When Jesus says, "protect them by the power of your name," He is asking God to assume direct responsibility for these men while He is personally absent from them, so that they may be kept by the infinite resources of God. Why do they need to be "kept" by God? So that they will experience true *unity.* "Protect them . . . ," Jesus prays, "so that they may be one as we are one."

While Jesus was with them, He was the unifying factor that bonded them together and guarded them from spiritual danger. That is what He means when He says, "While I was with them, I protected them and kept them safe by that name you gave me." So He is concerned that they remain unified and faithful after He leaves, and that is why He asks the Father to protect them.

Jesus also expresses the fact that He has been successful in His mission among the eleven. They have been called, trained, and mentored, and every one of them has remained faithful—except one, "the one doomed to destruction so that Scripture would be fulfilled." Judas was never truly part of the Twelve; he was there to fulfill the predicted role of traitor. All those who were truly given to Jesus as His own have remained faithful, and as a result, He says they have received the full measure of His own inner joy. He has not lost a single one of the disciples.

The Hostility of the World and the Devil

But what is it that Jesus wants His disciples to be kept and protected from? In the following verses, Jesus says that the danger to the disciples comes from the hostility of the world and the schemes of Satan.

17:14–16 *"I have given them your word and the world has hated them, for they are not of the world any more than I am of the world. My prayer is not that you take them out of the world but that you protect them from the evil one. They are not of the world, even as I am not of it."*

Jesus clearly saw the danger these men faced—both physical danger and spiritual danger. He understood that the world would hate them, fight them, and undermine them every way it could. Why? Because He had entrusted the Word of the Father to them. It is that Word—which would, in coming years be written and compiled as the New Testament—that the enemy wishes to destroy or at least dilute.

The church rests upon the witness and the Word that was given to us by the apostles, these eleven disciples and that apostolic latecomer, the apostle Paul. The only errorless faith is the apostolic faith, the faith that was first set down by those who received it from the lips of Jesus himself. We do not have modern apostles, nor do we need them.

A woman once approached me and said, "Where does it say in the Bible that there are only twelve apostles and no more?" She had been brought up in the Church of Jesus Christ of Latter-Day Saints, which claims to have modern-day apostles. I referred her to the book of Revelation, which depicts the great city that God is building. There, in Revelation 21:14, John writes, "The wall of the city had twelve foundations, and on them were the names of the twelve apostles of the Lamb." The apostles have transmitted to us the pure essence of the Christian faith, and we are linked with them through that one pure faith. They have given us the Word of God, which the Spirit inspired them to write.

The most startling question I have ever been asked was put to me by a pastor at a pastors' conference where I was teaching on expository preaching. This pastor took me aside and said, "What should I do when I have analyzed a passage of Scripture, learned what it means, and found that I do not agree with it?" I almost had to pick myself up off the floor! I replied, "Well, if I found myself in disagreement with Scripture, the first thing I would do is ask myself, 'What is wrong with me that I don't agree with this passage?' "

The problem is never in the Word. Any problem that we have with God's Word is due to our finite understanding, our limitations, and perhaps even our sin, arrogance, and resistance to the truth. The belief that we have a right to pass judgment on God's truth is the deceptive work of the enemy, part of his subtle attack upon the Word. In this passage, Jesus reveals that His disciples will be hated by both the world and by the devil because they speak His truth.

There is a very important practical truth for us to understand in this prayer. Jesus prays, "My prayer is not that you take them out of the world, but that you protect them from the evil one." In other words, Jesus asks God to protect us in the very midst of an evil world. Many Christians over the centuries and right to this day mistakenly take the position that they must completely separate themselves from the world. So they put up walls around themselves and their family to keep the world out. They have no contacts or friendships with non-Christians. As a result, they have no impact on non-Christians.

Jesus makes it clear that we are not to isolate ourselves from the world. We are to be in the world but not of it. As Jesus once told His disciples, "I am sending you out like sheep among wolves."[2] No sensible shepherd would ever do that, because wolves are dangerous animals—and there's nothing a wolf likes better than tender, fresh lamb to eat! With one slash of his teeth, a wolf can rip a sheep's throat wide open. The world can do that to believers, too. We must never forget that this world is a dangerous place, and a hostile environment for those who follow Jesus.

But Jesus has made a commitment to protect us and to be with us and in us. The way to maintain our protection from the hostility of the world is to maintain a close love-relationship with Jesus. We must maintain our contact with the world, yet keep ourselves from the temptations and spiritual dangers of the world.

Behind the world's hostility, Jesus sees the malevolent, manipulative hand of the god of this world, the devil. "My prayer is . . . that you protect them from the evil one," says Jesus. Certainly, He wants them to be protected spiritually. But He also asks for their physical protection, because the devil will destroy God's people any way he can—by luring them into deception and self-destructive sin, or by destroying them physically. Death is Satan's weapon, and Jesus has called him a murderer.

Our assurance is that Satan has no claim on us, anymore than Satan had a claim on Jesus Himself. Satan could not deflect Jesus from His course or alter God's plan. And Satan cannot hurt us if we center our will on His will. "They are not of the world," says Jesus of His followers, "even as I am not of it." God has His shield over us, and Satan has no power to penetrate it.

That doesn't mean we are invulnerable to death. Certainly, all of our Lord's followers must eventually die. Some die young. Some die as martyrs. Some die under circumstances of torture and suffering. But Satan cannot take the life of any Christian before God calls that believer home. Satan cannot disrupt God's timing or penetrate God's protection of the life of a believer.

Sanctified for God's Use

Our Lord's next request for these men is that they may be sanctified.

17:17–19 *"Sanctify them by the truth; your word is truth. As you sent me into the world, I have sent them into the world. For them I sanctify myself, that they too may be truly sanctified."*

"Sanctify" is a religious-sounding word that many people misunderstand. Some people think of it as involving a kind of a religious fumigation where all evil is somehow cleansed from our lives. Some have actually believed that after they have gone through "sanctification," they now were incapable of sinning. But what does "sanctification" mean, according to God's Word? It means to separate or set apart a person or object for a specific purpose and to use it for that intended purpose. In a secular sense, I sanctify my comb when I comb my hair—that is, I use my comb for its intended purpose.

When we talk about people being "sanctified," the principle is exactly the same. We are sanctified people when we are put to our intended use, when we are set apart for our specific, intended purpose. And what purpose were we intended for? What purpose did God have in mind when He made you and me? He made us to be used as instruments of His will. He made us to be miniature manifestations of His character.

When we abuse our bodies with drugs or overeating, or when we fill our minds with impure entertainment, or when we misuse our sexuality, or when we give vent to rage or filthy language, or when we take advantage of other people with unscrupulous business practices—then we are not putting ourselves to the use that God intended. We are not being sanctified. But when we determine to commit ourselves—body, mind, and soul—to God's service, then that is sanctification. In this passage, Our Lord prays that these eleven men will be personally, willingly committed to the work of being used by God.

What's more, He Himself is their model for sanctification. "As you sent me into the world," He says, "I have sent them into the world. For them I sanctify myself, that they too may be truly sanctified." He was sent into a dangerous and broken world to live among hurting, broken people—and now He sends His disciples out into that same dangerous and broken world to carry on His work. And He has exemplified true sanctification for their sakes, so that they will follow His example and sanctify themselves for God's use.

For All Believers

In the closing section of His prayer, Jesus reaches out to embrace all believers of all time, including you and me.

17:20–23 *"My prayer is not for them alone. I pray also for those who will be-lieve in me through their message, that all of them may be one, Father, just as you are in me and I am in you. May they also be in us so that the world may believe that you have sent me. I have given them the glory that you gave me, that they may be one as we are one: I in them and you in me. May they be brought to complete unity to let the world know that you sent me and have loved them even as you have loved me."*

Notice the inclusiveness of these words. Jesus says, in effect, "I do not pray only for these eleven men, but for everyone who will ever believe in me through their word." This prayer encompasses literally millions and millions of believers down through the ages, including you and me. And the primary thrust of this prayer is that we all may be *one,* unified in Christ.

As I travel around the world, I meet people with different languages, dif-ferent cultures, different skin colors than mine, yet the minute we meet, I know they are my brothers and sisters, and that we share a profound inner reality through Jesus Christ. That is the unity for which our Lord prays. He is not speaking of an outward union, of institutional or organizational bonds, or of ecumenism. He is talking about the unique quality of life which is in each of us as believers—a life that comes through the Holy Spirit.

Notice that the focus of this unity is *love:* "May they be brought to com-plete unity," says Jesus, "to let the world know that you sent me and have loved them even as you have loved me." When we love one another, that love produces the unity God desires, and it is that loving unity which witnesses to the world.

Jesus prays for the ultimate destiny of His church next.

17:24 *"Father, I want those you have given me to be with me where I am, and to see my glory, the glory you have given me because you loved me before the creation of the world."*

Here we catch a glimpse of the great cosmic significance of the church. Jesus prays that the church will be with Him, a phrase which refers to the promise given us by the apostle Paul when he wrote, "For the Lord himself will come down from heaven, with a loud command, with the voice of the archangel and with the trumpet call of God, and the dead in Christ will rise first. After that, we who are still alive and are left will be caught up with them in the clouds to meet the Lord in the air."[3] To be with Jesus—that will be heaven! And that is our ultimate destiny, the destiny He prays for when He says, "I want those you have given me to be with me where I am."

When we finally join Jesus to be with Him, we will see His glory. That means that we shall, as the apostle Paul tells us, see Jesus "face to face."[4] As George MacDonald writes,

> Then shall my heart behold thee everywhere.
> The vision rises of a speechless thing,
> A perfectness of bliss beyond compare.
> A time when I nor breathe nor think nor move.
> But I do breathe and think and feel thy love.

That is what it will be. We will become part of the glory, for we shall know fully, and we shall see Jesus face to face.

Jesus concludes in the following verses.

17:25–26 *"Righteous Father, though the world does not know you, I know you, and they know that you have sent me. I have made you known to them, and will continue to make you known in order that the love you have for me may be in them and that I myself may be in them."*

Intimacy with the living God is the key to vitality and fruitfulness. That intimate relationship with God begins with a recognition that Jesus is sent from God. It develops as our awareness of God's power and love grows in us. It finds its deepest expression in our love for one another, which is the source of our unity, the wellspring of our witness to those around us.

Love is the hallmark of the true church. If we want to show the world that we have been with Jesus, that we know Him and we manifest His character, then we must become a community of love. When we do that, then this prayer of Jesus—this long yet beautiful and powerful prayer in John 17—will be answered in your life and in mine.

Chapter Forty-Four

The Way to the Cross

John 18:1–19:3

W e now approach the climax of the drama of the life of Christ. In John 18, we will witness the arrest of Jesus, the denials of Peter, and the trial of Jesus before Pilate—all of which form a prelude to the crucifixion in John 19. You cannot read these two chapters, John 18 and 19, without noting that John has very carefully selected the events he chooses to relate. He leaves out many of the incidents the other gospels include, while supplying details they omit.

In these pages, we will not be focusing on the familiar details of this account, as recorded in the synoptic gospels. Rather, we will focus on the special eyewitness perspective that John gives us in his gospel. While there is no contradiction between the accounts of John and the other gospel writers, it is clear that the apostle John has a specific purpose in mind, a certain impression he wants to create, a certain theme he wishes to underscore in his account. It is John's unique slant on these events that will be our focus in this passage.

Jesus in Control

The chapter opens with the account of our Lord's arrest in the Garden of Gethsemane.

18:1–11 *When he had finished praying* [that is, his prayer for himself and his followers recorded in John 17], *Jesus left with his disciples and crossed the Kidron Valley. On the other side there was an olive grove, and he and his disciples went into it.*

Now Judas, who betrayed him, knew the place, because Jesus had often met there with his disciples. So Judas came to the grove, guiding a detachment of soldiers and some officials from the chief priests and Pharisees. They were carrying torches, lanterns and weapons.

Jesus, knowing all that was going to happen to him, went out and asked them, "Who is it you want?"

"Jesus of Nazareth," they replied.

"I am he," Jesus said. (And Judas the traitor was standing there with them.) When Jesus said, "I am he," they drew back and fell to the ground.

Again he asked them, "Who is it you want?"

And they said, "Jesus of Nazareth."

"I told you that I am he," Jesus answered. "If you are looking for me, then let these men go." This happened so that the words he had spoken would be fulfilled: "I have not lost one of those you gave me."

Then Simon Peter, who had a sword, drew it and struck the high priest's servant, cutting off his right ear. (The servant's name was Malchus.)

Jesus commanded Peter, "Put your sword away! Shall I not drink the cup the Father has given me?"

What is the most striking feature of this account? To me it is not what John records but what he leaves out: the agony of Jesus in the shadows of the Garden of Gethsemane. Each of the other three gospels relates the story of Jesus taking Peter, James, and John aside and asking them to watch and pray with Him in the Garden. Then, going off alone, Jesus knelt and prayed, asking that—if possible—the cup of the cross might pass from Him.

John was there; the other three gospels agree on that fact. Yet John says nothing of the Lord's anguish, His tears, or the bloody sweat that fell from His brow. John does not record His prayer in the garden or of the angel who came to strengthen Him near the end of His ordeal.

The reason John does not mention these incidents is two-fold: (1) These incidents were already well reported in the other three gospels, and (2) these incidents reveal the humanity of Jesus as He faced the most terrible ordeal imaginable. While John does not deny the humanity of Jesus, he wants to focus on the glorification and majesty of the Son of God. He skips past the agony in the Garden to the moment when Jesus—having already worked through His anguish and having already been strengthened by the angel mentioned in the synoptics—strides out in dignity and in full command of events.

Here is the scene John sets for us: Jesus is in the olive grove with His disciples when Judas arrives with a group of soldiers and officials carrying torches, lanterns, and weapons. Judas has brought these enemies to the very haven and sanctuary Jesus had always used as His secret place of prayer.

There is a ridiculous contrast here: On the one hand, we have a detachment of Roman soldiers—probably fifteen or twenty armed men—plus some temple guards and high officials from among the chief priests and Pharisees.

And on the other hand we have . . . an itinerant preacher and eleven very frightened followers. What is wrong with this picture? Why does it take such a large armed detachment to arrest one wandering preacher? What are these people afraid of?

Here, John paints a picture of the absurd contrast between the expectations of these soldiers and the dignified majesty with which our Lord conducted Himself. Jesus meets this armed crowd with a question: "Who is it you want?"

"Jesus of Nazareth," they answer.

"I am he," Jesus replies simply.

Notice that while the other gospels focus on Judas' symbolic act of betrayal—the traitor's kiss—John does not even mention it. John does not want to distract us from the bold, aggressive attitude and actions of Jesus in this drama. The kiss—Judas' prearranged signal to the soldiers to indicate which of the twelve men in the Garden was Jesus—was quite unnecessary. The kiss, which probably took place before Jesus said, "Who is it you want?", had little meaning for Jesus, because He was already on an unalterable collision course with His enemies. There is boldness and determination in His words, "I am he." Jesus willingly, assertively offers Himself to those who will kill Him.

The response of the soldiers to Jesus' reply is either dramatic or comedic, depending on your point of view: They fall down! Some Bible commentators suggest that the reason these men fall over one another is that they are awestruck by Jesus' statement: "I am he." Some say that He is actually speaking the name of God, "I AM," an echo of the Lord's name for Himself, spoken to Moses out of the burning bush in Exodus 3:14. According to these commentators, when Jesus says, "I AM he," a dramatic revelation of His deity takes place which bowls these soldiers off their feet.

While these commentators may be correct, I lean to a different interpretation of this incident. I view it this way: These men have come with a massive force to overpower a man they have heard much about: a Wonder-Worker, a Man who has evaded previous attempts to capture Him and stone Him. These men are going up against the Unknown, a figure about whom many legends have grown—and they are anxious and even fearful. Is this man truly invincible? He has reportedly raised a man from the dead with His word alone! Might He be able to strike a man dead with His word as well? These men didn't know what to expect—and the Unexpected was what made them afraid.

But of all the things they imagine Jesus might do, He does the most unexpected thing of all: He boldly steps forward and hands Himself over to them! He does so in such a commanding way that the soldiers and priests are startled into taking a step back—and they stumble and fall over one another like characters in a slapstick movie! These highly trained, battle-hardened soldiers must feel like utter fools after being felled by the impressive calm and dignity of Jesus.

While they are still in disarray, Jesus again asks them who they want, they again reply, "Jesus of Nazareth," and He responds, "I told you that I am He. If you are looking for me, then let these men go."

The most striking aspect of this scene is the fact that Jesus is in complete control. He gives orders and the soldiers obey Him! They don't lay a hand on Jesus' followers, and so, as John notes, the words Jesus prayed are fulfilled: "I have not lost one of those you gave me."

Though John does not say so, it is clear that the disciples take full advantage of the soldier's bewildered obedience of Jesus' command, and they flee as fast as they can. Peter, however, cannot leave. He has already crawled out on a limb by vowing to defend Jesus to the death. So he draws his sword and aims a blow at the head of the high priest's servant, probably intending to separate the man's head from his collar! But the man ducks and loses only an ear. (John verifies his credentials as an eyewitness by noting that it was the man's *right* ear.)

Peter has proved that he possesses a certain rash courage—but his actions leave him looking like a fool. Jesus orders him to put his sword away and rebukes him for trying to interfere with God's plan. "Shall I not drink the cup the Father has given me?" He says.

Judas Versus Peter

It is significant that the apostle John, as he did in chapter 13, uses the dramatic figures of Judas and Peter for contrast. Here we see Judas at the very depths of treachery, arriving in the Garden and acting as if it is perfectly normal for him to travel in the company of Roman soldiers, chief priests, and Pharisees! And here we see Peter at the very height of his foolhardy courage and impetuousness, leaping to his Lord's defense, yet thwarting the Lord's purposes.

John very deliberately draws this contrast between Judas and Peter. Twice, in verse 2 and verse 5, John refers to Judas as a betrayer. He is cold and calculating. He has thought this entire plan out in advance. And ultimately, he has outwitted himself. It is already too late for Judas. He has passed the point of no return. Soon he would be dead, and his soul would be consigned to eternal night.

But observe Peter—brave, foolhardy, hasty Peter. He makes a stupid mistake—a seemingly irreparable mistake. But Jesus, the Lord of Life, the Lord of Healing, can undo even such a terrible act as the mutilation of the high priest's servant. He picks up the severed ear and, according to the other accounts, places it back on the man's head—and the ear is healed! This is not only a mercy for Malchus, the wounded servant, but for Peter, who would have had to pay for his actions later had not Jesus intervened in a healing way.

Throughout this account, Peter is referred to as "Simon Peter." Wherever the Bible refers to him as "Simon Peter," we see him acting in the flesh, according to his old Simon nature. Simon Peter acts according to his own strength and tries to do things his own way.

But before judging Peter too harshly, we have to confess that there are times when we, too, "lop off an ear" now and then in a misguided attempt to serve our Lord. It might be a sharp word to someone in the church who does not do things as we think they should be done. It might be an argument with a friend or family member, in which we try to debate rather than love that person into the kingdom. There are many ways that we lop off the ears of those around us, both Christians and non-Christians, in an attempt to defend our Lord with worldly methods. As Jesus makes clear to Peter, that is no way to serve Him!

The good news is that Jesus has the power to heal the wounds we cause. He often can undo the mistakes we make. Of course, it is better to stay in tune with our Lord's program right from the beginning. We should take to heart His rebuke to Simon Peter: "Put away your sword! That's not the way I work. I am not here to destroy, to cut people apart. I'm here to put people back together again."

The Beginning of an Avalanche

John now summarizes the trial before the Jewish priests.

18:12–14 *Then the detachment of soldiers with its commander and the Jewish officials arrested Jesus. They bound him and brought him first to Annas, who was the father-in-law of Caiaphas, the high priest that year. Caiaphas was the one who had advised the Jews that it would be good if one man died for the people.*

It is not the trial before the high priest that occupies John's attention, however, but the actions of Peter.

18:15–18 *Simon Peter and another disciple were following Jesus. Because this disciple was known to the high priest, he went with Jesus into the high priest's*

courtyard, but Peter had to wait outside at the door. The other disciple, who
was known to the high priest, came back, spoke to the girl on duty there and
brought Peter in.

"Surely you are not another of this man's disciples?" the girl at the door
asked Peter.

He replied, "I am not."

It was cold, and the servants and officials stood around a fire they had
made to keep warm. Peter also was standing with them, warming himself.

There is undoubtedly a kaleidoscope of emotions swirling through Simon Peter. Certainly, he is concerned about the fate of his Lord. Perhaps he is also resentful and stung by the rebuke of Jesus. And he is probably feeling confused because his well-intentioned but over-zealous efforts have been ineffectual.

The mention of "another disciple," who was on familiar terms with the high priest, is probably a reference to John himself, though we cannot be certain. We know that John was present, along with Mary, the mother of Jesus, at the foot of the cross. So it may well be that John followed Christ throughout His ordeal, including the trials and the crucifixion itself. The fact that John knew the name of Malchus, the high priest's servant, may be an indicator that John was on familiar terms with the high priest, as this other disciple was.

The dialogue between Peter and the young lady by the fire is fascinating. Here is a man who risked his life, drawing his sword in front of a bunch of Roman soldiers and mutilating the servant of the high priest—yet in this scene he is intimidated by the innocent question of a servant girl! "Surely you are not another of this man's disciples?" she asks. Peter had no reason at all to deny it. He was in no danger. But something had been broken inside this man. His former zealous spirit and his courage had completely wilted. So Peter tells a lie.

Here, Peter is like the little boy who mixed up his Scriptures, believing, "A lie is an abomination to the Lord but a very present help in time of trouble!" Many of us agree with that philosophy. The problem is, once you tell one lie it's hard to stop. One lie leads to another. The first lie needs to be backed up and covered by another lie. Soon you are riding an avalanche of lies down a steep and slippery slope. That is what happens to Peter: Here is his first lie, the first snowball of the avalanche. Soon his lies will proliferate until he is completely swept away into the most disastrous experience of his life.

How To Turn the Other Cheek

By contrast, John describes Jesus' behavior before the high priest.

18:19–24 *Meanwhile, the high priest questioned Jesus about his disciples and his teaching.*

"I have spoken openly to the world," Jesus replied, "I always taught in synagogues or at the temple, where all the Jews come together. I said nothing in secret. Why question me? Ask those who heard me. Surely they know what I said."

When Jesus said this, one of the officials nearby struck him in the face. "Is that any way to answer the high priest?" he demanded.

"If I said something wrong," Jesus replied, "testify as to what is wrong. But if I spoke the truth, why did you strike me?" Then Annas sent him, still bound, to Caiaphas the high priest.

As John points out, Annas was not really the high priest but the father-in-law of the high priest. He had been the high priest some years before, but because of his corruption he had been removed from office by the Romans. Now he was the "power behind the throne," so the soldiers brought Jesus to him for a kind of preliminary hearing.

Annas begins this interrogation on a totally illegal basis. Like American law, Jewish law never required anybody to testify against himself, yet that was what Annas did with Jesus. It is interesting to note a contrast here: Peter was asked a fair, simple, nonthreatening question, yet he answered with a lie. Jesus, on trial for His life, is subjected to devious and illegal questioning, yet He replies openly and honestly. His honest answers, however, are only met by contempt and by a violent blow to the face.

Jesus' response is powerfully instructive, especially in light of His teaching in the Sermon on the Mount: "Do not resist an evil person. If someone strikes you on the right cheek, turn to him the other also."[1] Many people interpret this counsel of our Lord's to mean that we are to be living doormats, meekly allowing evil people to wipe their feet on us, never raising a single peep of protest.

But this account in John explains what Jesus meant. While John does not indicate that He literally "turned the other cheek," it is clear that He does so in a figurative sense. After being struck in the face for answering honestly, Jesus does not say, "Hit me again." He turned the other cheek by repeating the very same statement which got Him unjustly struck in the first place! He confronts the injustice of His interrogators. "If I said something wrong," says Jesus, "testify as to what is wrong. But if I spoke the truth, why did you strike me?"

That should be our guide in responding to evil. Jesus does not strike back—but He doesn't let evil go unanswered either. He confronts injustice without resorting to injustice in return. What a beautiful model of both *grace* and *truth* Jesus gives us here!

Two More Denials

Annas saw he was getting nowhere, so he sent Jesus across the courtyard to the hall of Caiaphas, where by this time the Sanhedrin had gathered. Interestingly, John ignores the entire trial before the high priest (we have to turn to the other gospels for that story). Instead, he focuses on the actions of Peter.

18:25–27 *As Simon Peter stood warming himself, he was asked, "Surely you are not another of his disciples?"*

He denied it, saying, "I am not."

One of the high priest's servants, a relative of the man whose ear Peter had cut off, challenged him, "Didn't I see you with him in the olive grove?" Again Peter denied it, and at that moment a rooster began to crow.

This is a highly condensed account, probably covering a period of an hour or more. While warming himself at the fire with the soldiers and servants, Peter's Galilean accent betrays him. He stands out like a Texan in Boston! Everyone instantly knows where he came from. According to the other accounts, he has to deny being a disciple of Jesus because he sounds like one.

By this time Peter is becoming frustrated and rattled. Finally, according to the other accounts, he resorts to blasphemy in order to lend credibility to his lies—and that is when the rooster crows and Peter remembers that Jesus had predicted his denials. According to the other accounts, it was at this same moment that Jesus was led across the courtyard and caught Peter's eye—and the love and compassion in those eyes shattered Peter's soul. He went out into the streets of Jerusalem, weeping bitterly.

What Is Truth?

With verse 28, John turns to the account of Jesus before Pilate.

18:28 *Then the Jews led Jesus from Caiaphas to the palace of the Roman governor. By now it was early in the morning* [probably 4 or 5 o'clock in the morning], *and to avoid ceremonial uncleanness the Jews did not enter the palace; they wanted to be able to eat the Passover.*

This statement has confused many people, because the Passover had actually been eaten the night before. But John refers to the Feast of Unleavened Bread, which accompanied the Passover, and for which it was necessary to keep oneself undefiled from leaven. This is why the Jews did not want to enter the place of a Gentile, because they might touch leaven and be defiled. John draws a clear contrast between the Jews' sanctimonious piousness over ceremonial defilement versus their complete lack of concern about the transgression of sending an innocent man to His death.

18:29–32 *So Pilate came out to them and asked, "What charges are you bringing against this man?"*

"If he were not a criminal," they replied, "we would not have handed him over to you."

Pilate said, "Take him yourselves and judge him by your own law."

"But we have no right to execute anyone," the Jews objected. This happened so that the words Jesus had spoken indicating the kind of death he was going to die would be fulfilled.

The Jews, of course, want Pilate to rubber-stamp their sentence against Jesus without any further hearing. Pilate refuses. He has no fondness for these Jewish leaders, so to exasperate them, he throws it back at them: "Take him yourselves and judge him by your own law." John says God used this situation to bring about what had been predicted a thousand years earlier by the psalmist, who prophesied that Messiah would die not by the Jewish method of stoning but by the Roman method of crucifixion. Psalm 22 describes it very clearly, right down to the piercing of His hands and feet. John is saying that God is in control of all these events, despite human sin and human free will.

18:33–35 *Pilate then went back inside the palace, summoned Jesus and asked him, "Are you the king of the Jews?"*

"Is that your own idea," Jesus asked, "or did others talk to you about me?"

"Do you think I am a Jew?" Pilate replied. "It was your people and your chief priests who handed you over to me. What is it you have done?"

Pilate seems genuinely curious. He looks at Jesus and wonders what is behind all this turmoil. And the question he asks Jesus—like so many prickly questions that have been put to Him during His earthly ministry—is a minefield. There is no safe answer to it. If Jesus says no, then He would be denying His kingship, His messiahship. But if He says yes, then Pilate will assume that He was claiming kingship according to the Jewish standards, and that He was a threat to Caesar. So Jesus answered the question with a question: "How are you asking that question?" He says, in effect. "Are you asking it as a Jew or as a Roman?"

Pilate's response: "Do I look like a Jew? Your own people delivered you to me. What is going on? What did you do?"

Jesus answers Pilate's question directly.

18:36–38a *Jesus said, "My kingdom is not of this world. If it were, my servants would fight to prevent my arrest by the Jews. But now my kingdom is from another place."*

"You are a king, then!" said Pilate.

Jesus answered, "You are right in saying I am a king. In fact, for this reason I was born, and for this I came into the world, to testify to the truth. Everyone on the side of truth listens to me."

"What is truth?" Pilate asked.

This is the critical moment for Pontius Pilate. Jesus tells him, in effect, "Yes, I am a king—but my kingship is not of this world. It is not the kind you think. But I am a king. I was born for the purpose of unveiling the truth, of making people face reality as it truly is. So every person who loves the truth will listen to me."

Pilate responds with a cynical, world-weary answer: "What is truth?" This is the response of a man who has seen many troubles and injustices in his lifetime. He has no confidence in religion or politics or ethics or philosophy. He is a pragmatist, not an idealist—and he is a tired and dispirited pragmatist at that.

Truth Condemned to the Scaffold

Continuing verse 38, John tells what Pilate does next.

18:38b *With this he went out again to the Jews and said, "I find no basis for a charge against him."*

This is a verdict of acquittal. Had Pilate been a man of truth and integrity, he would have dismissed the charges and Jesus would have gone free. Unfortunately, Pilate was not a man of integrity. He was a pragmatic politician.

18:39–40 *"But it is your custom for me to release to you one prisoner at the time of the Passover. Do you want me to release 'the king of the Jews'?"*
They shouted back, "No, not him! Give us Barabbas!" Now Barabbas had taken part in a rebellion.

Barabbas was a terrorist, a violent troublemaker who had caused trouble throughout Jerusalem.

John greatly compresses these events compared with the accounts in the other gospels. In the synoptics we read that Pilate received a warning from his wife to have nothing to do with Jesus, because she had experienced bad dreams about this situation; that Pilate sent Jesus to King Herod for questioning, who then sent Him back to Pilate; that Pilate tried to find some way to release Jesus, but finally caved in to political pressure from the Jewish leaders. Finally, as John records here, Pilate does a terrible thing.

19:1–3 *Then Pilate took Jesus and had him flogged. The soldiers twisted together a crown of thorns and put it on his head. They clothed him in a purple robe and went up to him again and again, saying, "Hail, O king of the Jews!" And they struck him in the face.*

Here is the beginning of the physical torment of our Lord, predicted in Isaiah 53:5: "The punishment that brought us peace was upon him, and by his wounds we are healed." The Romans scourged their victims with leather whips braided around pieces of metal and bone. These whips left our Lord's back in bloody ribbons. A crown of thorns was pressed upon His head, and the soldiers mocked and taunted Him.

We can see in this account that many choices are being made, but only one will is being imposed: the will of God. Pilate chose compromise and political expediency; he ended up with the blood of an innocent man on his hands. The crowd chose an evil man named Barabbas; they ended up crucifying the Son of God. Jesus chose the cross, and the end of His story is that He is crowned King of kings and Lord of lords.

We all make our choices, either to join God or oppose Him. But we cannot overturn God's will. We cannot outwit God. If we choose sin and folly, then we will bear the consequences of our sin and folly—but God will weave our sin and our folly into His plan and bring His own good out of it.

The truth of this account is best summed up in the words of James Russell Lowell, who wrote:

> Truth forever on the scaffold,
>> Wrong forever on the throne.
> Yet that scaffold sways the future,
>> And behind the dim unknown
> Standeth God among the shadows,
>> Keeping watch above His own.

"What is truth?" asks Pilate—and then he condemns the Truth to die, nailed to a Roman scaffold. Truth has been scourged and bloodied. Truth has been mocked. Truth is being led to the hill of Calvary to be pierced and murdered.

But God is keeping watch.

Stay tuned.

Chapter Forty-Five

The Battle on the Hill

John 19:4–42

Beneath the buildings that presently occupy the north side of the temple Mount in Jerusalem, archaeologists have uncovered a pavement stone that bears markings of an ancient game—a game rather like tick-tack-toe—which was played by soldiers of the Roman Empire. Historical researchers have established with almost complete certainty that this stone is the actual pavement upon which the judgement seat of the Roman governors rested. It is the place where Jesus Himself stood as He was unjustly condemned to death by Pilate. This paving stone is called "Gabbatha," which is Hebrew for "pavement."

In chapter 19, John leads us from Gabbatha to Golgotha, from the place where Jesus was condemned to the hill where He was crucified. In these verses, we reach the climax of John's eyewitness account of the life of Jesus.

Pilate and the Mob

As we pick up the scene in chapter 19, we see Pilate bringing Jesus before the multitude. Our Lord is bloodied and torn by the scourging He has suffered, and He wears a crown of thorns and the purple robe which the soldiers placed on Him in mockery of His kingship.

19:4–9a *Once more Pilate came out and said to the Jews, "Look, I am bringing him out to you to let you know that I find no basis for the charge against him." When Jesus came out wearing the crown of thorns and the purple robe, Pilate said to them, "Here is the man!"*

As soon as the chief priests and their officials saw him, they shouted, "Crucify! Crucify!"

But Pilate answered, "You take him and crucify him. As for me, I find no basis for a charge against him."

The Jews insisted, "We have a law, and according to that law he must die, because he claimed to be the Son of God."

When Pilate heard this, he was even more afraid, and he went back inside the palace.

It is clear in this account that Pilate was desperate to find some way to release Jesus. Twice in this passage (and once in chapter 18), he declares that he has found no crime in Him. A comparison of all the gospel accounts reveals Pilate pronounces Jesus guiltless no less than *seven times* during this trial. Pilate knows the right thing to do, but he is unwilling to face the political pressure that a moral and just verdict would bring on him.

Sooner or later, all of us are called upon to make a similar choice—to take a stand for Jesus and for what's right regardless of cost and pressure, or to give in. It is frightening to realize how easily we can slip into the weakness and compromise of Pilate.

In this passage, John also shows us the murderous hatred of the Jewish leaders. First, they manipulate the crowd. They are expert agitators, and they use a technique that agitators and rabble-rousers still employ today: They begin by chanting a slogan. Watch any television newscast of a demonstration by some pressure group, and you will see a simple chant repeated again and again. So as Pilate seeks to acquit and release Jesus, these Jewish leaders start up a chant and the crowd takes it up: "Crucify! Crucify!"

The leaders of this mob also succeed in breaking down the psychology of this superstitious Roman. "We have a law," they say, "and according to that law he must die, because he claimed to be the Son of God." Pilate did not understand the term "Son of God" in the same way the Jews meant it. To them, the term symbolized an act of blasphemy on Jesus' part, since He was claiming equality with the one true God. But Pilate, this pagan governor, believed in many gods and in the possibility that some human beings were actually the children of the gods. To Pilate, the "son of a god" would be a demigod possessing supernatural powers—including the power to take revenge on anyone who displeased him.

Pilate's superstitious heart was struck with fear. Pilate had already judged Jesus as innocent, then had Him subjected to humiliation and torture. If this man really was a son of a god, then what sort of revenge would He take out against Pilate?

Ignorance and Guilt

Caught between the rock of political pressure and the hard place of his superstitious fears, Pilate went back into his palace to question Jesus further.

19:9b–11 *"Where do you come from?" he asked Jesus, but Jesus gave him no answer. "Do you refuse to speak to me?" Pilate said. "Don't you realize I have power either to free you or to crucify you?"*

Jesus answered, "You would have no power over me if it were not given to you from above. Therefore the one who handed me over to you is guilty of a greater sin."

Pilate tries to impress and intimidate Jesus with his own political and judicial power. "Don't you realize I have power either to free you or to crucify you?"

In quiet dignity, our Lord simply replies, "You would have no power over me if it were not given to you from above." Jesus is unimpressed by Pilate's so-called power, since he holds his power only by the permission of God the Father.

We all need to have this view of life and those who hold authority over us. Remember the reply of Jesus when your boss misjudges you, when the professor assigns more reading than you can handle, when the policeman gives you that ticket you don't think you deserve, when the president or the Congress saddles you with higher taxes or bothersome regulations. In a thousand and one circumstances, we need to remember that God is in charge of human life, and no one exercises authority over us that God does not permit.

This perspective helps us as we wrestle with problems of mistreatment, injustice, sorrow, cancer, war, and death—whatever the oppressive or injurious circumstance might be. This is not a perfect world, nor is God engaged at this time in making it a perfect world. Someday, He will dry every eye and heal every hurt and restore the world to its original perfection, as it was before the Fall. But for now, there is injustice and there is pain. Jesus is our model for facing unjust, painful circumstances. Our response to evil circumstances and evil people should be the same as that of Jesus: "You would have no power over me if it were not given to you from above."

Jesus also states before Pilate the principle that to him who knows more, more will be required. He says, "The one who handed me over to you is guilty of the greater sin." Jesus refers, of course, to Caiaphas and the other Jewish leaders who handed Him over to Pilate for judgment and execution. Pilate, Jesus implies, is ignorant of how God operates, and therefore incurs less judgment. But the priests have Moses and the Law, and they are not ignorant of the fact that God demands justice and mercy. Delivering an innocent man over to pagans for crucifixion, says Jesus, is the greater sin.

"We Have No King But Caesar"

In the next scene the wolves close in for the kill.

19:12–16a *From then on, Pilate tried to set Jesus free, but the Jews kept shouting, "If you let this man go, you are no friend of Caesar. Anyone who claims to be a king opposes Caesar."*

When Pilate heard this, he brought Jesus out and sat down on the judge's seat at a place known as The Stone Pavement (which in Aramaic is Gabbatha). It was the day of Preparation of Passover Week, about the sixth hour.

[Note: This does not mean that the Jews were preparing to eat the Passover feast, which they had already done the night before. This refers to the day of preparation for the Sabbath which fell within Passover week, which is why they needed to remain ceremonially undefiled.]

"Here is your king," Pilate said to the Jews.
But they shouted, "Take him away! Take him away! Crucify him!"
"Shall I crucify your king?" Pilate asked.
"We have no king but Caesar," the chief priests answered.
Finally Pilate handed him over to them to be crucified.

John paints this drama in vivid colors. We can almost hear the shouting priests, their faces contorted with anger. We can see the worry lines furrowing the face of this vacillating, compromising Roman politician—so much like the politicians of our own age—as he desperately tries to find a way out of the mess the Jewish leaders have handed him. As Jesus awaits the inevitable outcome with quiet dignity, the priests increase their pressure on Pilate, threatening him with political ruin and suggesting that a move to acquit Jesus would be disloyal to Caesar.

In this account, John strips away the facades, revealing the hypocrisy and lies of these religious leaders. That is how the cross operates in the lives of men and women to this day. God brings the hidden things into the light. The pressures of this climactic event do not create the character flaws we see in Pilate and the Jewish leaders. These pressures only unveil the defective character that has been there all along. As the great coach Vince Lombardi once said, "Character is not made in a crisis; it is only displayed there."

Pilate wants to play the role of a wise, fair, impartial Roman judge, so he engages in a game of wits with these priests, hoping to out-maneuver them and preserve the public peace, his career, and the last remaining shreds of his conscience. What happened to Pilate after these events? Historical records show that he was later dismissed as governor and summoned to Rome to answer charges lodged against him by the Roman emperor Tiberius. On his way, Tiberius suddenly died and the charges against Pilate were dropped. Pilate later went to southern France, which was then known as Gaul. There, according to tradition, he took his own life.

This account clearly shows the Jewish priests for what they are: men of religious ambition rather than faith, eager to be viewed as righteous, but jealous and murderous inside. In their struggle with Pilate, they are driven to reveal their true motives: they are willing to commit murder in order to protect their own selfish interests. In the end, they are forced to openly forswear their loyalty to God and to embrace the hated rule of Caesar: "We have no king but Caesar!"

The closer people come to the cross, the harder they find it to maintain their deception. Jesus had earlier said, "There is nothing concealed that will not be disclosed, or hidden that will not be made known."[1] For all of us, a time must eventually come when God will strip away all pretense and reveal us for what we really are.

"What I Have Written, I Have Written"

Now, with reverent hearts, we venture upon the scene of the crucifixion itself.

19:16b–22 *So the soldiers took charge of Jesus. Carrying his own cross, he went out to The Place of the Skull (which in Aramaic is called Golgotha). Here they crucified him, and him with two others—one on each side and Jesus in the middle.*

Pilate had a notice prepared and fastened to the cross. It read: JESUS OF NAZARETH, THE KING OF THE JEWS. Many of the Jews read this sign, for the place where Jesus was crucified was near the city, and the sign was written in Aramaic, Latin and Greek. The chief priests of the Jews protested to Pilate, "Do not write 'The King of the Jews,' but that this man claimed to be king of the Jews."

Pilate answered, "What I have written, I have written."

John carefully selects certain symbols which underscore the meaning of this soul-wrenching scene. The place to which they led Jesus is called The Place of the Skull. The skull has always symbolized death. I don't think it is an accident that God chooses The Place of the Skull as the setting for His decisive battle with Death.

You can visit the hill of Golgotha today. It stands a few hundred yards outside the Damascus gate of Jerusalem, a low mound with two large excavations on its side which give the appearance of eye sockets. It is fascinating to recall that this hill is the exact spot where Abraham was called to offer his son

Isaac as a sacrifice to God, but was stopped at the last moment by the voice of God. In that Old Testament story, Isaac had to carry the wood for the sacrifice up that hill, just as Jesus had to bear His own cross up that hill.

Today, a road passes along the foot of that hill, following the track of the ancient road where travelers could pass on their way to the city gate. Though it is impossible to know with precision where the crosses were positioned, historians believe they were placed close enough to the road so that every passerby could read the inscription that Pilate ordered placed over the cross.

God wanted the whole world to know that Jesus was indeed King of the Jews, so He put it in Pilate's heart to write the inscription in three languages so no one could miss it. When the Jews tried to force Pilate to change the wording, the Roman governor refused to budge. He had already given these vexatious Jews everything else they demanded, but he would not change the inscription. His reply to the priests carries a weight of double meaning: "What I have written, I have written."

What is the double meaning? Pilate had written the inscription and he was unwilling to change it. But he had also written a page of history, and he was forever unable to change it. And the same is true in your life and mine. You cannot take back words you have said. You cannot take back actions you have taken. What we have written, we have written. This is a sobering truth. The past cannot be changed. It can be forgiven, by God's grace, but it cannot be changed.

The Humiliation of the Cross

John again underscores the Old Testament predictions that were fulfilled in the crucifixion of Jesus.

19:23–24 *When the soldiers crucified Jesus, they took his clothes, dividing them into four shares, one for each of them, with the undergarment remaining. This garment was seamless, woven in one piece from top to bottom.*

"Let's not tear it," they said to one another. "Let's decide by lot who will get it."

This happened that the Scripture might be fulfilled which said,
"They divided my garments among them
and cast lots for my clothing."
So this is what the soldiers did.

Here, John cites Psalm 22, that amazingly precise description of the cruci-fixion of the Messiah, written centuries before the tree which provided the wood of the cross was even a seedling! "They divide my garments among them," says Psalm 22:18, "and cast lots for my clothing." The way John describes the division of the garments and the seamless undergarment of Jesus by the soldiers makes it clear that Jesus hung naked in full public view—thus still more shame and humiliation was heaped on top of torture and murder. Moreover, His nakedness was a fulfillment of Old Testament scripture.

Last Words

John's focus in this account now turns to the words of Jesus from the cross. By comparing the gospel accounts, we learn that there were seven statements Jesus made from the cross, but John selects only three of these statements which reveal the depths of the heart of Jesus as He hung dying.

The first statement of Jesus is one which was burned into John's memory, because it is addressed to Jesus' mother and to John himself.

19:25–27 Near the cross of Jesus stood his mother, his mother's sister, Mary the wife of Clopas, and Mary of Magdala. When Jesus saw his mother there, and the disciple whom he loved standing nearby, he said to his mother, "Dear woman, here is your son," and to the disciple, "Here is your mother." From that time on, this disciple took her into his home.

It is difficult to contemplate the terrible agony of Jesus on the cross, hour after unbearable hour. Yet, despite His agony, the thoughts of Jesus in the last moments of His life were for His mother. As a last will and testament, He commended His mother into the care of His best friend. One wonders about Mary's other four sons: Why didn't they take care of her? John doesn't say. But it is apparent that John could give Mary what they could not—comfort and a compassionate understanding of her sorrow in this terrible hour.

It is also remarkable to note that John's own mother was standing there as well—the second woman mentioned, "his mother's sister." This woman is the mother of James and John, who were cousins of Jesus—yet Jesus commends His own mother to John. The apostle John—"the disciple whom Jesus loved"—accepts the responsibility and takes her into his own home. This is a beautiful insight into the deep humanity of Jesus, His deep human love for His mother, and His deep identification with our own humanity.

Next, John selects a statement which reflects the unrelenting torment and physical agony of the cross.

19:28–29 *Later, knowing that all was now completed, and so that the Scripture would be fulfilled, Jesus said, "I am thirsty." A jar of wine vinegar was there, so they soaked a sponge in it, put the sponge on a stalk of the hyssop plant, and lifted it to Jesus' lips.*

Scientists tell us that thirst is the most agonizing of all pain. Every cell in the body cries out for relief, and the pain grows steadily worse as the body dehydrates. The thirst of the long hours on the cross was accelerated by the loss of blood from His wounds, which further depleted the liquid from His body.

Finally, John records Jesus' last word from the cross, a word of triumph and achievement.

19:30 *When he had received the drink, Jesus said, "It is finished." With that, he bowed his head and gave up his spirit.*

This word, "It is finished," is just one word in the original language. There is a note of relief in that word. The agony is over, the terrible ordeal is finished—and the work is completed.

John does not record those mysterious three hours when the sun hid its face and a strange darkness covered the whole land, when Jesus uttered that haunting cry, "My God, my God, why have you forsaken me?" It was during those hours that Jesus grappled hand to hand with the power of evil.

But now it is over. The foundation of redemption has been laid. It is finished.

That said, Jesus dismisses His spirit from His body. Jesus has made it clear that He does not have to die. No one can take His life from Him against His will. "I have authority to lay it down," He told His Jewish opponents once before, "and authority to take it up again."[2] And Paul tells us He "became obedient to death."[3] That could never be said of you or me, for we have no choice in the matter. When death comes for us, we submit to it. But Jesus did not have to submit to death. He was obedient to death of His own free will, and He willingly dismissed His spirit. His body was still fastened to the cross, but Jesus Himself was gone.

Scripture Fulfilled

John goes on to give another prophecy of Old Testament Scripture being fulfilled.

19:31–37 *Now it was the day of Preparation, and the next day was to be a special Sabbath. Because the Jews did not want the bodies left on the crosses during the Sabbath, they asked Pilate to have the legs broken and the bodies taken down. The soldiers therefore came and broke the legs of the first man who had been crucified with Jesus, and then those of the other. But when they came to Jesus and found that he was already dead, they did not break his legs. Instead, one of the soldiers pierced Jesus' side with a spear, bringing a sudden flow of blood and water. The man who saw it has given testimony, and his testimony is true. He knows that he tells the truth, and he testifies so that you also may believe. These things happened so that the Scripture would be fulfilled: "Not one of his bones will be broken," and, as another Scripture says, "They will look on the one they have pierced."*

The apostle wants us to understand that it is impossible for Scripture to be broken. Again and again in this account, John says this happened or that happened so that Scripture would be fulfilled. In this passage, we have two more such instances.

Further, John wants us to understand that Jesus really was dead. He wants to drive a stake through the heart of that unbiblical theory that Jesus only became unconscious on the cross, and that His resurrection was merely a matter of regaining consciousness in the cool of the tomb. John goes so far as to say, "The man who saw it has given testimony and his testimony is true," meaning that John himself—the eyewitness author of this account—gives his affirmation as if he were swearing an oath in court. He even makes a point of the fact that the plasma and hemoglobin of His blood had separated by the time His side was pierced—a circumstance that only takes place when the circulation has stopped and death has occurred.

Burial

John goes on to record what was done with the body of Jesus.

19:38–40 *Later, Joseph of Arimathea asked Pilate for the body of Jesus. Now Joseph was a disciple of Jesus, but secretly because he feared the Jews. With Pilate's permission, he came and took the body. He was accompanied by Nicodemus, the man who earlier had visited Jesus at night. Nicodemus brought a mixture of myrrh and aloes, about seventy-five pounds. Taking Jesus' body, the two of them wrapped it, with the spices, in strips of linen. This was in accordance with Jewish burial customs.*

Following the death of Jesus, something remarkable happens: Two secret disciples—who were afraid to confess Jesus while He was alive—did in death what they did not have the moral strength and courage to do while Jesus was alive: openly acknowledge that they belonged to Him. It must have taken great boldness for Joseph to go to Pilate and ask for His body, while Nicodemus, at great expense, gathered the burial spices. They lovingly washed and prepared the body of Jesus, wrapping it in a cloth which was saturated with spices. Whereas they had previously been afraid to acknowledge their connection with Jesus, now they didn't care who knew it.

In verses 41 and 42, John concludes his account of the burial of Jesus.

19:41–42 *At the place where Jesus was crucified, there was a garden, and in the garden a new tomb, in which no one had ever been laid. Because it was the Jewish day of Preparation and since the tomb was nearby, they laid Jesus there.*

Again, John selects three highly symbolic details to convey in this portion of the story: (1) Our Lord was buried in a garden; (2) He was buried in a tomb where no one had ever been buried before; (3) and it was near to the cross. What is John conveying by this?

The Bible records that sin began in a garden—the Garden of Eden, where the serpent tempted Eve and Adam and sin had its genesis. Death came into our race in the Garden of Eden. I am convinced John has this long-ago garden in mind as he records that Death has met its conqueror in a garden.

In this garden in Jerusalem was a brand-new tomb where no one had ever lain. Jesus had suffered torture and humiliation beyond belief in the last hours of His life—yet in death He was given the honor of a burial place which had been prepared for His use alone. And it was there, in that special place, that Death was conquered.

It is interesting that John notes that the tomb was near to the cross. There, in that beautiful garden, just a few yards from the site of Jesus' agony, was this tomb. The cross represented failure and despair. Certainly, that was the mood of all those who had followed Jesus throughout His earthly ministry, only to see all their hopes nailed to a Roman cross.

But, though Jesus' friends and followers didn't know it then, the place of resurrection was just a few yards from the place of despair and hopelessness. And so it is with you and me.

Perhaps you are feeling a complete bankruptcy of spirit as you read these words. Perhaps you are in a situation which leaves you feeling hopeless. Perhaps you have been "crucified," unjustly treated by the world around you. Your spirit may be broken, and you see no future ahead of you.

Let me assure you of this: There is a resurrection in your future. You can't see it now, but it is not far away. The empty tomb is near the cross. When you stand close to the cross of Jesus, when you choose to follow the will of God wherever it leads, the Day of Resurrection is just around the corner!

Chapter Forty-Six

The Living Hope

John 20:1–18

Some years after the death of Abraham Lincoln, graverobbers broke into the Lincoln family crypt and stole the body of the sixteenth president. The thieves held the body for ransom, throwing the entire nation into shock and dismay. The crisis ended when the ransom was paid and the body was recovered and buried again, this time under tons of concrete, in Springfield, Illinois.

The shock that the nation felt when the body of Lincoln was stolen is much like that which the followers and friends of Jesus felt when His tomb was discovered to be empty just three days after His death. When we celebrate Easter, we tend to think of that first Easter morning as an event of good news—and it was. But in those first few moments after the empty tomb was discovered, it did not seem like good news at all. It was absolutely *terrible* news: The body of Jesus had been stolen!

An Empty Tomb

Some fifty years had passed between the time of these events and the time that the apostle John took pen in hand to write them down. Yet the narrative of that first Easter in John chapter 20 is as vivid and fresh as the morning news!

20:1–11a *Early on the first day of the week, while it was still dark, Mary of Magdala went to the tomb and saw that the stone had been removed from the entrance. So she came running to Simon Peter and the other disciple, the one Jesus loved, and said, "They have taken the Lord out of the tomb, and we don't know where they have put him!"*

So Peter and the other disciple started for the tomb. Both were running, but the other disciple outran Peter and reached the tomb first. He bent over and looked in at the strips of linen lying there but did not go in. Then Simon Peter, who was behind him, arrived and went into the tomb. He saw the strips of linen lying there, as well as the burial cloth that had been around Jesus'

*head. The cloth was folded up by itself, separate from the linen. Finally the oth-
er disciple, who had reached the tomb first, also went inside. He saw and believed. (They still did not understand from Scripture that Jesus had to rise from
the dead.)*

*Then the disciples went back to their homes, but Mary stood outside the
tomb crying.*

If you go to modern Jerusalem and ask to be shown the tomb of Jesus, you
will be guided to a place called The Church of the Holy Sepulchre, a dismal
and garishly overdecorated palace of a church that squats upon a piece of real
estate which supposedly encompasses both the original site of the cross and of
the tomb. That church was first built by Constantine the Great in 336, then
destroyed by the Persians in 614, then rebuilt and redestroyed several more
times over the centuries, with the present building having been constructed in
1810. It is used by the Roman Catholic Church and various Orthodox groups
as a house of worship.

There is great room for doubt, however, that this is the actual site of the
crucifixion and the tomb. There was a persecution and mass exodus of Christians from Jerusalem in A.D. 66, and then the city was destroyed by the
Romans in A.D. 70. The next several centuries were marked by war and disor-
der, and many walls and landmarks in the area were destroyed. So it is impossible to fix the site of the tomb with any objective certainty. You can visit the
hill of Golgotha and the garden nearby, but the area is sufficiently large and
has been so altered over the years that the best any visitor can say is, "The site
of the cross and the original tomb were located *somewhere* in this area."

Not far away from the Church of the Sepulchre, however, there is a mod-
est and unadorned tomb called the "Garden Tomb." It is certainly the same
type of tomb in which the body of Jesus would have been laid, and—given the
turbulent history of Jerusalem and the uncertainty of the archaeological
remains in the area—it is as good a candidate as any nearby cave for that
honor.

John only focuses on the visit of one woman, Mary of Magdala, to the
tomb of Jesus. According to the other gospel accounts, however, other women
besides Mary went to the tomb on that first Easter morning. When they
arrived—probably around 5:00 or 5:30 a.m.—the sun was just rising and in
the first slanting rays of morning they saw that the mouth of the tomb was
open. The tomb should have been sealed by a great disk-shaped stone weigh-
ing over half a ton, which had been rolled along a groove-like track in front of
the tomb until it covered the opening. But as Mary arrived, she saw that the
stone had been rolled back and the tomb was empty.

Shocked by this discovery, Mary left the other women there and ran to tell Peter and John that the tomb had been plundered and the body of Jesus had been stolen. According to the gospel accounts, the other women stayed and met two angels who told them that Jesus had risen. But Mary left before she could receive that news.

On hearing Mary's news, both Peter and John immediately left for the tomb, running through the streets of Jerusalem and through the Damascus Gate to the tomb. John, the younger of the two, outran Peter and, stooping down, he looked into the tomb. If this was indeed the Garden Tomb, you do have to stoop to look into it. It is a fairly large chamber, hewn out of the rock, with three rock shelves for bodies. As he peered in, John observed the burial cloths still lying on the rock shelf where the body of Jesus had lain.

John does not tell us what he thought at that moment, but he may have thought, at first, that Mary was mistaken. The grave cloths were still lying in their proper place, and—given his awkward vantage point and the poor lighting conditions, it might have appeared to him that the body was still there. Perhaps this is why he did not enter the tomb immediately.

But Peter—as impetuous as always—arrived at the tomb, puffing and gasping from his early morning run, and without waiting for John, scrambled through the opening of the tomb and examined the shelf where the body of Jesus had been placed. The burial cloths John had seen were lying there, as well as the napkin which had cradled Jesus' head.

John Believed

At this point John entered the tomb. According to his own account, when he saw these cloths he "believed." We have to ask, "What did he believe?" Many read these words and assume John is saying that he believed in the resurrection. I used to think so myself. But that interpretation does not explain the next verse: "They still did not understand from Scripture that Jesus had to rise from the dead." This verse suggests that John still did not believe in the resurrection, even after seeing the empty tomb.

So what did John believe? He believed that someone had stolen the body of Jesus! Here's the sequence of events from John's perspective, as I interpret them: Mary finds the empty tomb and runs to tell Peter and John. The apostle John instantly concludes that Mary is distraught and hysterical, and that what she reports is impossible. But something has clearly happened at the tomb of Jesus so he runs to investigate, followed by Peter. Arriving at the tomb, he looks inside, sees the grave clothes, lying on the shelf in the shadows. Just like the old trick of arranging wadded clothing on a bed to give the appearance of someone sleeping, John is fooled into thinking that the body of Jesus is there. Mary, he thinks, was wrong. Then after Peter goes in and calls out that the body is gone, John goes in and "believes"—but he doesn't believe in the resurrection. Rather, he believes Mary's story: the body of Jesus has been stolen!

That being the case, there was nothing for the disciples to do but go home. And that is what they did: "Then the disciples went back to their homes." There is no note of Easter triumph in this account. Instead, a mood of despair and dejection now settles over the scene.

Mary's Despair

John now returns his attention to Mary of Magdala. After the other disciples returned to their homes, she remained at the tomb, weeping in despair. John's account continues.

20:11b–18 *As she wept, she bent over to look into the tomb and saw two angels in white, seated where Jesus' body had been, one at the head and the other at the foot.*

They asked her, "Woman, why are you crying?"

"They have taken my Lord away," she said, "and I don't know where they have put him." At this, she turned around and saw Jesus standing there, but she did not realize that it was Jesus.

"Woman," he said, "why are you crying? Who is it you are looking for?"

Thinking he was the gardener, she said, "Sir, if you have carried him away, tell me where you have put him, and I will get him."

Jesus said to her, "Mary."

She turned toward him and cried out in Aramaic, "Rabboni!" (which means Teacher).

Jesus said, "Do not hold on to me, for I have not yet returned to the Father. Go instead to my brothers and tell them, 'I am returning to my Father and your Father, to my God and your God.' "

Mary of Magdala went to the disciples with the news: "I have seen the Lord!" And she told them that he had said these things to her.

This brief account focuses first on Mary's despair—then on the transformation of her tears of sorrow into tears of joy. Notice that moments before, when Peter and John had searched the tomb, it was empty. Now there are two beings inside, speaking to her. Then a man—Jesus Himself—comes up behind her and speaks to her, and she mistakes Him for the gardener.

Twice, Mary is asked why she is weeping, once by two angels who wait in the tomb, and once by Jesus Himself. There is a gentle rebuke inherent in that twice-asked question, a subtle implication that Mary could and should have known that this is not a time for weeping, but rejoicing. The morning which Jesus repeatedly promised has arrived: It is Easter at last!

One of the striking phenomena of the gospels is the deafness of His disciples to the repeated revelations of Jesus concerning His resurrection. Again and again, He told them He was going to die, then rise again. Perhaps they thought He was speaking figuratively, or perhaps they were so sure of their own conception of Jesus as a conquering Messiah that His words and His meaning rolled off them without making an impression. In any case, despite His repeated predictions, the disciples were completely unprepared for both the tragic reality of Jesus' death and the exhilarating reality of His resurrection.

I cannot criticize Mary for her lack of comprehension. If you and I were in her situation, would we have fared any better? I'm certain we wouldn't. In fact, I believe you and I have already faced—and failed—the same test Mary now finds herself in. We all know the experience of going through a distressing crisis, when the sky seems gray and the landscape dark, when all hope is gone. It is so easy for us to forget the promises of God, to feel sorry for ourselves, to become anxious, upset, and depressed.

Martin Luther once spent three days in a black depression over some problem in his ministry. On the third day, his wife came downstairs dressed in black mourning clothes. "Who has died?" Luther asked in alarm.

"God," she replied.

"What are you saying?!" he sternly rebuked her. "How can you say that God is dead? God cannot die!"

"Oh?" she said. "Well, the way you've been acting, I was sure He had!"

Many of us have been caught in a trap of spiritual despair. I've been there. I'm sure you have, too. And that is where Jesus finds Mary as she weeps outside the opening of the empty tomb.

The Last Adventure

How does Jesus open her eyes? With a single word: "Mary." Mary instantly recognizes His voice, just as any one of us would recognize a loved one's voice on the telephone, speaking our name. Responding in Aramaic, Mary flings herself at His feet and cries, "Rabboni!" (which means "Teacher"). She seizes Him by the feet and again she weeps—but now she weeps tears of joy!

Jesus gently disengages Himself, saying, "Don't hold on to me, for I have not yet returned to the Father." Much theological guesswork has gone into this statement of Jesus. We know from the other gospels that forty days would elapse before He ascended to the Father. He would appear several times to the disciples in Jerusalem, to two disciples on the road to Emmaus, to Peter several times, and to the disciples over seventy miles away at the Lake of Galilee. In all, over five hundred believers saw Him on the mountainside there. Forty days after the resurrection, after the disciples returned to Jerusalem, Jesus ascended from the Mount of Olives and was taken into the heavens, where a cloud received Him out of their sight. Thus, He "returned to the Father."

Jesus does not let her touch Him because a new relationship must now exist between them. "Mary," He says, in effect, "I am leaving, and I can no longer be a source of comfort and consolation to you. An embrace right now would give you emotional support, but I am ascending to the Father soon, and you must transfer your trust and dependence to the Holy Spirit. Now, go tell my brothers this same truth."

Notice that Jesus no longer calls them "my disciples" but "my brothers." Having passed through death, having been glorified by the cross and the tomb and the resurrection, Jesus expresses an even deeper identification with humanity than ever before. The resurrection is not only the Good News, it is the best news imaginable. The death and resurrection of Jesus gives us a glorious hope to fix our eyes upon as we move closer and closer to death's door.

As Ron Ritchie has said, there are three essential questions we all ask of ourselves at one time or another:

"Where do I come from?"

"Why am I here?"

"Is it really necessary to leave?"

Most of us are deeply reluctant to answer "Yes" to the third question. We live out most of our lives in denial of the obvious truth: No one gets out of this world alive. All must pass through death. *All.*

So the hope of the believer's resurrection is clearly one of the central implications of that first Easter. Yet that hope is not even on the minds of Mary and the other disciples at this point in the story. All they could think of was, "Jesus is back again! We haven't lost Him after all! He will always be with us!"

That is the truly good news of Easter. Through two thousand years of Christian history, that truth has sustained the hearts of millions: Jesus can enter our lives and be personally present with us through the trials, pressures, tears, and joys of life right here on earth. We do not have to go through life— or death—alone.

During World War I, a German submarine fired a torpedo into the unarmed British passenger ship *Lusitania,* dooming the ship and nearly 1,200 men, women, and children to a watery grave. One of those doomed passengers was the famous Broadway theater manager Charles Frohman. A survivor of the disaster later reported that Frohman stood on the afterdeck with a number of fellow passengers as the ship was settling into the water. Many of the people were weeping or screaming in panic, but Frohman shouted to them, "Don't fear death, my friends! Death is only a beautiful adventure!"

Jesus has gone before us in that great adventure called death—and He has emerged triumphant on the other side. Now He says to us, "Don't be afraid, for I will be with you, in life and in death. You are never alone."

The continuing, eternal companionship and presence of Jesus alongside us, throughout all the adventures of our lives and even in that last great adventure called death, is our greatest joy and our living hope. That is the message of the first Easter.

Chapter Forty-Seven

The New Commission

John 20:19–31

Do you believe in ghosts?

If so, you are far from alone. Even in our high-tech age of computers, lasers, space shuttles, and genetic engineering, the belief in occult phenomena is at an all-time high. Can the dead return and appear to the living? A recent survey indicates that a majority of people believe that ghosts are real, and over a quarter of those surveyed claimed to have actually had contact with a ghost!

Many people reading the gospels for the first time wonder if the story of the resurrection appearances of Jesus are not ghost stories. For that reason, I want to examine this account in John chapter 20 with extreme care and precision.

A Surprise Visit

We pick up the narrative on the evening of Easter Sunday. The disciples are excited and bewildered by the rumors sweeping Jerusalem that something has happened to the body of Jesus. Four different individuals or groups of individuals already claim to have seen Jesus alive:

(1) Mary Magdalene.

(2) Peter and John.

(3) The other women who were at the tomb and who saw and worshiped Jesus (as recorded in Matthew 28, Mark 16, and Luke 24).

(4) The two believers on the road to Emmaus—Cleopas and probably his wife—to whom Jesus ministered and explained the Scriptures concerning His death and resurrection (see Luke 24).

So it is no wonder the disciples gather together in the evening in the Upper Room to discuss what had happened. John, who was there, gives us this account.

20:19–20 *On the evening of that first day of the week, when the disciples were together, with the doors locked for fear of the Jews, Jesus came and stood*

among them and said, "Peace be with you!" After he said this, he showed them
his hands and side. The disciples were overjoyed when they saw the Lord.

No doubt John's statement that they were glad is true—but other gospel
accounts say their first reaction was not gladness but fear. Luke reports that
when Jesus suddenly appeared in their midst they were frightened. We would
be too if we were visited by someone who was undeniably dead. We would
think we were being visited by a ghost!

Notice the emphasis on the time and the day when Jesus appeared to the
disciples: the evening of the day of the resurrection—that is, Sunday. But
John goes on to stress that it was the "first day of the week." It is significant
that John mentions this fact, for from this time on in the gospels and throughout the book of Acts we find that the disciples began to gather for worship on
the first day of the week. This marks a transition in the lives of these believers: They ceased worshiping on Saturday, the Hebrew Sabbath, and began to
gather for worship on Sunday. Some say this change did not take place until
the third or fourth century, but this account makes it clear that, because of the
profound importance of the resurrection, the disciples began to meet on Sun-
days right from the beginning.

"Peace Be With You!"

The scene John sets for us has the feel of a classic ghost story: The disciples have gathered in the Upper Room, they have locked the doors, they are
afraid. Suddenly, Jesus appears!

Where does Jesus come from? Most of us have grown up with the imagery of Jesus somehow passing through the door—and perhaps He did, but
John does not specifically say so. He says that "Jesus came and stood among
them." From this bone-spare description, it is possible that Jesus suddenly
materialized among them, as if from another dimension.

Or perhaps Jesus was present yet unseen among them, and simply made
Himself visible among them. This possibility would surely be in line with
what He had promised when He said, "For where two or three come together
in my name, there am I with them."[1] This promise is true today, and it may be
the explanation of why He seems to have suddenly, unexpectedly appeared
among the disciples.

John underscores the words of Jesus' greeting: "Peace be with you!" (or,
in the original language, "Shalom"). While it is true that "Shalom" was a standard greeting in the Middle East then as it is today, in this brief account Jesus
greets these disciples no less than *three times* with these words. In the early

section of the Upper Room discourse, He frequently talked about peace. "My peace I leave with you," He said. "My peace I give unto you." Peace—inner serenity that transcends all our circumstances—is our inheritance. That is His resurrection gift to us.

Jesus identifies Himself by showing the disciples His hands and His side, where the wounds of crucifixion are still visible on His body. Surely, this fact answers the charge that this is merely a ghost story, that the disciples were hallucinating. The body in which Jesus appeared was the same body that had been put in the grave. It is a body restored from the dead in a new dimension of existence, bearing upon it the marks of crucifixion.

"Receive the Holy Spirit"

Why did Jesus appear to the disciples? Was it to reassure and comfort them? No. John tells us His purpose in coming to them.

20:21–23 *Again Jesus said, "Peace be with you! As the Father has sent me, I am sending you." And with that he breathed on them and said, "Receive the Holy Spirit. If you forgive anyone his sins, they are forgiven; if you do not forgive them, they are not forgiven."*

There has been much debate over what Jesus means. Many have asked, "If Jesus gives the Holy Spirit to the disciples here, what happens on the day of Pentecost, forty days later? Why did Jesus tell them to wait in Jerusalem until the Spirit came upon them on the day of Pentecost?" Others wonder about these strange words on forgiving and not forgiving sins. There is a mystery at the heart of this account.

We cannot answer these questions unless we carefully observe all that Scripture—especially the New Testament—says about the ministry of the Holy Spirit. The Spirit comes for various purposes and, according to the Scriptures, we must distinguish those purposes. To understand what takes place when Jesus breathes on the disciples and says, "Receive the Holy Spirit," let's first look at the activity of the Spirit in the book of Acts. By understanding how the Spirit comes to us and both *baptizes* us and *fills* us, we can better understand what Jesus means in this passage in John.

Forty days after the events in John 20, when the disciples were gathered in the temple courts, there was a mighty wind and tongues of fire appeared on their heads, and they all began to speak with other tongues under the influence of the Spirit. At His ascension in Acts 1:5, Jesus predicted that the believers would be *baptized* with the Spirit, and in Acts 2:4 it is said that the believers were *filled* with the Spirit and began to speak in other tongues.

The baptism of the Holy Spirit has to do with *identifying* us with the Lord Jesus, and it takes place at conversion. In 1 Corinthians 12:13, for example, Paul says, "For we were all baptized by one Spirit into one body." You do not necessarily feel anything extraordinary take place when you are baptized by the Spirit, when you are added to the body of Christ. You feel at home, you have a sense of belonging to God and His family, but there is not necessarily an emotional tingle when this event takes place.

But the filling of the Spirit is often accompanied by inward and outward manifestations, such as the tongues of fire when the disciples spoke by the Spirit in Acts 2. The filling of the Holy Spirit has to do with certain ministries that the Spirit does through us, and in Acts that filling takes place in preparation for a powerful *witness* to take place (see also Acts 4:8,31; 9:17;13:9). We should always be ready to be filled with the Spirit, so that we can be available to God to do His will. That is why Paul, in Ephesians 5:18, says, "Do not get drunk on wine . . . [but] be filled with the Spirit." The Spirit does in a positive way what strong drink can do to us in a negative way: He takes over and controls. This filling of the Spirit for specific acts of service and witness is also sometimes referred to as an anointing of the Spirit.

As we have seen in previous chapters, Jesus has predicted that a day would come when the Holy Spirit would not only dwell among the disciples but *within each disciple.* I believe that is what takes place here. When Jesus breathes upon them, He imparts to them the gift of the Person of the Spirit. From this moment on, the Spirit no longer comes from without, but from within. There is a clear parallel between what Jesus does with His disciples—breathing upon them, so that the Spirit comes upon them—and the account in Genesis where the Lord God forms the body of man from the dust of the ground and breathes the breath of life into him. Here, in John 20, Jesus breathes new life, the life of the Spirit, into His disciples.

Scripture sometimes calls this indwelling of the Spirit the "seal of the Spirit." This seal is our mark of ownership by God, a sign that we belong to Him and that the Spirit dwells in us. We are sealed by the Spirit the moment we place our trust in Christ. "Having believed," says Paul, "you were marked in him with a seal, the promised Holy Spirit."[2] Just as the coming of the Spirit in the likeness of a dove at His baptism marked the beginning of Jesus' Spirit-led ministry, so His breathing of the Spirit upon these disciples marks the beginning of their ministry—even though the full manifestation of the Spirit in all His power and attributes awaits the day of Pentecost.

What is this Spirit-led ministry? Jesus tells us in the words, "As the Father has sent me, I am sending you." Just as Jesus drew His very life from the

Father, so we are to draw our life from the Son. Just as He was sent into a lost world to touch broken lives and speak the truth and set people free, so are we to do as imitators of Christ. Just as He was empowered by the Spirit, so we will be empowered by the Spirit. He is our model and example. We are His ambassadors.

"If You Forgive . . ."

The central truth of our message to the world is the truth of forgiveness. Our task is to preach repentance, forgiveness, and release from sin and guilt. When people are liberated from guilt, they experience wholeness not only in their spirits, but in their minds, emotions, and even their bodies. Psychologists and medical doctors say that as many as half of those who are mentally and physically sick in hospitals have, as one component of their illness, a deep sense of unforgiven guilt. Our gospel can help people experience not just eternal life but a deep and satisfying sense of wholeness and wellness throughout life.

Jesus affirms the centrality of forgiveness to our message with these words: "If you forgive anyone his sins, they are forgiven; if you do not forgive them, they are not forgiven." These are wondrous words, but they are also mysterious. What does Jesus mean? Is He really saying that we have the power to determine whether people are forgiven or unforgiven? This is an issue we need to examine closely and carefully.

Forgiveness is a beautiful cleansing experience. It is a blessing I avail myself of every single day without fail. Each morning, I rise and step into the shower and I not only wash my body, I wash my spirit and my soul! I think back over the previous day and week, and I confess my sins. I ask God to bring to my mind any sharp words, loveless deeds, selfish attitudes, or malicious thoughts. While rinsing off, I receive God's forgiveness and He washes away every residue of guilt from my conscious and subconscious mind. Using the shower as a confessional is a good daily habit, but we must not forget to claim that forgiveness anew, moment by moment, a dozen times a day, as the need arises.

Not only do we claim God's forgiveness, we offer it to people. "If you forgive anyone his sins," says Jesus, "they are forgiven; if you do not forgive them, they are not forgiven." I have practiced this statement of Jesus many times. This does not mean I have authority to say to one, "You are forgiven," and to another, "You are not." Some have interpreted it that way, saying that priests are empowered to forgive some sins and let others stand unforgiven.

But Jesus is not saying that. He is telling us we have the power to declare the gospel of the forgiveness of sin, and if any man, woman, or child receives

Jesus as Lord and Savior upon hearing our gospel, we have the authority to say, "Your sins are forgiven." I have done that. I have said to people who were deeply troubled over their past and who prayed and asked the Lord into their lives, "Rejoice, your sins are forgiven."

On the other hand, if someone refuses to believe, or merely pretends to believe, and his life shows no sign of change, we are authorized to say to him, "You have not yet been forgiven of your sins. The struggle in your life can be traced to the fact that you have never truly believed and trusted in Jesus Christ." That is why John stresses this statement so strongly here.

The Skeptic

John now turns to the account of the man history has come to know (perhaps a little unfairly) as "Doubting Thomas."

20:24–25 *Now Thomas (called Didymus), one of the Twelve, was not with the disciples when Jesus came. When the other disciples told him that they had seen the Lord, he declared, "Unless I see the nail marks in his hands and put my finger where the nails were, and put my hand into his side, I will not believe it."*

That text, by the way, is a preacher's dream! It reveals the tremendous importance of not missing the Sunday evening service! That's what Thomas did. He was not there at the Sunday evening service and had to go through a week of pain and heartache before he believed that Jesus was risen from the dead.

Thomas has taken a lot of criticism over the years for his hard-nosed skepticism about the resurrection. But I am personally grateful to Thomas for his courage and outspokenness in voicing the doubts many of us feel, yet are too timid to speak aloud. Thomas was not expressing atheistic unbelief. Rather, he wanted to examine the evidence for himself, so that he could know beyond doubt that he was not being misled. Once convinced, he became a witness and an apostle to all who would later doubt.

We would all do well to practice a little bit of Thomas-like skepticism in matters of faith. As A. W. Tozer writes in *The Root of the Righteous,*

> In our constant struggle to believe, we are likely to over-
> look the simple fact that a bit of healthy disbelief is sometimes
> as needful as faith to the welfare of our souls.

I would go further and say that we would do well to culti-
vate a reverent skepticism. It will keep us out of a thousand
bogs and quagmires where others who lack it sometimes find
themselves. It is no sin to doubt some things, but it may be fatal to believe everything. . . .

Faith never means gullibility. The man who believes everything is as far from God as the man who refuses to believe
anything. . . . I have met Christians with no more discrimina-
tion than the ostrich. Because they must believe certain things,
they feel that they must believe everything. Because they are
called upon to accept the invisible they go right on to accept
the incredible. God can and does work miracles; ergo, everything that passes for a miracle must be of God. God has spoken to men, therefore every man who claims to have had a
revelation from God must be accepted as a prophet. . . . This
is the dangerous logic of the gullible Christian. And it can be
as injurious as unbelief itself.[3]

So a little doubt, a little "reverent skepticism," is a healthy thing in a
believer. Still, I think it is clear that Thomas took his skepticism too far.
Notice how he puts it: "Unless I see the nail marks in his hands and put my
finger where the nails were, and put my hand into his side, I will not believe
it." There is a note of stubbornness in these words. He wants to set the terms
of the evidence. If the evidence for the resurrection does not match his crite-
ria, then he will reject it.

You also catch a glimpse of Thomas's pessimistic streak. No one would
ever mistake Thomas for Norman Vincent Peale or Robert Schuller. For him
the glass is clearly half-empty, not half-filled. He is the one who said, in John
11, "Let us also go [with Jesus to Bethany], that we may die with him." The
man is a born pessimist!

Later, when Jesus appears again, He rebukes Thomas—not for being
careful, not for being reverently skeptical, but for going too far and rejecting
perfectly good evidence, and for being pessimistic about the promises Jesus
had made to come back after His death.

What was the perfectly good evidence that Thomas rejected? *Corroborated testimony,* a whole parade of witnesses whose testimony would have
convinced any jury in the land! Moreover, this testimony came not from a
bunch of strangers, but from Thomas's own brothers and sisters in Christ,
people he could and should have trusted, people who had seen Jesus face to
face, who had touched Him and spoken with Him. Jesus rebuked Thomas
because he took his skepticism one or two steps too far!

We see the Lord's reappearance and His rebuke—His tender, loving, patient rebuke!—of Thomas here.

20:26–29 *A week later his disciples were in the house again, and Thomas was with them. Though the doors were locked, Jesus came and stood among them and said, "Peace be with you!" Then he said to Thomas, "Put your finger here; see my hands. Reach out your hand and put it into my side. Stop doubting and believe."*

Thomas said to him, "My Lord and my God!"

Then Jesus told him, "Because you have seen me, you have believed; blessed are those who have not seen and yet have believed."

John does not say whether Thomas actually reached out and touched Jesus, examining the evidence as he said he would. Many people read this account and conclude that Thomas simply saw Jesus and fell to his knees in complete belief. Perhaps he did.

But I believe Thomas actually reached out and examined the evidence. Jesus graciously invited him to do so, without scolding or punishing him for his pessimistic unbelief, and I think Thomas accepted that invitation. But I also believe one touch was enough. With that touch, this disciple was flooded with the realization of how foolish and stubborn he has been not to believe the credible testimony of his friends. He confesses this realization immediately with words that affirm the complete sovereignty and deity of Jesus, "My Lord and my God." Thomas not only believes Jesus is alive, he believes He is God!

In Jesus' reply, we see that His purposes are not only immediate but eternal. He looks beyond the people in that room, and He sees the faces of believers who will come after them—centuries and centuries of believers. He sees your face and mine. And He says, "Because you have seen me, Thomas, you have believed. But blessed are those who have not seen and yet have believed." This is a blessing Jesus pronounces on you and me and all who have placed their faith in Jesus without ever having the opportunity to touch the physical evidence of the resurrection with our fingers. We have heard the testimony, and the testimony has convinced us: Jesus is alive. He is our Lord and our God.

The Invitation

Now John sums up the evidence he has presented in his gospel.

20:30–31 *Jesus did many other miraculous signs in the presence of his disciples, which are not recorded in this book. But these are written that you may believe that Jesus is the Christ [the Messiah], the Son of God, and that by believing you may have life in his name.*

Here is John's purpose in writing his eyewitness memoir of the life of Christ. Here is his evidence for the Christian faith, carefully selected from among the abundance of acts and works and words of our Lord. John's purpose is to inspire belief—the saving belief that results in eternal life for the one who believes.

If, like Thomas, you have withheld your belief until the evidence is in, then I pray that you will make your decision now. The evidence is clear. It is profound. It is amply corroborated. Jesus died for you. He was raised again. He lives today. He offers life and forgiveness to all who receive Him and believe in His name.

He invites you to step closer, to touch Him, to place your trust in Him. I urge you to accept His invitation today.

Chapter Forty-Eight

By the Sea

John 21

Mark Twain was an avid fisherman and an even more avid teller of fish stories. Once, while spending a few weeks at a lakeside lodge in the Maine woods, Twain was relaxing beside a crackling fire. A big, rugged stranger in a plaid flannel shirt and denim britches had come into the lodge and was sitting in the chair across from him.

"You look like a fisherman to me," said Twain, eager as always to strike up a conversation.

"Ayuh," said the other man. "I fish some. 'Tain't fishin' season now, though."

"Fishing season!" laughed Twain. "Fish'll bite in season and out. If fish don't care what season it is, neither do I!"

"Oh?" said the other man, perking up and leaning forward. "You take a catch out of the lake today?"

"A catch?" said Twain proudly. "More like a haul! I've got it on ice in the larder!" And he proceeded to launch into an embellished recounting of all the fish he had taken in. The more Twain exaggerated, the more interested the other man became.

"Ayuh," said the man at last, "you certainly did have yerself a good day at the lake. Seems an awful shame I have to spoil it."

"Spoil it?" said Twain. "What do you mean? I just—Say, who are you, anyway?"

The man grinned, turned over the lapel of his flannel shirt, and revealed a gleaming badge. "I'm the state game warden, sir. Now, just who might you be?"

"Me?" Twain said sheepishly. "Why, I'm the biggest liar in the whole United States!"

The apostle John has chosen to close his gospel with a fish story—an even bigger and more amazing fish story than the one that landed Mark Twain in trouble with the game warden. But John's fish story is true. It is significant. And it packs a powerful weight of meaning for your life and mine.

A Big Catch

From this vantage point, having reached the final chapter, we can see that John's gospel reads like a modern novel. It is a story of rising conflict, in which the hero battles against overwhelming odds and intense opposition. It reaches its dramatic climax at the moment of the crucifixion, when it seems all is lost and the hero's quest has ended in failure. But then comes the triumphant and unexpected resolution of the climax: the resurrection of Jesus. But even though the key conflict of this drama has been resolved, there are important plot threads that need to be tied up. That is what John does in chapter 21.

The scene is the Sea of Galilee, to which the disciples have come in obedience to Jesus' word to Mary Magdalene after He rose from the dead: "Go and tell my brothers to go to Galilee; there they will see me."[1]

21:1–3 *Afterward Jesus appeared again to his disciples by the Sea of Tiberias. It happened this way: Simon Peter, Thomas (called Didymus), Nathanael from Cana in Galilee, the sons of Zebedee, and two other disciples were together. "I'm going out to fish," Simon Peter told them, and they said, "We'll go with you." So they went out and got into the boat, but that night they caught nothing.*

These are my kind of fishermen! They caught nothing!

Much of the fishing in the Sea of Galilee was done at night in those days, as it is often done today. Fishermen used torches to attract the fish to the boat, then netted them. Although they were expert fishermen, these disciples had labored throughout the night and had caught nothing—certainly an unusual and disappointing experience for them.

Yet, as this account makes clear, it was the Lord's intention that they catch nothing on this occasion. He had something to teach them, a lesson which involved a symbol that was very familiar to these men: fishing. Failure is a very demoralizing experience, and these men had failed miserably at the one thing they did best. Though failure is a painful experience, there is nothing like failure to get a person's undivided attention and to render that person teachable.

As the account continues John shows how our Lord plans to use this experience of failure in the lives of His friends.

21:4–8 *Early in the morning, Jesus stood on the shore, but the disciples did not realize that it was Jesus.*

He called out to them, "Friends, haven't you any fish?"

"No," they answered.

He said, "Throw your net on the right side of the boat and you will find some." When they did, they were unable to haul the net in because of the large number of fish.

Then the disciple whom Jesus loved said to Peter, "It is the Lord!" As soon as Simon Peter heard him say, "It is the Lord," he wrapped his outer garment around him (for he had taken it off) and jumped into the water. The other disciples followed in the boat, towing the net full of fish, for they were not far from shore, about a hundred yards.

Some Bible commentators suggest that this was a natural occurrence, that Jesus could somehow see a school of fish swimming past the right side of the boat that the fishermen themselves could not see. Such a suggestion is impossible to accept. Jesus could hardly have seen a school of fish under the water from a distance of a hundred yards—the length of a football field! The slanting rays of early dawn would make it even more difficult to see into the waters from the shore. It seems clear that an exercise of supernatural power takes place here. I'm convinced that our Lord summoned these fish to be there—and the fish obeyed their Lord without hesitation, filling the nets of the disciples.

The enormous catch they found on the right side of the boat was a sign to the disciples that the Lord was at work—and that was what sparked recognition in the eyes of "the disciple whom Jesus loved," the apostle John. When their nets filled with fish, John's mind must have flashed back to the event recorded in Luke 5, when Jesus commanded Peter, John, and James to let down their nets and they caught so many fish their nets broke and their boat began to sink. As he was having this *deja vu*-like experience, John realized that such an occurrence could only be the work of one man, so he shouted, "It is the Lord!" In response, Peter wrapped his robe about him, leaped into the sea, and swam for shore. (It seems, from this account, that John is quicker to understand, but Peter is quicker to *act*.)

Lessons for Fisherman

The meaning of this event becomes clear in the following verses.

21:9–14 *When they landed, they saw a fire of burning coals there with fish on it, and some bread.*

Jesus said to them, "Bring some of the fish you have just caught."

> *Simon Peter climbed aboard and dragged the net ashore. It was full of large fish, 153, but even with so many the net was not torn. Jesus said to them. "Come and have breakfast." None of the disciples dared ask him, "Who are you?" They knew it was the Lord. Jesus came, took the bread and gave it to them, and did the same with the fish. This was now the third time Jesus appeared to his disciples after he was raised from the dead.*

When Jesus first called the disciples, He used the symbol of fishing to describe the job He had for them: "Come, follow me," He said, "and I will make you fishers of men."[2] Here, at the end of John's gospel, we see several symbolic parallels to this concept of "fishing for men."

First, when the disciples landed, the charcoal fire was already lit, and fish and bread were lying there. This symbolizes the fact that all we have comes from the hand of God. We did not provide this world or the food that is in it. We do not provide the opportunities that come our way. Many of them come to us seemingly "out of the blue." But behind it all is the hand of God, working behind the scenes. We live and work and minister by His grace and according to His good will.

Second, Jesus then invites the disciples to bring the fish they have caught. This is a beautiful picture of the way God works in partnership with people. As I read through the Scriptures, I am continually astonished at the privilege God gives us of being co-laborers with Him. Human labor was involved in almost all of the miracles of Jesus—when He turned water into wine, when He multiplied the bread and fish to feed the multitude, and even when He raised Lazarus from the dead. God could easily do it all Himself, but He extends to us the great privilege of being in partnership with Him.

Third, the work of fishing blesses the fisherman. As Jesus gathered these men on the shore, He invited them to feast with Him. Undoubtedly, this simple meal of loaves and fishes reminded them of His miraculous feeding of the multitudes. As they ate the combined food which both Jesus and they themselves had provided, their physical hunger left them, and they felt satisfied and blessed.

Fourth, and most important: Success is impossible without acknowledging and relying upon God's power. As the psalmist wrote, "Unless the Lord builds the house, its builders labor in vain. Unless the Lord watches over the city, the watchmen stand guard in vain."[3] When the disciples cast their nets on the left side of the boat, according to their own insight, they caught nothing. When they cast their nets according to the Lord's direction, the catch exceeded their wildest dreams. The same is true in all our endeavors for God, and especially in our efforts to witness and win others for Christ. If we go in our own strength, we are doomed to fail. If we go in God's power and God's will, He will take care of the results.

"Do You Love Me?"

John now turns to the theme of shepherding, and to the restoration of Peter. In this scene, John ties up the plot threads left dangling after Peter's three-fold denial of Christ.

21:15–17 *When they had finished eating, Jesus said to Simon Peter, "Simon son of John, do you truly love me more than these?"*

"Yes, Lord," he said, "you know that I love you."

Jesus said, "Feed my lambs."

Again, Jesus said, "Simon son of John, do you truly love me?"

He answered, "Yes, Lord, you know that I love you."

Jesus said, "Take care of my sheep."

The third time he said to him, "Simon son of John, do you love me?"

Peter was hurt because Jesus asked him the third time, "Do you love me?"
He said, "Lord, you know all things; you know that I love you."

Jesus said, "Feed my sheep."

Jesus clearly intends to cancel out Peter's three-fold denial by inviting Peter to make a three-fold expression of love for his Lord. It is interesting to note the parallels between this scene and the incident of the three denials. Both events took place around a charcoal fire. In both of these accounts, Peter is called "Simon Peter" (the Spirit of God, who inspired the writing of this gospel through John, always uses the name "Simon" to indicate the natural Peter, the old Peter, the Peter who vacillates, not Peter the Rocklike Apostle). In both accounts, Peter is questioned three times, and must answer three times—either three denials or three affirmations of his love.

It is important to note the specific language that is used in this story. In the English translation, we see only the word *love* used by Jesus and Peter. But in the original language, we see two different words for love: *agape,* meaning the decision a person makes to commit oneself completely to another person's benefit; and *phileo,* which means a deep but natural affection, like brotherly or family love. The first two times He asks the question, Jesus asks, "Simon, do you truly *agape* me?" and Peter answers, "Yes, Lord, you know that I *phileo* you." The third time Jesus asks the question, He descends to Peter's word and asks, "Simon, do you *phileo* me?" and Peter again answers with the word *phi-*

leo. Peter's old boastful bravado has been destroyed, and in its place we find *shame.*

This is an extremely significant issue, because it shows us the state of Peter's heart and his own view of himself. Before the crisis of the cross, Peter stated his loyalty and love for Jesus again and again in ardent, zealous terms. Then, in the depths of the crisis, when all the chips were down, Peter's bravery turned to Jello. Now, Peter is ashamed and broken, and he cannot bring himself to say, "I *agape* you, Lord."

Notice, too, Jesus' first question—a question which has sparked controversy among Bible commentators: "Simon son of John, do you truly love me more than these?" The commentators have long debated what Jesus means by "these." Some insist Jesus is asking, "Do you love me more than these fish? Or these boats?" In other words, "Do you love me more than your fishing business? Are you willing to leave all this behind in order to follow me and be my apostle?"

But it seems to me much more likely that Jesus is asking, "Do you love me more than these men love me?" Remember that before he denied Jesus, Peter had claimed to love Jesus more than all the other disciples. "All men will forsake you, Lord, but I will lay down my life for you," he had said. Clearly, Peter has regarded himself as more faithful and more committed than the others disciples. He boasted that even if all his other disciples deserted Him, he would always be there. As it turned out, Peter's defection was the worst. He even sealed it with an oath.

Peter has learned some painful but valuable lessons. He has seen his own weakness, and his pride has been shattered. Moreover, he has learned not to judge himself in relationship to the others. Now, he only looks within—and he is no longer smugly satisfied with what he sees there. When Jesus says, "Do you love me more than these other men?"—a pointed invitation to compare his love with that of the other disciples!—poor humbled Peter reads his own heart and says simply, "Yes, Lord, you know that I *phileo*-love you." Three times he gives that answer, and he makes no mention of the others.

Another lesson Peter has learned: He has learned to read the heart the Shepherd. Once, he thought he was serving his Lord by attacking Jesus' enemies with a sword. But now he knows he has a higher calling than that of an armed warrior. He has been called to be an assistant shepherd to the Great Shepherd. He has been given the responsibility to feed the sheep of Jesus.

The Cost of Following Jesus

Jesus has just restored Peter as a disciple, and He has made him an apostle and a pastor, charging him with the responsibility to feed His sheep. Now He goes on to reveal to Peter just where he will have to go and what price he will have to pay to follow Jesus Christ.

21:18–19 *"I tell you the truth, when you were younger you dressed yourself and went where you wanted; but when you are old you will stretch out your hands, and someone else will dress you and lead you where you do not want to go." Jesus said this to indicate the kind of death by which Peter would glorify God. Then he said to him, "Follow me!"*

For Peter, following Jesus would ultimately involve pain, privation, and a hard, gruesome death. This prediction of our Lord's was historically fulfilled. This book was almost certainly written after the death of Peter, and John appears to assume his readers are aware of the manner of Peter's death. Eusebius, the church historian, tells us that when Peter went to Rome near the close of his life, he was imprisoned, his hands were bound, and he was led out to the place of execution and crucified. At his own request he was crucified upside down because he did not feel worthy to die in the same way that his Lord died.

Peter once promised that he would lay down his life for Jesus. Here, Jesus prophetically says to Peter, in effect, "Yes, Peter, you will keep your promise and you will lay down your life for me. But you will not die for me as you thought you would, with a sword in your hand, defending me against the Jewish priests and the Roman soldiers. You will be bound and led out to die just as I was. You will lay down your life, not in battle, but in martyrdom."

"You Must Follow Me"

But Peter still has more to learn.

21:20–23 *Peter turned and saw that the disciple whom Jesus loved was following them. (This was the one who had leaned back against Jesus at the supper and had said, "Lord, who is going to betray you?") When Peter saw him, he asked, "Lord, what about him?"*

Jesus answered, "If I want him to remain alive until I return, what is that to you? You must follow me." Because of this, the rumor spread among the brothers that this disciple would not die. But Jesus did not say that he would not die; he only said, "If I want him to remain alive until I return, what is that to you?"

Peter wants to know what God has planned for John's life. But Jesus wants Peter to mind his own business. He says, "Don't worry about what others are doing. Just be faithful to what God has shown *you,* to what God is doing in *your* life."

Here we see the beginnings of a problem that continues to afflict the church today: competition and rivalry between brothers and sisters in Christ. When the church behaves like the world, warring and struggling within itself, faction contending with faction for power, the gospel is diminished and Satan—not God—becomes exalted!

In a symphony orchestra, a violinist cannot go around to the trombonist and say, "Play louder here." The cymbalist cannot go to the oboist and demand, "More pianissimo!" That is the conductor's job, and the entire orchestra must keep focused on the conductor or the result will be discord! If everyone plays his or her own part and keeps watching the conductor, the result will be beautiful, harmonious music.

This is how the church should operate, how it *must* operate! We are each to use and fulfill the gifts God has given us—not focus on the other person and how he or she is using his or her gifts. It's God's job to put all of our individual notes together and make music, not ours.

It is amazing to think how effective the church would become if we would all follow the word that Jesus gave to Peter: "Don't mind your brother's business. Just follow me."

The End—and the Beginning

In the final verses John brings his gospel to a fitting close.

21:24–25 *This is the disciple who testifies to these things and who wrote them down. We know that his testimony is true.*

Jesus did many other things as well. If every one of them were written down, I suppose that even the whole world would not have room for the books that would be written.

The wording of these closing words suggests that they were written partly by John and partly by those who were associated with him, probably in Ephesus. It is John who writes, "This is the disciple who testifies to these things and who wrote them down." This is John's last word in his eyewitness account of what Jesus said and did.

But those who were associated with him—possibly the elders of the church in Ephesus—added their own postscript to John's gospel: "We know that his testimony is true."

Whether in John's voice or the voice of the elders, the gospel ends with the statement that Jesus did many other things—so many wonderful, intriguing things that if they were all recorded, the accounts would have so intrigued men that they would have endlessly written and filled all the libraries of the world! What a marvelous life our Lord lived. Though we have received only four condensed accounts of that amazing life—the gospels of Matthew, Mark, Luke, and John—we have all the truth about Jesus that we need. We have enough of the words and the works of Jesus to convince us, to guide us, to inspire us, to encourage us, to empower us, to lead us to saving belief in Him.

Here, John closes his account of the greatest story ever told, the greatest life ever lived. This is the end of John's gospel, but it is just the beginning of the story of the church—a story that will continue in the book of Acts, and beyond. From that shore in Galilee, where Peter and John and the other disciples share one last meal with their Master, these men will go out and change the world. The fisherman will become a shepherd. The disciple whom Jesus loved will become an evangelist. A handful of believers will become a church.

Baptized and filled with the Holy Spirit, that church will grow: On the day of Pentecost, it swells to 3,000 in the city of Jerusalem. Soon afterward, it numbers in the thousands and tens of thousands in Judea and Samaria and Galilee. More years pass, and it spreads to the uttermost parts of the earth, numbering in the millions.

The story that begins in John 1:1 with the words, "In the beginning . . ." does not end here in John 21:25. It continues, an unbroken, unending story, sweeping through twenty centuries of history. It embraces your life and mine. The same Lord who was present with these disciples is present with you and me today. This same Spirit whom Jesus breathed upon them in the Upper Room is within you and me today. The same power that propelled them in ministry to a lost and broken world is available to us today.

Jesus did many things in His lifetime, so many that John and the other evangelists could not hope to record them all. And He is still at work today. He is at work though you and me. Let us go out into our neighborhoods and our workplaces and our world. May our touch be a healing touch; may our witness be bold and unashamed; and may our love be pure and selfless as we write the next chapter in this great saga with our prayers, with our obedience, with our love, and with our lives.

Notes

Chapter 1: **Who Is Jesus?**

1. John 10:10.
2. John 14:26.
3. Hebrews 1:1–2.
4. 1 Corinthians 2:7.
5. For Old Testament passages which likely refer to the pre-incarnate Son, see Genesis 12:7;17:1; Psalm 2:12; 34:7; Daniel 10:5ff.
6. Genesis 1:26.
7. C. S. Lewis, *Miracles,* collected in *The Best of C. S. Lewis* (Washington, D.C.: Canon Press, 1969), p. 283.
8. J. I. Packer, *Knowing God* (Downers Grove, Ill.: InterVarsity Press, 1975), p. 58.
9. Colossians 1:17.
10. Hebrews 1:3.
11. 1 John 5:12.

Chapter 2: **Hello, Darkness**

1. 2 Corinthians 4:5.
2. Zechariah 13:6.
3. 1 John 5:12.

Chapter 3: **The *Real* Jesus**

1. Dick Van Dyke, *Faith, Hope and Hilarity: The Child's Eye View of Religion,* ed. by Ray Parker (Garden City, NY: Doubleday, 1970), p. 13.
2. Ibid., p. 14.
3. Dorothy Sayers, *Creed or Chaos?* (New York: Harcourct Brace, 1949).
4. 1 John 4:2–3; cf. 2 John 7.
5. John 3:16.
6. 1 Timothy 6:16.

Chapter 4: **Call the First Witness!**

1. 1 Timothy 4:1.
2. Luke 1:17.
3. Isaiah 40:4.
4. Isaiah 9:6.
5. John 7:37–39.

Chapter 5: The Man Other Men Followed
1. John 3:30.
2. John 2:25.

Chapter 6: Water Becomes Wine
1. See Hosea 6:2.
2. John 19:26.

3. C. S. Lewis, *Miracles* (from *The Best of C. S. Lewis,* Washington, D.C.: Canon Press, 1969), p. 332.
4. Ibid., p. 330.

Chapter 7: The Temple Cleanser
1. Malachi 3:1–3.
2. 1 Kings 8:27.
3. 1 Corinthians 6:19.
4. 1 Corinthians 6:19–20.

Chapter 8: Born of the Spirit
1. Colossians 1:13.

Chapter 9: The Best Possible News
1. 2 Corinthians 5:19.

Chapter 10: A Woman with Modern Problems
1. Matthew 9:13.

Chapter 11: The Encourager of Faith
1. Philippians 2:6–7.

Chapter 13: The Secret of Jesus
1. Hebrews 2:8–9.

Chapter 14: He's Got the Whole World in His Hands
1. Revelation 5:11–14.
2. 1 John 5:11–12.

Chapter 15: The Credentials of Jesus
1. Deuteronomy 19:15.

Chapter 16: **The Testing of Faith**

1. C. S. Lewis, *Miracles* (from *The Best of C. S. Lewis,* Washington, D.C.: Canon Press, 1969), pp. 334–35.
2. Deuteronomy 18:15.

Chapter 17: **Treading Water**

1. Mark 6:45.
2. C. S. Lewis, *Miracles* (from *The Best of C. S. Lewis,* Washington, D.C.: Canon Press, 1969), p. 339.

Chapter 18: **What Are You Working For?**

1. Luke 16:15.
2. John 15:5.

Chapter 19: **Life With God**

1. John 15:16.
2. John 14:20.

Chapter 20: **To Whom Shall We Go?**

1. John 2:19.
2. John 3:7.
3. John 3:4.
4. Matthew 13:12.

Chapter 21: **Is Jesus For Real?**

1. Cal Thomas, *Uncommon Sense* (Brentwood, Tenn.: Wolgemuth & Hyatt, Publishers, Inc., 1990), p. 50.
2. Isaiah 50:4.

Chapter 22: **For Those Who Thirst**

1. Acts 18:10.
2. 1 Corinthians 10:4.

Chapter 23: **Judging the Judges**

1. C. S. Lewis, *Mere Christianity* (from *The Best of C. S. Lewis,* Washington, D.C.: Canon Press, 1969), p. 483.
2. Matthew 8:20.
3. Jeremiah 16:13.

Chapter 26: **The Choice**

1. 1 Peter 2:23.

Chapter 27: **Believing Is Seeing**
1. Matthew 11:25.

Chapter 28: **The Shepherd and His Sheep**
1. John 1:23.
2. John 1:29.
3. Psalm 23:4.
4. Matthew 28:18.
5. Matthew 10:16.
6. Hebrews 13:20–21.
7. Ephesians 4:4–6.
8. Matthew 26:39.

Chapter 29: **A Mere Man—Or the God-Man?**
1. See Isaiah 35.

Chapter 30: **The Strange Ways of God**
1. Philip Yancey, *Disappointment with God* (Grand Rapids, Mich.: Zondervan, 1988), p. 26.
2. Revelation 13:8.
3. 1 Thessalonians 4:13–14.
4. John Claypool, *The Light Within You* (Waco, Texas: Word, 1983), pp. 85–86.

Chapter 31: **The Conquest of Death**
1. 1 Corinthians 15:55.
2. Romans 12:15.
3. John 11:15.
4. See John 5:27–29.

Chapter 32: **God's Will or Our Will?**
1. See Luke 16:19–31.
2. 1 Corinthians 2:7.
3. Isaiah 53:6.

Chapter 33: **Worship or Waste?**
1. Colossians 3:23 KJV.
2. Mark 14:6–9.
3. M. Scott Peck, *People of the Lie* (New York: Simon & Schuster, 1983), note on pp. 76–77.

Chapter 34: **Triumph or Tragedy?**

1. Matthew 21:10–11.
2. Daniel 9:25.
3. A. W. Tozer, *The Root of the Righteous* (Harrisburg, Penn.:Christian Publications, 1955), p. 66.
4. Luke 9:23.

Chapter 35: **Faithful Belief—and Fatal Unbelief**

1. Matthew 26:38.
2. Matthew 26:39.
3. Luke 22:43.
4. Matthew 3:17.
5. Luke 9:23.
6. Isaiah 9:6–7.
7. Isaiah 53:5.
8. Isaiah 6:9–10.

Chapter 36: **Servant Authority**

1. Luke 22:25–27.
2. Galatians 6:13.
3. Matthew 18:15.
4. Galatians 6:1.
5. James 5:16.

Chapter 37: **The One Commandment**

1. Matthew 7:22–23.
2. Matthew 26:25.

Chapter 38: **The Cure for Heart Trouble**

1. 2 Corinthians 4:17–18.
2. 1 Thessalonians 4:16–18.
3. Acts 7:56.
4. John 14:20.
5. 2 Peter 1:4.
6. Luke 22:42.

Chapter 39: **Another Is Coming**

1. John 7:37–39.
2. Hebrews 13:5.
3. Matthew 28:20.
4. Philippians 3:10.

Chapter 40: **The Vine and the Fruit**
1. Psalm 80:8.
2. 1 John 2:19.

Chapter 41: **Love and Hate**
1. 1 Corinthians 13:6.
2. Mark 14:34.

Chapter 42: **The New Strategy**
1. Acts 17:6, author's paraphrase.
2. Philippians 4:6–7.

Chapter 43: **The Longest Prayer**
1. John 1:14.
2. Matthew 10:16.
3. 1 Thessalonians 4:16–17.
4. 1 Corinthians 13:12.

Chapter 44: **The Way to the Cross**
1. Matthew 5:39.

Chapter 45: **The Battle on the Hill**
1. Matthew 10:26.
2. John 10:18.
3. Philippians 2:8.

Chapter 47: **The New Commission**
1. Matthew 18:20.
2. Ephesians 1:13.
3. A. W. Tozer, *The Root of the Righteous* (Harrisburg, PA: Christian Publications, 1955), pp. 119–21.

Chapter 48: **By the Sea**
1. Matthew 28:10.
2. Mark 1:17.
3. Psalm 127:1.

Note to the Reader

The publisher invites you to share your response to the message of this book by writing Discovery House Publishers, Box 3566, Grand Rapids, MI 49501, USA. For information about other Discovery House books, music, or videos, contact us at the same address or call 1-800-653-8333. Find us on the Internet at http://www.dhp.org/ or send e-mail to books@dhp.org.

Other Discovery House Books by Ray C. Stedman

God's Final Word: Understanding Revelation

Everyone likes a good mystery, but no one wants to get to the end of a book and have the mystery remain unsolved. We don't have that dilemma with the Bible. Dr. Stedman offers this sensible, easy-to-understand explanation of the book of Revelation and the completion of God's plan of redemption.

Waiting for the Second Coming: Studies in Thessalonians

Many find it difficult to think of God as loving and powerful when all around them they see suffering. In 1 and 2 Thessalonians, the apostle Paul explains this apparent contradiction and encourages believers to wait and watch for Jesus' soon return when He will right every wrong. Dr. Stedman explores this powerful promise and inspires us to tell others who live without hope.